· 国家社科基金项目《别现代语境中的英雄空间解构与建构问题研究》阶段性成果

· 上海高校高峰学科建设计划资助“中国语言文学”阶段性成果

· 上海师范大学艺术学理论重点学科成果

别现代：空间遭遇与时代跨越

BIE-MODERN: SPACE ENCOUNTERS AND TIMES SPANS

王建疆 著

中国社会科学出版社

图书在版编目（CIP）数据

别现代：空间遭遇与时代跨越/王建疆著. —北京：中国社会科学出版社，2017.9

ISBN 978 - 7 - 5203 - 0956 - 1

Ⅰ.①别… Ⅱ.①王… Ⅲ.①社会形态学—研究 Ⅳ.①C912

中国版本图书馆 CIP 数据核字（2017）第 220257 号

出 版 人 赵剑英
选题策划 刘 艳
责任编辑 刘 艳
责任校对 陈 晨
责任印制 戴 宽

出 版 中国社会科学出版社
社 址 北京鼓楼西大街甲 158 号
邮 编 100720
网 址 http://www.csspw.cn
发 行 部 010 - 84083685
门 市 部 010 - 84029450
经 销 新华书店及其他书店

印 刷 北京明恒达印务有限公司
装 订 廊坊市广阳区广增装订厂
版 次 2017 年 9 月第 1 版
印 次 2017 年 9 月第 1 次印刷

开 本 710×1000 1/16
印 张 22.75
插 页 2
字 数 322 千字
定 价 89.00 元

自　序

在中华文化复兴的伟大历史进程中思想的创新、理论的创新愈发重要，并且已经成为全民族的共识。而思想的创新和理论的创新首先是话语的创新。说不同的话，做不同的事，就可能有不同的思想和不同的理论。相反，说同样的话，做同样的事，还指望思想和理论的创新就如同缘木而求鱼。

话语的创新，其极致就是哲学的创新。所谓哲学，不仅是世界观和方法论，而且首先是概念，是主义，是一种言说方式。所谓唯物主义、唯心主义，就是最基本的概念、最基本的主义和最基本的言说方式。因此，概念是哲学的第一要素。哲学家如果未能提炼出属于自己发明的概念，或未能对已有的概念做出新的解释，那么，这个哲学家将如何彰显自己的存在？

“别现代”（Bie-modern）理论，包括别现代现实与别现代主义（Bie-modernism）两部分，是由中国学者提出并在国内外引起反响的话语创新，是与西方的现代、前现代、后现代相对应的涵盖性理论，包含告别伪现代性、具足真实现代性和建构别样现代性三个方面的含义。中国社会经济结构中所有制的多元并存，加上前现代文化传统、制度理念和后现代思潮，使得现代、前现代、后现代以不同占比杂糅在一起，这种占比按主导性力量的价值倾向而随机变化，很难用西方现代性作为中国社会形态的理论坐标。因此，别现代的“别”，既告别虚妄的现代性，具足真实的现代性，又包含构想在人类普遍价值认

同基础上的别样的中国现代性；既是对现实的描述，又是对更新超越属性的概括。

现代性理论始自西方，并在不断发展。如艾森斯塔特（S. N. Eisenstadt）的多元现代性，乌尔力希·贝克（Ulrich Beck）的第二现代性，哈贝马斯（Jürgen Habermas）的未完成的现代性，弗里德里克·詹姆逊（Fredric Jameson）的多元现代性，路易·皮埃尔·阿尔都塞（Louis Pierre Althusser）的另类现代性，安东尼·吉登斯（Anthony Giddens）的反思的现代性，齐格蒙特·鲍曼（Zygmunt Bauman）的流动的现代性，C·詹克斯（C. Jencks）的晚期现代性，威尔施·沃尔夫冈（Wolfgang Welsch）的后现代的现代性等。改革开放以来，现代性成了中国学者考察和界定中国社会形态的理论坐标，成为哲学人文学科的重大课题，并取得了显著的成绩。但就中国现代性研究中比较突出的"新现代性""复杂现代性""另类现代性""混合现代性"观点而言，都从西方现代性理论出发，首先肯定了中国的现代性，但在肯定现代性的同时却忽略了中国的前现代因素和后现代因素与现代性同时并置，而且它们之间的占比在随机变化的现状，看不到中国现代性尚在路上的事实，因而把虚妄不实的现代性当成了具足的而又真实的现代性。

相对于西方的现代取代前现代而后现代又超越现代的断代式发展，中国是现代、前现代、后现代三个不同时代在同一空间中的共存或时间的空间化。在这个空间共存中，由于现代与前现代之间的根本对立，后现代与前现代之间的天然隔膜，三者间的杂糅必然处于既和谐又对立的交集纠结状态，并在经济体系、管理制度、思想意识、文化形态、道德规范、审美现象、文学艺术等方面全方位地表现出来，从而构成和谐共谋期、对立冲突期、更新超越期等发展阶段。近年来蜚声海内外的中国电影、电视连续剧、小说、美术作品，以及生活世界中的奇葩建筑、门神年画等，从思想内容到艺术手法无不表现出现代前现代与后现代既杂糅又矛盾对立的状态。最近热播的电视连续剧

《人民的名义》中表现出来的强烈的和谐共谋与对立冲突，以及反腐的正能量，都可以说是对别现代时间空间化理论和社会发展阶段论的图解。从张艺谋的《秋菊打官司》到冯小刚的《我不是潘金莲》，时隔30年，但现代执法遭遇前现代文化的尴尬依然如故，加之后现代的戏谑、戏仿，构成了别现代的别具一格的审美杂糅——冷幽默。徐峥的囧类电影、贾樟柯的纪实影片、众多的抗日神剧、莫言小说等，无不具有典型的别现代特征。2016年9月至10月在上海举办的《别现代作品展》更是对别现代最为直观的美学和文艺学阐释。

正是由于别现代从中国现实出发而非从西方现代性理论出发，因而在学术上就有了一系列别出一路的话语创新：

（1）改造问题。跳出“是中国哲学/美学还是哲学/美学在中国”的“崇无”与“尚有”之争，提出“待有”的问题，即中国哲学/美学还缺少什么的问题，从而突破了西方在此问题上的话语设定。

（2）转换时空。指出中国社会的时间空间化特质以及这种空间化依靠自身矛盾和内在动力向历史阶段演变的必然性和轨迹，从而赋予哲学人文学科包括美学时空变幻中的动态功能和特点。

（3）刷新视野。主张从后现代之后回望的超前眼光审视现代、前现代、后现代，既不回归前现代，又不顺从现代和后现代，而是有选择地取舍借鉴，期许哲学人文学科包括美学上的时代超越和集成创新。

（4）思维革命。针对跨越式发展，提出跨越式停顿。对经济、技术、军事领域与生态、文化、制度领域的跨越与不可跨越做出界分，并将其演变为非遗和艺术风格领域的“切割”理论。

（5）形态优先。指出社会形态对审美形态的决定作用，又指出审美形态对美学理论创新的影响，试图首先从中国经验和形态学找到中国美学的创新点。

别现代的话语创新，引起了国内外学者的研究和讨论。著名西方哲学家、美学家艾尔雅维茨（Aleš Erjavec）以及恩斯特·曾科（Er-

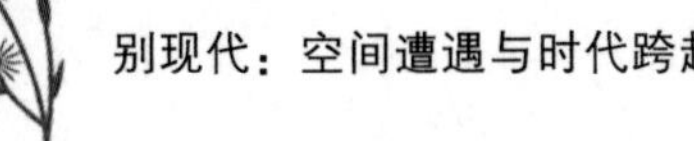

nest Ženko）、基顿·韦恩（Keaton Wynn）、洛克·本茨（Rok Bencin）等，国内的夏中义、吴炫、刘锋杰、王洪岳、陶国山等，近年分别在欧洲名刊《哲学通报》（*Filozofski vestnik*）、《艺术加媒体》（*Art + Media*）和中国的《学术月刊》、《文艺理论研究》、《探索与争鸣》及网站上撰文12组60余篇与我讨论别现代问题，有20余篇被转载。艾尔雅维茨的《主义：从缺位到喧嚣——与王建疆教授商榷》（*Zhuyi: From Absence to Bustle? —Some Comments on Jianjiang Wang's Article "The Bustle and the Absence of Zhuyi"*）一文在与别现代的讨论中提出"哲学四边形"论，将中国纳入其中，从而突破了德里达的中国无哲学论和舒斯特曼（Richard Shusterman）的"哲学三帝国"论。美国学者基顿·韦恩的《别现代时期相似的艺术的不同意义》（*Differing Modernisms: Similar Art, Different Meaning Zhuyi for a Bie-modern Age*）运用别现代理论为遭到美国艺术评论界指责的中国艺术辩护。美国佐治亚州西南州立大学于2017年初正式成立了中国别现代研究中心（CCBMS），国家社科基金项目《后现代语境中英雄空间的解构与建构问题研究》已经审批将"后现代"改为"别现代"。

尽管别现代理论还在讨论中，但从社会形态出发研究思考问题的方法对中国的理论研究创新不无启发。比如，从社会形态出发，由于中国尚处于别现代时期，因而无法跟随西方后现代进行理论的解构，相反，中国的学术研究更需要理论的建构，这就为中国的学术研究创新找到了时代根据。再如，从社会形态出发，我们可以首先考察"作为美学范畴枢纽"的审美形态。中国传统的审美形态如中和、气韵、神妙、意境、空灵、飘逸，当代的"囧"等，都在西方审美形态体系如悲剧、喜剧、崇高、荒诞之外，建立在这种审美形态基础上的审美形态理论也应该不同，这样一来就为我们探索别样现代性的中国美学找到了一条可行的路径。进而言之，别现代理论主张从"后现代之后回望"超前地审视现代、前现代、后现代，通过批判继承汲取这三个时代中合理的、符合中国实际的元素，实现更新超越，构建中国式

原创的、全球通约的现代哲学人文学科包括美学。正是由于从社会形态出发，别现代主义的构想就有可能把中国的理论创新落到实处。

总之，别现代与中国的理论创新紧密相连，是中国学术创新的一个新视域和一条新路径，如果深入下去，很有可能实现全面的理论原创。这种原创可能会以从社会形态研究到哲学形态研究、审美形态研究为突破口，以汲取现代、前现代、后现代中的积极成果而形成大的集成创新。

目前，别现代的话语创新已经引起国内外哲学界、文学界、艺术界学者的深入探讨，甚至个别法律界、经济界的专家学者也参加进来，说明这个问题具有辐射力和带动性。从跟着西方走到西方随我说，表现出来的是中国学术话语权的逐步形成和理论自信的确立，对于形成全域性的国际学术对话，推动中国话语创新，社会意义和学术意义之重大不言而喻。

主义，这个与哲学、美学和艺术靠得最近的概念或言说方式，是一个涵盖性很强却又多质多层次性的表达。在英语中，"主义"就是名词后缀"-ism"，包括哲学、思想、主张、观点、风格、流派、运动、潮流等许多方面，渗透在哲学、艺术、美学以及广泛的社会生活中。主义并一定很大，但要求具有明确的主张，不可重复的原创性，特征明显，而且具有影响力。印象主义起始于批评家对它的不屑一顾的评价——"不过是一些印象而已"。立体主义也就是对一种画法的标识而已。但它们对世界艺术史的影响却非同小可。虽然，在学术意义上，主义并不具有神性，也不具有魔性，但作为一种言说方式，若按法国大思想家福柯的说法，话语即权力，因此，主义也就是体现权力的话语和概念，往往成了哲学思潮、艺术流派、美学学派的代名词。所谓西方的话语霸权，主要就是这个主义的话语权的行使，并将主张、思想、创造、个性、影响力等凝聚在了一起，具有很大的能量。就美学而言，以"主义"冠名并对中国产生了影响的美学，据笔者统计，就有35种之多。相反，纵观当代中国学术，尤其是哲学

人文学科在全球的地位，其久不尽如人意者，或曰欠发达者，与本土的哲学上的、学术上的、艺术中的“主义”的缺位不无关系。虽然，我们在主义以下的地方，也就是在“论”和“学”的方面已经做了许多了不起的工作，但在主义之上还是有许多空白。要实现与西方的学术对话，如果没有来自自身的主义及其话语权力，形成你来我往的平等交流，也就是说建立一个已故英国诺贝尔经济奖得主罗纳德.科斯（Ronald Coase）所说的思想市场，而非思想的饲养场，则很难想象这种对话的效果。因此，学术上的主义，是文化软实力的关键所在，是一个不应该在学术研究中忌讳的话题。

别现代，一个源自于对中国社会形态的认识和概括，在话语创新的背后却是认识的创新、思想的创新、理论的创新。这个创新由一系列概念构成：别现代、别现代性、别现代主义、时间空间化、跨越式停顿、发展四阶段理论、中西马我主张、传承、借鉴与创新中的切割理论等，涉及哲学、美学、伦理学、政治学、社会学、文艺批评等众多领域，是一个关于社会发展历史阶段的新思想、新理论。

别现代的“别”曾经被不少学者误读为不要现代、告别现代、另一种现代。但就别现代所能概括的现实内涵而言，别现代并不是真正意义上的现代。在一个混合着前现代、现代、后现代因素的社会形态中，单独提取某一要素而不顾及其他要素的以偏概全，是不具合理性的。但是，如果因为不能以偏概全，就否定元素的存在，也是有违客观事实的。因此，别现代就是别现代，它是中国的时代特征和社会形态，而不是什么另类现代性、混后现代性，也不是什么复杂现代性或新的现代性，而是一种对于特殊社会形态和特殊社会历史阶段的概括，而非一种西方现代性理论的延伸。

与别现代现状相联系的是别现代性。别现代性是指，由时间的空间化导致的前现代、现代、后现代的和谐共谋与对立冲突所构成的多元并存属性、和谐共谋属性和内在张力属性、对立冲突属性、多变量及难以预测属性。不同于别现代和别现代性，别现代主义则是建立在

自我更新和自我超越基础上的理论主张，其实质是自我超越主义和自我更新主义以及作为现代社会必备条件的兑现主义。

中国自上世纪改革开放以来，已经开始向现代性迈进，但完全现代性的获得尚需要一个很长的历史时期。在完成现代性之前，前现代的梦魇还会不时地侵扰我们、妨害我们。因此，我们时代的问题也可以简约为现代、前现代、后现代三者之间的占比以及这种占比的此消彼长。如果现代性的占比愈来愈大，那么，中华民族的伟大复兴就愈来愈有希望，相反，前现代的占比愈来愈大，现代性的占比愈来愈小，那么，中华民族的停滞和倒退也将不可避免，遑论复兴。因为从根本上讲，“复兴”绝不是复古，也绝不是复辟！因此，中国的现代性建设任重道远。

物质的现代化无法取代精神的现代性。地球上那些拿着最现代化的武器在进行着恐怖袭击的暴徒们，那些挥金如土已将消费符号化了的“大国小民”们，无不在展示现代化的悖谬。别现代与别现代主义正是在这一悖谬基础上的同床异梦。别现代是指一种客观的社会现实和历史阶段，而别现代主义却是对别现代的改造、更新、超越。别现代只是为了认识世界，而别现代主义却是为了改造世界，包括改造别现代。也就是要在现代、前现代、后现代的空间遭遇中，最终实现时代的跨越。正是别现代主义的这一基本价值倾向，才会有别现代时期的别开生面、别具一格、别出一路、别有洞天的哲学思想、美学理论、艺术评论、学术主张。

在未曾想到的国内外学者对于别现代的讨论中，笔者已经感到，别现代问题正如艾尔雅维茨所说，并不仅仅是中国的问题，也是全球的问题。现在，别现代的问题已经被抛出，那就不管它是砖头还是金条，都已无法收回，就任由中外学者自由地讨论吧。

作者

2017年夏于沪上古美斋

目　录

第二编　别现代美学

第三编　别现代评论

Contents

导　论

别现代别在哪里？

王建疆

别现代，英译 Bie-modern（Bie-modernity，Bie-modernism），是关于社会形态和历史发展阶段的创新性理论。自 2014 年在中俄高层文化论坛上提出以来，别现代引起了国内国外学术界的热烈讨论。尤其值得注意的是，别现代在找不到“别”字最恰切的英文对译而不得不用汉语拼音 BIE 来代替后，竟然被欧美国家一些著名的学者如阿列西·艾尔雅维茨等在他们发表的文章中采用了。美国佐治亚州还成立了“中国别现代研究中心”（CCBMS，The Center of Chinese Bie-Modern Studies）。正如《文艺争鸣》有关 2016 年文艺学年度学术总结所说，别现代主义这一“创新性、建构性的理论议题，被中外学者持续关注和热议”[①]。反响之余，还有问题：别现代别在何处？别现代为什么要别？别现代如何才能别？我认为，这些问题不是负担，相反，将是别现代理论发展的动力。

一　别现代别在哪里

1. 汉语之“别”。

别现代的“别”词义颇多。直观的有不要、告别，错别字等；隐

① 可晓锋：《在自信与对话中构建当代中国文论》，《文艺争鸣》2017 年第 3 期。

晦一点的有别扭、另外等。“另外”是古义今用。古代汉语中没有“另”字，所有另字的功能都被“别”字所代替。别裁、别传、别墅、别动队等，都是另外的意思。“别”有这么多的词义并不奇怪，原因在于“别”字最早表达的是人拿着刀剔骨让骨肉分离的意思。[①]这个意思后来一被引申自然就成了不要、区别、告别、另外、别扭、各是各、人家的等意思。但词义只是词义，作为学术术语则需要界定，尤其是要在具体的语境（context）或文脉中确定。

2. 现实之“别”。

别现代乍一看很容易产生不要现代、告别现代的意思。但实际上恰好相反。我们不是不要现代，而是渴望作为对现代这一时间概念进行质的规定的东西，也就是现代性。现代性始自欧洲的启蒙运动和工业革命，以科学理性精神、社会契约制度、自由平等观念和社会福利制度为标志。现代性作为人类进步的标志，是一个时代之所以为这个时代而非其他时代的内在根据。由于不同国家、不同民族处于不同的发展阶段，因此，虽然同处于一个编年时代，但它们所具有的现代性却会在程度上、性质上有所不同。作为一个发展中国家，它的现代性程度有多高，往往要通过与前现代的占比有多大进行对比才能得以确定。

我们虽然处于编年史阶段的现代的时空维度中，物质的现代化程度也很高，但前现代的思想、意识、制度等仍占据着社会的空间，使得真正的现代性被遮蔽、被扭曲。我们距离真正的具足的现代性还很远，只能说我们尚在通向现代性的路上。2017 年春季热播的电视连续剧《人民的名义》实际上就是对这种现代性尚在路上的社会现状和历史发展阶段的艺术写照。法学教授出身的省委副书记兼政法委书记高玉良，尽管讲起法律来头头是道，口口声声任何时候都不能突破法律的底线，但其思想的深处不过就是前现代的人身依附观念、报恩

---

① 见图一。

思想，他所遵循的用人制度还是封建社会的门生故吏、裙带连襟那一套，他所做的一切都在维护能够保护既得利益集团的前现代制度。至于将他提携到省委副书记位置的前省委书记赵立春，就更是一个以赵家的公子为核心的封建宗法制思想和制度的化身了。一切为了自己和自己的小圈子的利益，与民争利，侵害民利，将体现现代性的人的权力视而不见、任意践踏，将保护人的权力的法律弃如敝履，这与真正的现代性有天壤之别。剧中汉东省的这个犯罪利益集团的最为突出的特点就是，处于统治地位打着法律的旗号违法乱纪，以人民的名义祸害人民，具有明显的虚伪性和欺诈性。由于法律、人民这些概念都是现代性的具体范畴，而在现实中，人民和法律总是被架空、被遮蔽、被替代，所以该剧中暴露出来的并不是真正的、真实的、具足的现代性，相反，是现代社会中虚妄不实的现代性。也就是吃大肉的和尚在念经。因此可以说，中国目前的腐败问题实质上是一个比腐败更为深刻、更为复杂的现代性缺失的问题，是一个别现代问题。

改革开放以来的中国已经处在迈向现代性的过程中，但就目前而言，中国的现实仍旧是现代、前现代、后现代交集纠结的杂糅状态，边际模糊，很难说它就是纯粹的现代或前现代，更不能说它是后现代，只能说它是别现代。这里的“别”就有与现代性相分别的意思。别现代主义就是要与这种虚妄不实的现代性做一种分别、别离和切割，从而具备真正的现代性，使中国进入新的历史阶段。正是在这个意义上说，中国的改革开放就是与前现代告别而奔向现代的过程。因此，提出别现代就不是文字游戏，而是对现实的反映和概括，符合历史发展的趋向，是一种进步的价值观。

3. 理论之别。

任何理论都不仅仅是对现实的反映，而且更主要的还在于对现实的概括。别现代根植于当代中国现实，其理论的根在于中国的现实，而非西方的理论体系。西方的理论体系对建构中国的理论体系具有启发、引导等作用，但由于西方理论产生的背景不同、社会形态不同、

历史发展阶段不同，因而其理论的普适性就会受到限制。因此，立足于中国现实的理论建构就要有别于西方的理论体系。

与西方的断代式发展相比，中国是共时性存在，是时间的空间化或时代的空间化。西方的现代是对前现代的否定和切割，而西方的后现代又是对现代的超越。这样一来，西方的前现代、现代、后现代之间的分别十分清楚，是一部断代史。相反，中国却是现代、前现代、后现代交织扭结的社会形态，没有断代，只有混合和杂糅。这种时间的空间化性质就需要符合它的理论概括。别现代理论把这种社会形态称为时间的空间化。这个时间的空间化理论由于来自中国的现实，因而与西方国家的空间理论判若两仪。

别现代的时间空间化理论并没有停留在对社会形态的性质和特征的概括上，而是在时间的空间化现状中引入了辩证发展的历史观。由于现代与前现代的根本对立，后现代与前现代的天然隔膜，现代与前现代、后现代处于既和谐共谋又矛盾冲突的历史进程中。在这一历史进程中，出现了和谐共谋期、对立冲突期、和谐共谋与对立冲突交织期、更新超越期四个阶段。与这四个历史阶段相伴随，美学和艺术的功能也会发生变化。如在和谐共谋期注重发挥现实主义美学和后现代戏仿美学的功能，对社会现实的真实再现，对和谐共谋假象的讽刺和揭露，就有利于针砭时弊，分流清浊，抑恶扬善；在对立冲突期，注重对悲剧、崇高等审美形态的张扬，就有利于唤醒人民的自尊和自信，凝聚正能量，维护社会的健康发展；在和谐共谋与对立冲突交织期，注重冷幽默手法的应用，就会有助于释放社会积怨、抚慰心灵。《人民的名义》形象地演绎了这四个历史阶段。由于既得利益集团的和谐共谋建立在对大风场工人利益侵害的基础上，对立冲突日趋激化，反腐与反反腐的较量交织在一起。该剧的意义不在于能够战胜腐败而且战胜了腐败，而在于主导性力量并未满足于战胜腐败后的胜利，而是开始思考对权力的监督问题，透露出自我反思和自我更新的气息。实际上，中国的现实无处不在印证着时间空间化所带来的这四

个历史阶段的存在。医患冲突、环境污染、制假售假、窜改历史、重大安全事故等，都是在成套的法律和一系列的条例下面发生的，有着和谐共谋以及和谐共谋与对立冲突相互交织的特点，同时，推进改革的力量也在不断壮大。正是别现代的历史阶段论，才使得别现代的时间空间化理论摆脱了不符合实际的抽象，摆脱了替西方背书的尴尬，而与中国的地气相接。自然，别现代的时间空间化理论也就有别于西方自列斐伏尔开始的一系列空间化理论，成为一种原创的理论，是中国的空间理论。①

4. 别中之别。

别现代之“别”不仅注意在同一个层面上的不同事物之间的平面之别，而且注重在立体层面上的超越之别。

别现代有一个反响不小的理论叫跨越式停顿。所谓跨越式停顿就是在事物发展的高级高速阶段，在顺风顺水甚至如日中天之际，进行自主性的突然停顿。跨越式停顿的事例我们可以在中国古代的“急流勇退”和禅宗的顿悟成佛中找到，可以从当今全球无水日、无车日、无烟日的演习中看到，从一些国家和地区的专制制度突然解体中感到。② 跨越式停顿实际上是对跨越式发展的一种矫正。因为它发现经济、技术、军事方面的跨越式发展不能代替文化传统、自然生态、社会制度的非跨越式发展。文化上的、自然生态上的、社会制度上的跨越式发展所带来的脆败和解体比比皆是。相反，及时汲取这方面的教训，进行跨越式停顿，则可以避免脆败和解体，实现平稳运行、长治久安。跨越式发展已经是对追随式发展的区别和超越，而跨越式停顿却又是对跨越式发展的区别和超越，是区别中的区别、超越中的超越。因此可以说，别现代之别是别中之别。

别现代的别中之别还有一个例子，就是别现代主义与别现代之

① 王建疆：《别现代：时间的空间化与美学的功能》，《当代文坛》2016 年第 6 期。
② 王建疆：《别现代：跨越式停顿》，《探索与争鸣》2015 年第 12 期。

别。别现代堪称伪现代性（pseudo modernity，简称 P），以中国 315 打假日为标志，以假货的普遍存在可以窥见西方现代性在中国的虚妄不真。同时，别现代主义是去除虚假的现代性（Deter-pseudo modern，简称 D）而建立真正的现代性（the real modernity，简称 R）。所以，别现代翻译成英语就是 P（Pseudo）modern，而别现代主义翻译成英语就是 D（Deter-pseudo）modern 和 R（Real）modern. 从 P 到 D 再到 R，就构成了别现代理论的全部。别现代是对现代、前现代、后现代杂糅状态的概括，而别现代主义却是对别现代的批判，是对别现代的超越。别现代是现实，别现代主义却是价值倾向。别现代主义与别现代之别就是别中之别，是超越与被超越之别。正是这种别中之别和超越之别，构成了别现代理论的既告别虚妄不实的现代性又期许和建构别样的真实的现代性的有机整体。告别虚妄不实的现代性，是对现代性和人类共同价值的认可；构建别样的现代性，又是与西方现代性的同中有异，从而构成中国现代性的特点。别现代的别中之别使别现代理论不断地处于自我更新和自我超越中，从而永葆理论创新的青春。别中之别应该成为一种创新机制、创新方式、创新路径。

别现代除了以上的时间空间化理论、历史阶段论、美学功能论、跨越式停顿论外，还有一些理论范畴，如发展论中的后现代之后论、[①] 思想资源上的中西马我主张、[②] 艺术传承创新和借鉴创新中的切割理论、英雄空间理论、消费日本理论等，[③] 都是建立在"别"的基础上的新理论。这些别样的理论虽然别出一路，但并不另类，亦非为了标新立异，而是趋向理论创新的本质，这就是要有别于别人的思想和主义。我曾说过，中国的学术思想欠发达现状就在于主义的欠发达。[④]

---

① 王建疆：《别现代：美学之外与后现代之后》，《上海师范大学学报》2016 年第 1 期。

② 王建疆（Wang Jianjiang）：*Quadrilateral in Philosophy, Aesthetics and Humanities and Bie-modernism*，*ART & MEDIA STUDY*，*forthcoming*。

③ 王建疆：《"消费日本"与英雄空间的解构》，《中国文学批评》2017 年第 2 期。

④ 王建疆：《欠发达时代的学术策略》，《中国社会科学评价》2015 年第 4 期。

因此，提出别现代就是一种创建主义的尝试，有关别现代的理论主张都可以归在别现代主义的名义下。

总之，无论是从语言上，还是从现实中，从理论上，从思维方式上，别现代都在做着发现“别”，建构“别”的工作。“别”是一种思想、一种方式、一种主义，它是由现实的发展所决定的，也是由中国的国情所决定的。打破闭关锁国、走向世界的中国，急需来自现实、符合现实、指导现实的思想和理论，急需有独立见解、构成话语系统的学说、理论、思想、主义。所谓的独立，所谓的独创、所谓的话语，都离不开“别”的存在。在世界范围内，任何一个国家都应该有自己的别。在学术领域里，每一个学者也都应该有自己的别。无论大别还是小别，新别还是旧别，有别才有独立存在，有别才有可能创新。正是从这个意义上讲，“别”就是主体性，“别”就是创新性，“别”就是话语权，“别”就是理论自信。

二　别现代为什么而别

从目的论的角度讲，主体的活动都有一个目的。就别现代理论而言，为什么而别，也是绕不开的问题。

第一，别现代是为了寻求差异性和主体性。别现代讲分别，也就是讲差异。差异或差别属于哲学认识论范畴。差异性是与同一性相对的范畴。中国古代《国语·郑语》就主张和而不同，如说“和实生物，同则不继”。庄子十分重视差异性问题，并把同异性问题纳入相对主义范畴。他说：“自其异者视之，肝胆楚越也；自其同者视之，万物皆一也。”（《德充符》）欧洲的莱布尼茨说，不可能在同一棵树上发现相同的树叶，当时的德皇并不相信，动员所有大臣和宫女去寻找相同的树叶，但事实证明莱布尼茨的说法是对的。从这个意义上讲，别现代主义的别，具有哲学的普遍意义。我们就是要有差别性意识和差别性概念，以差别性来确立自我、确立对象，从而形成主

体性。

差别不仅是哲学认识论，而且还是哲学价值论。正因为认识到差别的重要性，我们才要努力寻求差异性，保持差异性，在差异中确立自己，在差异中保持本色。差异的主体性价值在于，即使是高度认同的领域，比如信仰领域，个人的情感、个人的理解、个人的表达，还是同样重要，不可被剥夺的，否则，历来的宗教改革将不可能发生。阐释学就来自对《圣经》的不同理解。佛教对于佛教经典也有很多不同的注本。因此，差异性问题从价值论角度看，实质上是存在的需要，也是发展的需要。在与同一性相对立而形成的张力中，确保了个我的存在和有个人轨迹及其特点的发展。

第二，别现代是求异性思想的产物，寻求思想市场的建立。如上所说，求异是一种需要，是一种价值倾向。求异的价值倾向植根于求异的现实需要。如果抽象地讲求异可以获得自我与他人的区别，从而确立我的存在，这还只是一种假设，那么，就某一个相关行业的现实而言，则可进一步厘清这种自我确认的必要性和可能性。就以我国教育体制而言，高中之前的教育完全是认同教育，即饲养场式的教育。这种教育的形式就是在规定的教科书、教学大纲、考试大纲、试题答案范围内进行填鸭式教学，不允许学生和老师有任何差异性思维。原因在于，高考制度所规定的标准答案。标准答案就是红线，谁触及红线，谁就倒霉。考试通不过，一切免谈。这样一来，我国大学教育以前的学校教育是完全同质化、单一化的。当学生通过标准化考试进入大学后，这种同质化教育带来的单一、僵化等弊端开始暴露。很多大学生不知道如何学习，不知道如何写论文。即使在得到论文写作培养后，还是写不出来有自己独立见解的文章来，原因就在于同质化教育的深入灵魂，已经形成了学生和老师的共同文化行为方式，带来思想的枯竭。

这种求同性状况到了研究生阶段更为严重。多年来指导培养博士生、硕士生的经验告诉我，大多数文科研究生的学位论文，往往是述

而不论，不像是论文，而像是叙事文。没有论点和论证，只是过程和材料的排序，是叙述，而非思辨。而且论文写作著作化、教材化，面面俱到，纲目清楚周全而较少学术创新点和思想的闪光点。可以说，中国从小学到博士的全方位创新缺位，都与同质化教育猖行而求异性思维匮乏密切相关。这种同质化教育带来的求异性思维的泯灭，导致了整个教育的实质性落后。大批的中国学生宁愿让父母支付昂贵的学费竞相去欧美读书也不愿意继续接受国内高等教育，就说明了这一问题的无法回避。

因此可以说，建立在求异性基础上的别现代之别，并非刻意为之之别，相反，是现实需要之别，是人才培养之别，是教育大计之别。别现代别什么？在不同的语境中都有具体的指涉。在教育方面，为什么而别？就是为了与同质化教育而别，为了与求同性思维而别。跨出教育一隅，别现代之别就是为了存在和发展的需要而别。

别不仅是区别，而且更重要的在于告别求同性思维，树立求异性思维。在思想领域里讲，就是告别思想的饲养场而建立思想市场。英国已故诺贝尔经济奖得主龙纳德·科思在其 101 岁时通过网络对中国观众说，思想市场的缺乏最终会导致中国经济的危局。咋一看似乎危言耸听，但细细想来，实质上就是说要有个思想市场，相互间平等地交换思想，砥砺思想，从而开拓思路，活跃思想，不断寻求最佳的发展经济的路径。思想的市场大概是与思想的饲养场相对的。市场是等价交换，前提是你有我有，而且你有的跟我有的不同，也就是有别于你我的，否则也就无所谓市场交换。而思想的饲养场相反，是用同一种饲料和同一种方法来喂养，不允许有独立的思考和不同的要求。虽然科思是想给中国一个忠告，但就目前西方学术话语霸权而言，中西之间并不存在这样的思想市场，只有西方思想的饲养场。就文论界的“失语症”而言，就美学和哲学界的疑问“是中国哲学/美学还是西方哲学/美学在中国”而言，都说明了由于思想欠发达而造成的单向度接受，以及思想市场的缺失与思想饲养场的独大。再就我国目前研

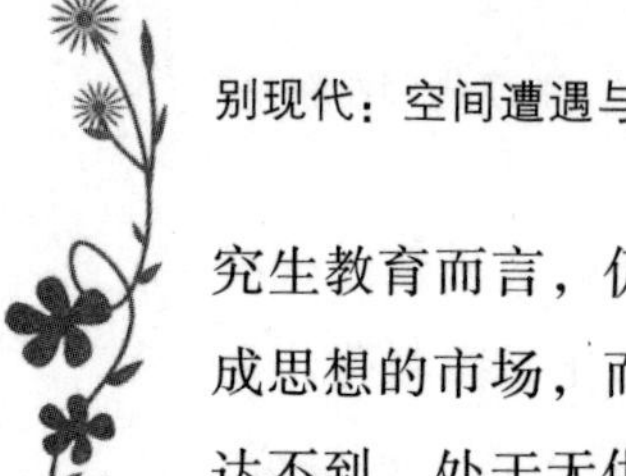

究生教育而言，仍有很大市场的小农作坊式门派在师生之间也没有形成思想的市场，而是思想的饲养场。甚至可以说，连思想的饲养场都达不到，处于无供料状态。所以说，别现代的别就是离开思想的饲养场而进入思想的市场。是用求异性思维，来确立自我的存在，保障创新的进行。

第三，别现代的别，就是要告别虚妄不实的现代性。时下关于中国的现代性研究中，出现了许多新的术语，如新现代性、混合现代性、复杂现代性、另类现代性等，力图从不同的角度去发现并界定中国的现代性。这些努力是值得肯定的。但其中的问题也不能忽视。有关中国现代性研究中的一个最大的问题在于，中国是否已经具有真正西方意义上的现代性，是否具足西方意义上的现代性？现代性自西方启蒙运动、工业革命而来，其核心范畴和核心价值是社会契约、科学理性、人权保障、博爱精神、社会福利制度、议会民主、三权分立、司法独立、言论自由等。正是这些核心范畴规定了西方的现代性。与之相比，中国是否具有这种西方意义上的现代性，或者在多大占比或程度上具有这种现代性，就是一个十分需要考量的问题。如果从中国的现实出发，即社会主义初级阶段的事实出发，而不是从西方的现代性理论出发，来考察中国的现代性现状，则发现，与西方的断代式发展不同，中国是一个现代跟前现代、后现代杂糅在一起的社会形态，因此，很难有真正的、纯粹的或具足的现代性。相反，前现代的噩梦时刻在缠绕着我们，许多社会腐败现象、重大安全事故的背后都有前现代的宗法制度、威权意识、迷信思想、裙带关系、人情世道、有法不依而行潜规则等在作祟。因此，不管如何修饰“现代性”，如用“新”“混合”“另类”“复杂”的形容词，但被修饰者是否就是现代性自身，却成了问题。当前现代性、后现代性与现代性同时存在时，无视前两种而只言后者，就难免以偏概全，逻辑上也讲不通。在这种杂糅的状态中，你只讲现代性，却忽视了前现代和后现代的存在和占比，这就如同将所有到过庙里的、住过庙的都叫和尚一样，却忽视了

大肉和尚、行方便法门者的非和尚存在及其更大的占比。将真正意义上的受过具足戒的和尚与普通的信众相混同，实际上是对“和尚”一词的误解。从思想史和文化史来看，来自西方的现代性至今一点也不新，不混杂，不另类，也不复杂，相反，西方的现代性概念非常清晰、简明，所谓复杂、另类、混同、新旧等，是研究者忽视了现代、前现代、后现代并置的现实及其不同占比，而对属于别人而非属于自己的现代性进行限定和修饰。但这种限定和修饰恰好掩盖了非现代性的、伪现代性的真相，给人以某种地地道道的现代性的错觉，这种错觉类似于一个书写中的别字，不易被发现。因此，别现代的别就是要与这种不真实的、非具足的、虚妄的现代性相区别、相告别，揭示真实的社会形态。

第四，别现代主义就是要建构真正的而又别样的现代性。别现代理论的价值不仅仅在于指出一种杂糅的社会形态，而且还在于通过揭示这种社会形态而找到了它的哲学基础和社会结构。别现代的时间空间化理论就是对别现代社会形态的哲学概括。这个哲学概括来自中国的别现代现实而非西方的空间理论。别现代理论不仅是哲学化的，而且因其揭示了时间空间化所具有的社会结构，因而又是系统化的。别现代理论所揭示的现代跟前现代之间的矛盾所带来的既和谐共谋又对立冲突的结构和功能，为别现代主义的价值观找到了合理的依据。同时，别现代的时间空间化哲学具有历史发展观，这就是别现代的社会发展阶段论，即建立在和谐共谋期、对立冲突期、相互交织期、更新发展期基础上的自我更新、自我调节、自我超越，并兑现历史承诺，建构真正的现代性。由于时间空间化哲学的本土性和现实性，有可能最终导致有一定中国文化特点而又符合现代性标准的现代性。这种别样现代性首先是一种真正的、纯粹的、具足的现代性，然后才是在某些方面有别于西方的现代性。这样一来，别现代理论的“别”就在区别和告别虚妄的现代性与建构别样的现代性上统一了起来。这种统一是历史与逻辑的统一，是认识论与价值论的统一，是普遍价值与民

族特点的统一。

第五，别现代的别是一种不为什么的现实之别，是一种不别而别。别，作为基于差异性哲学的识别概念或行为之别，表面上看是有为而为，但实际上却包括有别而别与无别而别两种情况。老子哲学强调无为以期无为而无不为。庄子发展了老子的学说，提出“有天道有人道，无为而尊者天道也，有为而累者人道也”的说法，主张天道自然。但庄子通过大量的故事说明“道者，进乎技矣”，即通过有为而为进入天道自然的无为而为。除了前述为什么而别外，别现代还有不为什么而别的别。这就是达到自然之别，是事物本然之别。别到极致则无别。正如庄子《齐物论》所云，在道的终极层面上，已无所别。但是，在大道自然的无所别之前，又首先必须有别。老庄的无为思想具有辩证法智慧，是有别之别与无别之别的辩证统一。别现代的别出于对虚妄不实的现代性之别和对别样现代性的建构之别，看起来是有为之别，但是，当别现代理论从时间空间化的现实中抽离出来的时候，已经不再是有意为之，有意而别，相反，是现实之别，是空间之别，是本然之别。在现实之别和本然之别面前，人的有为而别已不再有任何意义。只有当这种来自现实和本然的不别而别时，就如无为而无不为，会成为一种哲学，一种别哲学。同理，当“别”成为人们自觉或非自觉的行为方式时，就会生成一种文化，这种文化就叫别文化。

当别哲学和别文化生成时，创新、创造就开始了。而所有创新的开始都体现为话语创新。话语创新就是有别于他说的创造。语言是存在的家，话语离不开语言，因此，创新性语言在创造中具有决定性。作为别现代的首创者，笔者近年来除了别现代的理论创新和思想创新外，也进行话语创新。在 2017 年元旦和春节来临之际，撰写祝福词寄给大家，避免了数亿人共用相同的几条祝福词的尴尬。此处备忘，继续祝福所有读到此文的先生女士。

2017 年 1 月 1 日祝词：

别现代祝您新年里别梦依稀别来无恙别出心裁别具一格别开生面

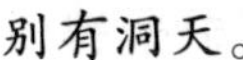
别有洞天。

2017年1月27日祝词：

别现代王建疆衷心祝福您和您的亲人丁酉年：生命别样鲜活、智慧别出一路、日子别有滋味、幸福别无选择——高兴别忘点赞。

总之，别现代为什么而别？是为话语而别，是为思想而别，是为理论而别，是为哲学而别，是为文化而别，是为创造而别，是为生存和发展而别，是不为什么而别，是不别而别，是无别而无不别。有别而别，无别而别，别别与共。别在创造者，创造在别中。

三　别现代怎样别

在明白了别现代别在哪里，别现代为什么而别之后，如何去别，将是题中之义。马克思主义哲学的不满足于认识世界，还要改造世界，就是对如何而别的精神召唤。别现代如何别、怎样别，从以下几个方面可见一斑。

1. 提出别现代理论而与前现代、现代、后现代相别。

别现代是关于社会形态和历史发展阶段的理论，它的提出在于对西方话语体系中前现代、现代、后现代的划分不满。原因即在于这种划分不符合中国的现实。与西方断代式的社会发展史相比，即与现代取代前现代、后现代超越现代的历史相比，中国是共时态的社会存在，是前现代、现代、后现代的既和谐共谋又对立冲突。这种社会的杂糅形态不是现代，也不是后现代，更不是前现代，只能是别现代。别现代就是杂糅的社会形态。由于别现代时期现代、前现代、后现代以不同的占比共存，社会的发展方向会因为某一个因素的占比过大而发生倾斜。如现代性倾向趋大，则社会会朝向真正的现代性迈进；如前现代倾向过大，则社会朝向前现代性的可能大增。但在现代、前现代、后现代三者交织而又较量的过程中，究竟哪一种形态会从占比上领先，往往具有随机性。这种随机性构成了未来中国发展的多项选择

性，也就成了别现代主义更新超越中人的因素决定论的现实根据和理论依据。

别现代之别其意义不仅在于揭示了社会形态的真实面目，而且，建立了别样的话语系统。别现代作为术语如果真能与前现代、现代、后现代并驾齐驱，那么，话语创新、话语权的问题将迎刃而解。

2. 提出时间的空间化理论以有别于西方的空间理论。

别现代理论的哲学基础是时间的空间化。即前现代、现代、后现代的杂糅扭结，既和谐共谋又矛盾对立的现状。这种现状是现代化和全球化的直接后果。但古老的封建王国被帝国主义的船坚炮利征服后，西方现代化的物质文明、制度文明被强行植入，并与前现代的腐朽思想、落后文化携手而行，从而形成了硬件的现代化与软件的封建化在相当一段历史时期共存的状态。这一状态是西方的空间理论所不能概括的。无论列菲伏尔、福柯，还是哈维，他们所讲的空间化理论并不关涉中国的社会形态。他们的理论所关涉的社会形态是一个断代特征十分明显的社会形态，不存在现代与前现代和后现代相互杂糅纠结的情况。因此，别现代的时间空间化就是与西方理论的第一别。这个第一别，别就别在是关于中国社会形态的共时态理论，而非空间生产理论、个人微空间理论、网络空间理论、时空压缩理论以及空间叙事学理论。正是由于这个第一别，才有了别现代理论发展的空间和建立中国式创新理论的可能性与现实性。

3. 提出别现代时期的四阶段论以展示别样的社会结构与功能。

建立在时间空间化哲学基础上的别现代理论，从对现代与前现代的必然对立以及前现代与后现代的历史隔膜中发现，这里存在着既对立又和谐的张力结构。按照现代系统论关于结构决定功能的思想，由于这个结构并非固定不变，而是在随机变化中出现振荡和偏离倾向，或者倾向现代，或者导向前现代，都完全取决于主导性力量的理念、意志，因此，别现代社会的走向难以预知。但是，在这样一个杂糅而又充满张力的结构中，由于现代、前现代、后现代的不同占比及其相

互较量，会必然形成和谐共谋期、对立冲突期、和谐共谋与对立冲突交织期、自我更新超越期四个历史阶段。别现代主义的最终出路在于超越这四个历史阶段，也就是否定别现代，进入现代性阶段。这个现代性阶段既符合人类历史进步趋势，又兼及优秀的中国文化精华，从而在一定程度上是有民族文化特点的现代性。现代性的具足之时，也就是中国的现代化之日。别现代的这种历史发展阶段论，是在人类所有的社会发展阶段论中别出一路的。

4. 提出后现代之后回望反观现状的新视野。

虽然别现代理论认为，西方是断代式的社会发展过程，而中国是共时态社会，但并不主张中国要以西方的现代和后现代为追求目标。相反，别现代认为后现代总有终结的时候。正如西方思想家德勒兹已经提到的后现代之后一样，后现代也只是西方社会发展进程中的一个环节。现在，“后后现代”一词在全球已很流行，是对后现代的否定和超越。别现代理论并不是追随西方的历史进程，走完西方的每一个历史阶段，而是要在时间空间化状态中，即在现代、前现代、后现代交织在一起的时候，审视后现代、反思后现代，要站在后现代之后的立场，从后现代之后回望和反观今天我们所处的时代，从而对我们的未来做出预判。这就是超前思维，也是时代跨越。身处别现代时期尚未达到真正的现代，却要跑到后现代之后去反观和回望别现代，这在一般人看来根本不可能，甚至荒唐。但是别忘了，思想、思维具有超前性和预判性。只有在思维上、思想上跨越了西方的现代和后现代，才能从西方的后现代之后回望、反观今天的别现代，从而为我们走出别现代，告别别现代，进而建构别样的现代性提供思想准备。否则，跟着西方的历史进程亦步亦趋，不仅不可能，而且会邯郸学步。因此，别现代的后现代之后的回望反观论就是一种全新的视野，也是一种跨越的哲学，一种别哲学。

5. 提出跨越式停顿以别于跨越式发展。

跨越式发展理论来自西方经济学的后发理论和蛙跳理论，认为后

发国家可以避免发达国家走过的实验性的弯路而奋起直追，甚至取得青出于蓝胜于蓝的效果。中国改革开放以来的经济、技术、军事的发展已经证明了跨越式发展的可能性和现实性。但别现代理论之别在于，针对跨越式发展提出跨越式停顿。跨越式停顿是指在高端高速的发展中突然主动终止前进，甚至改弦易辙。跨越式停顿是一种发展哲学，也是一种处世哲学，是生存智慧。老子讲功成身隐，儒家讲急流勇退，禅宗讲言语道断、截断横流，都是在高级和超高级阶段上的跨越式停顿。跨越式停顿来自增长的极限，因而需要及早停顿和退出，而非等到相反的后果横陈在你的面前。跨越式停顿又基于技术、军事、经济的可跨越式发展，而自然生态、文化传承、社会制度的不可以跨越式发展。苏联就是因为陶醉于自己在军事、技术、经济方面的跨越式发展而忽视了社会制度、自然生态、文化传承的不可跨越式发展，最终走向解体。跨越式停顿也不是什么转向、转型，在跨越式发展的高速行进中，突然的转向意味着毁灭。跨越式停顿就是主动消解运动的惯性，停下来。只有先停下来，才有之后的转向、转型。俄罗斯的再生、台湾的民主转型，都是跨越式停顿的产物，都是首先停顿后的转向和转型，而非突然的转弯。跨越式停顿可以用来阐释终结危险之旅、改造思维惯性、树立创新意识和革命性改造等，也可用在艺术流派的出现、学术上主义的产生和文化创意等领域，是一种具有横向性的哲学方法论。

6. 主张艺术和学术上的切割之别。

与跨越式停顿相联系的是，别现代在艺术创作中主张切割之别。通过对西方艺术史的考察，别现代理论发现，西方的艺术往往以主义或流派的方式存在。如现实主义、超现实主义、未来主义、达达主义、现成主义、立体主义、印象主义、抽象主义等。正是这些主义或流派，构成了西方艺术巨大的影响力和丰富的内容以及不断创新的形式、手法。与中国现当代艺术的没有主义和流派的现实相比，西方的主义和流派就建立在分别、切割的基础上，即在传承之后被传承者切

割，从而形成独立的具有知识产权的主义和流派。相反，中国的艺术界更多地强调了传承，而未能与被传承者之间形成切割，因而边界不清，独立性不强，原创性难以见到，也就形成不了主义和流派。传承——创新的口号被喊得山响，但却忽略了在传承与创新之间的一个最重要的因素，这就是在传承之后必须与被传承对象之间进行切割。切割就是划界，切割就是独立，切割就是创新。切割的理论往哲学上靠，就是跨越式停顿。当学到了老师的看家本领后，是守家看户呢，还是自立门户，自成一体，自成一派呢，这就要看艺术家本人的素质，他的抱负，他的志向，他的能量，看他是否会在顺风顺水之时甚至如日中天之际来个跨越式停顿了。吴天明导演的《百鸟朝凤》说的就是传承了独门绝活的徒弟，因为未能与恩师在艺术上切割而自创一派，最后整个独门绝活被时代抛弃而只能成为活化石的悲剧性故事。中国艺术不能再靠什么秘方、绝活来自大了，而是要冲出自闭的牢笼，引入更多的哲思和主义。做徒弟的要有切割的思想准备，做老师的也要有被弃置、被切割、被超越的思想准备和希望后辈超前辈的胸怀，否则，艺术的流派何以形成?

与艺术上的切割相比，学术流派的产生更需要切割。真正的学术流派都建立在批判的基础上。只有批判，才能厘清边界，才会有自己的思想和自己的阵地，才有资格用自己的思想到思想市场上去进行交换。中国的文化艺术传统是通变和变通。通变就是讲先通后变。通就是与源头相通。源头就是四书五经之类的。变就是在通的前提下进行变化。刘勰、严羽、郑燮，所谈虽有不同，但基本上不出通变的范围。别现代认为，正是通变这种传统的制约，导致了中国突变观念的式微。而要突变，首先就要在传承的基础上进行切割。就以在中国流行的现象学哲学而言，从黑格尔到胡塞尔，再到海德格尔、伽达默尔、姚斯，一路走来，无一不是后学对前辈的超越，无一不是后来学说对之前传承的切割。因此，别现代主义之别是彻底的别，而非藕断丝连的杂糅。

7. 主张审美形态之别。别现代主义美学基于中国审美形态范畴与西方审美形态范畴的考察认为，中国的审美形态有别于西方的审美形态，尤其是中国古代的审美形态要比西方的还要丰富，往往是西方有的中国也有疑似的，如悲剧、丑等，而中国有的西方却没有，如中和、神妙、气韵、意境、阴柔与阳刚等。但是在2000年以前的中国美学教科书中，基本上都是西方的审美形态而无中国的审美形态。至今也有不少的教材没有写入中国的审美形态。这是一个很大的缺陷。因为审美形态范畴就是美学范畴中最为基本的也最容易被把握的范畴，学习美学最好的入口就是审美形态。别现代美学一直注重对审美形态的研究，曾主持完成过两个与审美形态相关的国家社科基金项目。一个是中国诗歌意境的生成和流变，一个是中国审美形态研究。做这些项目的目的就是发现有别于西方的审美形态，进而掌握中国美学的特点和发展规律。在审美形态范畴研究方面，我有两个产生过影响的理论，一个是诗歌意境生成理论，一个是内审美理论。这些理论都有着坚实雄厚的中国古代审美形态的基础，也有着明显的中国美学的特点。我始终认为，突破“中国美学还是美学在中国”这一诘难的入口还是对中国审美形态的研究。因为中国审美形态非常典型，个性分明，正好与西方审美形态相区别，进而可以生发出不同于西方的美学体系。

8. 主张中西马我之别。

中国哲学、美学乃至整个人文学科研究都有着较西方更为丰富的学术资源和思想资源。这是因为，中国学者对于西方学术的了解远远超过了西方学者对于中国学术的了解。固然这与汉语较之英语更难学有关，但更主要的原因在于西方中心主义作怪，导致西方学者对于中国学术资源的藐视和忽视。与西方学者的学术资源仅限于西方的和马克思主义的不同，中国学者的学术资源除了西方的和马克思主义的之外，还有中国的，包括中国古代资源和近现代资源。因此，坚持中西马的学术资源观，就具有了相较西方学者而言的优势，这个优势就是

差别所带来的种类上的优势。但是，别现代主义在中西马我资源论的基础上更进一步，提出了中西马我的主张。① 而且进一步认为，在中西马我中，我更具有中心的地位。因为中西马都需要研究者“我”来理解、我来利用、我来创造，所以，在中西马跟西方的西与马之别之后，又来个中西马我与中西马的区别，从而把别现代之别贯彻到底。说到底，人文学术是个我研究思考的事，有时需要合作，但更主要的还在于依靠个我的劳动。因此，提出中西马我的学术资源观，并非为了标新立异，而是做符合学术研究规律的事，充分调动和发挥个我从事学术研究的主观能动性。通过中西马我之别，更有利于深入而又全面的学术创新、思想创新。

9. 防止以别为由对共同价值的否定、遮蔽和改造。

目前我国的学术研究正处于一种悖论中。一方面，强调中国特色，坚持走特色道路，与西方保持距离；但另一方面，在学术研究上却往往唯西方马首是瞻，盲目认同西方，邯郸学步，陷于“失语症”的尴尬，是中国美学/哲学还是美学/哲学在中国的诘难依然在困扰着我们，更谈不上什么特色的问题。特色必须建立在真实性基础上，如果不真实，是个伪现代，特色就失去了意义。真伪不辨，这种现状正是思想欠发达的表现。其结果就是学术研究上的无别可言。无别可言导致拿不出自己的东西，进行思想市场上的交换。西方的政要们说过，中国只能做大国而不可能做强国，因为中国人只能输出商品和劳力，不可能输出思想。西方的学界至今也是这个看法。著名美学家阿列西·艾尔雅维茨在与我商榷的一篇文章中引述亚里士多德和雅克·朗西埃的话，对我的别现代主义先是肯定，之后就从声音与语言的区分上指出，尽管我已经向世界发出了建构别现代主义的声音，但距离真正的语言尚有距离。在西方传统学术观念中，发出声音是人和动物

① 王建疆：《哲学、美学、人文学科四边形与别现代主义》，《探索与争鸣》2016年第9期。

都能够做到的，而语言，并且只有语言才是人所具有的。[①] 这种先扬后抑的论述技巧潜藏着一种对中国学术的不信任。这种不信任主要来自西方学者认为，我们是在否认人类共同价值的前提下又按照五年计划的政府主导的方式来做学术包括主义的，因此，充其量也就是发出点声音告诉世界，中国也要进行学术上的、思想上的、主义上的创造，而实际上并非真正去建立什么主义或流派。

艾尔雅维茨的质疑虽然刺激，但也提醒我，坚持特色是否会与坚守真实性和坚守人类共同价值相矛盾，坚持别现代主义之别是否就意味着一定要否定、遮蔽、改造人类共同价值。显然，这是一个历史性的选择。但作为别现代理论有关如何去别的话题，我坚持认为，人类具有某些共同的价值和价值观，这种共同的价值和价值观不能因为要有所别而被否认、被遮蔽或者被改造。相反，要通过建立在真实性基础上的别来体现共同价值、遵守共同价值，要坚决防止以别为由而对共同价值和共同价值观的否定、遮蔽和改造。

当艾尔雅维茨读过我对他的反驳后，他又写了一篇文章，题目是《对王建疆别现代主义的再评论》。他说，我的别现代主义触及他的神经深处的痛点，他突然感到不管是在中国还是在西方，我们的脚下缺少了什么。但一时也找不到，想不起来，到底缺少了什么。[②] 我想，艾尔雅维茨所感到的缺失，就是我所说的别。正是我所说的别，使他感到了前所未有的冲击。

中西之间各有所本，也各有各需，但西方人也好，中国学者也好，大家最容易犯的错误仍在于对于现实的忽视。因忽视而认识不到，因而总是感到缺了点什么，但又说不清楚究竟缺了什么。可能这

① 王建疆：《哲学、美学、人文学科四边形与别现代主义》，《探索与争鸣》2016 年第 9 期。

② Aleš Erjavec: *Some Additional Remarks Concerning Issues Opened by Prof. Jianjiang Wang*, International Academic Seminar on Discourse Innovation and Bie-modern Problems in Art and Aesthetics, pp. 100 – 105.

种缺失就在脚下的现实中，因而难免危险。

别现代理论就是立足于对脚下缺陷的清醒认识，然后始于足下，建构自身，形成别现代主义。如果说，别现代是杂糅的，那么，别现代主义却是纯一的，这种纯一就是自我更新主义、自我调节主义、自我超越主义和实事求是的兑现主义。

别 bié

〔附〕彆 biè

本义是“分剖”。甲骨文的字形，一边是“刀”；一边是“冎”，即骨头。《说文》：“㓨，分解也。”段玉裁注：“分别、离别皆是也。”《淮南子》：“宰庖之切割分别也。”简化字“别”字还兼代“彆”。

甲骨文
秦简文
小篆
隶书
楷书
草书
行书
简化字（同楷书）

图一

Introduction

What is "Bie" in Bie-modern?

Wang Jianjiang

Bie-modern theory (Bie-modernity, Bie-modernism)① is an innovative theory about the current social form and the stage of historical development in China. Since the putting forward of the notion in the Sino-Russian High-level Cultural Forum, Bie-modern has arisen heated discussion in domestic and foreign academic circles. More noticeably, the notion had to take the Pinyin (Chinese phonetic alphabet) "Bie" for not finding the most appropriate English equivalent to the Chinese Character "别", which was then unexpectedly adopted by the famous scholars in some European and American countries in their articles such as Aleš Erjavec. The Center of Chinese Bie-modern Studies (CCBMS) was established at Georgia Southwestern

① Bie-modern is translated from Chinese character 别现代 (bie xian dai), which contains Bie-modern and Bie-modernism. Bie-modern is different from Bie-modernism. "Bie-modern" is pseudo modern certified by the annual National Public Day of Anti Fake Commodity on March 15 in China, while "Bie-modernism" is deter-pseudo modern and sets up the real modernity. Therefore, "Bie-modern" is P (Pseudo) modern, but "Bie-modernism" is D (Deter-pseudo) modern and sets up R (Real) modern. From P modern to D modern and then to R modern, there is the Bie-modern theory throughout. Zhang Xiaogang, Wang Guangyi, Yue Minjun, Fang Lijun, etc., are typical Bie-modernist artists for criticizing the reality and uncover the pseudo modernity. "Bie-modern" is the generalization of the entangled state of modern, pre-modern and postmodern, while "Bie-modernism" is the criticism on and transcendence over the Bie-modern. Bie-modern is reality, but Bie-modernism is value orientation.

State University (GSW) in the U. S. As said in the article of annual academic conclusion of theory of literature and art published by *Literature and Art Forum*, Bie-modernism "as an innovative and constructive theoretical theme is gaining continuous concern and discussion among Chinese and overseas scholars."① In addition to the warm feedback, there still exist some questions: What is "Bie" in Bie-modern? For what is there "Bie" in the concept? How is Bie-modern distinguished by itself? In my opinion, these questions are not a burden; instead, they will be the driving force for the development of Bie-modern theory.

What is "Bie" in Bie-modern?

1. "Bie" in Chinese

"Bie" in Bie-modern has multiple meanings. Literally, it means not, farewell, or wrongly written words; more implicitly, it refers to awkward, or another, etc. For the meaning of "the other" or "another", it is as a matter of fact today's usage of an ancient meaning. There is no character of "ling" (另) in classical Chinese, and all its functions has been replaced by "Bie" (别). For example, in Biecai (别裁), biezhuan (别传), bieshu (别墅), biedongdui (别动队), the character "Bie" all stands for "another". It is not strange for "Bie" having so many meanings, as the character "Bie" at first expressed the connotation of making bone and flesh separated (see also the attached figure 1). The word was then expounded to have more meanings, such as no, different, distinct, farewell, another, awkward, separated, other one, and etc. However, meaning is meaning,

① See Ke Xiaofeng, "To Build Contemporary Chinese Literary Theory in the Self-confidence and Dialogue," *Literature and Art Forum*, no. 3 (2017).

as an academic term, it needs to be defined, especially in the concrete context.

2. "Bie" in reality

At the first glance, the notion of Bie-modern is likely to generate the meaning of refusing modern or bidding farewell to modern according to the Chinese original meaning. But in fact it has the opposite connotation. We are not refusing modern; instead we are eager for something of qualitative stipulation on the temporal concept of "modern", that is, modernity. Modernity starts from the Enlightenment movement and industrial revolution in Europe, marked by scientific rationality spirit, social contract system, freedom and equality concept and social welfare system. Modernity, as the symbol for human progress, is the intrinsic reason why it is this era rather than other times. Since different countries and different nations are in different development stage, they are unequaled in the degree or quality of modernity in spite of being in the same chronological age. As a developing nation, to measure the degree of its modernity, a contrast has to be made with the proportion of the pre-modern.

Although China is in the temporal and spatial dimensions of chronicle stage and material modernization has reached a high level, the pre-modern thought, consciousness and system are still occupying the social space, leaving the real modernity hidden and distorted. China is far from the genuine and sufficient modernity, and we can only say that we are on the road to modernity. The TV series, *In the Name of People*, which was popular in the spring, 2017, is actually the artistic reflection of current social situation and historical development stage that modernity is still on the road. Gao Yuliang, Deputy Secretary-General of CPC Handong Provincial Committee and Secretary of the Political and Legal Committee, originally a law professor, though his talks about the law are always closely reasoned and well ar-

gued, and despite his proclaim that the legal bottom line cannot be breached at any time, is following in the personnel system the intimate party (former disciples and subordinates) and nepotistic relations in the feudal society with the concept of pre-modern personal bondage and the idea of requiting rooted deep in his thought, and everything he has done is to maintain the pre-modern system that could protect the vested interests groups. As for Zhao Lichun, the former provincial Party secretary who supported Gao to the position of deputy provincial Party secretary, he is the embodiment of feudal patriarchal ideology and system who has asked all officials to serve his son. In doing all the things just for the benefit of himself or his coterie, competing with the people and violating their interests, turning a blind eye to and even trampling on the human rights that reflect modernity, and abandoning the laws that protect people' s rights, there is much difference with the real modernity. The most outstanding characteristic of the criminal interest group in Handong province is that they violate the laws and break the rules holding high the banner of laws, harm people in the name of people, featuring obvious falsity and fraud. Because the concepts such as the law and people are the specific dimensions of modernity, while in reality, the people and the laws are always undermined, obscured and replaced, thus the modernity exposed in the play is not the real, genuine and sufficient modernity, on the contrary, it turns out to be a false and disloyal modernity in modern society. That is like monks eating meat are chanting Buddhist scripture. Therefore, China' s current corruption is essentially a problem lack of modernity, a Bie-modern problem, more profound and complicated than corruption itself.

China, since the reform and opening-up, has been in the process of moving towards modernity, but for now, the reality of China is still a entangled state mixed with the modern, pre-modern and postmodern, without a clear boundary, thus it is hard to be characterized as pure modern or pre-

modern, nor postmodern, so we can only say that it is Bie-modern. "Bie" here has a meaning separated from modernity. Bie-modernism represents a distinction, separation and incision from the false and disloyal modernity, so as to possess the real modernity and promote China to enter a new historical stage. It is in this sense that China's reform and opening-up is a process bidding farewell to the pre-modern and heading for the modern. Therefore, the putting forward of Bie-modern is not a game of words, but a reflection and generalization of reality, which is in line with the trend of historical development and is thus of a progressive value.

3. "Bie" in theory

Any theory is not only a reflection of reality, but also more importantly a generalization of reality. Bie-modern is rooted in current China's situation, and the root of the theory is China's reality rather than the Western theoretical system. Western theoretical system has an enlightening role in constructing China's theoretical system, but because of its different background, social form and historical development stage, the universality of its theory will be limited. Therefore, the theoretical construction based on Chinese reality should be distinguished from the Western theoretical system.

Compared with the Western period-cut development, China is a synchronic existence, the spatialization of time or times. Western modern is the denying and incising of the pre-modern, while its postmodern is a transcendence over the modern. As a result, the distinctions between the pre-modern, modern and post-modern in the West are very clear, so the Western history is in fact a period-cut history. On the contrary, China is intertwined with the modern, pre-modern and postmodern in its social form, with no division of history into periods but mixture and combination. The spatialized feature of time requires the corresponding theoretical generalization that accords with it. The social form is called time spatialization in Bie-modern theory. This time spatialization theory comes from the reality of China, thus completely different from those space theories of the Western countries.

The time spatialization of the Bie-modern does not stay in the generalization of the nature and characteristics of the social form, but has introduced the dialectical view of history development in the current situation of time spatialization. Due to the fundamental incompatibility between the modern and pre-modern as well as the natural diaphragm between the postmodern and pre-modern, they are as a matter of fact in the historical process of both harmonious conspiracy and opposing contradiction. In this process, there appeared four phases of the Bie-modern, namely the harmony andconspiracy, the conflict and contradiction, the interweaving of harmony and conflict and the self-renewal and transcendence. Accompanied with the four phases, the functions of aesthetics and art have also changed. In the phase of harmony and conspiracy it gives full play to the functions of realism aesthetics and postmodern parody aesthetics, and also emphasizes the true reflection of social reality as well as the irony and exposure of harmonious conspiracy illusions, which are conducive to pointing out the problems, distinguishing the clear and the muddy, suppressing the evil and praising the good. In the conflict and contradiction phase, it stresses the promotion of tragedy and sublimity and other aesthetic forms, which contribute to the awakening of people's self-respect and self-confidence, the cohesion of positive energy, and the maintaining of the healthy social development. In the interweaving phase of harmony and conflict, Chinese cold humor is attached with great importance which helps to release the social grievances and soothe the mind. The TV series *In the Name of People* vividly depicted the four historical phases. Because the harmony and conspiracy of the vested interest group was established on the basis of encroaching on the interests and rights of workers in Dafeng factory, the conflicts between the two parties were increasingly inten-

sified, with the intertwining of anti-corruption and the fight against it. The significance of this play did not lie in the fact that corruption could be overcome and had been overcome, but that the dominant force was not content with the victory after defeating corruption, and began to think of the supervision over power, revealing the sign of self-reflection and self-renewal. In fact, China's reality is ubiquitously confirming the existence of the four historical phases brought by the time spatialization. Doctor-patient conflict, environmental pollution, the production and sales of counterfeit goods, the distortion of history, and major security accidents, etc. all happened in the framework of a set of law and regulations, featuring a harmonious conspiracy and the interweaving of harmony and conflict; at the same time, the force promoting the reform was also growing. It is the theory of Bie-modern historical stage that has made the Bie-modern time spatialization get rid of the unpractical abstraction and the embarrassment of reciting for the West, and get down to earth with China's situation. Naturally, the Bie-modern time spatialization has become a kind of original theory and China's own space theory distinguished from a series of Western space theories starting with Lefebvre①.

4. "Bie" in differences

"Bie" in Bie-modern pays attention to not only the plane difference of things at the same level, but also the vertical difference that goes beyond.

Great-leap-forward Pause in Bie-modern theory has aroused some feedback, which implies a sudden autonomous stop in the advanced or high-speed developmental stage or in its booming and flourishing growth. The cases of Great-leap-forward Pause can be found in the strategy of drawing back

---

① See Wang Jianjiang, "Bie-modern: Time Spatialization and Aesthetic Functions," *Modern Literary Forum*, no. 6, 2016.

wisely from the most illustrious moment in official career and the idea of attainingBuddhahood in the way of sudden enlightenment in Zen Buddhism, seen from the exercises of No-Water Day, No-Tobacco Day and No-Vehicle Day in the globe today, and felt from the sudden disintegration of autocratic systems in some countries and regions①. Great-leap-forward Pause is actually a correction of Great-leap-forward Development as it has been recognized that the leapfrog development in economy, technology and military cannot replace the non-leapfrog development in cultural tradition, natural ecology and social system, so it is not rare to see the collapse and failure caused by the leapfrog development in the latter aspects. Instead, drawing on the lessons and conducting Great-leap-forward Pause can avoid failure and collapse, and achieve smooth running and long-term stability. Great-leap-forward Development is different from following-up development and transcends over it, while Great-leap-forward Pause is a difference from and transcendence over Great-leap-forward Development, which is a difference in difference and transcendence in transcendence. Therefore, "Bie" in Bie-modern is "Bie" in difference.

There is another example in "Bie" in difference of the Bie-modern, that is, the difference between Bie-modernism and Bie-modern. "Bie-modern" is the generalization of the entangled state of modern, pre-modern and postmodern, while "Bie-modernism" is the criticism on and transcendence over Bie-modern. Bie-modern is reality, but Bie-modernism is value orientation. "Bie-modern" is pseudo modernity certified by the annual National Public Day of Anti Fake Commodity on March 15 in China, while

① See Wang Jianjiang, "Bie-modern: Great-leap-forward Pause," *Exploration and Free Views*, no. 12, 2015, pp. 9 - 14, reprinted by Principles of Philosophy, *Periodical Literatures Reprinted by RUC* in no. 3, (2016).

"Bie-modernism" is deter-pseudo modernity and sets up the real modernity. Therefore, "Bie-modern" is P (Pseudo) modern, but "Bie-modernism" is D (Deter-pseudo) modern and R (Real) modern. From P modern to D modern and then to R modern, there is the Bie-modern theory throughout. The difference between Bie-modernism and Bie-modern is "Bie" in difference and the difference in surpassing and being surpassed, which constitutes the organic whole of the Bie-modern theory, deterring the false and disloyal modernity, expecting and constructing real differing modernity. The former, indicates the recognition of modernity and common human value; the latter, building differing modernity, manifests the differences among similarities with the Western modernity, thus forming the characteristics of Chinese modernity. "Bie" in difference makes Bie-modern theory continually involved in self-renewal and self-transcendence, thus maintaining the youth of theoretical innovation forever. "Bie" in difference should become a kind of innovation mechanism, innovation method, and innovation path.

In addition to such theories as time spatialization, historical stage theory, aesthetic function theory and Great-leap-forward Pause, there are some other theoretical categories, like the "after Post-modern" theory in development①, Sino-West-Marxism-I ("Chinese Traditional Philosophy, Western Philosophy, Marxism and Individual") ② in ideological resources, "cutting" theory in artistic innovation through inheritance and reference, hero

---

① See WANG Jianjiang, "Bie-modernism: Beyond Aesthetics and after Postmodernism—On Reaction to an International Aesthetics Trend led by Welsch Wolfgang," *Journal of Shanghai Normal University* (*Philosophy & Social Sciences Edition*), no. 1 (2015), pp. 5 – 14, reprinted by *Social Sciences Weekly*, 3rd page, Apr. 9, 2015.

② See WANG Jianjiang, " Quadrilateral in Philosophy, Aesthetics and Humanities and Bie-modernism" . *ART & MEDIA STUDY*, forthcoming.

space theory and "consumption on Japan" theory[①], which are all brand-new theories established on the basis of "Bie" . These differing theories are novel and originative, but never weird, or unconventional or unorthodox, and they tend to embrace the essence of theoretical innovation, that is, to build the thought or *Zhuyi* different from others' . I once said that the less-developed academic thought in China lies in the underdeveloped *Zhuyi*[②]. Therefore, the putting forward of Bie-modern is an attempt to build *Zhuyi*, and all the theories relevant to Bie-modern can be categorized in the name of Bie-modernism.

In short, whether from language, reality, theory or the way of thinking, Bie-modern is doing the job of discovering "Bie" and constructing "Bie" . "Bie" is a kind of thought, way and*Zhuyi*, decided by the development of reality and by China' s national conditions. China, breaking the isolation and walking towards the world, is in urgent need for thought and theory that comes from reality, conforms to reality and guides reality, and for the doctrine and *Zhuyi* that involves independent thinking and constitutes its own discourse system. The so-called independence, originality, and discourse cannot exist without "Bie" . In the whole world, any country should have its own "Bie" (difference) . In the academic field each scholar should have their own "Bie" . Whether the "Bie" is big or small, new or old, the existence of "Bie" will be definitely leading to the independence and innovation. In this sense, "Bie" is subjectivity and originality, "Bie" is discourse power and theoretical confidence.

---

① See Wang Jianjiang, "Consumption on Japan and Deconstruction of Hero Space", Chinese Literary Criticism, no. 2, 2017.

② See Wang Jianjiang, "Academic Tactics in an Era of Intellectual underdevelopment: The Case of Aesthetics," *Chinese Social Sciences Review*, no. 4, 2015, pp. 93 – 104.

For what is there "Bie" in Bie-modern?

From the perspective of teleology, the activities of the subject all have a purpose. As far as the Bie-modern theory is concerned, "For what is there 'Bie' in the concept?" is also a question that cannot be avoided.

First, "Bie-modern" is to seek diversity and subjectivity. It focuses on the distinctions, namely differences. Distinctions or differences belong to the category of philosophical epistemology. Difference is a category opposite to identity. As said in the ancient Chinese classic, *History of State of Zheng*, *National History*, "Harmony actually fosters new things and similarity doesn t sustain", harmony in diversity is advocated. Zhuangzi attaches great importance to the differences, and brings the problem of identity and difference into the category of relativism. He says in *Signs of Complete Integrity* that "seen from the aspect of differences of things, the closely related liver and gallbladder though in the same body are wide apart just like the State of Chu and the State of Yue; while from the aspect of similarities, all the things in the world are almost the same." Leibniz, the great thinker said that it is impossible to find the same leaves in a tree, but Kaiser at that time did not believe him, mobilized all the ministers and maids to search the same leaves, but Leibniz was then proved right. In this sense, "Bie" in Bie-modernism has universal philosophical significance. We should have the consciousness and concept of disparity, with which to establish ourselves and establish the object, thus forming a kind of subjectivity.

Disparity is not only philosophical epistemology, but also philosophical axiology. It is in recognizing the importance of disparity that we strive to seek and maintain distinction and establish ourselves and remain our own distinctive character in differences. The subjective value of disparity signifies

that even such highly acknowledged fields as belief, personal emotion, understanding and expression are equally important which cannot be deprived of, otherwise, the past religious reforms would be unlikely to happen. Hermeneutics arises from the different understanding of the Bible. Buddhism also has different annotations for Buddhist scriptures. Therefore, the issue of disparity from the perspective of axiology is essentially the need of existence and also the need of development. In the tension formed by the opposition to identity, the existence of individual self and the development of individual trajectory and characteristics are ensured.

Second, "Bie-modern" is the product of the ideology of seeking differences and divergences, pursuing the establishment of marketplace of ideas. As mentioned above, seeking differences is a need and also a value orientation. The value orientation of dissimilarity is rooted in the practical need for dissimilarity. If it is abstractly claimed that seeking dissimilarity will help to gain the difference between self and others and then establish one's own existence, this is just a hypothesis, so in terms of the reality of a related industry, the necessity and possibility of this self confirmation can be further clarified. As for the educational system in China, the education before high school is entirely an identity education, that is, "feedlot" education, the form of which is conducting cramming method of teaching in the range of the prescribed textbooks, teaching syllabus, examination syllabus and suggested answers, without allowing any differential thinking. The reason lies in the standard answers stipulated by the college entrance examination system. The standard key is like a red line, and whoever touches the red line is unlucky. Failure in the exam means there is no way to go. As a result, the school education before university is completely homogenous and singularized. When students enter the university through standardized examination, the weaknesses such as singleness and ossification from the homogenous education start

to be exposed. Many students do not know how to study, or how to write papers. Even after being trained in writing, they still cannot compose articles with their independent views, because the homogenous education has invaded deep in their soul, and constituted common cultural behavior pattern of both students and teachers, leading to the exhaustion of ideas.

The conformity behavior is more serious in the stage of postgraduates. The experiences of guiding and cultivating students of PhD and master told me that the dissertations of most postgraduates of liberal arts are usually narration rather than argumentation, not like a paper, but a narrative text. With no argument and evidence, but the ordering of process and materials, they are narration instead of speculation. Moreover, the writing of dissertations tends to be like writing a book, or a textbook, trying to cover all aspects of a matter. The dissertations usually have a clear and detailed outline, but are mostly short of academic innovation points and intellectual shining points. Thus we can say, the lack of all-round innovation from primary school to PhD students in China is closely related to the rampancy of homogenous education and the shortage of divergent thinking. The extinction of divergent thinking resulted from the homogenous education lead to the substantial backwardness of the entire education. A large number of Chinese students would rather ask their parents to pay the expensive tuition to study in Europe and America than continue to accept the domestic higher education, which explains the unavoidability of this problem.

Therefore, it can be said that the "Bie" in Bie-modern based on the divergence-seeking is not deliberately for the sake of it, on the contrary, it is the "Bie" (difference) in practical needs, talent cultivation, and education planning. What is "Bie" in Bie-modern? In different context, it has specific references. In terms of education, for what is there "Bie"? It is for the difference from homogenous education and identical thinking. Extended to other fields than education, "Bie" (difference) in Bie-modern is for the demand of existence and development.

"Bie" is not only distinction, but more importantly means deterring identical thinking and establishing divergent thinking. In the domain of ideology theory, it implies to say goodbye to the feedlot of thought and build a free market of ideas. Ronald Coase, the late British-born Nobel Laureate in economics in his 101 – year – old said to the Chinese audiences through the network that the lack of marketplace of ideas will eventually lead to China's economic crisis. At first glance, it appears to be alarmism, but after consideration we found that it actually signifies that a marketplace of ideas is required to facilitate the equal exchange of thought and the tempering of thought, so as to develop and activate ideas and constantly seek the best path of developing economy. The marketplace of ideas is probably opposed to the feedlot of ideas. Market offers the exchange of equal values, with the premise that we both have things and what you have is different from mine, otherwise it cannot be called market exchange. However, the feedlot of ideas is just the opposite, feeding with the same feed-stuff and the same method, without allowing independent thinking and different requirement. Although Mr. Coase was trying to give China an advice, but in terms of the hegemony of Western academic discourse, such free market of ideas does not exist between China and the West where only the feedlot of Western thought can be found. As far as the aphasia in literary theory world, and the question in aesthetic and philosophical circles whether it is Chinese philosophy and aesthetics or Western philosophy and aesthetics in China are concerned, they illustrate the one-dimensional acceptance, the lack of marketplace of ideas as well as the dominance of the feedlot of thought caused by underdeveloped thought. As for the present postgraduate education in our country, there are still a large number of small-scale workshop-like schools, with no

market of ideas between teachers and their students, but only the feedlot of thought. It can be even said that the feedlot of thought is absent and offers no feeding. Thus, "Bie" in Bie-modern means leaving the feedlot of thought but entering the free market of ideas, that is, using divergent thinking or different approaches to construct the marketplace of ideas, establish the existence of self and guarantee the advancing of innovation.

Third, Bie in Bie-modern implies a farewell to false and disloyal modernity. Nowadays, in the research about Chinese modernity, there sprung up many new terms, such as new modernity, mixed modernity, complicated modernity, and alternative modernity, etc., trying to find and define Chinese modernity from different angles. These efforts are commendable, but the problems in them cannot be ignored. One of the biggest problems in the study of Chinese modernity is whether China has already had the truly Westernized modernity, or sufficient modernity in the western sense. Modernity arose from the Western enlightenment movement and industrial revolution, the core categories and values are social contract, scientific rationality, human rights protection, humanity spirit, social welfare system, parliamentary democracy, the separation of powers, judicial independence, and freedom of speech, etc. It is this core category that rules the Western modernity. By contrast, whether China has this kind of modernity in the Western sense, or to what extent or degree it has such modernity, remains a problem that needs to be given careful consideration. If started from the reality of China, namely, the fact of primary stage of socialism, rather than from the Western modernity theory, to investigate present situation of Chinese modernity, we will find that China is a social form entangled with modern, pre-modern and postmodern, which is different from Western period-cut development, thus, it is difficult to have real, pure or sufficient modernity. Instead, pre-modern nightmare is still haunting us, and behind a lot of social corruption and seri-

ous safety accidents, there are pre-modern patriarchal clan system, authoritarianism, superstitions, nepotism, human world, disobedience to law and unspoken rules, etc. Therefore, no matter how to modify "modernity", for example, using such adjectives as "new", "complex", " alternative", "complicated", but whether the modified is modernity itself has become a problem. When pre-modernity, post-modernity and modernity exist at the same time, talking only about the last one instead of the first two is unavoidably biased, and it doesn' t make sense logically. In a state of the mixture, you only talk about modernity, but ignore the existence and proportion of the pre-modern and postmodern, just like calling those who went to temples or stayed in temples monks, and neglecting the fact that the meat monks and fake monks who abuse the practice for their own interests are occupying a larger proportion. Confusing those trained monks in the real sense with the ordinary believers is actually a misunderstanding on monks. From the point of ideological history and cultural history, the modernity from the West is not new at all, not complex, alternative, or complicated, on the contrary, the Western modernity concept is very clear and succinct; the so-called complicated, alternative, confused, old and new, are actually indicating that the researchers ignored the juxtaposition of the modern, pre-modern and post-modern and their different proportions, but to restrict and modify Western modernity rather than Chinese own. But this restriction and modification just covers the truth of non-modernity, and pseudo-modernity, giving them some illusion of authentic modernity; and this illusion is similar to a wrongly-written word which is not easy to be found. Thus, "Bie" in Bie-modern is to distinguish from and bid farewell to the non-sufficient and disloyal modernity and reveal the real form of the society.

Fourth, Bie-modernism is to build the real and different modernity. The value of Bie-modern theory does not only point out a mixed social form, but

also find its philosophical basis and social structure through revealing this social form. The Bie-modern time spatialization theory is the philosophical generalization of the Bie-modern social form, which comes from the Bie-modern reality rather than the Western space theories. Bie-modern theory is not only philosophical, but also systematical for revealing the social structure featured by time spatialization. The structure and functions of both harmony and contradiction resulted from the conflicts between the modern and the pre-modern suggested in the Bie-modern theory give a reasonable explanation for the value of Bie-modernism. At the same time, the philosophy of time-spatialization in Bie-modern theory has an outlook of historical development, and this is the social development phase theory of the Bie-modern, with self-renewal, self-regulation, self-transcendence, redemption for historical promise, and construction of the real modernity established on the basis of the harmony and conspiracy phase, the conflict and contradiction phase, the interweaving of harmony and conflict phase and the self-renewal and development phase. Due to the aboriginality and realism of time spatialization philosophy, it will be likely to lead to the Bie-modernity with some Chinese cultural characteristics that also accords with the standards of modernity. Bie-modernity is first of all the authentic, pure and sufficient modernity, and then a modernity that differs from the Western modernity in some extent. In this way, "Bie" in Bie-modern theory is united within itself on both differentiating from and bidding farewell to the disloyal modernity and constructing the unique modernity. It is the unity of history and logic, epistemology and axiology, common value and national characteristics.

Finally, "Bie" in Bie-modern is the difference of reality for nothing, and a distinction of no distinction. "Bie", as a different recognition concept or behavior based on the differences in philosophy, seems to act for willful action on the surface, but in fact it encompasses two cases of both a "Bie"

of difference and a "Bie" of no difference. The philosophy of Laozi emphasizes inaction, expecting to reach action through inaction. Zhuangzi developed Laozi' s theory, put forward the idea that "there are natural law and human world, that respected for inaction is natural, while that tired for action is humane", proclaiming the naturalistic ideology (that is, being natural and letting things take their own course) . But Zhuangzi, cited a lot of stories to illustrate that "Tao (the natural law) that I favor, has surpassed my pursuit for techniques", that is reaching the action through inaction and entering the nature of heaven by acting for willful action. In addition to "Bie" for something, there is "Bie" for nothing in Bie-modern theory. This is, to attain natural difference, which is the inherent difference of things. When "Bie" achieves at the extreme, there is no "Bie" (distinction or difference) . Just as said in Zhuangzi, *On the Uniformity of All Things*, there is no "Bie" (distinction or difference) on the ultimate level of Tao. But before reaching no distinction of natural law, there has to be distinction at first. Thus, the inaction thought (a Taoist concept of human conduct) of Laozi and Zhuangzi has the wisdom of dialectics, so it is a dialectical unity of both a "Bie" of difference and a "Bie" of no difference. "Bie" in Bie-modern means the distinguishing from pseudo modernity and implies a distinctive construction of a unique modernity, which seems to be "Bie" of action, but when the Bie-modern theory is drawn away from the reality of time spatialization, it is no longer difference out of intention, or "Bie" of purpose, but the "Bie" of reality, of space, of nature. In front of realistic "Bie" and natural "Bie", human' s "Bie" of action has no meaning at all. Only when a distinction of no distinction from reality and nature comes into being, just like action through inaction, could it become a philosophy or Bie-philosophy. Similarly, when "Bie" becomes a behavior pattern of human consciousness or non-consciousness, it will produce a kind of culture;

this culture is called "Bie" culture.

When Bie-philosophy and Bie-culture were generated, the innovation and creation began. And the beginning of all innovations is embodied as discourse innovation. Discourse innovation is the creation distinguished from other doctrine. Discourse cannot be separated from language, thus innovative language is also crucial in creation. As the initiator of Bie-modern, I have worked on discourse innovation in recent years in addition to the theoretical and ideological innovation of the Bie-modern. In 2017 New Year' s day and Spring Festival approaching, I wrote some greeting words and sent them to people, avoiding the embarrassment of a few same greeting messages shared by hundreds of millions of Chinese. So I take two excerpts from them, and bless all those who read this article.

New Year greetings on Jan. 1, 2017

Bie-modern wishes you a vague Bie-dream (beautiful dream), hope that you are Bie-well (extremely well), invent a Bie-idea (original idea), have a Bie-style (unique style), break a Bie-path (new path), and create a Bie-world (different world)!

Spring Festival greetings on Jan. 27, 2017

Wang Jianjiang of Bie-modern sincerelywishes you and your family on the year of Dingyou (according to the Heavenly Stems and Earthly Branches in the lunar calendar that is 2017): a Bie-life (lively life), Bie-wisdom (special wisdom), Bie-time (great time) and Bie-happiness (only happiness). Bie-forget (don' t forget) to give likes to such a message if you are happy with it.

In a word, for what is there "Bie" in Bie-modern? For the sake of discourse, thought, theory, philosophy, culture, creation, and of survival and development, for the sake of nothing, thus it is a distinction of no distinction, a distinction through no distinction. A "Bie" of difference and a

"Bie" of no difference, the two kinds of "Bie" (distinction or difference) have something in common. "Bie" relies on creator and creation lies in "Bie".

How is Bie-modern distinguished by itself?

After understanding what is "Bie" in Bie-modern and for what there is "Bie" in the concept, "How is Bie-modern distinguished by itself?" will be the central key in the issue. Marxist philosophy is not contented with understanding the world, but also aims to change the world, that is the spiritual evocation of how Bie is conducted. How Bie-modern is distinguished by itself can be seen from the following aspects.

1. Putting forward the Bie-modern theory which is opposite to the pre-modern, modern or postmodern

"Bie-modern" is a theory about social form and historical development stage, and the claim of this theory arises from the dissatisfaction or no full faith of the division of pre-modern, modern and postmodern in Western discourse system. The reason is that this division does not conform to the reality of China. Compared with the Western period-cut development that is modern replacing pre-modern, postmodern transcending modern, China is a synchronic social existence, encompassing both the harmony and conspiracy, and the contradiction and conflict of pre-modern, modern and post-modern. The mixed social state is neither modern, nor postmodern, or pre-modern, and can only be Bie-modern. The Bie-modern is the intertwined social form. Because the modern, pre-modern and postmodern coexist in different proportion, the social development direction will be likely to tilt for the larger percentage of one factor. For instance, if the modern has a larger proportion, the society will tilt towards the real modernity; if the pre-modern tendency is

too large, the possibility for the society going towards pre-modernity will increase. But in the process of interweaving and battling of the modern, pre-modern and postmodern, which one will take a lead in proportion usually tends to be a random thing. This randomness has constituted a multiple choice for the development of future China, and also become the realistic and theoretical evidence for the determinism of human factor in the renewal and transcendence of Bie-modernism.

The significance of Bie in Bie-modernism lies in that it has not only revealed the true face of social form, but also established the unique discourse system. If Bie-modern as a term can keep pace with pre-modern, modern and postmodern, then, the problems of discourse innovation and discourse power will be readily resolved.

2. Putting forward the time spatialization theory which is distinguished from the Western space theories

The philosophical basis of Bie-modern theory is time spatialization. That is, the interweaving and entangling of pre-modern, modern and post-modern, the current situation of both the harmony and conspiracy and the contradiction and conflict. The situation is the direct result of modernization and globalization. But when the old feudal kingdom was conquered by the imperial military power, the Western modernized material civilization and systematic civilization were forcibly implanted, mixed with the decadent pre-modern thought and backward culture, thus forming the coexistence of the material modernization of "hardware" and the feudalization of "software" for a quite long historical period. This state cannot be generalized by the Western space theories. Whether Lefebvre, Foucault or David Harve's space theory is, none of them concern Chinese social form. The social formation that their theories speak of is one obviously characteristic of period-cut features, so there is no mixture or entanglement of the modern, pre-modern and

postmodern. Therefore, time spatialization of the Bie-modern is the first "Bie", distinguished from the Western space theories. The first "Bie" (distinction or difference) signifies that it is a synchronic theory about Chinese social form, rather than space production theory, personal micro-space theory, Network space theory, space compression theory and spatial narrative theory, etc. It was the first "Bie" (distinction or difference) that provided the space for the development of Bie-modern theory and the possibility and feasibility of establishing Chinese innovation theory.

3. Putting forward the four-phase theory of the Bie-modern to illustrate the unique social structure and function

Bie-modern theory established on the philosophical basis of time spatialization, seen from the inevitable confrontation between modern and pre-modern and the historical diaphragm between pre-modern and postmodern, there is a tension structure of both conflict and harmony. According to the modern system theory that structure determines function, as this structure is not fixed, but appears oscillation or deviation trend in the random changes, tilting toward the modern, or directing to the pre-modern, which all depends on the thought and will of the dominant power, thus, the trend of Bie-modern society is hard to be predicted. But in such an intertwined structure full of tension, due to the different proportion and mutual competing, it will be bound to form the four historical phases, namely, the harmony and conspiracy, the conflict and contradiction, the interweaving of harmony and conflict and the self-renewal and transcendence. The ultimate way out for Bie-modernism is to go beyond the four historical phases, that is, denying the Bie-modern and entering the stage of modernity, which not only conforms to the tendency of human historical progress, but also combines with excellent Chinese cultural essence, thus to some degree it is modernity with national cultural characteristics. When modernity is sufficient, the day of Chinese mod-

ernization will come. The historical phase theory of the Bie-modern is very unique among all the theories relating to the stage of human social development.

4. Putting forward the new horizon of reflecting on the current situation after postmodern

Although Bie-modern theory holds that the West is a period-cut social development process while China is a synchronic society, it does not advocate that China should pursue the Western modern and postmodern as goals. On the contrary, it believes that post-modern will face an end one day. Just as the term "after-postmodern" mentioned by the famous Western thinker, Deleuze, postmodern is only a link in the process of the evolution of the Western society. Now "after-postmodern" is very popular in the whole world, which implies the denying and transcending of the postmodern. Bie-modern theory does not follow Western historical process, or go through every historical stage of the West, but in a state of time spatialization, that is, in the interweaving of modern, pre-modern and postmodern, examines and reflects on postmodern; standing in the position of after-postmodern, looks back and reviews our present age, and makes predictions about our future. This is a forward thinking and also time leapfrog. Despite being located in Bie-modern yet not reaching the real modern, going to the after-postmodern to review and look back on the Bie-modern looks impossible or even ridiculous for ordinary people. But don't forget, thought and ideology have forward thinking and predictability. Only when the Western modern and postmodern are crossed in mind and thought, can we review and examine the present Bie-modern from the Western after-postmodern, so as to provide ideological preparation for us to go out of and bid farewell to the Bie-modern, and help us further construct the unique modernity. Otherwise, following the Western historical process blindly not only is impossible but will also cause someone to lose his own originality when imitating others. Thus the after-postmodern retrospect and review theory of the Bie-modern is a brand-new field of vision, a philosophy of transcendence, and a Bie-philosophy.

5. Raising Great-leap-forward Pause theory so as to distinguish itself from Great-leap-forward Development

Great-leap-forward Development theory comes from the late-developing theory and leapfrog theory in Western economics, holding that the backward countries can avoid the experimental detours that the developed countries walked through and catch up with them, even achieve the effect of "the pupil outdoes the master". The development of economy, technology, military since China's reform and opening-up, has proved the possibility and feasibility of the Great-leap-forward Development. However, the "Bie" (distinction or difference) of Bie-modern theory lies in that it put forward the Great-leap-forward Pause against the leapfrog development. Great-leap-forward Pause theory implies a sudden stop in its booming and flourishing growth and even a change in its route of development. Leapfrog pause is a kind of development philosophy, a philosophy of life and also existential intelligence. Laozi insists on retiring after success, Confucians speak of bravely drawing back from the most illustrious moment in official career. Zen upholds the highest principle which cannot be explained in words, and advocates the truncating of cross flow, which are all Great-leap-forward Pause in advanced and super-advanced stage. Great-leap-forward Pause arises from the limit of growth, which demands pause and retreat as early as possible, rather than to wait until the opposite consequences lay in front of you. It is based on the leapfrog development of technology, military and economics on the one hand, but absolutely on the non-leapfrog development of natural ecology, cultural inheritance, and social system on the other hand. Soviet Union went to collapse precisely because it reveled in the leapfrog develop-

ment on military, technology and economics but ignored the non-leapfrog development of social system, natural ecology and cultural heritage. Great-leap-forward Pause is not a great direction change or transformation, for in the high-speed leapfrog development, a sudden turn means destruction. It tries actively to relieve its force of inertia and come to a stop. Only after a stop, can there be the following turn or transformation. Russia' s regeneration or Taiwan' s democratic transition is a product of leapfrog pause, the direction change and transformation after a pause, rather than a sudden turn. Great-leap-forward Pause can be used to interpret and terminate the dangerous journey, transform the thinking inertia, set up innovation consciousness and carry out revolutionary transformation, etc. , and it can also be applied in such fields as the emergence of art schools, the generation of academic*Zhuyi* and cultural creativity, etc. , thus it is a kind of horizontal philosophical methodology.

6. Advocating the distinction of the incision in art and academics

Associated with Great-leap-forward Pause, "Bie-modern" advocates the distinction of incision in the artistic creation. Based on the research of the history of Western art, it is found in the Bie-modern theory that Western art often exists in the form of doctrines (-isms, equivalent to Chinese *Zhuyi*) or schools, for example, realism, surrealism, futurism, Dadaism, cubism, impressionism, and abstract expressionism, etc. It is these doctrines (-isms) or schools that have generated the enormous influence, and constituted the rich content and innovative technique of Western art. Compared with the reality of Chinese modern and contemporary art with no *Zhuyi* or schools, Western doctrines (-isms) and schools were established on the basis of separation and incision, that is, being cut by inheritors after inheritance, consequently forming distinctive doctrines (-isms) or schools with their own intellectual property rights. On the contrary, the Chinese art world

attached more importance with inheritance, and failed to be cut from the object being inherited, thus having unclear boundary, weak independence and rare originality, so *Zhuyi* and schools were not likely to come into being. The slogan of inheritance and innovation was shouted loudly, but one of the most important factors between inheritance and innovation was ignored, that is, after inheritance, incision has to be made with the object being inherited. Incision is demarcation, independence, and innovation. If the theory of incision leans to philosophy, it turns out to be Great-leap-forward Pause. Whether the artist keeps watching homes or sets up his own school of thought, has a style of his own and creates his own system after learning the master' s special skills actually depends on the quality of the artist himself, his ambition, his ideal, his energy and if he can have a Great-leap-forward Pause in the smooth or flouring period of development. *Song of the Phoenix* directed by Wu Tianming, tells a tragic story that a disciple, who inherited the unique talents, was not cut from his master in art nor created his own style, and the unique talents he learned was finally discarded by the times and became a living fossil. Thus, Chinese art can no longer rely on secret recipe or special skills to brag itself, but to run out of the closed cage and introduce more philosophical thought and *Zhuyi*. A disciple should have the ideological preparation for incision, and a teacher should also be prepared in thought to be abandoned, cut or surpassed and have a breadth of vision that younger generations exceed their predecessors, otherwise, how will the schools of art be formed?

Compared with the incision in art, the generation of art schools needs more incision. The true academic schools were established on the basis of criticism. Only being criticized, could their boundary be clarified, and they could have their own thought and positions and be qualified in exchange for others with their own thought. Culture and art tradition of China is to "con-

nect and change" as well as "being flexible". "Connect and change" refers to connect before change. Connect means connecting to the source. The source is the Four Books and the Five Classics of Confucianism. Change occurs in the premise of "connection". What Liu Xie, Yan Yu or Zheng Xie, the Ancient Chinese Writers and thinkers talked about, despite the differences, cannot go beyond the range of "connect and change". Bie-modern theory holds that it is the constraints of "connect and change" tradition that lead to the decline of Chinese conception of mutation. To realize mutation, cutting has to be made on the foundation of inheritance. So in terms of philosophy of phenomenology that is popular in China, from Hegel to Husserl, to Heidegger, Gadamer, and Jauss, along the way, none of them is not the transcendence of the latter over the former, or the incision of the latter theory on the former. Therefore, "Bie" in Bie-modernism means the complete distinction rather than thearbitrary entanglement that is not entirely cut off.

7. Advocating the distinction in aesthetic forms

Bie-modernism aesthetics based on the exploration of Chinese aesthetic morphology and Western aesthetic morphology holds that Chinese aesthetic forms are different from Western aesthetic forms; in particular, Chinese ancient aesthetic forms are richer than the Western forms. Usually, corresponding to the Western aesthetic forms such as tragedy, and ugliness, etc., China has similar and resembling ones; while the West does not have equivalents for those Chinese aesthetic forms, such as Zhong He (mediation and harmony), Shen Miao (miracle and wonder), Qi Yun (spirit and vitality), Yi Jing (artistic conception), Yin Rou (female gentleness) and Yang Gang (male strength), and etc. However, in the textbooks of Chinese aesthetics before 2000, most of which essentially include Western aesthetic forms rather than Chinese aesthetic forms. Until now quite a few teaching

materials have not contained Chinese aesthetic forms. This is a big flaw. Because the aesthetic category on morphology is the easiest to grasp, the best entry for learning aesthetics is through aesthetic forms. Bie-modern aesthetics have always paid attention to the study of aesthetic forms, which carried out two relevant national social science fund projects. One is the generation and evolvement of the artistic conception of Chinese poetry, the other is on Chinese aesthetic morphology. The purpose of these projects is to find the unique aesthetic forms that are different from the West ones and then grasp the characteristics and development law of Chinese aesthetics. In the research of aesthetic morphology, I have produced two influential theories, one is the theory of the generation of the artistic conception of poetry, and the other is inner aesthetic theory. Both of them have a solid foundation of ancient Chinese aesthetic forms, and obvious characteristics of Chinese aesthetics. I always think that the entrance of breaking through the question "Chinese aesthetics or aesthetics in China" lies in the study of Chinese aesthetic forms. Because Chinese aesthetic forms are very typical and have rich individual characters which differ from the western ones, it will be likely to generate an aesthetic system different from the West.

8. Advocating the distinction of Sino-West-Marxism-I

Chinese philosophy, aesthetics and the whole humanities, have more abundant academic resources and ideas than the West. It is because Chinese scholars' understanding of Western academics is far more than what Western scholars know about Chinese academics. It is certainly related to that Chinese is more difficult to learn than English, but the more important reason is the Western centralism, leading to the contempt and ignorance of Chinese academic resources. Different from the Western scholars' academic resources limited to the West and Marxism only, Chinese scholars have Chinese elements in their academic resources, namely, Chinese ancient re-

sources and modern and contemporary resources. Thus, the insistence on the view of the Sino-West-Marxism academic resources makes Chinese scholars have an edge over the Western scholars, which is an advantage in categories brought by the differences. However, Bie-modernism explores much further on the basis of the Sino-West-Marxism academic resources, by putting forward the claim of Sino-West-Marxism-I ("Chinese Traditional Philosophy, Western Philosophy, Marxism and Individual Thought")① . And it further argues that "I" is in a central position compared with the other three resources. Because all the Sino-West-Marxism academic resources require "I " to understand, utilize and create, so following the difference between Sino-West-Marxism academic resources and the Western West-Marxism resources, the other difference between Sino-West-Marxism-I and Sino-West-Marxism comes up, which carry out the Bie (distinction or difference) in Bie-modern to the end. After all, the humanities academic is a thing for individual research and thinking, sometimes calling cooperation, but more importantly depends on one' s own work. Therefore, putting forward the view of the Sino-West-Marxism academic resources is not to do something unconventional or unorthodox, but do something that accords with the law of academic research, fully mobilize and give full play to the subjective initiative of individual "I" engaged in academic studies. Through the distinction of Sino-West-Marxism-I, it will be conducive to the in-depth and comprehensive academic and ideological innovation.

9. Preventing the denial, shielding and transformation of common values for the sake of characteristics

At present, China' s academic research is in a paradox. On the one

① See Wang Jianjiang, "Philosophy, Aesthetics and Humanities Quadrilateral and Bie-modernism", *Exploration and Free Views*, no. 9, 2016.

hand, it emphasizes the Chinese characteristics and adheres to the distinctive road with Chinese characteristics, keeping a distance from the West; but on the other hand, it usually follows the lead of the West in academic studies, blindly agrees with the West, imitates the West and loses its own originality, finally falling into the embarrassment of aphasia, with the question of "Chinese aesthetics or philosophy vs. aesthetics or philosophy in China" still haunting us, let alone the issue of characteristics. The characteristics depends on the reality, if no distinction between true and false, the characteristics will no reason to exist. It is that no discern on true and false is the reflection of underdeveloped thought. The no discern will result in there is no "Bie" (distinction and special characteristics) in academic research, and scholars cannot take out their own things and to exchange ideas on the market. For this, the Western politicians said that China can only be a big power rather than a great power, as China can only export goods and labor, instead of thought. The Western academic circle has also had the same idea so far. Aleš Erjavec, the famous aesthetician, cited the words of Aristotle and Ranciere in an article commenting on me. He first regarded my Bie-modernism as positive, but later on pointed out from the distinction between voice and speech that though I have made a voice of constructing Bie-modernism to the whole world, but there is still a distance from the real speech. In the Western traditional academic concept, making a sound is what both humans and animals are able to do, but speech and speech only is what humans are equipped with①. The discussing technique of negation after praises is hidden with distrust on Chinese academics of the Western scholars. In their mind, we are building academics or *Zhuyi* under the premise of deny-

① See Wang Jianjiang, "Philosophy, Aesthetics and Humanities Quadrilateral and Bie-modernism", *Exploration and Free Views*, no. 9, 2016.

ing the common human value and according to the five-year plan dominated by the government, therefore, we are at best making a voice to the world that China will also conduct creation on the academics, thought and *Zhuyi*, rather than to establish any real *Zhuyi* or schools.

Though the questioning of Aleš Erjavec is a bit poignant, it reminds me to think whether the adherence to the characteristics is contradictory to the common human values, and the persistence in the "Bie" of Bie-modernism definitely means denying, obscuring, or transforming common human values. Obviously, this is a historic choice. But as for how Bie-modern is distinguished by itself, I insist that humans have some common values, and these common values should never be denied, obscured, or transformed for having to be "Bie" (distinct or special) . Instead, common values should be reflected and observed through "Bie", meanwhile the denying, obscuring and transforming of common values for the sake of "Bie" should be resolutely prevented.

When Aleš Erjavec read my comment on his review, he wrote an article, titled*Some Additional Remarks Concerning Issues Opened by Prof. Jianjiang Wang*. He said that my Bie-modernism has touched upona neuralgic spot in his mind. He suddenly felt that whether in China or in the West, a part of the ground beneath us is missing. But somehow he could not find or even remember what is missing. Isuppose the missing that Aleš Erjavec felt is the "Bie" that I elaborated. It is my "Bie" that made him feel the unprecedented impact.

China and the West have their own root and also have different demands. But for either the Westerners or Chinese scholars, the mistake that they are likely to make is the ignorance of the reality. They cannot recognize it due to their ignorance, so they always feel that something is missing, but they cannot tell what is missing. Probably this missing is hidden in the reality underfoot, thus inevitably dangerous.

Bie-modern theory is based on the clear understanding of the missing in the ground beneath us, then begins with one step and constructs itself, constituting Bie-modernism. If the Bie-modern is intertwined, Bie-modernism is homogeneous, which means actually *Zhuyi* of self-renewal, self-regulation and self-transcendence as well as of practical and realistic redemption.

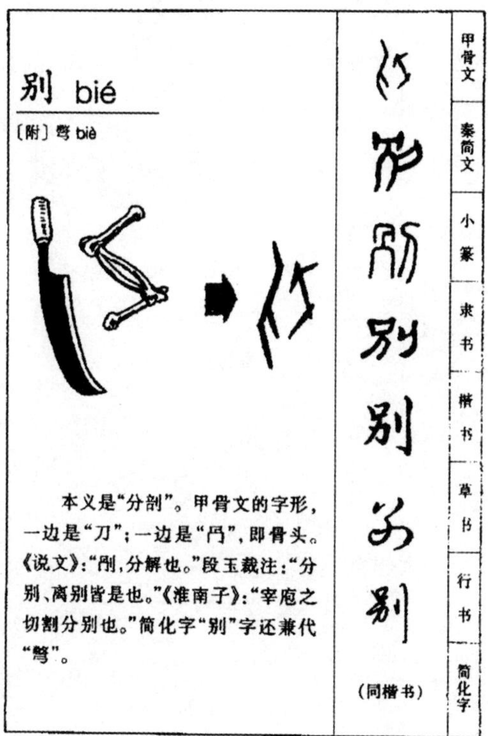

Figure 1: Bie (别) 's more than 2000 years history. Bie (别) is one of ancient Chinese Hieroglyphics showing separation of flesh and bones by knife.

第一编

别现代哲学

第一章

别现代：学术思想欠发达问题及其出路

——以美学为例*

第一节　学术思想欠发达的具体标志

学术，是指系统专门的学问，是对事物的本质和规律的学科化及研究。所谓学术思想，是指这种系统专门的学问或学科背后的抽象思辨、价值判断、叙事方式，在哲学、人文学科和社会科学中最为显著，构成了整个学术的基础。它与国家战略策略、路线方针等，既有联系又有区别。联系在于，学术，尤其是哲学、人文社会科学，都离不开国家战略策略、路线方针的影响，有时还要以它们为研究对象；不同在于，学术思想属于系统化、专门化，同时又是个体化、个性化的研究成果，广泛存在于社会生活和生产实践的各个领域，跟国家战略策略和路线方针的制定、宣传、落实保持距离，并不直接参加政治活动。由于思想有保守与进步、活跃与懒惰、创新与陈旧这些质的区分，又有各个质素的表现程度以及质素间的差异程度和对立程度的不同，还有影响力的不同，因此，学术思想的发达、不发达或欠发达，都只具有比较的意义和相对的意义，而无绝对的意义。学术思想的欠发达是指在特定时期内，通过与

---

* 本章部分内容曾以《思想欠发达时代的学术策略——以美学为例》发表于《中国社会科学评价》2015 年第 4 期。

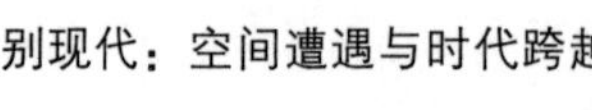

本国其他领域的整体发展水平相比，尤其是与经济发展水平相比、与科技发展水平相比，包括跟国家策略、路线方针的政治影响力相比，都处于相对落后的状态。又通过与发达国家思想活动情况的横向比较，确定本国思想领域的发达与否。

第一，与中国改革开放以来近40年取得的伟大成就相比，并与指导这些成就的国家策略、路线方针的影响力相比，中国的学术思想领域并没有取得与之同步的成就。中国国内生产总值（GDP）已超越了日本，稳居全球第二，并且坐二望一，有可能在不远的将来取代美国成为世界第一。事实上，中国经济近年来已经成为拉动世界经济发展的火车头。随着“一带一路”战略的推进，中国经济的影响力和国家战略主导性愈来愈明显。但与国内经济繁荣发达和国家战略的影响力相比，中国的学术思想并没有达到相同的水平，没有产生与欧美国家同等水平的思想流派，没有形成影响世界的社会思潮，对国际人文社科领域的影响微乎其微。据我的粗略统计，仅就美学而言，也仅以西方以“主义”（英语后缀-ism）冠名并对中国产生影响的美学思潮、美学方法和美学流派而言，且不考虑以“论”（如生命论美学、符号论美学、系统论美学、信息论美学等）和“学”（如阐释学美学、图像学美学、人类学美学）冠名的就有人文主义美学、新人文主义美学、科学主义美学、古典主义美学、新古典主义美学、启蒙主义美学、理性主义美学、非理性主义美学、现实主义美学、浪漫主义美学、自然主义美学、感伤主义美学、表现主义美学、心理主义美学、形式主义美学、直觉主义美学、新康德主义美学、新黑格尔主义美学、新托马斯主义美学、结构主义美学、解构主义美学、取消主义美学、存在主义美学、马克思主义美学、西方马克思主义美学、经验主义美学、实用主义美学、怀疑主义美学、新理性主义美学、新感性主义美学、女权主义美学、后殖民主义美学、现代主义美学、后现代主义美学、人本主义心理美学等，约有35种之多，表现出西方美学在主义方面的独占鳌头和话语统治权，也显示了西方美学思想的发达和对世界美学潮

流的引领。而中国以主义冠名且在国内产生了影响的美学就只有在20世纪50年代美学大讨论中出现的主观（唯心）主义美学和客观（唯物）主义美学。但是，这种最为古老的、原初的美学主义，基本上被消融在了哲学基本问题，即物质与精神、存在与意识孰为第一性的问题中，而无现代思潮、现代方法和现代流派的特征，因而很难作为具有原创性的主义而对世界美学产生影响。因此，仅就主义的影响力及话语权而言，中国美学处于思想欠发达状态也是一目了然的。其他人文社科领域我没有做统计，但叫得响并在国际上产生了很大影响的中国哲学上的、经济学上的、历史学上的、宗教学上的、军事学上的、管理学上的、心理学上的、社会学上的、法律学上的主义，我还未曾听说过。当然，在学术上，与主义平行的还有“某某论”“某某说”，虽然我们不能说只有主义才具有原创性，其他的论和说不具原创性，但是，论和说可以沿着别人的论点和学说展开论述或“接着说”，而主义却必须是概念原创、话题原创、观点原创、论证原创的，否则就不叫主义。主义是思想的提炼和理论的升华，是价值倾向的凝聚，是一个具有强烈界分的不与他人混同的识别标志。而论和说，更多的是对某一个观点的论述、阐释。因此，在西方语境中，许多重大学说最后都被纳入主义的名下。就以19—20世纪最伟大的三个社会科学的学说，即达尔文的进化论、马克思的剩余价值理论、弗洛伊德的精神分析学说，最终都构成了达尔文主义、马克思主义、弗洛伊德主义的一部分。因此，如果以主义的有无作为衡量思想的发达与否的标准之一，那么，中国属于学术思想欠发达国家应该是没有什么问题的。

第二，与新时期以来中国科学技术的发达相比，若按国际流行的量化标准，中国人文、社科包括美学成果海外发表率低，排在世界第13位，[①] 与中国自然科学研究论文海外发表率排在世界第二位（据

① 郑海燕：《三大国际检索工具收录我国论文统计分析》，《中国社会科学院院报》2008年8月7日第2版。

SCI 统计）很不协调。这些社会科学成果大都分布在管理科学、社会学、民族学、医药卫生、统计学和一些以实证和认知为主的学科领域，而且，作者大多来自中国科学院和理工科大学。王宁教授根据从汤姆森路透集团得到的“中国高校和科研机构发表 SSCI 和 A&HCI 论文排名（2012 年）”最新数据统计，提出这样的问题：“为什么专事自然科学研究的中国科学院能够雄踞所有中国大陆高校之上呢？为什么素来以理工见长的清华大学、上海交通大学和浙江大学高居于那些素来以人文社科见长的高校呢？”① 另外，张哲、邱长波、边鸿宾在《处于主导地位的 SSCI 收录的我国社会科学文献的影响力研究》一文中指出：

> 以 1992—2010 年 SSCI 收录的中国参与的国际合作论文为样本，运用文献量学的方法，从数量分布、时间、学科等方面对中国主导论文（通讯作者是中国学者的合作论文）和中国从属论文（通讯作者不是中国学者的合作论文）的被引频次进行对比分析，发现中国主导论文同中国从属论文相比影响力较差，不仅高被引论文比重较低，总体平均被引频次较低，在大部分年份与学科中平均被引频次也处于劣势。②

余莉在她的博士论文中选取 2010 案例分析，进一步指出：“与欧美发达国家相比，我国 SSCI 文献占世界份额仅为 1.09%，远低于美国的 36.33%，英国的 9.46%，德国的 5.69%。由此可见，我国在世界舞台上的社会科学研究成果与欧美发达国家相比还存在较大差距。”③ 又据

---

① 王宁：《中国文化走出去，外语学科大有作为》，《中国外语》2013 年第 2 期。

② 张哲、邱长波、边鸿宾：《处于主导地位的 SSCI 收录的我国社会科学文献的影响力研究》，《情报科学》2013 年第 7 期。

③ 余莉：《SSCI 收录我国社会科学文献的基本状况研究》，博士学位论文，吉林大学，2013 年，第 60 页。

中国社会科学报对中国法学文章的海外发表转载引述率偏低的最新报告，起始于1975年6月，终止于2015年6月的40年间，中国法学文章在SSCI和A&HCI上被国外学者引述共计仅86次，无疑说明情况的确堪忧。[①] 一般来说，法学文章要比哲学人文学科的文章较易在国外引述和转载。但仅就法学文章而言，国际影响力也如此之低，遑论中国的哲学和人文学科了。在这样一个低频引状态下，想让中国当代的学术思想有大的国际影响几乎是不可能的。

第三，比以上经济与科技方面的数据更要紧的是，海外尤其是欧美人文社科文献的汉译、介绍、引述、转载一直呈几何数字增长。西方的思想已经渗透中国学人的大脑和血液，成了中国学人立论的根据、思想的指导、谈论的对象和美学大讨论的话题，甚至成了话语中不可或缺的名词，出现了不引用、不借用西方名词、思想、原理，中国学者就不会说话的所谓“失语症”。

第四，更有甚者，中国哲学和美学至今未能走出是有中国哲学和美学还是无中国哲学和美学的困惑，“是中国美学还是美学在中国”的疑问一直未能消除。“美学在中国”不等于中国美学。就如一个欧洲人来中国旅游，而非中国人一样。实际上，这个问题的起始可能在蔡元培那里，而非金岳霖那里。作为中国美学学科创建人之一的蔡元培于1923年写了《五十年来中国之哲学》的文章，认为，由于近五十年缺乏中国人独创的哲学，因此，“五十年来的中国之哲学一语，实在不能成立”[②]。这里的“哲学”自然应该包括具有学科形态的美学。因为早在1901蔡元培的《哲学总论》一书中已经将美学和美育

---

① 耿海英：《中国法学期刊国际影响力初探——基于Web of Science的引用数据分析》一文指出：根据检索截至2015年6月1日的检索结果显示，“中国法学学科期刊的国际影响力整体偏低”。《中国社会科学报》2016年7月5日，第6版。

② 中国蔡元培研究会编：《蔡元培全集》第5卷，浙江教育出版社1997年版，第137页。

归入哲学学科。[1] 蔡元培这种将美学归结为哲学学科，但又否定中国有哲学的存在，这跟他本人并未否认有中国美学之间，的确存在着明显的矛盾，这也说明中国哲学的“合法性”问题也是美学无法回避的问题。但这样一个 20 世纪 20 年代的问题，到了 21 世纪，直到今天仍然存在，就不能不说，中国哲学和美学至少是欠发达的。如果哲学欠发达，整个民族的思想会是发达的吗？

第五，这种欠发达最为明显的表现是伪发达或虚胀。中国美学的特色现象在于，只要是一门学科、一个行业，就都可以被冠以“美学”之名。如什么数学美学、物理美学、生物美学、地理美学、环境美学、旅游美学、美容美学、足疗美学、饮食美学、厕所美学、工业美学、农业美学、科学美学、技术美学、商业美学、军事美学、医疗美学、证券美学等，不一而足。虽然也不排除极个别的行业美学如技术美学的实用性，但就绝大多数而言，这些所谓的美学既缺乏学理支撑，又不具有实用美学的功能，因而是一种毫无灵魂的徒有虚名的美学，意在为所谓的美学名分而圈地。这种徒有虚名的美学及其大量出版的专著，形成了一种虚假的繁荣，似乎中国美学极其发达，但实际上其内涵却非常空虚，没有思想，没有原理。

以上现状即使是出现个别相左的案例，如李泽厚美学的影响，也仍然无法改变目前整体上思想欠发达的状况。众所周知，李泽厚先生在法国和美国哲学界有影响，[2] 被认为是近代以来最了不起的思想家和“中国现代美学的第一小提琴手”[3]。但李泽厚的未定因素仍然在于，他的一系列重要的学说和范畴，目前还只有学说的意义，尚未形

---

① 中国蔡元培研究会编：《蔡元培全集》第 1 卷，浙江教育出版社 1997 年版，第 355 页。

② 1988 年李泽厚当选巴黎哲学院年度院士，2010 年出版的《诺顿理论和批评选集》（第 2 版）选录李泽厚的著作，李泽厚成为美学、马克思主义和身体理论这三个类别目录下唯一的非西方哲学家。

③ 刘再复：《李泽厚美学概论 · 自序》，生活 · 读书 · 新知三联书店 2009 年版，第 i 页。

成一个主义，也尚难断定今后是否会形成李泽厚主义，因而他的学说能否在一个哲学的高度上对人类的思想产生广泛而又持久的影响，还需要观望。

学术思想欠发达不等于策论和技术的欠发达，同样，策论与技术的发达也不能掩盖学术思想的欠发达。策论，不论是国家层面的还是国际层面的，也不论是单位需要的还是个人需要的，都是针对性很强的应用性策略和方法，主要针对具体国情、具体问题，因而能够根据现实需要而迅速跟进。同样，应用技术也因为跟国计民生的关系密切而又直接，从而总是处在不断的更新和升级中。改革开放以来，中国在如何改革的策论方面，在应用技术方面都取得了令人瞩目的成就，有力地推动了社会发展。但是，无论如何，策论和技术再发达也不能代替学术思想的发达，这是因为学术思想是人类全面进步的基础，对一切策论和技术都具有决定作用，一个国家的智库水平取决于该国的学术思想水平。因为学术总是在相对独立的、专门的立场上考察问题、研究问题，较之智库的急功近利式的对策研究，更需要思想的深厚。虽然，思想与现实的需要之间总有一定的距离，尤其是哲学思想，更是以高度抽象的方式，以反思的方式，即黑格尔所说的密涅瓦的猫头鹰总是在黄昏才起飞，以远离现实的假象在关注现实和指导现实。因此，人们往往以现实的当下急需而专注于策论和技术的发展，很容易造成对思想和哲学的忽视，但是，正如大哲学家罗素所认为的，要想了解一个民族，就首先得了解这个民族的哲学。哲学是人类的最高智慧，对整个人类的智慧都具有统摄性，策论和技术因其对于智慧的依赖而将自己的根扎在哲学。如果哲学欠发达，应用技术、策论即便一时发达也仍然处在思想欠发达的地位。事实上，西方后现代哲学兴起后，对中国的文学创作和艺术创作都有明显的影响，彰显着思想的统摄力。后现代的去中心、反权威、反宏大叙事和多元主义思想就已经渗透了中国的文艺作品。张艺谋导演的电影《英雄》，近年热播的电视连续剧《王大花的革命生涯》《二炮手》等，其中颠倒、

错乱的英雄观和由超大量的随机事件构成的戏仿、戏谑、解构的喜剧性手法，颠覆了传统的革命文艺的正剧手法和悲剧手法以及高大上全的美学原则，从思想到艺术，再到技术手段，无不打上后现代思想的烙印。因此，对于思想的发达程度的评估应该与对策论和技术的发达程度的评估区别对待，避免以策论和技术的发达来掩盖思想的贫乏。

当然，思想欠发达是个具有时间性的问题，不一定是个固化了的缺陷。正如中国经济经过近40年的改革开放，已经摆脱了欠发达状况，中国的科学技术成果也在逐步缩小与发达国家的距离一样，学术思想的欠发达也会逐步改善，这在19世纪的欧洲曾有过先例。当时英法在经济上远远超过了德国，但是，德国却如恩格斯所说，在哲学上“扮演着第一小提琴手”的角色。而且，20世纪以来，德国的经济和科技也都处于世界领先地位。

但是，思想欠发达和发展不平衡问题在当下中国必须引起高度重视。因为大国复兴从来都不是简单的经济实力雄厚和军事、科技、政治力量强大，而且还需文化软实力的配合。否则，大国复兴将跛足而行。因此，学术思想欠发达问题不应该属于任其自然或不作为区间，而是要重视之，并努力改变之，使之适应中华复兴的历史进程。

思想欠发达问题的严重性还在于经济学上所谓的短板原理的制约。一只水桶到底能装多少水，不是取决于最上边的桶沿有多高，相反，而是取决于最下面的桶沿有多高。因此，在中华民族复兴的过程中，思想的短板，不发达，是不得不予以克服的问题。面对中国的崛起，来自西方主流世界的中国威胁论、中国衰败论、中国大而不强论纷纷出笼。表面上看，这些论调之间格格不入，甚至相互对立，但实质上都与对中国崛起方式的判断有关。在许多西方人眼里，中国是通过向世界输出劳力、商品和资本来发财致富，并靠强化武力来实现大国梦的，而不是靠输出文明、输出思想来实现大国梦的，因此，中国只能做一个充满了不可预见性的大国，而不可能成为一个对世界不具有威胁的强国。可见，思想的欠发达问题，并非一个简单的先进还是

落后的问题，而是一个事关文化复兴、世界认同、民族崛起的大课题。

除了短板原理提供的不得不为的理由，更重要的还在于，思想是统帅，是灵魂，唯有思想的发达才能提供源源不断的卓识和远见，才能为政治安邦、经济强国、军事守成提供智力支撑。因此，按照实事求是的原则和文化自信、理论自信的主张，应该承认目前阶段我国学术思想欠发达的现状，但又不甘于现状，而是面对现状，改造现状，将不发达变成发达，将思想输入国变成思想输出国，使中国从目前的制造业大国，成为创造性大国，成为思想市场大国。我们将不仅向世界输出劳动力、商品和资本，而且要输出思想，到世界上去建立更多的思想市场。只有当中国到了向外输出思想的时候，中华民族的伟大复兴，才算指日可待。因此，就像当年中国坦率地自称是第三世界发展中国家一样，坦诚地面对思想欠发达问题，努力改变这种状况，应该是当代人文社科学者的历史使命。

第二节　学术思想欠发达的原因

从问题域的角度看，目前中国的经济发达而学术思想相对欠发达的问题，实际上印证了马克思主义的艺术与经济发展不平衡的理论。如果从不平衡的高度看问题，那么，思想的发展程度会在不同的历史阶段具有不同的表现，即使是欠发达问题，也只能是发展中的不平衡问题，而不是不发展的问题。因此，目前中国的学术思想欠发达问题本身属于马克思主义经典理论域内问题，也是有可能运用辩证唯物主义和历史唯物主义方法来解决的问题。一方面，我们不能将思想欠发达与经济发达直接挂钩，而是用历史的眼光和发展的眼光看待目前的思想欠发达问题，不再像过去曾经有过的追求 GDP 那样去刻意追求学术思想的发展速度，而是给思想的发展一个酝酿和准备的时期，留有创造的空间。思想意识形态与经济基础的联系是在最终的意义上实

现的，而非在具体的进程中体现的。相反，意识形态与经济基础之间往往在发展过程中出现背离现象，出现不成比例和不平衡现象。因此，我们在探讨学术思想欠发达问题时，更应该注重意识形态方面的直接的原因，而把经济发展只是作为思想发展的大背景和基础，这样才能保证对学术思想欠发达问题自身原因的揭示。另一方面，也不能忌讳经济发达而思想欠发达的现实，相反，要根据不平衡规律，按照现实的需求，克服短板制约，努力用这种欠发达的现实去唤醒思想发展的意愿，去激活思想发展的潜能，从而在合目的性与合规律性之间保持平衡，达到和谐。合乎规律又合乎目的，就要求我们既不能苛责学术思想的欠发达，又不能任其不发达，而是要在承认不发达的前提下努力去克服不发达，从而达到发达的目的，实现中华文化复兴的大自由。

根据思想发展与经济发展不平衡原理，就首先应该探讨学术思想欠发达问题的内在原因。这一内在原因，可以概括地归结为以下几点。

第一，原创性不够，没有形成主义和流派。思想来自对意识的凝聚、提炼和升华，思想需要以理论的形式存在，而思想的最高理论形态就是主义。主义，是理论的升华，是思想的凝聚，是价值倾向的旗帜，是行动的纲领和口号。因此，主义是思想成熟和达到相当高度的产物，是思想发达与否的标志。原创性是指思想的发端和应用成果都具有与别人的思想发端和应用成果不可重复的特征。同时，原创性都具有一定价值，并非每一项别人没有做过的事和别人没有讲过的话你做了你说了就有原创性。前述那些圈地式的所谓美学，虽然也在填补“空白”，但没有价值，因而也就没有原创性。我国50年代的“美学流派”，也是在最为古老和原始的唯物主义和唯心主义之争中形成的，不具有现代原创意义的主义和流派。

在人类众多的主义中，有自觉形成与非自觉形成的。前者产生于近现代，后者处于人类思想形成的原始期。唯物主义和唯心主义就属

于后者。这种非自觉的原始的主义如果按照恩格斯的说法则没有普遍的意义。恩格斯在他的《费尔巴哈和德国古典哲学的终结》中指出，只有在涉及哲学基本问题即物质是第一性的或者存在是第一性的，还是精神是第一性的或者说意识是第一性的时候才有意义，否则，就没有意义。相反，自觉形成的主义却在哲学基本问题之外仍有意义。因为它关联着事物实在的运行过程，这个过程是离不开这种主义的主导的。尽管随着后现代思想的兴起，反本质主义很时髦，但真正能对人类思想和行为产生重大影响的无非自觉形成的主义，离开了自觉的主义，我们几乎无法确定自己的立场和方位。

主义除了自觉与非自觉之外，还有层次之分。唯物主义和唯心主义就是自人类有了世界观后自发地形成的，因此可以说是最原初的主义。而人类于近代所创建的主义，基本上都是自觉的、原创的、有针对性的具体的主义。50 年代美学大讨论实际上是在唯物主义和唯心主义的对垒中发出的，具有主义的原初性，缺乏原创性。而且若按恩格斯关于唯心唯物的意义范围的说法，这种唯物与唯心的争论是否在美学层面上有效，值得怀疑。事实上，现代美学绕开了简单的唯心与唯物之争，却取得了巨大的进步。因此可以说，与西方近代以来的主义包括马克思主义相比，50 年代的美学大讨论，处在主义的原初层面上，与现代的具有知识产权意义的主义相去甚远。

与 20 世纪 50 年代美学大讨论的缺乏原创性相比，80 年代之后西方的形形色色的主义在中国泛滥，以至于本科生和研究生的毕业论文大都以西方的主义为研究对象，或以西方的主义阐释中国经典，或以引用西方的主义为博学、为光荣，但这种貌似主义的繁荣，实则是国门打开后西方思潮在中国如入无人之境，西方的主义在中国的舞台上表演，而中国美学只有做看客的份儿。在学术思想贫乏的情况下，面对“西方美学在中国”而非中国美学，如何与西方美学对话，如何不失语？因此，缺乏原创性的主义应该是中国哲学和美学欠发达的首要因素。

第二，主观原因在于缺乏建立原创性主义的意识。50 年代的美学大讨论有个鲜明的特征，就是大家都在争主义，都在争取自己的立场和观点属于唯物主义（曾经等同于客观美论），而论敌的立场和观点属于唯心主义（曾经等同于主观美论）。这种主义争夺战，今天看来与真正的学术流派的建立并无多少关联，因为前述恩格斯的话已做了权威性的回答。但吊诡的是，争主义与无主义之间，看似有着逻辑的连贯性，即没有我们才去争，但实则悖谬得很。原因在于大家在捍卫一个无知识产权的、无原创性的、价值有限的主义，而自己却在主义原创方面一贫如洗。也许有人会说，“我有马克思主义”，但是，我们且不管马克思的国籍，他是不是中国人，也不管马克思是否姓马，仅就中国美学而言，你能否拿着马克思主义代表中国美学去与西方美学对话？因此，50 年代美学大讨论中的主义之争，不是原创性的主义之争，而是在特定政治环境中安身立命的举措。事实上，时至今日，再也没有哪个美学家，包括当年那些为了唯心还是唯物争得不可开交的美学家，还在坚持和捍卫这种主义的美学了。这种现象恰好说明，中国当代美学思想的贫乏，就在于主义的贫乏，在于原创性思想的贫乏。这种原创性思想的贫乏就来自对于原始性的、无原创性的主义的过度迷恋，而缺乏建立属于自己的、具有原创性的主义的意识。连创建主义的意识都没有了，哪里还有原创性的主义？

第三，客观原因在于思想禁锢。20 世纪 50 年代美学大讨论中的唯物唯心之争并非简单的学术之争，而是立场之争，是命运之争。事实上，个别被认定为唯心主义（实则是主观主义美论）美学立场的学者，在接下来的反右斗争中得到了“非学术”待遇。在这种情况下，对主义讳莫如深也就是情理中的事了。虽然新时期伊始，思想解放运动轰轰烈烈，冲决了极“左”禁锢，但是时至今日，创建主义，仍然是一个敏感的问题，许多有历史记忆的学者仍然心有余悸。这里无疑需要抛弃一种观念：任何一种原创性的主义都是与马克思主义对立的，都有可能降低马克思主义的威信。这实在是误会。实际上，西

方的主义五花八门，其中就有不少是继承和发展了马克思主义立场和观点的。如西方马克思主义美学、消费主义美学等。总之，对主义的禁忌无疑会影响到思想建设的高度，导致思想欠发达现状的继续存在。

第四，解禁之后的学术思想惰性和缺乏自信。中国自解放思想、改革开放以来，思想自由、学术繁荣，有目共睹。但问题仍然在于为什么在这种历史转型期没有出现具有原创性的主义。除了以上讲到的主义意识没有觉醒之外，还有人文学者的情商问题。这就是思维惰性和自信心缺失。思维惰性表现在只接受某种观点，然后保持这种观点，而不是像马克思所说的不断地去进行反思和批判，也不是如罗蒂所说的去改造一个问题。时至今日，还有不少人在不断地重复着胡适“少谈些主义，多谈些问题”的名言，却并不知道胡适本人的自由主义思想，不能不说是一件令人惋惜的事。① 这种将胡适与主义相分离的做法，实质上是思维惰性在作祟。借名言而远离主义，既是逃避，又是懒惰。惰性大了，创新的动力自然消弭。较之胡适的少谈主义，会堕落到不谈主义，甚至不谈思想的地步。这种思维的惰性还表现在当了看客后的释然。20 世纪 80 年代中国曾经出现了方法论热，即运用西方的横向科学原理来探讨文学艺术和美学中的问题，著名科学家钱学森也是始作俑者，引领潮流，轰轰烈烈，但后来由于在文理交叉中人文学科学者对于自然科学的一知半解和理工科学者对于文学艺术的天然隔膜，导致了生搬硬套，于是这一令人耳目一新又取得了不少优秀成果的探索就在一片唏嘘中退潮了。看着潮起潮落，看客不仅是看热闹，而且感到释然，会为自己的稳重未试水而感到惬意。这样一来无疑强化了原本就有的惰性。

与思维惰性相比，还有一个不自信的问题。所谓的不自信也有两

---

① 有关胡适的问题与主义之争，参见本书第二编第四章第二节“主义的问题与问题的主义”。

个方面的突出表现。一是对中国传统文化的不自信。如面对西方话语霸权，提出中国古代文论的现代转型。如何转？无非是去适应西方的话语系统。因为用古代汉语写成的文论、诗论、画论、乐论等，面对西方话语，不仅仅是个语言的译转问题，而且更主要的是文化底蕴、民族精神的西方化问题。真的能在中西方之间形成转换吗？结论是不可能的，除了证明我们的不自信外，并不会有任何成功的转换。二是认为德国人的思辨能力我们华人无法企及，我们根本不可能创造出主义来。尽管我国理论界近年来一直在做马克思主义的中国化工作，但落实到个人，就往往是应和应和而已。殊不知马克思主义的中国化就是鼓励创建符合中国实际的原创性的思想，而不自信者却反其道而行之，以为谨记马克思的教导就万事大吉了。这种思想的惰性和信心缺失有时会比来自外界的限制和抵触更可怕，因为它已从根本上消解了人的创造意志、泯灭了学者的创造热情。

第五，学术体制存在不完善之处。中国改革开放以来最大的进步在于突破了全民国有制的铁板一块，允许并鼓励私有经济的存在和发展，从而使中国经济产生了前所未有的活力。但与中国目前的中外公私并存的经济体制不同，在学术界，目前我们还很少有不依靠政府薪水而独立工作的学者。一个从事哲学和理论美学研究的工作者一旦脱离现有学术体制，则其所从事的基础学科、基础理论的研究就可能难以为继。相比较而言，在一些欧美国家，许多科研成果来自独立的科学家，许多思想创建来自独立的思想家。在当前的学术体制下，这是值得我们借鉴和反省的。但是，无论如何，我们都可以确认，由于学术体制而导致的学术平台的缺乏和学术支持的不足，也是造成目前我国学术思想欠发达的原因之一。

第六，为求安稳坐实的数据考证和急功近利的策论需求影响到思想的发育和成熟，尤其是影响到玄妙的形而上学智慧的生成。由于学术思想的欠发达，考据与资料整理盛行，甚至影响到社科基金项目立项政策的倾斜。“小学”盛行而“大学”隐匿，这于思想的建设而

言，或者被数字化，或者被策论化，或者被考证化，而唯独没有形而上学化。有的从事文献整理和经籍考证的学者，公开声称哲学、美学、文艺学就不是学问，其问题就出在这些学者对于形而上学的忘记，缺乏对形而上学的敬畏感。中国古代有《大学》一书，被宋代程子认为是“孔氏之遗书”，其旨在于“明明德”，即道德学问，治国之学。而后的音韵训诂之学相对大学被称之为“小学”。如果只顾小学而忘了大学，重于技而忘乎道，要出现大的思想家是不可能的。在数据化和策论化的背后，是思想的弱化，而其在经济利益上的诱导更容易麻痹思想的创新，使学者要么闭门造车，要么追逐现实利益，从而远离思想的高蹈，丧失形而上的品格，甘于平庸，又何来学术思想的发达。

第七，邯郸学步，落入后现代主义的陷阱。中国思想界的思维惰性和自信心缺失，是非常渴望找到解构理论的温床的。事实上，中国思想界追随后现代的进程，在没有完成启蒙的前提下，提前进入了后现代去中心、反本质、反理论的反现代性阶段，不以建构理论为责，反以为累；不以发展思想为荣，反以为耻，从而将思想建设的历史使命抛到九霄云外。可是，当中国的人文社科学者也在跟着西方人背后嚷嚷进入“后理论时代”时，却已经不自觉陷入了后现代的理论陷阱。西方人讲不要理论的时候，实际上背后就是理论，不过是一种多元化了的理论①。人们真的以为在后理论时代就可以免除理论思辨的痛苦，从此就可以万事大吉了，但事实并非如此。实际上，迄今为止，还没有哪一种理论比后现代理论在自我反思方面，在自我批判方面，在多元化建构方面能够超越后现代。后现代的策略就是在“后”

---

① 沃尔夫冈·威尔施指出：“后现代是这样一个历史阶段，在这个历史阶段中，作为社会的基本状态的彻底的多元性事实上已经得到了承认，因此多元的意义和行动模式变得紧迫，甚至占统治地位和必不可少。如果把这种多元化仅只解释为解题过程，这就完全错误了。它反映了一种非常积极的预示未来的幻景。它和真正的民主是密不可分的。”［德］沃尔夫冈·威尔施：《我们的后现代的现代·第三版前言》，洪天福译，商务印书馆2004年版，第7页。

和“反”的过程中确立自己的思想的。[①] 再说，与西方相比，我们不是理论过剩，而是理论贫乏。近代以来中国哲学、美学理论、文学理论、艺术理论，无一不是从西方来的，无一不打上西方的烙印。但是，许多审美形态范畴，如意境、气韵、空灵、飘逸等，是中国独有而西方所无的，又如何从西方美学中找到理论根据呢？因此，中国要想摆脱这种困境，就必须自己创建理论，而非跟着西方后现代主义者去逃避理论、解构理论。如果我们不知道这一点，而跟着西方学者去反对理论建构，无疑会邯郸学步。

第八，技术层面上缺乏新的话语系统，尤其缺乏哲学层面上的既创新而又能使人耳熟能详的叫得响的名词和话语。自 20 世纪 80 年代文艺学美学新方法论被诟病以来，创造新的词汇似乎成了不光彩的事。殊不知，早在清末民初，王国维就提出了造新语的主张。王国维在 1905 年发表的《论新学语之输入》中指出，“我国学术尚未达自觉之地位也”，“故我国学术而欲进步乎，则虽在闭关独立之时代犹不得不造新名，况西洋之学术骎骎而入中国，则言语之不足用固自然之势也。”[②] 如果没有新语，何来新的思想？因此，造词方面的消极也是思想欠发达的原因之一。

以上八个方面就是中国当代学术思想欠发达的现实，要想改变这种现实，就不得不寻求行之有效的对策。

第三节　改变学术思想欠发达现状的策略

明白现状但又不甘于现状，而是努力改造现状，这是哲学的最为

---

① 齐格蒙·鲍曼指出：“现代性最出色的、最忠诚的子孙与其说表达了子女的忠诚，不如说变成了其掘墓人。他们越是专注于现代性着手建立的技巧的构建，他们越是削弱了大厦的基础。现代性从一开始就孕育了其后现代的扬弃（Aufhebung）。从遗传学的角度说，她的子孙决定成为她的诋毁者，并最终成了她的破坏分子。”［英］齐格蒙·鲍曼：《后现代性及其缺憾》，郇建立等译，学林出版社 2002 年版，第 90 页。

② 姚淦铭、王燕主编：《王国维文集》下册，中国文史出版社 2007 年版，第 23 页。

重要的使命。面对当代中国学术思想欠发达的现实，可能会有不同的态度。一种是不承认这种不发达，依然故我，故步自封。另一种是面对现实而不顺从现实，相反，要批判现实，改造现实。批判现实和改造现实，这是马克思主义的精神，是其活的灵魂。针对目前思想欠发达现状，我认为要从以下几个方面着手去解决。

第一，要承认思想的多样性和主义的多样性，要在多中求一，在一中求多。多中求一，就是在承认思想和主义多样性的前提下，建立自己的主义，这个主义就是一。因为任何主义都具有独一无二性和排他性，如果是折中、骑墙或跨界，就不可能形成主义，就会被别的主义所同化或被别的主义所遮蔽。因此，在多中求一，就是原创，就是独树一帜，这应该是发展思想的不二法门。一中求多，就是在建立主义的同时，不搞仙鹤独立，而是要与其他主义相磨抵荡，甚至展开论战，将自己的思想和主义放在一个众多主义的大背景中，接受多方面的挑战和洗礼。多中求一和一中求多，表面上看似对立，实际上都在体现百花齐放和百家争鸣，既反对无自我的思想和主张，又反对唯我独尊、独霸一方。思想只有在舍我其谁，而又参与比较、交流、摩擦、碰撞、较量中存在，在争鸣中发育成熟、茁壮成长，在对比中彰显合理性，在磨难中完成洗礼。主义本身既具有高度的排他性，又具有最为广泛的比较性，因而在本质上是一与多的统一，是对禁锢和专断的最好的阻隔。要想中国人文社会科学的发达，要想中国美学占据世界美学一席之地，就首先应该唤醒主义意识，创造自己的主义“一”，然后跻身世界学术思想高地的“多”。

第二，突破对立性思维的藩篱，把握主义建构的价值选择。主义作为思想的凝聚、理论的升华和行动的旗帜，具有明确的思想边界和价值倾向，因而很容易被纳入意识形态的防卫识别区，甚至引起恐慌。但是，众多的主义处在一个广大的空间中，并非一定要跟什么过不去，非要对立起来不可。当然，习惯于意识形态对立和阶级斗争的人，总是要将主义进行阶级的和社会形态的划分，如无产阶级美学与

资产阶级美学的划分，社会主义美学与资本主义美学的对立，等等。但是，美学作为具有通约性的人文学科，它的存在和发展并不是通过意识形态的对立来实现的，相反，是通过对美学原理的共识和共享来实现的。因此，应该尊重主义的多种属性和多重价值，有选择地建立美学上的主义，避免为主义贴社会意识形态和社会性质的标签。

第三，从中国的审美形态出发提炼中国美学精神、发掘中国美学内涵，建构中国美学的主义。中国美学思想源远流长，其思想基础是儒道禅。发端于春秋时代的儒道思想，是地地道道的中国本土的主义，被译为 Confucianism 和 Taoism。禅宗也是中国化了的佛教。儒道禅在当今西方世界受到高度的重视，被广泛传播。许多西方大学者，大思想家，包括伏尔泰、海德格尔等，都承认中国哲学的伟大之处。实际上，后现代的去中心、解构的思想，海德格尔存在主义的新天人思想，生态主义的回归自然的思想，空想社会主义的大同思想，也都能在老子、庄子、孔子的思想中找到根据。不同于西方的审美形态范畴主要来自文艺体裁，中国的审美形态范畴主要来自儒道禅的哲学思想。神妙、中和、气韵、意境、飘逸、空灵、阴柔与阳刚、清丑等，无不是中国哲学思想的体现。因此，中国美学研究的出发点就不应该是西方的主义，而是中国的审美形态，是中国的审美历史和现实经验。要在中国的审美形态和审美现象中提炼美学思想，建立中国美学上的主义，而不是追随西方的主义，把西方的主义当成了我们的出发点。只有通过对中国美学思想的传承和发展，才能建立起有中国特色的美学。

第四，秉持“别现代”主义原则，错位发展，避开西方解构主义陷阱，在唯西方主义与唯民族主义之间保持必要的张力，实现从特色学术向范型学术的转换。“别现代”的“别”不仅不是“不要”的意思，而且也不是告别的意思，除此之外还有深厚的至今仍在使用的古义，这就是“别样”的意思。但是，如果从中国的现实看，则既不是不要现代性，也不是另一种现代性，相反，它是前现代、现代和后

现代的杂糅。这种杂糅就是各有占比，随机变化，很难定于一尊，如果说是现代性而不顾前现代性和后现代性，或者只说前现代性而不顾现代性和后现代性，就都是不周全的表达。因此，建立在别现代基础上的别现代主义就是不同于西方现代主义、后现代主义以及东方前现代主义的一种主张、思想、理论。它的原则之一就是在前现代、现代和后现代之间保持独立性，既不滞后，又不随行，而是立足于中国现实，提炼主义，发展思想，最后超越别现代性而实现真正的别样的现代性。因此，别现代同时包含了既告别或不要虚妄的现代性，又建构别样现代性的理论主张。

这种别样的现代性表现在学术研究上就是独立性和个性。比如，面对后现代的后理论主张，别现代就绕开这一陷阱，不当跟班，不去盲目地否认思想、解构思想，而是根据中国学术思想欠发达的现实，反其道而行之，大力加强理论研究和思想建设，提炼哲学上的、美学上的主义。同时，别现代并不认为只有民族的才是最伟大的，而是坚持一与多的原则，既重视民族特色的重要性，但又不唯民族性，而是以思想的成就为准则，在民族性与现代性之间保持必要的张力。但是，别样现代性并不是只讲特色而忽视通约。相反，在学术价值认同上，注重从特色向范型的转变。所谓范型就是规制。西方美学之所以雄视天下，就在于它们掌握了美学的规制。这种规制就是主义。主义是规制，是纲，是统帅，是灵魂。强调特色，虽然具有一定的意义，具有“和而不同”的立足点，但过分地强调特色而掩饰规制的缺乏，就只能是护短的权宜之计了。法兰克福的特产——法兰克福学派和欧洲中央银行，就是学术上的规制，也是欧洲货币的规制，较之牛肉拉面、二锅头之类的特产，哪种特色更具有影响力，也是不言而喻的。一个正在谋求复兴的大国，要保持自己的特色，走自己的路，但是又不能老把自己局限于特色，而是要在特色的基础上建立规制，要对别人有影响力。只有你能拿出规制来，你的思想，你的美学，才有与人平等交流的资格，否则，也就只能拿着所谓特色独步六合，当一个被

猎奇的角色，聊以自慰了。因此，与美学上的主义建设相同步的应该是实现从特色学术向范型学术和主义学术的转变。

第五，克服思想惰性，增强学术自信，坚持话语创新，鼓励体制外学术力量的发展。中国自先秦诸子百家争鸣以来，几千年的封建社会就再也没有什么与社会制度相左或无关的主义诞生。宋明理学虽然延续道统，但与近代意义上的主义尚有距离。20 世纪 30 年代兴起的新儒家、新道家，也很难说是具有独创性的主义。中国古人有不讲主义，只讲“家”（农家、医家、小说家等）的习惯，也在无形中消解了主义的要义，这就是形而上学性和独一无二性。这种传统习俗，构成了中国人在创建主义方面的懒惰，过分地依赖前朝旧制，谨守一家，维护道统，不思进取，不敢进行话语创新。近代以来学术上的不自信与西学东渐有关，西方的哲学、自然科学、技术成果，都在中国引领潮流，独占鳌头，中国的学者一直在模仿和学习西方，也有人唯西方马首是瞻，言必西方，而无自己所说，这无疑是没有自信的表现。当然，也许囿于体制，有的人也有想法，也有原创的冲动，但考虑到存在规则，也就得过且过，和光同尘了。在这种情况下，鼓励学者进行话语创新，并为话语创新提供更加丰富的平台和更加多元的支持，无疑有益于新时代的思想繁荣。

第六，在策论与形而上之间保持必要的张力。战国时代的张仪和苏秦，纵横捭阖，谋变天下，但就思想家而言，却无他们的份儿。思想，不仅需要从现实中激发灵感，从现实中吸取营养，而且也需要在书斋中沉思，要像密涅瓦的猫头鹰那样只有在黄昏才起飞。在中国社会快速发展的今天，我们需要更多的谋士，需要更大的智库，也需要更多的策论。但是，谋士、智库、策论，毕竟属于实用层面和技巧层面，不属于形而上的所谓反思、理式等，因此，学术思想的发展既要务实，又要务虚，只有务虚，才能与纷繁复杂的现实拉开距离，冷静地观察现实，才能透视现实，反思现实，凝聚思想，形成理论，提炼主义，创造哲学。如果学者们都忙于经世致用之学，那么，思想的翅

膀谁来放飞，哲学的宫殿谁来打造，主义的旗帜谁来树立？因此，既要经世致用，直接服务于社会，又要远离社会，反观社会，在实用与玄思之间保持必要的张力，做到翔于天而立于地，使思想在不同的层面上得到全面的发展。

总之，学术思想欠发达问题的学术策略，受制于特定的社会现实，也受制于特定的发展阶段，因此，需要从实际出发，根据需要不断地进行自我调节，从而取得事半功倍的效果。

第四节　学术上主义创建的尝试

别现代系列论文自 2014 年年底发表以来，已经引起了国内和国际学者的讨论，产生了一定的影响。

什么是别现代呢？别现代是对一定历史阶段和社会形态的概括，也是在前现代、现代、后现代的交集纠葛中，别出一路的思想发现、理论建构和主义创造。当人们第一次接触佛教禅宗经典中的“教外别传”时，此“别”很可能被误读为“不要”，以为佛教之外不要传法。而读到“别墅”“别动队”这些名词时，也会对“别”字产生好奇。实际上，别现代的“别”字从古代汉语到现代汉语，很可能引起更多的联想，如告别现代、告别后现代；不要现代、不要后现代；另一种现代性、另一种后现代性；另一种现代主义、另一种后现代主义；别扭的现代性；以上都不是，等等，不一而足，表面上看，具有比德里达（Jacques Derrida）延异更为复杂也更难以把握的分歧、变异、模糊，而且更有甚者，“别”本身就具有主观价值判断和价值选择的别出一路的意思，也就是具有“主义”的蕴含，因而，别现代与别现代主义有时会成为一个词。但是，别现代主义的思想内涵却恰恰与后现代解构主义相反，是建构主义，包括本文所讲的要改变中国思想欠发达状态的想法，就不是对现状的承认，而是改造；不是描述，而是主义。因此，别现代不仅在构词上，而且在思想的表达上和

主义的建构上围绕着告别虚妄的现代性和构想真实的现代性这一中心思想，别出心裁、别具一格、别出一路、别开生面。

别现代的建构主义体现在“预设在后现代之后以回首俯视的方式，展开自己的话语体系和主义建构”。“要像处在19世纪的马克思思考和预测世界文学的来临那样，要在前现代中思考现代，在现代中思考后现代，在后现代中思考后后现代或另一种后现代。只有这样，才有可能保持思想独立和理论创新。”① “在后现代之后”，不同于“后现代主义之后”的或者追随后现代主义或者期待在后现代主义之后出现什么新的主义，而是一个基于中国社会历史现状的时间的空间化概念。在时间的空间化面前，现在是过去的未来，未来是过去的现在。因此，别现代将现代、前现代、后现代放在同一个空间考察，克服从前现代到现代再到后现代的线性思维方式，超越后现代和“后理论时代”的专注解构不问建构的陷阱，以超前思考和预设的方式，探寻中国的哲学人文学科和美学之路。

后现代之后就是要在前现代、现代、后现代之间特立独行，保持自己的“别”。中国同时处在现代、前现代和后现代犬牙交错的时代，加之学术思想欠发达和西方话语霸权，很容易对西方的理论和主义亦步亦趋，最后却落得个邯郸学步，因此，别现代主义特别强调在现代、前现代、后现代之间保持独立的立场。前现代是别现代主义要永别的目标，后现代是别现代主义要超越的对象，现代只是别现代主义的起始目标。现代取代前现代是历史的必然；但现代工具理性的弊端已在后现代的批判中暴露无遗；后现代对于现代的解构对于尚未具足现代性的国家来说可能是一场灾难。因此，别现代以后现代之后的视域保持“别”的思想方式，就是它自己存在的理由。

别现代主义的特立独行之“别”是“别后重逢”，先“别”后

① 王建疆：《别现代：美学之外与后现代之后——对威尔施·沃尔夫冈引领的一种国际美学潮流的反动》，《上海师范大学学报》2015年第1期。

“逢”。别现代主义不可能因为要保持特立独行而拒绝接受人类文明成果，相反，要在吸纳人类文明成果的基础上发展自身。但不同于以往的先继承后出新，而是先有别，再相逢。原因在于别现代时期是一个现代、前现代、后现代交集纠葛的时代，因此，对其进行具有判别的处理乃为当务之急，否则将会迷失于这种杂糅混沌之中。再相逢，是指吸收、继承现代性合理的能够与时俱进的文明成果，吸收后现代与现代保持张力的自然生态思想，吸收前现代民族文化的精华，从而发展一种集现代、后现代和前现代人类文明成果之大成的别现代主义。这种别现代主义还如前述，强调多中求一和一中求多，即永远保持个性和独创，把主义当成自己的事而不是别人的事。要建构属于自己的主义，就既要学习和吸收西方先进的思想和方法，但又不能盲目崇拜西方，跟着西方人的主义瞎胡转，而是要有主体精神和自我意识。同时，别现代不仅认同思想市场，而且提倡思想间的碰撞，在碰撞中壮大自己。近代以来，西方在政治、经济、军事、文化等方面的强大，即使在“中国人民站起来了”之后，仍然极大地压缩了中国学术思想的创造空间，使我们不想、不敢、不能创造自己的主义，从而导致了学术思想的欠发达。现在，随着中国的崛起，思想和主义的崛起都是早晚的事。抓住历史机遇，大胆创新，也许是改变学术思想欠发达现状的起步之作。

别现代的提出，是主义建构的一种初步尝试，它是汉语的创造，又有中国文化的传统和背景。中国文化是一种“化”的文化，如“物化”（《庄子·齐物论》）、“大而化之”（《孟子·尽心下》）、“独化于玄冥之境”（《庄子注·齐物论》）、“化腐朽为神奇”（《庄子·知北游》）等。这种化的最大成就，古代有佛教的中国化，出现了禅宗这一中国式佛教，现当代有马克思主义的中国化，取得了中国革命的胜利。佛教的中国化已成历史，而马克思主义的中国化正在进行中。人们对马克思主义中国化的理解不一定完全一样，但马克思主义中国化肯定不是照搬马克思主义，也不是除了马克思主义就没有任何

其他思想的发展。相反，马克思主义中国化就是创建有中国特点的、符合中国实际的中国学派和中国思想，包括中国的各个思想领域的主义。尤其面对当前西方话语霸权和学术思想欠发达问题，更应该尝试突围，建构自己的话语领地。正是在如此的意义上，别现代的提出应该是自我先行，是一种抛砖引玉。

第二章

别现代：主义的诉求与建构*

第一节　别现代：不仅仅是汉语的创造

近年来在多次国际国内的文化、美学、文艺学会议上，我提出的“别现代”已被叫响。中央编译局的专家说愿意在最短的时间里将“别现代”这一具有中国原创的学术用语及其系列成果介绍到国外去，争取话语权。与此同时，对于别现代的首发也成了几家刊物的意愿。这的确是笔者所未料到的。

别现代不是对外来术语的翻译，而是受到古代汉语和现代汉语的词义启迪之后的创造。别现代起因于汉语中古代没有“另”字，“另”字的意思皆由“别”来表达。如“教外别传”“别开生面”“别裁”“别体”“别传”等。同时，别现代也是一次灵感的碰撞与对接，与德里达式解构主义的“延异”（différance）① 不谋而合。如告别现代、告别后现代；不要现代、不要后现代；另一种现代性、另一种后现代性；另一种现代主义、另一种后现代主义；别扭的现代性；以上都不是，等等。汉语词汇的表现力于此可见一斑。但别现代的思想内涵却恰恰与后现代解构主义相反，是建构主义，即在西方话语霸

---

* 本章曾以《别现代：主义的诉求与建构》发表于《探索与争鸣》2014 年第 12 期，并为《人大复印资料·社会科学总论》2015 年第 2 期转载。

① 雅克·德里达：《论文字学》，汪堂家译，上海译文出版社 2005 年版。

权中努力发出自己的声音。这种貌似文字游戏的别现代实则是我国学术界长期酝酿突破的结果，是主义诉求①的回音。

能够提出别现代，并非一时的灵感和巧智，而是有着深刻的历史文化背景、迫切的社会现实吁求和理论创造的需要。

第一，名称是识别标志之首，欲行文化创新、思想创新、理论创新，就不可不重视新概念的创造。与“名者，实之宾”相反，名在现代学术中有着极为重要的功能。王国维早在上世纪初就指出，中国的学术意识尚未觉醒，不懂得学术术语创造的重要性。这种状况在面对西学在中国全方位展开和本土固有习惯语已无法表达新的概念时，愈发严峻，因此，必须创造新的概念，即“造新名”。这里的“造新名”就是学术上的发明和对这一发明的冠名。王国维的“造新名”说，是一种高度的学术自觉和对学术发展、民族文化存续的洞见。西方话语霸权，主要来自名词霸权。发明了名词者具有优先使用权和统治权，而随从者只有依附和唱和的份儿。因此，寻求新名，是叙述和表达的双重需要，是学术创新、理论创新、思想创新、主义创新的第一要义。如果没有好的名称，再好的思想也会被淹没，再好的理论也终将离散。因此，王国维所云造新名，确实是历史转折时期中国文化存续的需要，是中国学术谋求发展的需要，也是新学自立的需要，于此世界文化大变革时期，不能不予以高度的重视，并积极尝试之。就中华泱泱大国而论，成为名词大国，不仅在情理之中，而且在迫切需要之时。原因就在于目前中国生生不已的创造力和对名词概念的需求。近年来我国许多学者呼吁要把中国新时期以来创造的新名词梳理一遍，评估一下，看看我们取得了哪些有创造性的人文社会科学成果。我觉得这是一个很好的想法，很有必要。

第二，思想的发展需要凝聚和升华为理论，理论靠术语存身、立

① 王建疆：《中国美学：主义的喧嚣与缺失》，《探索与争鸣》2012 年第 2 期；王建疆：《中国美学：主义的缺位与重建》，《探索与争鸣》2012 年第 7 期。

身，而由思想和理论构成的话语系统更需要能够统冠的名称。别现代是全新的现实吁求、思想主张、价值判断、主义建构、理论原创。它力图在前现代、现代和后现代之间保持必要的张力，讲述中国故事，整理中国经验，提出自己的主张，建构自己的理论，解决自己的问题，本身就是一种从实践到理论，从思想到口号，从观念到主义的全新的建构。这种全新的建构首先需要冠名，这种冠名是为了表达思想、彰显系统、独树一帜。只有在别现代的术语下，纷繁复杂的、本土的、原创的、有中国特色的、与西方中心论离散悖谬的思想和理论才能得到整合，得到建构，否则，面对西方理论体系，仍免不了一盘散沙。一个谋求复兴，又正在复兴的文明古国，不应该名词匮乏，还得去跟别人借，而是首先应该有表达自己思想和理论的现代话语体系，而这个话语体系的第一特征就是有的学者所渴望的"涵盖性理论"，[①] 这个涵盖性理论因其是涵盖的或曰统摄的，所以就必须是简约的、明白的、叫得响的、有人气的。正因为如此，别现代的提出等于给中国的现代性话语系统冠了名，立了户口。这个冠名和户口的意义就在于，我不管你说的什么现代、后现代，我就讲我的别现代；你也不要一上来就问我"你是现代的还是后现代的"，我说我讲的是别现代。别现代是什么，你听着就是了。如果我们起了一个名，别人感兴趣了，才有可能进行交流。否则，你用别人家孩子的名给自己家孩子起名，岂不太贫乏、太无能了吗？

第三，后现代所带来的中国理论界和思想界的迷茫，需要不同于现代和后现代的理论和思想予以解惑或脱魅，而目前我们尚无这种思想和理论，因此，别现代的适时提出，无疑是思想建设的需要，是时代进步的需要，是中国文化复兴的需要。本来，按照依次跟进、循序发展的西方现代化逻辑，在中国尚未具足现代性，尚未结束现代化进

---

① 杜维明、黄万盛等：《发展真正有涵盖性的人文社会理论》，《开放时代》2006 年第 3 期。

程的时候，是不可能与后现代牵手的，但现实却是，如美国学者安德森在他的《后现代性的来源》一书中所说，20 世纪 50 年代中国革命刚刚成功时，有一位叫查尔斯·奥森（Charles Orson）的美国诗人提出了一个主张，认为20 世纪的上半叶是现代，下半叶是后现代，后现代的动力不是西方，而是第三世界，特别是中国的革命。① 但究竟是什么原因导致了这种牵手呢？那要后现代自己回答，无须我们妄猜。实际上，将中国革命与后现代牵手的西方论著很多，最典型的就是阿尔都塞的毛泽东的另类现代性即后现代性说。② 虽然，后现代是否如西方学者所说的就是中国的时代，无法判定，但后现代理论是最受中国理论界和文化艺术界关注和争议的主题，却是不争的事实。但这种争议都是在“后现代”的名称所圈定的论域和框架中进行的，是在后现代批判现代的过程中展开的，因此，难免中国的历史和现状被肢解、中国的本质被扭曲、中国的思想被同化、中国的现代化被后现代化的可能。这种可能性将会成为催生中国文化虚无主义的助剂。就我看来，在中国尚未结束前现代而已开始实现现代化的历史进程中，后现代的出现所造成的时代交叠和观念错乱使得我们无所适从，困惑和迷茫由此而起。进而言之，这种困惑和迷茫来自语界，即语言边界的消失所带来的被同化。

文化人类学的研究认为，语言是文化的识别标志，没有识别性语言的文化是最容易被同化的文化。我这里讲的“语界”，就是一个在全球背景下用于表示民族文化、时代差异、思想边界的一个超大概念。这个超大概念就是能够与现代、后现代、前现代并列而又不同的概念。由于在全球化背景下中国当代文化中语界的未有或缺失，使极具特色的中国当代文化，无法有效地进行自我表达，相反，却是在听

① 李欧梵：《当代中国文化的现代性和后现代性》，《文学评论》1999 年第 5 期。

② 刘康：《毛泽东和阿尔都塞的遗产：辩证法的问题式——另类现代性以及文化革命》，田立新译，《湖南科技大学学报》（社会科学版）2005 年第 6 期。

从西方后现代研究者的摆布，难免迷茫。但是，一个有着深厚历史文化传统和社会形态特征且正在崛起的大国是不会永久地迷茫的，相反，它会努力寻找自己的语界，去发现一个来自自我的、能够表达自我的有涵盖性的、有统摄性的理论和名称。别现代就是这样的语界标识，它不仅是汉语的创造，而且是主义的建构。

别现代的提出并非只是对话语系统缺失的一种补白，而是有着明确的目的性和价值取向。其动机在于用西方后现代性的理论和方法去解构西方的后现代，去除西方中心论而代之以本体中心论或中国中心论。别现代的提出不是因应目前流行的“在西方主流话语中注入中国元素”的自豪，而是相反，要形成中国主流话语，并且吁求“在中国主流话语中注入西方元素”。也就是要在中国的功夫和熊猫中注入美国元素，而非相反。西方的主流话语有哪些呢？信仰、启蒙、理性、自由、民主、公正、存在、现代性、解构、去中心。对比之下，我们有什么？还缺少什么呢？我们又比西方的主流话语多出些什么？对这些问题的回答，就是别现代的具体内涵的生长点。这些生长点，都需要在别现代的展开中发育成长。

第二节　多级跨越中的主义诉求与建构

别现代既不是现代，也不是后现代，更不是前现代。但它包含了这三种模式的因素，而别现代主义却是一个建立在中国文化背景上的现代思想，是有的学者讲的“涵盖性理论”。别现代主义就是否定和超越前现代，实现具足的现代性，又超越和否定后现代的离散和解构的一种建构。是在后现代之后的一种主义形态和文明范型。因此，别现代主义虽然产生于前现代、后现代、现代共处的共时形态，但它的思想取向面向未来。别现代主义既是构想也是方法；是价值观也是真理观；是理论也是实践；是主张也是主义。这种主义究其形态特征而言是立足于中华本土的跨越了前现代、现代和后现代的跨越主义和未

来关怀。

别现代主义处在前现代、现代和后现代的纠葛之中，但不囿于现代与后现代之间的理性与反理性、本质与反本质、中心与去中心、权威与反权威、体系与反体系、进步与反进步、解放与反解放、启蒙与反启蒙、一元与多元、高雅与大众之间、宏大叙事与微叙事之间的诸多对立，而是关注当下的现实问题和理论建构，展望后现代之后的未来前景，制定当下的文化策略和发展道路。

中国作为从封建社会直接跨入社会主义的社会形态，在思想观念、制度政策、行为方式都还没有完全与前现代脱离就进入现代社会，作为后发国家还没有实现现代化，就遇到了后现代的裹挟，因而，从存在样态到面临问题再到发展前景，中国都有不同于西方的处境，很难从西方那里得到灵丹妙药。新时期以来中国经验的概括表达就是跨越，既跨越前现代又想跨越现代，在跨越中实现局部性的超越，用几十年的时间走完西方几百年的道路，出现了经济、技术、军事上的中国奇迹。正是这种中国经验和中国奇迹，使建立本土理论体系有了坚实的基础和丰厚的内涵，也使别现代不可能成为一个空洞的口号。

伟大的时代不仅需要伟大的思想，而且需要涵盖性的和统摄性的理论，需要建立在理论基础上的主义，而这个理论之所以是理论，这个主义之所以为主义，就在于能够提出问题，然后去解决问题。在中国进行多级跨越式发展的时候，有关这种跨越式发展的理论却并没有出现，这无疑是理论落后于时代的表现。但这种理论上的落后所带来的却是在面对西方的怀疑和轻看时的尴尬。西方的政要们就曾说，中国只能做一个大国，但永远不可能成为一个强国。因为中国人只能向世界输出他们的产品和劳动力，而不可能输出思想。当然，这里讲的思想是指近现代以来的思想，包括当代的学术思想。为什么会出现这种论断，显然与中国学术思想还在西方的主义中兜圈子而缺乏原创有关。思想建构、理论创新就是从大国向强国转变的关键所在。而在思想建构、理论创新中，主

义的建构更是迫在眉睫。这是因为，思想和理论只有凝聚为主义才能形成它的涵盖性和统摄性，形成顶级形态和与其他主义的对话平台。因此，主义建构就是思想和理论发展的必然归宿。近年来顺应中国文化复兴的历史性要求，中国特色的主义建构诉求不绝于耳，也出现了源自西方马克思主义否定辩证法的否定主义美学和源自马克思主义生产消费论的审美生产主义美学等，中国式主义建构适逢其时，也可以说千载难逢。但从大处着眼，首先要看到，由于中国特殊的文化历史和现实状况，需要有中国本土的有中国特色的哲学思想和文化理论的创构。这种创构依据中国的传统文化资源和现实需求，借助西方的学术思想和方法，提出和解决中国的问题，就有可能形成中国本土的有中国特色的主义。

事实上，别现代主义就是一个借道西方现代和后现代而又不同于西方哲学体系和价值体系的具有创新型理论建构和中国本土特征的主义。别现代主义关注中国的问题，从政治意义上讲，是在西方体制和中国两千年的“秦政与荀学”“外儒内法”之间和之外寻求新的立足点和发展道路，也是在“西儒会融，解构法道互补”的探索中的另外一种思路。在社会发展上讲，将是跨越式发展与跨越式停顿的新型儒道互补。在文化上讲，借用一位学者的话说，就是考虑全球性的未来[①]。别现代主义就是未来关怀，但这个未来是什么呢？我认为答案可能很多。但别现代与一般的发展观不同，是从后现代之后的观点看问题，认为，别现代不仅意味着现代结束，也意味着后现代的结束。后现代在现代性被自己否定之后，自己却面对无法摆脱的危机而最终被否定。后现代之后的主要问题是人与自然的关系问题、人与科技之间的关系问题，包括斯洛文尼亚哲学家齐泽克的所谓系统暴力问题和赵汀阳所说的服务对人的统治问题。别现代主义除了对人与人和人与社会之间矛盾的关注，还关心网络对人的统治问题、能源枯竭和全域（包括地下、海洋和大气层）污染

① 赵汀阳：《现代性的终结与全球性的未来》，《文化纵横》2013年第4期。

之后的荒原问题、星际穿越的多维度纠缠问题、个人修养及其返璞归真等全球性的问题。除了全球性问题之外，别现代更关心中国问题。中国问题包括中国梦想、中国现实、中国未来，从上层建筑到经济基础，从存在到发展，从实践到理论，从理论到主义等，非常宏观，又非常具体，但绝不另类。这些问题都不是在否定本质、离散中心、反对权威的后现代与现代的钩心斗角中存在的问题，而是现实中的问题。后现代并不关心这些问题，它只关心与现代性对立的问题，是西方二元对立传统在当代的延续。后现代犹如庞贝城即将被火山淹埋之时还在斗兽场决斗的勇士，而不是一个关心存续和未来的哲人。因而，后现代的被否定和被抛弃是必然的事。而后现代之后的人类命运和人类存活状态及其理论建构才是别现代主义所关心的问题。

别现代理论所以要在西方后现代理论盛行之时被提出，是基于中国与西方在发展层级上的代差而导致的主义上的诸多错位。如在我们尚未实现西方启蒙时代就已形成的现代性之时，西方学者已经开始反思和批判启蒙运动了；我们在 20 世纪 70 年代对人道主义还是讳莫如深的时候，西方已经用生态主义开始批判和超越人道主义了；当我们还在以马克思主义者自居反对西方霸权时，后殖民主义却把马克思主义作为西方文化霸权的一部分来审视了①；当我们坚定地认为毛泽东是反对资产阶级法权的无产阶级革命家的时候，西方后现代却把他纳入了“另类现代性”或后现代谱系②。这不仅是时间上的代差，而且更主要的是观念上的代差。在如此这般的代差中，中国要跟着西方的思想观念、理论表达走，就难免与自己的传统断裂，而又无法与西方同步，从而出现错乱。

中国与西方在现代性上的错位导致了许多盲目、困惑和尴尬。如

① 刘康、金衡山：《后殖民主义批评：从西方到中国》，《文学评论》1998 年第 1 期。

② 刘康：《毛泽东和阿尔都塞的遗产：辩证法的问题式——另类现代性以及文化革命》，田立新译，《湖南科技大学学报》（社会科学版）2005 年第 6 期。

在自己还没有人道主义的时候不是去补课而是跟着后现代去批判人道主义，在自己还没有完全实现社会主义核心价值观中的民主自由的时候不是努力实现之，相反，而是跟着后现代去批判自由化和宪政民主，就真有点堂吉诃德大战风车的味道。这种盲目、困惑和尴尬同样在美学研究中出现。如轰轰烈烈的“日常生活审美化”大讨论，就是在还没有搞清楚谁的日常生活审美化的时候出现的盲目冲动。还有就是要否定和超越美学经典理论回归自然和社会的美学回归说、回潮说、美学行动说[①]，无不是不顾中国美学缺少理论建构的现状而跟着西方后现代由于理论过剩而否定理论建构的论调走，去做艺术家和设计师才能胜任的工作，而与中国的美学理论建构愈行愈远。因此，必须要有自己的表达方式。这个方式就是别开生面、别出一路的别现代。舍此，则很难想象建立自己的涵盖性理论。

值得注意的是，中国在实现经济上的跨越式发展的时候形成了思想的空洞症。在既与传统隔绝，又对西学一知半解的情况下，徒有西方的概念和口号，而无自己的思想内涵，形成了石灰岩般的空洞。用这个空洞去支撑一个经济上快速发展而在思想和理论上相对羸弱的大国，难免不出问题。时下随着拜金主义而出现的唯利是图、贪污腐化、违法乱纪、虚无主义等，无不与此空洞症有关。这种空洞症在现代文论中也是屡见不鲜。如所谓“失语症”（实际上准确的表达应该是“背书症”），离开了西方话语就不会说话。还有什么“古代文论的现代转型（换）”，就让人感到莫名其妙。转什么型？换什么？那些形成于古代奴隶社会和封建社会的中国文论，有着凝固了的语码，怎么转型去适应现代西方的文论？如果从别现代主义看问题，中国文论就是中国文论，不能转型，也无须转型。凡是在当代有生命的自然

---

① 这些说法主要来自威尔施·沃尔夫冈引领的国际美学潮流，可参见其《重构美学》《美的回潮》《超越美学的美学》（*Aesthetics beyond Aesthetics*）等论著。笔者对此将有专论，参见王建疆：《别现代：美学之外与后现代之后——对一种国际美学潮流的反动》，《上海师范大学学报》（哲学社会科学版）2015 年第 1 期。

会被提起、会被关注、会被引用。而那些已经死去的无用的理论自然会被遗忘，又何必为了适应西方文论体系而去做什么转型工作呢？还有反本质论，反宏大叙事论等，也只适合理论过剩、民族观念式微的西方，而不适合中国。中国目前是实践有余而理论不足，有许多成功的经验尚未上升到理论；国家统一、民族振兴尚待实现，我们仍需要用悲剧、崇高、英雄去提振民族精神，而不是解构悲剧、解构崇高、解构英雄。思想的空洞症是非常可怕的。既可以导致信念的塌方，又可以被其他的思想填充、占领，从而误导人们的行为。因此，别现代的提出，不时地提醒人们，自己是有话要说的，是有话可说的，不必借用别人名称和话题去迎合别人的意图，这样一来，起码会在语界的意义上避免这种思想空洞症所带来的危险。

就思想建构而言，别现代具有重要的、迫切的现实意义。原因在于，中国古代的思想一直在国际舞台上辉煌闪耀着，而相形之下，近现代以来的思想却不能同享尊荣。中国古代儒家思想曾在启蒙时代受到西方青睐，如杜维明所说：西方的启蒙运动，从伏尔泰、卢梭、莱布尼茨、狄德罗及其他百科全书派，有一个共识，就是儒家是最重要的参考思想，中国社会是最重要的参考社会，这是毫无疑问的，所以才有魁奈，就是重农学派的魁奈，把孔子像摆在他的书房里面。有伏尔泰，还有莱布尼茨，有的学者认为他的思想和《易经》有关系，反正有这么一套思想。对康德，以前秦家懿做过，我不知道她的材料是怎么找来的，但是有句话说，康德是从 Konigsberg（哥尼斯堡）来的伟大的中国人，用英文说是 A Great Chi-nese from Konigsberg，这句话大概是尼采讲的。[①] 但近现代以来的中国思想却不再风光。原因何在？原因就在于儒家的后代们未能创造出顶级的具有现代性和民族性的新思想，从而失去了作为西方文化思想参照系的机会。进一步的原

① 杜维明、黄万盛等：《发展真正有涵盖性的人文社会理论》，《开放时代》2006 年第 3 期。

因是，中国学术界除了表达政治经济的治国策论外未能创造出系统的思想和别具一格的哲学。而系统的思想和别具一格的哲学恰好是西方启蒙主义思想的特点。如英法德诸国在这一时期出现了大量的影响至今的独立思想家和独立的人文学派，而且这一传统一直延续到今天。可以说，西方延续了古希腊时期或人类轴心时代思想独立、思想者独立的传统，而中国自20世纪30年代以后，先秦时代的思想者独立和思想独立的传统没有得到继承和发展。也就是说，在中国，政治思想和纲领及其策论不断得到强化和发展，而独立知识分子的思想却没有形成足以引起世界注意的地方。作为思想的最高形态，主义是西方学术、文化最普通的表达，而在中国，就是李泽厚这样有国际影响的思想家，也没有形成自己的主义。这样造成的结果是，当代中国学者最了不起的发现所得到的最高评价无非“为西方主流话语增添了中国元素”。这无疑是在西方话语霸权中甘拜下风。别现代的提出，就是对西方思想文化进行甄别、批判、学习、利用，从而创造出有价值的思想，使别现代理论本身不流于一个空洞的口号，而是具有思想内涵、对话功能、引领作用的主义。

第三节　别现代的系统识别与理论张力

别现代不同于西方所谓的另类现代。别现代立足于后现代之后的建构而非解构，它的理论指涉是面向未来的。而那种对戊戌变法以来的中国式现代性的描述并没有涉及后现代的转型等超前问题，因而仍在西方现代性的框架中谈现代和后现代，与中国的历史和现状脱节。而别现代不仅在时代上而且在思想上超越了现代和后现代，是别开生面的主义建设。别现代之妙就妙在“别”字的“延异”及其这种延异所勾连的思想文化背景、理论内涵和主义诉求。

在别现代提出之前，已经有了“另类现代性”的表述，如前引刘康阐释阿尔库塞的文章，把毛泽东思想中的文化部分作为另类现代性，

至少对于中国人来说是难以想象的。而据李欧梵的说法，另类现代性的提出还要更早①。但是，这种另类现代性是指后现代性②。都是针对某个人的现代性表现或某种社会历史形态的现代性而言的。而别现代不同，与另类现代性的个别性相比，具有普遍性，并不关注某一个人、某一国家、某一个时代的特别的现代性，如所谓的斯大林关注的另类现代性或者中国的“文化大革命”这类另类现代性，而是关注在全球视野中的现代性。同时，别现代相较于另类现代性的具体性，更侧重于别现代作为主义的抽象性。又与另类现代性的倾向于描述过去，别现代倾向于预设未来，即在后现代时代思考和规划后现代过时之后的事情。因此，别现代是一个思想体系或理论体系，是与现代主义和后现代主义并驾齐驱的新的主义。它不例外，也不另类，而是中国的一个主义。它的译名应该是“Bie-modern”（别现代）和“Bie-modernity”（别现代性）以及与之相对立的“Bie-modernism”（别现代主义），而不是 Other modernity（另一种现代性），更不是 Alternative Modernity（另类的现代性）③。

别现代主义既与现代、后现代、前现代有着不可分割的联系，又与现代主义、后现代主义、前现代主义有着质的区别。它不得不顾忌前现代依然存在的现状，又极力吸收资本主义现代性的启蒙成就和科技成果，同时采取后现代的对资本主义文明的警惕和批判。别现代理论在中西之间保持距离，又在现代与后现代及前现代的纠葛中保持独立，因而理论的空间极其巨大，并能在各种理论之间游刃有余，保持既联系又对立的态势，从而形成思想的张力，彰显了别现代主义兼容并包而又泾渭分明的理论特点和理论畛域。

别现代作为一个主义具有具体的内涵和系统的识别功能，并具有

---

① 李欧梵、季进：《现代性的中国面孔》，《文艺理论研究》2003 年第 6 期。

② 刘康：《毛泽东和阿尔都塞的遗产：辩证法的问题式——另类现代性以及文化革命》，田立新译，《湖南科技大学学报》（社会科学版）2005 年第 6 期。

③ 李欧梵、季进：《现代性的中国面孔》，《文艺理论研究》2003 年第 6 期。

自己的特征。

（1）时代前瞻性。即处于前现代、现代和后现代之间而率先研究后现代之后的事情。别现代有个信念，就是后现代一定会结束，而且一定有个后现代之后的时代来临。无论是在时代的不可逆上，还是辩证法的原理上，都不可能存在一个亘古不变的后现代。为了后现代之后这个时代的来临，别现代要未雨绸缪，做好适应未来并引领未来的准备。正是这一前瞻性，使目前任何囿于西方标准的现代和后现代的探讨都无法替代别现代。同时，任何关于以往中国和现代中国的现代性表现的研究也不能与之重合。别现代就是一个在后现代之后的预设和信念。这是它最大的特点。舍此，将很难与现代和后现代脱离瓜葛。别现代的这种预设和信念来自后现代自身存在的无法克服的问题。后现代性作为“一个特殊历史时期”是“一种思想风格”与此相联系的后现代主义，被伊格尔顿概括为“一种无深度的、无中心的、无根据的、自我反思的、游戏的、模拟的、折中主义的、多元主义的”“文化风格”①。正因为如此，后现代总会有终期，后现代之后又是什么，就成了别现代主义要关注和解决的问题。别现代主义是对现代和后现代这两种出生在资本主义社会的思潮、主义、现象和风格的反思和跨越。别现代的最大特点就是，不是跟着后现代去研究后现代，而是走在后现代的前头反观后现代。

后现代之后会是什么图景？这是别现代的立足点和出发点。也许，会是罗马俱乐部担忧的“寂静的春天”；也许会是好莱坞大片所展现的星际穿越。但也许会是中国式大同实现的“至德之世”；会是老庄期待的自然生存、自然发展的时代；也可能是老庄想不到的跨越式停顿。但无论如何，别现代都是一次前瞻性的探讨，一次超时代的谋划，一次居高临下的回首。

（2）综合创造性。由于中国处于前现代、现代和后现代三种情况

① ［英］特里·伊格尔顿：《后现代主义的幻象》，华明译，商务印书馆2002年版。

并存的时代，因此，别现代就是基于对三种思潮的综合考虑和去粗取精、去伪存真、批判继承、创造性发展，是一种别开生面、别出一路、别有洞天的叙事。别现代既有中国古代传统，又有中国现代传统，包括马克思主义传统；既有封建中和、中庸、中道的思想，又有启蒙主义的自由、平等、民主思想；既是科学主义的，又是自然主义的；既有解构主义思想，又有建构主义思想，是一个全新的创造体。但别现代主义不是大杂烩，而是独立创造体，这是因为，别现代的精神旨归、理论目的、思想方式、价值取向，是早已确定好了的，不会与现代的、后现代的混同。别现代的名称本身就是一个创造。别现代将创造出自己的理论、方法、主义来。

（3）时代跨越性。跨越现代、后现代和前现代。在前现代尚未结束甚至在一定程度上、在某些方面还很盛行的时候跨上现代性的快车；在现代性受到质疑、挑战、批判的时候思考后现代之后的图景，无疑就有超时代的大跨越，而且还是多级跨越。但这种大跨越和多级跨越，并非“挟泰山以超百海”的夸张，而是“思接千载”而“视通万里”的胸怀和眼界。事实上，中国目前无论是在经济上还是在科学技术上，都是在现代、后现代之间的跨越中前进着，建立在这种历史性跨越现实基础上的别现代主义还有什么不可以跨越的呢？

（4）民族性。在西方世界大讲世界性之时，中国仍要讲民族独立性和国家统一性。这与中国的历史有关，也与中国人的情感有关。西方人不是在野蛮阶段侵略中国，而是在启蒙之后侵略中国，这就为中国铸定了民族国家信仰，从而铸定了中国的现代国家和现代民族观念。但别现代主义不是狭隘的民族主义或盲目的爱国主义，它遵循人类思想创建和发展的规律，尊重地方经验和地方价值，但又不否认普适经验和普世价值。别现代在经济上的立足在于，西方的经济学从来就没有预测到中国奇迹；别现代在政治上的存身在于，西方的政治学总是在近乎绝望中看着一个民族国家欣欣向荣；别现代在文化上，在美学和艺术学上的自信在于，那些不符合民族审美心理的西方叙事、

西方流派，无法在中国找到市场，那种“艺术终结”之类的宏论总是被相当一部分中国学者视为一种梦话或者是一个笑话。

（5）别现代主义除了以上鲜明的特点外，还有一个自我调节机制，这就是自省、自治、自我选择。自省应该是文明的一种功能。现代性就有强烈的自省性，从而在自身派生出自反性，催生后现代主义。同样，别现代主义也是继承了中华文化的自我反省传统，己欲达而达人，己所不欲勿施于人。深谙中国问题的复杂和中国梦想的邈远，深知西方近代文化的进步和发达，要在前现代、现代和后现代的包围中崛起，亦非易事，但又生生不已、自强不息。别现代的自治机制在于，它一开始就有强烈的语界意识，不会盲目认同，也不会跟随着某种思想潮流或文化风格去进行仰视的研究，相反，是在回望中的俯视和思索，是在后现代终结之处的超前展望。因而别现代主义始终是一种独立的思想方法和问题意识。别现代主义具有自我选择功能，首先表现在对现代、后现代范式和定论及原理的质疑。其次，表现在对本土文化诉求的警惕。比如，“中华文化的全面复兴”是一件激动人心而又任重道远的事，但这个“全面复兴”在别现代主义看来是肯定值得怀疑和思考的问题。全面复兴，是否也包括三班六房、三朝元老、三坟五典、三宫六院、三寸金莲、三国阴谋、三分天下、三里之城七里之郭、三寸不烂之舌、三教九流的全面复兴？因此，别现代主义是一个历史性的抉择，同时也将是一部选择的历史。

别现代是一个全新的表达、名称、理念、思想、理论、主义和口号，但它是一个开放的体系，是一个有待建构的框架。正如伊格尔顿、詹姆逊等都对于后现代理论有着各自不同的建构一样，别现代更应该是一个具有张力的思想容器。这一点是由它的前瞻性、综合性、创造性和跨越性所决定的。因此，就如别现代从字面上看，具有不要现代性、告别现代性、另一种现代性、别扭的现代性的奇异表象一样，关于别现代的思想建构，也将是一种延异。

别现代因其中国背景、中国诉求、中国表达、中国创意、中国主义，而又紧扣着现代和后现代的脉搏，因此必然会在全球化背景下受到关注、争议。但是，别现代所期待的都将会是别出一路的中国故事、中国经验、中国思想、中国理论、中国主义和别开生面的全球表达。

第三章

别现代：时间的空间化与美学的功能*

别现代学说自2014年起，引起学界关注，[①] 并吸引国内外学者参加研究和讨论。著名西方美学家艾尔雅维茨（Aleš Erjavec）以及恩斯特·曾科（Ernest Ženko）、基顿·韦恩（Keaton Wynn）等，国内的夏中义、吴炫、刘锋杰、王洪岳、陶国山等，近年分别在欧洲名刊《哲学研究》（*Filozofski vestnik*）、《艺术媒体》（*Art Media*）和中国的

---

* 本章部分内容曾发表于《当代文坛》2016年第6期。

① 潘黎勇：《“‘别现代’时期思想欠发达国家的学术策略”高端专题研讨会综述》，《上海文化》2016年第2期；“不服来辩”，《探索与争鸣》“学术争鸣”栏目（2—4月）别现代讨论征稿，2016年2月3日；王建疆别现代会议发言：《美学：后现代之后与别现代》，2014年4月，上海市美学学会主办美学研讨会发言，上海师范大学；《别现代：美学之外与后现代之后》，2014年12月，中央编译局、上海交通大学联合举办《经济全球化与中俄文化现代化比较论坛》，上海交通大学；《别现代与话语创新》，中华美学会年会，2015年5月，四川师范大学；《别现代的“别”与德里达的 différance 的区别》，2015年10月，复旦大学《法国文论在中国、北美的影响国际学术会议》，复旦大学；《中国美学：是现代性还是别现代性》，2015年10月，复旦大学《中国美学的现代性》会议，复旦大学；《从别现代角度看美学的传承与创新》，2015年10月，上海市美学学会《音乐美学的传承与创新暨上海市美学学会年会》，上海音乐学院；《别现代时期思想欠发达国家的学术策略》，2015年10月，中国文艺理论学会年会，华东师大；《别现代时期中国影视艺术的囧与神》，2015年11月，《全国“艺术：形态 精神 创意”学术研讨会》会议发言，上海师范大学；《别现代时期思想欠发达国家的学术策略》，2015年11月，上海师范大学美学与美育研究所《别现代时期思想欠发达国家的学术策略高端论坛》，上海师范大学；《别现代与别现代主义》，全国美学会议，2016年5月，四川师范大学；《别现代时期英雄游戏与英雄空间的解构》，第二十届世界美学大会，2016年7月，韩国首尔大学；《时间的空间化与别现代主义美学》，《艺术与美学的话语创新暨别现代问题高端专题国际学术研讨会》，2016年9月，上海师范大学。

《学术月刊》《文艺理论研究》《探索与争鸣》及网站上撰文6组近30篇与我讨论别现代问题，有十余篇被转载。艾尔雅维茨的《主义：从缺位到喧嚣——与王建疆教授商榷》（*Zhuyi*：*From Absence to Bustle*？—— *Some Comments on Jianjiang Wang's Article* "*The Bustle and the Absence of Zhuyi*"）一文在与别现代的讨论中提出"哲学四边形"论，将中国纳入其中，从而突破了德里达的中国无哲学论和舒斯特曼（Richard Shusterman）的"哲学三帝国"论。美国学者基顿·韦恩的《差异的现代：别现代时期相似的艺术与不同的意义》（*Differing Modernisms*：*Similar Art*，*Different Meaning Zhuyi for A Bie-modern Age*）运用别现代理论为遭到美国艺术评论界指责的中国艺术辩护。美国佐治亚州西南州立大学成立了当代别现代研究中心（CCBMS），国家社科基金项目《后现代语境中英雄空间的解构与建构问题研究》已经审批将"后现代"改为"别现代"。

随着讨论的深入，别现代的具体内涵、思想根据、理论创新、应用价值等都将被期待予以进一步的表达。尤其是别现代的哲学基础和哲学思想，作为别现代这一话语创新的本根所在，需要更明确地表达出来。

第一节　别现代的时间空间化与和谐共谋

别现代是个关于特定历史阶段和社会形态的新的表述①，来源于我们这个时代的既有现代因素，又有前现代因素，也有后现代因素，但同时既不是现代，也不是后现代，更不是前现代的现实，对这个混合杂糅的时代，只能用别现代来表达。别现代的"别"从字面上讲，对于具有古汉语基础的读者来说，容易联想到"另一种现代性"。但

① 作为特定历史阶段表述的别现代，起始于1978年以来中国的改革开放，西方的现代性、后现代性从此植入中国的各个领域。

如前所述，中国社会既不是现代，也不是后现代，更不是前现代，因此，用另一种现代性来表述中国社会特定历史阶段，概念上并不周延，也不准确，因为它忽视了前现代性和后现代的同时存在及其占比。因此，唯有别现代才能赋予它准确的含义，这就是既包含现代、后现代和前现代又不同于现代、后现代和前现代的社会形态或社会历史发展阶段。因此，那种将别现代理解成另一种现代性（other modernity）、另类现代性（alternative modernity）、复杂现代性（complex modernity）、特殊现代性（special modernity）以及混后现代性（mixed modernity）的说法，都是不符合别现代的具体现状的。因此，不同的杂志社在发表有关别现代的文章时，无论将别现代翻译成 bie-postmodernism①，还是 Don’t be modern②，bie-modernism③，都可能是针对具体文脉而言的，不一定会定于一尊，具有绝对的意义。别现代可以被理解为一种关于新时代或特别的社会形态理论。别现代的译法除了以上种种，也不妨以“一种关于新时代和历史发展阶段的理论”（a theory of the new times & the new historical development）④ 来表达。

社会形态、历史阶段、时代特征，也可以有多种表达方式。马克思主义的从社会生产力与社会生产关系的辩证关系及其发达程度来表示，西方现代主义的从现代性来加以界定，文化人类学的用文明形态来说明，都有一定的道理，但哪种表达方式更容易被接受，就要看这种表达方式是否最适合中国的历史和现状。

就文明形态论而言，似乎更适合于解释人类早期形成的以地域、

---

① 王建疆：《别现代：美学之外与后现代之后》（内容简介英译版），《上海师范大学学报》2015 年第 1 期。

② 王建疆：《别现代：话语创新的背后》（内容简介英译版），《上海文化》2015 年第 12 期。

③ 王建疆：《别现代：主义的吁求与建构》（内容简介英译版），《探索与争鸣》2014 年第 12 期。

④ Wang Jianjiang, “The Bustle and the Absence of Zhuyi. The Example of Chinese Aesthetics” *Filozofski Vestinik*, Letnik, XXXVII, 2016.

地理为背景而又与自然相区分的人类活动、符号系统及其遗迹，如华夏文明、两河文明、巴比伦文明、玛雅文明等，而不再适合近代以来以民族国家为背景的人类活动及其符号系统和遗迹，如中国文化、美国文化、法国文化、藏族文化、汉族文化等，就不好用中国文明、美国文明、法国文明、藏族文明、汉族文明来替代。

就生产力发展水平与生产关系的矛盾运动而言，中国自改革开放以来，以阶级、生产资料占有和利益分配来确定社会形态的理论遇到了不存在阶级和阶级斗争、生产资料占有和利益分配的国有、私有、外资混合形式的空前挑战，尤其是资本主义的按资分配以资本控股的形式取代了新中国成立以来社会主义的按劳分配原则及其劳动人民的“主人公”地位，加上中国也已如弗里德里克·詹姆逊所说的那种难逃“资本的逻辑统治了一切”的全球化现实，依据经典政治经济学对中国社会形态和历史阶段的界定已显得无力。因此，在中国就有了中国特色社会主义的理论。但是，随着外资、私营企业的占比扩大，尤其是当资本控股的地位愈发显赫，资本可以脱离实体劳动而又榨取实体劳动的利润而增值时，当本国资本可以与国际资本自由组合时，当资本以虚拟经济形式出现时，有关中国社会形态的已有看法就不断地受到质疑。

随着改革开放的深入，尤其是资本主义生产关系、市场经济在中国的成长壮大，中国社会开始有了来自西方资本主义近代文明的某些现代性特点。这种现代性包括对于资本主义生产方式、资本、市场、贸易、经营等的全面开放和接纳，对资本主义科学技术、知识和理性的学习模仿等。更主要的是，这种来自西方的现代性不仅未能对中国前现代的宗法制思想、裙带关系、人身依附、两性观念、封建迷信思想展开批判，划清界限，相反，现代性与前现代性和谐相处。同时，西方后现代艺术作品和艺术手法受到中国前卫艺术家、知识精英、青少年的青睐，具有后现代色彩的由大众随意界定的网络语言层出不穷。这种现代、前现代和后现代和谐相处的现状很难用是社会主义还

是资本主义的意识形态类概念来表达。相反，用现代性、后现代性、前现代性来表达似乎更为符合当前社会现实。但现代性、后现代性和前现代性实际上是交织在一起的，若只用其中任何一个去表述这个时代，都难免以偏概全。因此，用涵盖了现代、后现代和前现代的“别现代”这一术语，就不仅是对时代特征的揭示，也是对时代特征的概括，是一个具有涵盖性的理论。

别现代的现代、前现代和后现代的混合杂糅，造成了时间或时代的空间化。所谓时间的空间化或时代的空间化最为直观的镜像是现代、前现代、后现代的和谐共谋。别现代的“共谋”包括现代、后现代与前现代在同一个社会中的彼此适应、和谐共处；有法不依、放弃原则、彼此妥协、相互交易、达成媾和与共赢；不断更改规矩而又实行潜规则；有选择地遗忘和遮蔽历史；利益共同体的知法犯法、监守自盗等。前现代的思想观念和行为方式因现代制度的缺位而由后现代的跨越边界（cross border）、解构中心、消解政策和法规来加以表现，形成混沌的和谐。

和谐共谋的另一种形式在于沉默的假象。或不愿言、或不敢言，在好人主义盛行中形成社会的表面和谐。

和谐共谋的第三种形式就是共享与互害。在和谐共谋现状中由于对公共环境的破坏和对公义的漠视，导致环境污染、有害食品买卖、工伤事故、债务纠纷不断等，害人者和受害者最终都被拴在了一根链条上，其结果只能是互相伤害，走到了和谐的反面。

别现代的时间空间化理论对社会形态和历史阶段中和谐共谋现象的揭示，贯穿在整个社会形态和历史阶段中。

就经济基础而言，别现代的特征在于公有经济与私有经济并存，内资与外资融合，以股份占比的方式实现共谋共赢，使得以生产资料占有和生产资料分配为标准的社会形态划分因边界模糊而难以厘清。小农经济思想、家族企业方式、权力寻租手段与现代大工业模式、大农业模式、现代商业模式携手并进。同时，顺应后现代返璞归真思潮

的对手工制作、自然生态、有机食品的推崇及其相应的小作坊、小块农耕地的建立正与前现代的经济思想和经营手段并肩携手。

就道德伦理而言，一方面，一夫一妻的现代婚姻制度，与包二奶、养小三的前现代两性观念亲密无间，又与玩弄异性的后现代行为艺术手法和谐共谋；另一方面，英雄被空间化[①]，成为抽象的符号，失去了传统的本色和真实的内涵，成为游戏软件中的角色。

就文学艺术而言，前现代的思想观念与现代生活场景、现代社会理念、现代派手法、科技制作手段以及后现代艺术手法和谐共谋。在近年来走红的囧类电影和抗日神剧、古今穿越剧中，前现代的血缘宗亲制度、香火观念、家法手段、迷信思想、造神方式、大光明结局与现代社会场景、现代生活方式、现代战争观念、现代派手法以及后现代的戏仿、戏谑、恶搞等解构英雄的手法和谐相处。

就审美形态而言，前现代的中和、诙谐与现代的炫耀、虚饰，又跟后现代的冷幽默、搞笑、俗乐沆瀣一气，蔚然成风。批判现实主义式微，崇高被解构，悲剧绝迹，感官型审美盛行，境界型审美和内审美几近消失。这一点，在官媒高调赞美而网媒屡屡吐槽的春晚节目中得到了最为集中的表现。

总之，别现代就是别现代，它不是另一种现代性，不是另一种后现代性，也不是另一种前现代性，而是这三种形态的和谐共谋，是时间空间化的一种社会形态和历史发展阶段。

第二节　别现代是一种中国的空间理论

说到时间的空间化，习惯于为西方学说背书的中国学界总要追索任何一种学说的西方渊源。但事实上，别现代的时间空间化与来自物理学的和西方马克思主义的、后现代的空间理论并无直接的联系，它

---

① 王建疆：《后现代语境中的英雄空间与英雄再生》，《文学评论》2014 年第 2 期。

只是对当前中国社会现状的描述和概括，但是却有着现实的根据和独立的理论品格。

将时间纳入空间，是现代物理学关于空间维度的做法，但与社会形态的界定无关。目前空间物理学已将空间界定到了十一维。在四维空间理论中，已将时间纳入第四维度。虽然在十一维理论中，四维之后的其他七维被统称为理论维数，与具体维数（长度、平面、立体、时间四维）相对，但这种理论维数还是将时间纳入空间。比如，第十一维空间的超膜理论认为，十一维空间是由时间、空间、记忆与感知构成的。可见，除了具体维数的第四维即时间概念被纳入空间外，还有理论维数的第十一维也将时间纳入了空间，可被视为时间的空间化。但是，所有这些空间理论的时间空间化都是关于物质空间的，与社会空间无任何联系，也与别现代社会历史阶段的共存和社会形态的并置所表现出来的时间空间化无关。

虽然物理学上的时间空间化与别现代的社会形态和历史发展阶段的时间空间化没有联系，只是将时间视为空间的一个维度而已，但空间物理学的意义在于将时间与空间并置的常识打破，而将时间作为空间的一个维度来对待，从而动摇了时间与空间形影不离平行并置的观念，而赋予空间更大的转换功能和包容功能。这样一来，空间物理学对时间的空间化处理不仅为物理空间的拓展提供了广泛的可能性，而且也为社会形态的解释提供了诸多的可能性。在中国，自改革开放以来形成的多时代并置现象即别现代社会形态和历史发展阶段，为社会发展理论提供了新的现实基础。

20世纪以来，西方的空间理论在人文社会科学领域得到了长足发展。在西方的空间理论中，最早是关于时间和空间的自然属性的哲学思考，形成了柏拉图的绝对空间概念与亚里士多德的相对空间概念的不同，接着是莱布尼茨的经验空间与康德的先验空间的差别，再接着就是西美尔针对自然空间概念提出的社会空间概念。而始自法国新马克思主义学者亨利·列斐伏尔（Henri Lefebvre）的“空间生产”

思想，被认为是20世纪后半叶知识和政治发展中最为重要的事件之一。从此，人文学者开始把以前对于时间和历史以及社会关系的关注转移到空间上来，从而导致地理空间和哲学空间概念的社会化，被称为“空间转向”。列斐伏尔的巨著《空间的生产》论述了发生在社会生活的“精神”和“物质”空间的社会生产，成为影响至今的空间理论研究的重要思想来源。列菲伏尔认为，空间性不仅是被生产出来的结果，是在空间中生产的，而且是再生产者，即资本主义生产空间，空间也生产资本主义，资本主义的“生产”是一个超越地理空间而进行的“自我生产”，这种自我生产包括对资本主义生产关系的生产、对资本的生产、对市场的生产，从而构成诸多的空间如绝对空间、抽象空间、神圣空间、历史性空间、资本主义空间、身体空间、想象空间、矛盾性空间、差异性空间等。列斐伏尔还将空间化的历史过程概括为从自然状态的绝对空间，中经埃及式神庙与暴君统治国家的神圣空间和希腊式城邦、罗马帝国的政治国家的历史性空间，到资本主义财产的政治经济空间即抽象空间，再到当代全球化资本主义与地方化意义对立的矛盾性空间，以及未来的差异性空间六个阶段。

列斐伏尔的《空间的生产》发表后不久，福柯（Michel Foucault）作了《地理学问题》的访谈，他认为，在现代都市生活的人们处于一个同时性（simultaneity）和并置性（juxtaposition）的时代，人们所经历和感觉的世界，是一个人工建构的点与点之间、团与团之间互相纠结缠绕的网状空间，而不再是传统社会中的物质存在。福柯把空间问题当成建构历史的核心问题。但他不同于列菲伏尔的处理空间与社会生产的宏观思考，而是注重空间对个人的微观影响。他反对对历史做线性的目的论的解释，而是非常强调历史的非连续性和中断性。他认为空间既可能是统治的工具，也可能有助于人们的政治反抗。

列菲伏尔、福柯之后，又出现过许多空间理论，形成了列菲伏尔一系的西方马克思主义空间理论、福柯的后现代空间理论、曼纽尔·卡斯特尔（Manuel Castells）的网络空间理论和巴赫金（Mikhail Bakh-

tin）等的空间叙事理论。其中，列菲伏尔一系最为庞大，代表性人物有曼纽尔·卡斯特尔的城市消费空间理论、戴维·哈维（David Harvey）的空间压缩理论、弗雷德里克·詹姆逊（Fredric Jameson）的跨国性空间结构理论、爱德华·索亚（Edward W. Soja）的第三空间理论。尽管曼纽尔·卡斯特尔的网络空间理论和索亚的第三空间理论有着超越列菲伏尔和福柯的意旨，但这些后继的理论尚未在思想高度上超越列菲伏尔和福柯二位大思想家。在中国，叙事空间学在美学、文艺学和比较文学研究中得到了广泛的应用，但真正属于中国的空间理论还有待建立，而且相较别现代的关于时代特征的宏观时代空间理论，中国的空间叙事理论也只能是移植西方空间理论的一种微观研究。

以上列菲伏尔和福柯的空间理论虽然对人类空间理论将空间的容器功能理解为生产和再生产的功能，使空间概念从哲学和自然科学转向社会学发挥了历史性的作用，对中国的空间理论研究有着很大的启发，但就别现代的空间理论而言，总体上是与他们明显不同的。

（1）列菲伏尔的空间生产理论揭示了资本生产和扩张带来的全球范围内的资本主义空间的形成和不断扩大的历史现象，具有发展马克思主义政治经济学的某种进步意义。但是，空间生产理论还只是对单一资本主义空间特征和功能的概括，而非对于像中国这样更为复杂的社会形态的概括。在别现代理论中，不仅存在着资本的生产和扩张，而且还有前现代生产关系和后现代思想的生产和扩张，是多重生产和扩张带来的时代空间化，是前现代、现代和后现代的同时生产和扩张，因此，别现代的空间是由不同时代、不同生产关系、不同意识形态的并置及其矛盾冲突所造成的复杂空间，因而是一种超越了列菲伏尔空间理论的更大的空间生成和空间生产。

（2）列菲伏尔的空间理论中对于六个历史阶段的划分不符合中国的现实，因而完全可以被别现代的阶段论，即和谐共谋期、矛盾冲突期、和谐与冲突交织期、自我更新与超越期（见本文第三部分）所

代替。别现代能够取彼而代之的原因在于，别现代的时间的空间化理论并非来自西方，而是对中国特定社会形态和历史发展阶段的概括，是一种中国的空间理论。

（3）福柯的空间是个人微空间，而别现代的空间却是时代的大空间。福柯关于当代社会混杂的网状空间概念，道明了时间空间化的部分现实，即权利空间的存在及其功能，但别现代的空间网状却是现代、前现代、后现代相互联系而又对立的立体的时代网状空间，而非具体事物相关联的网状空间。别现代不同时代的并置共存是福柯未曾遇到的空间状态，因此，他的空间理论不可能是别现代的立体的时代网状空间，而只能是同时代或单一时代具体事物间关联的具体空间，是单一空间和小空间，是空间对个人的压迫、规训及个体反抗的微空间，而别现代的空间却是复杂立体空间，是大空间。

（4）福柯的历史中断论，符合西方的社会形态和历史阶段的事实，其空间理论有着明显的时代分别，但却不符合中国的实际。别现代时期是现代、前现代和后现代的并置和谐，前现代一直延续到现代，同时，后现代也进入今天的中国，这种社会形态和历史发展阶段与西方式的现代是对前现代的中断，后现代是对现代的中断的历史和现状完全不同，因此，别现代的时间空间化就是一个立足于现实的独特的理论，而非西方理论的翻版。

（5）列菲伏尔的空间生产还是个抽象的理论假设，还需要空间生产的反向动力来体现其具体的针对性。事实上，资本主义在全球扩张的过程中，不仅会遇到来自不同社会制度、不同意识形态的抵抗，而且也会受到不同利益集团的抵抗，形成地缘政治经济和特定的生产方式。相比之下，别现代的时间空间化不仅已经囊括了空间生产，而且还同时包含了空间的和谐与空间的对立。别现代从自身的张力结构中生产出新的社会关系、社会力量、社会发展方向、社会性质和社会功能，并形成和谐共谋期、矛盾冲突期以及自我更新超越期，因而是一个具有张力结构的既抽象概括又具体指涉的空间理论。

时间与空间是人类自有了哲学之后就有的概念，人们早就意识到世间万物都以时间和空间为转移，因此，时间与空间的概念具有普遍性。但是，任何理论都有现实的基础，任何时间都以特定的空间为转移，而不以抽象的空间为转移。因此，将时间特定空间化之后，就会生成许多新的观察视角和新的社会理论。别现代就是这种时间特定空间化的结果和新的理论表述。

总之，与西方人文社科领域中的空间理论相比，别现代的时间空间化具有时代的延续性而非中断性；具有来自对现实概括的直接性而非嫁接性——是对中国特定现实社会和历史发展阶段的直接的概括；具有全球范围的普遍性——就世界范围而言，具有时间空间化特征，除了中国，还有尚在改革路上的国家、东亚的现代化国家、伊斯兰现代国家等。从这个意义上说，别现代理论最适应中国现实，但也不止于解释中国，而是具有很大的适应范围的中国的空间理论。

第三节　别现代的四个发展阶段与美学的功能

原则上讲，别现代的空间理论来自中国的现实，是对中国现实的概括，但哲学史上西方哲学家对中国社会和历史的评价仍然是绕不过去的一道坎。最著名的就是黑格尔在其《历史哲学》《哲学史讲演录》《法哲学原理》中关于中国没有历史，有的只是改朝换代、轮流坐庄的“非历史的历史”，是社会共时态对历时态的侵占，而于社会的发展而言是停滞，是一种单一模式的循环。而与此相联系的则是，中国也没有哲学，等等，一直是中国哲学界、美学界为之焦虑的问题。黑格尔这种老调也许道出了中国封建社会的某些本质，但当今则有可能与时间的空间化理论相混同。因此，别现代的时间空间化需要具体的时空范畴，否则，中国社会很可能落入黑格尔时的抽象逻辑思辨中，从而掩盖了我们这个具有发展空间和进步能量的时代现实。

在别现代时期，除了现代、前现代、后现代之间的和谐共谋，还

有一个重要的特性就是现代、前现代、后现代之间的内在对立，从而赋予别现代特殊的属性，这就是由多维制度空间、物质空间和意识空间构成的既和谐共谋又内在紧张的多重复杂属性。包括时间空间化属性、多元并存属性、和谐共谋属性和内在张力属性、内在冲突属性、多变量属性、难以预测属性等，合称为别现代性。别现代的前现代、现代、后现代并存现状，导致时代的空间化，在这个空间形式中，现代与前现代的天然对立、现代与后现代的相互矛盾、后现代与前现代的文化隔膜，都被祈求社会安稳的民间愿望和官方意志不谋而合地黏合在了一起，因而会在某个历史时期总体上还是多元并置、和谐共处，但又会在某个历史时期必然出现现代与前现代之间、现代与后现代之间的矛盾和冲突，也会同时出现和谐共谋与矛盾冲突交织的状态，但最终别现代的混融现象会被自身的变革力量所打破、所超越。因而，跟西方断代式的前现代、现代、后现代相比，中国是现代、前现代、后现代媾和共谋的"三头怪"，是一个共谋而又内在分裂的共同体。这种情形恰如柏拉图在《斐德若篇》（*Phaedrus*）中描述的灵魂奔向天国的途中那架由良马和劣马一起拉着的马车，虽然是同一驾马车，但这些马匹的不同意志所导致的不同运行轨迹和发展前景却因为相互间的角力而前途未卜。别现代的这种既内在分裂又和谐共谋的结构特征，决定了别现代时期必然会出现矛盾和斗争，并在矛盾和斗争中形成主导性的力量，最后超越这种混合杂糅的时代。因此，别现代时期将会形成和谐共谋期、对立冲突期、和谐与对立的交织期、自我更新超越期。

1. 和谐共谋期

西方历史上从未出现过现代、前现代、后现代共时并置的现象。西方社会从来都是中断式的社会发展阶段，如现代替代前现代，后现代替代现代。而中国延续了两千多年的封建主义随着近代民主革命而从半封建、半殖民地国家突然进入社会主义阶段，这种跨越了资本主义历史阶段的社会形态，反而为前现代封建制度和封建意识的延续提

供了机会，从而造成现代与前现代的并置。同时，由于全球化背景和改革开放，为西方的后现代思潮进入中国提供了方便。如此一来，在西方本来是一个历史阶段替代另一个历史阶段，一种社会形态替代另一种社会形态的社会发展过程，在中国却变成了现代、前现代、后现代的和谐共处。这不能不说是一种社会历史的奇特现象。

别现代时期的和谐共谋具有二重性。共谋是本质，和谐是现象，互害是结果。不少重大储存安全事故，按照早已制定好的现代社会储存管理法规条例和层层关口是不可能发生的，但偏偏就发生了。人们不禁要问，那么多的审批关口、监管部门怎么就形同虚设呢？无疑，这就是和谐共谋带来的互害。

和谐共谋期虽然也有矛盾冲突，但绝大多数矛盾被前现代的权大于法、利大于法的潜规则所摆平，被面子文化、人情文化、裙带文化所遮蔽，从而造成和谐的假象。但是，正如社会学研究成果所表明的那样，这种冷漠心态的背后往往是暴力①。借用鲁迅的话说，是“地火在地下运行、奔突；熔岩一旦喷出，将烧尽一切野草，以及乔木”。（《野草·题辞》）是爆发前的能量积蓄，具有更大的危险性。

在和谐共谋期，美学最重要的功能就在于配合反腐倡廉揭穿“和谐”假象，以幽默讽刺的艺术手法批判社会丑恶现象，抑制负能量，褒扬正能量，以审美的方式维护社会的健康发展。

2. 对立冲突期

别现代的内在张力性和内在矛盾冲突性不仅建立在现代与前现代的天然对立之上，建立在现代与后现代的观念对立上，而且还建立在后现代与前现代的天然隔膜之上。这种内在张力和内在矛盾冲突通过对生产资料占有和利益分配上的不公表现出来，通过生产力与生产关系之间的不和谐表现出来，通过上层建筑和意识形态与经济基础之间的不匹配表现出来，通过行业竞争、私权保护以及各种社会矛盾表现

① 于建嵘：《警惕中国民众政治心态的两极化》，《探索与争鸣》2015年第11期。

出来，有时甚至还通过文艺评论表现出来，使重大文艺活动也往往成为各种矛盾对立的焦点。这种内在张力和内在矛盾冲突一方面是社会稳定与健康发展的必要结构保障；但另一方面，过度的紧张以及由此而带来的矛盾激化和表面化，就会打破别现代的和谐，导致社会的对立冲突。

别现代时期的对立冲突来自直接的利益冲突，如农民工讨薪无果、征地拆迁等。另外还来自间接的非关直接利益的不满。民众要求兑现改革开放的红利，要求兑现核心价值观中国家层面的“富强、民主、文明、和谐”和社会层面的“自由、平等、公正、法治”的允诺和期许等。对立冲突期存在的根本原因在于前现代的巨大惯性和现代性的尚未具足，现代核心价值观由于缺乏现代制度保障，民众的期许和政府的允诺都难以及时兑现。

在对立冲突期，美学的责任在于伸张正义，弘扬正气，批判丑恶，抚慰心灵，化解矛盾冲突，维系社会的稳态发展。这个时期是最容易产生崇高而且一定能够产生崇高这一审美形态的发展阶段。

3. 和谐共谋与对立冲突交织期

在对立冲突期，局部的对立冲突并非不可避免，和谐也不是一去不复返，相反，只要人们对公平正义还有信心，秉公执法还能够得到落实，民生工程能够发挥作用，那么，激烈的对立冲突就有可能减缓甚至避免。这里的关键在于：一是国家负责的民生工程能否发挥作用，解决老百姓的实际困难；二是取决于矛盾的能否及时化解，如信访、告状、诉求的得到回馈、问题得到及时解决；三是取决于公民对政府的监督权能否得到落实和保障。

说到化解矛盾的问题，我对于建嵘先生的冷漠与暴力的非此即彼是持保留意见的。这是因为除此之外，还有第三种途径——冷幽默的发泄。这种冷幽默与中国式的冷嘲热讽有一致的地方，是一种审美形态，但不同于西方的幸灾乐祸、令人绝望的黑色幽默，而是具有中国传统讽谏因素的发泄方式，作为一种审美形态构成了对要么冷漠要么

暴力的缓冲。冯小刚导演的《我不是潘金莲》，以一种冷幽默的方式告诉人们，幽默是一种智慧，不懂得幽默，过于严肃和紧张地对待女主角“我问牛了，牛说了不告”这句实话，就反而容易把无事变成有事，把有事变成大事。虽然这种缓冲只能是暂时的和局部的，但通过冷嘲热讽，积怨会得到一定的发泄，从而缓解矛盾，避免冲突，形成和谐共谋与对立冲突的交织。

既然冷幽默是冷漠与暴力之间的缓冲剂，是一种艺术的发泄，又与中国传统的疑似中和的政治讽谏和文艺上的温柔敦厚诗风以及大团圆抚慰观有着天然的联系，那么，近年来有的媒体对讽刺小品的盲目挤压，就实在是一件不太高明的举措。相反，注重审美形态对当下社会存在和发展的影响，注重对对立冲突缓冲方式的研究，也是别现代主义美学的担当。

作为喜剧形式之一的冷幽默，还有马克思所说的具有诀别旧时代的意义。马克思曾说：“世界历史形态的最后一个阶段是它的喜剧。”① 因此，以冷幽默的形式批判社会丑恶现象，凝聚正能量，建设理想社会，就是别现代的美学担当。

4. 更新超越期

别现代时期的内在矛盾和内在冲突，必然寻求走出矛盾冲突的自我解脱之路。这种自我解脱来自自我更新和自我超越。别现代的自我更新和自我超越期的必然来临既取决于经济基础和社会现状所带来的解压需要和发展需求，也取决于践行中国社会核心价值观的主导性力量的形成。

别现代进行自我更新和自我超越的可能性在于：第一，国民经济的持续中高速发展和城市化步伐的加快，有利于现代性替代前现代性，有利于民主和法制的建立和实行，有利于现代文明建设。第二，

---

① 马克思《黑格尔〈法哲学批判〉导言》，见《马克思恩格斯文集》第1卷，人民出版社2009年版，第7页。

践行核心价值观的主导性力量的形成。随着国民现代性意识的觉醒，包括民主意识、法制意识和逐渐积累起来的多方面的自信，导致别现代社会的主导者们的跨越式停顿①，即终止前现代的制度、思想、行为方式，从而导致社会的自我更新和自我超越，超越别现代时期，进入真正意义上的现代社会。目前中国进行的反腐倡廉和深化改革，都在昭示这种历史性的进步。第三，在国家层面上和在社会层面上的“富强、民主、文明、和谐、自由、平等、公正、法治”核心价值观的兑现，能够为实现中华民族的伟大复兴，提供良好的机遇。

别现代主义建立在结构分析和反思自我的基础上，因此它并不自满于别现代的现状，而是要努力改变这种现状，根绝前现代的思想干扰和制度障碍，建立现代思想和现代制度，将现有的核心价值观落到实处。因此，别现代主义的历史使命就是要自我更新，超越这个历史阶段，而不是停留在这个历史阶段。

在自我更新超越期，作家艺术家的创作能量全面爆发，一个摒弃了模仿中国古人和西方艺术的真正原创的时代来临了，中国文学和艺术将以历史上从未有过的气派、魅力、风格、形式开创一个人类文学艺术创作的新时期。

别现代是一种关于特定社会形态和历史发展阶段的理论，别现代性是对别现代时期复杂属性的概括，别现代主义则是对于别现代社会和别现代发展阶段的自我更新和自我超越，其目的在于进入更理想的社会形态和历史发展阶段，建立富强、民主、文明、和谐的现代国家，建立自由、平等、公正、法治的现代社会，塑造爱国、敬业、诚信、友善的公民。但别现代主义与前现代主义虚假的和谐共谋不同，是表里如一的本真主义，是实现期许和允诺的兑现主义，而不是表里

① 王建疆：《别现代：跨越式停顿》，《探索与争鸣》2015年第12期、《人大复印资料·哲学原理》2016年第3期。跨越式停顿是指在事物的发展如鱼得水、如日中天的时候一种建立在前瞻性基础上的主动的停顿，以换取更好的发展路径和发展前景。

不一的虚饰主义和心灵鸡汤的空想主义。

总之，如果说别现代是多和杂，那么，别现代主义则是一与纯；如果说别现代是虚与假，那么，别现代主义则是真与实。别现代主义就是自我更新主义，是自我调节主义，是自我超越主义，是实事求是的兑现主义。

第四章

别现代：跨越式停顿*

拙文《别现代：主义的诉求与建构》发表后被人大复印资料《社会科学总论》转载，并引起《探索与争鸣》在全国征文讨论。别现代作为一个新的思想体系或理论体系，究竟包括哪些范畴呢？这是同人一直关心的问题。本章仅就别现代主义诸多范畴中的跨越式停顿做一论述。

第一节　具有普遍性的跨越式停顿

跨越式停顿来自人类生存发展的需要，具有哲学的蕴含。随着人类环保和节能意识的增强，全球无烟日、全球无车日、全球熄灯日、全球停水日相继推出并得到了全世界众多国家和民众的响应。无烟、无车、熄灯、停水，都是在发展的惯性中突然停止，目的在于人们从突然的停顿和暂时的丧失中居安思危，反省自己的行为，寻求最佳的、长久的生存之道。这种突然的停顿是主动的选择，而非被动的接受。它只能发生在人类发展的高级、高速阶段，而非低级、低速阶段，充分反映了人类对于自己生存环境和发展前景的担忧，是一种高度自觉的行为。因而这种停顿是超越了按部就班思维方式的跨越式的

* 本章曾发表于《探索与争鸣》2015 年第 12 期，并为《人大复印资料·哲学原理》2016 年第 3 期转载。

停顿而非自然的终止，亦非被迫的中断。其跨越就是尚在过程中却与结果超前对接，按照可能性结果进行人为的干预、调节。虽然这只是人为设定的短暂的自我警醒之计或演习，但其中有着深刻的哲学蕴含，这就是对过程——结果、前进——停顿之间的思考。只是目前还没有人从理论高度对这种哲学蕴含予以揭示和概括而已。

跨越式停顿是一种生存哲学。类似跨越式停顿的现代思想，在中国古代的人生哲学中就有老子“功成，名遂，身隐，天之道”的表达，后来儒道互补的为官之道更被誉为“急流勇退”模式。即在高速、高度发展的时候突然停顿，不再前进，而是突然转向。它把归隐作为生命存在方式转化的条件，跨越了勇往直前的直线思维，突然改变了原有生命的运行轨迹，以停顿的方式迈入“仙”“道”“佛”这类超高级生命行列。

跨越式停顿产生的现实基础在于增长的极限和“成住坏空”的宿命因缘。跨越式停顿不是发生在不得已的情况下，或终止，或转向，相反，是在欣欣向荣之日，甚至是在如日中天之际，突然停顿。这种突然停顿来自对未来结果的预见。如果建功立业，一路精进，到头来也可能功高震主而不得善终。同样的道理，科技的发展会给人假象，好像人定胜天，永无止境，因而导致科学家沿着一条道走到黑，结果却总是被别人超越。原因就在于事物的发展总有极限，总有尽头，而人的认识总有局限。因此，及时停顿，才不至于输得很惨。当中国高铁走向世界，每小时400公里成为现实时，人们的期待可能是500公里、600公里，而不质疑增速的极限。但事实上，美国人的1.2千公里时速的高铁已在加利福尼亚试验成功。甚至2万公里的真空高铁也在论证中。但这种2万公里的极速也难逃跨越式停顿规律的制约。这是因为，在物质速度以光速为最快之外，还有超光速，这就是意念波。因此，跨越式停顿是一个向前发展的超阈值策略。跨越式停顿，是谋求更大发展，但这种更大的发展只能首先建立在停顿的基础上，是对原有路线的中断。只有终止既定路线上的惯性才能改弦易辙。

跨越式停顿是思维的革命。随着大城市人口膨胀，交通压力成为首要问题。城市地面马路拓宽、增道工程不断进行，地铁不断增加，但是，何时才是尽头？这里还有跨越式发展的空间吗？与其不能，还不如中断这种拓宽和增道的思路，来个跨越式停顿，转向高架，于是特大城市的交通状况有了很大的改善。但高架也有限度，还是无法根治特大城市的交通顽疾。因此，人们遵循跨越式停顿规律，在发达国家的个别区域，已经转向空中运输。但空中运输也只能是个补充而非可以替代其他交通方式。除了以上几点极尽其能的发展策略外，按照现代物理学的虫洞理论和十一维空间理论，物质及其运输的隐形化将进入考虑范围。在隐形化状态下，物体的运输将不再占有空间。因此，跨越式停顿是思维的质变和飞跃，具有革命性的特质。

跨越式停顿具有普适性。在教育上，与其做一个循规蹈矩而无大出息的好学生，不如做一个别出一路的专家怪才。历史上的伟大人物，许多学历不高，或者弃学或中断了常规教育。由于不受常规教育的束缚，他们的天才和创造力得到了发挥，成为一代天骄。不识字的中国禅宗开山祖师慧能就是这方面的代表。

一个政权，也要在不断论证自身统治合法性的同时，突然中断这种合法性论证，而是要反问自己，什么是合法？原因在于“法无定法”。这种跨越式停顿，会促使我们不断地反省自己、修正自己，从而找到真正的合法性，而非自我论证、自我满足的合法性。亚洲某地区政党领袖领导下的政权曾经把专制权力用到了极端，血腥暴力，甚至在美国暗杀持不同政见的记者，引起全球惊骇，但他本人的一次跨越式停顿，即所谓的“最后一次专断”就结束了专制统治，开启了这个地区的民主新时代，从而免予崩溃式瓦解。

跨越式停顿在竞技、战争方面尤其重要。与其跟着别人去研究别人的方法而不得，不如提早抛弃这种方法，放弃这种跟进，而别出一路。如跟着别人去打对称的战争或比赛，打不过，怎么办？就只好摒弃原来的路数，打不对称的战争和比赛，即以险、奇和个别优势战胜

平、常和整体优势。这在比赛和战争中屡见不鲜。其做法就是突然放弃了做徒弟的身份，来个跨越式停顿，从做题者变为出题者，变为考官去考验对手。

人类科学研究的发展亦遵循跨越式停顿规律。不沿着既定路线前进，突然中止前进的惯性，不破解现成命题，而是另起炉灶，改造问题，提出新问题，这在人类科学史、社会科学史、人文学科史上屡见不鲜。按照托马斯·库恩的说法，人类科学的发展都是一个范式对另一个范式的革命。其实，社会科学和人文学科也有这种范式革命。如曾经沾沾自喜于建立在贫穷基础上的社会主义中国，在面对世界的繁荣而感到惭愧时突然停顿下来，提出贫穷不是社会主义的观点，寻求一种通过致富来强国并用经济引领世界的理论；当面对“全球化”的问题时，将其改为“化全球”；而当我们面对“化全球”时，又将其改为“去全球”，即将全球问题改为星际问题。这就是对既有思路和既有范式的跨越式停顿，即中断了现成的思路而另辟蹊径；跨越了这个时段的问题而思考未来将要出现的问题。就以笔者从事多年的美学研究而言，面对“是中国美学还是美学在中国”的难题时，不是一味地跟着这个问题找答案，而是相反，将其改造为“是西方美学还是中国美学在西方”，就是中国美学研究的未来走向。

跨越式停顿是一种新的时空观，而非肯定——否定、前进——倒退等一系列被庸俗化了的所谓辩证法。跨越式停顿的核心机密在于多种思路并进所形成的时间之矢的平行、并置、交叉，从而终止了线性思维的独霸而将时间转化为空间，在多种维度中，消解了先后的顺序，从而为思维的跨越提供了可能。时间是线性的从起始到终端具有先导性的延续过程，而空间却是一个平等的共享平台，它终止了时间先来后到的次序统治，而将过去、现在、未来放在平等的位置上重新开始谋划。因此，在某种意义上说，跨越式停顿就是空间对于时间统治的颠覆。毛泽东“数风流人物，还看今朝”的豪言壮语，在跨越式停顿的世界观那里，可以表达为“未来考古，尽在今朝”。不是沿

着纵向比较的时间之矢自说自强，而是将时间空间化，让未来和历史所构成的空间在评判谁最强。

别现代跨越式停顿的哲学基础之一是老子所讲的“反者，道之动”。即从反向认识事物，改造事物。这种“反动”的思维方式，也是后来禅宗六祖慧能所表达的“对法”，即“问有将无对，问无将有对”①。这种“反动”的思维方式，在对待时间问题上，特别突出。就是终止时间之矢的线性，不再延续，将时间空间化，从未来看过去，而非从当下看过去看目前，凸显时间平行的、复合的维度。

跨越式停顿也来自佛禅的顿悟思维。停止静心修养的“时时勤拂拭”程序，秉持“本来无一物”的釜底抽薪，中止渐悟而进入顿悟。顿悟即飞跃，即由跨越式停顿带来的另一种新的飞跃。

跨越式停顿受益于《易经》中“生生之为易”② 和《尚书·盘铭》“苟日新，日日新，又日新”以及《诗经》“周虽旧邦，其命维新”思想的影响。中国先秦传统思想的主流是一种不断革新、发展、变化的发展观。但这里的“易”（变化）和“新”（更新、革新）的前提就是跨越式停顿，是对旧的终止。古人的思想因为缺少现代的逻辑论证而只是停留在价值判断和希望、幻想上，而到了现代社会，这种“易”和“新”就有了具体的内涵。跨越式停顿，就是把惯性消解，别出一路，从而别开生面，别有洞天。

尽管跨越式停顿离不开西方经济学思想和中国传统哲学思想的影响，但跨越式停顿有着与现代西方思想和传统中国思想的不同。

首先，与西方的跨越式发展或后发理论不同。跨越式发展是针对别人的超越，而跨越式停顿是面对自我的更新。前者是省略了别人的路程和程序而赶超别人，但走的是同一条路，比如追求 GDP 增长等。而后者却中断了对别人的跟进，而另辟蹊径，走自己的路。如摒弃了

---

① 《六祖坛经·付嘱品第十》，至元本。
② 《易·系辞上》：“日新之为盛德，生生之谓易。”

唯 GDP 之路，而走生态式发展之路；终止了地域生态观而转向星际生态观。跨越式发展来自对历史记录以及经验的总结，确实有过跨越发展的无数实例，中国经济在这方面尤其突出。但跨越式发展只顾及事物的一个方面，即发展、发展，前进、前进，而忽略了发展的极限这一问题。因此，跨越式发展总有尽头。但跨越式发展恰恰忽略了对自身未来的考虑，很容易导致盲目乐观或者盲目跟进，在时间之矢上做直线延伸。相比之下，跨越式停顿则因为新的时空观和对自己未来的及早考虑，即对结果的评判而绕开了由于增长的极限而带来的末路。这一点，在人们已经开始探索星际移民的今天，显得十分明确。因此，跨越式停顿比跨越式发展更具有战略的长远性和发展的可行性。

跨越式发展来自对科学发展观的顺应，总认为发展、增长是绝对的，人本身具有绝对的可靠性和无限的可能性。而跨越式停顿更多的是来自对自然发展观的遵循，总认为发展、增长是相对的，人本身并不是万物的尺度，也不是宇宙的主宰，人本身并不具有绝对的可靠性和无限的可能性。因此，在“将漆黑桶兜底打穿”之后，跨越式停顿仿佛是在拼死追赶超越的无边苦海中回头见岸，而跨越式发展却在一去不复返地加速走向了那个自己也不知道的“漆黑桶底”。

跨越式发展是沿着别人的思路、经验、路径前进，可以省略和避免由于试验、探索、不成功、走弯路带来的成本和时间，因而相较于发达国家和地区，出现快速增长，这种增长被视为跨越式发展，即站在别人的肩膀上翻墙。但跨越式停顿却是最终放弃了别人的思路、经验、路径的别出一路的发展。它停顿的是被效仿者的道路，而发现或创造了一条更适合发展的自己的道路。因此，如果跨越式发展是模仿和改进的话，那么，跨越式停顿就是创新和革命。跨越式发展是因循之路，而跨越式停顿却是别现代的创造之旅。

其次，与熔断机制不同。熔断机制是西方金融界在高风险行业中设置的自动暂时中断功能，在达到危险阈值时，暂时停止营业、运

营。这种方式在全球股票市场交易中曾普遍使用。当暴跌达到危险或有可能导致崩盘时，暂时中断交易半个小时或中止当日交易。同样，当股市暴涨到一定程度时，也要进行人为的干预，中止交易半个小时。熔断机制就如电路上的保险丝一样，起到稳定股票市场的作用。但跨越式停顿不是保险丝，并不在一个封闭的系统中进行自我调节，如自动中断，又自我恢复，而是彻底中断现有程序和路径，建立新的程序，开辟新的路径。是在一个开放体系中的新的创造。

再次，与道家的返璞归真不同。老子所谓“大曰逝，逝曰远，远曰反”终止了西方哲学的那种以往而不返的线性思维方式，而是到一定程度后自动返回，也就是要归根复命，返璞归真。但是，老子的思想是一种反对发展的逆向运动，与跨越式停顿的向前发展，甚至是寻求更大的发展具有不同的价值观。而且这种返璞归真的思想更多地带有幻想色彩。因为朴散为玉，而玉永远不可能还原为璞。因此，跨越式停顿是当代的发展的思想，与古代回归自然的逆向运动的思想有着实质性的区别。

最后，跨越式停顿虽然借鉴了禅宗的思想，但与禅宗的顿悟有所不同。顿悟是突然明白，洞见真理，进入澄明之境，思维发生了飞跃。跨越式停顿也是顿悟的结果，但是，禅宗的顿悟是要“见父母未生时本来面目”，是对生命来历、归宿的洞彻，是方外之事，可谓“跳出三界外，不在五行中”。而跨越式停顿是方内之事，是人间俗事，并无宗教目的，因而是世俗的发展观，而非宗教的解脱观。

跨越式停顿是未雨绸缪。沿着别人的路走，或者沿着自己制定的既定路线走，只是一种惯性，这种惯性背后潜藏的危机是什么，我们可能不知道。这就需要我们在高速运转时运用跨越式停顿思维时时警醒自己、反思自己、检查自己，而不是等待真正的危机凸显了再去找应对之策。

为什么要强调跨越式停顿？主要原因在于人类处于高速发展，新旧代替越来越频繁的时代，因此应居安思危。在发展中、尤其是在领

先时及时停顿，谋求换代、更新、转型、升级，而非自足自满，等待别人快要超过自己了才去改弦易辙、另谋出路。我们眼见的无数个曾经的辉煌已经烟消云散了。这跟缺乏跨越式停顿有关。不待人类地球资源耗尽而转向探讨外星际，这就是跨越式停顿的具体表现。

总之，跨越式停顿，表面上是停顿的，但实质是飞跃，是跨越，跨越的幅度是超地球的，是跨星际的。但它不是简单的超前思维，而是将时间空间化，把过去、现在和未来放在同一个空间中看，从而产生不同的思路，制定不同的策略。但无论如何，在跨越、超前、时间空间化之前，首先要做的还是突然停顿。

第二节　跨越式停顿：别现代的全球视野

别现代的思想是在国际范围内的现代性讨论中形成的。但什么是现代性？这是一个源自西方连带着多元价值观而又歧义纷呈的概念。目前国内外已有众多不同的表达：

艾森斯塔特（S. N. Eisenstadt）的多元现代性。

乌尔力希·贝克（Ulrich Beck）的第二现代性。

哈贝马斯（Jürgen Habermas）的未完成的现代性。

詹姆逊（Fredric Jameson）的多元现代性。

阿尔都塞（Louis Pierre Althusser）的另类现代性。

吉登斯（Anthony Giddens）的反思的现代性。

齐格蒙特·鲍曼（Zygmunt Bauman）的流动的现代性。

C. 詹克斯（C. Jencks）的晚期现代性。

以上现代性，尽管名词不同，表达各异，但在思维方式上并没有太大的区别，都是强调各自现代性的独特性和对立性，都具有明显的地域性和意识形态性。这种地域性和意识形态性首先表现在非西方国

家。正如沃尔夫冈·威尔施（Wolfgang Welsch）所说："惊异来自对这个定理的非西方的接受。它指明这个定理的西方的拥护者们没有想到的一些方向。许多日本人今天对我们说，他们早就赞成后现代，因为日本的文化在其整个的历史中是最好的折中主义的和杂交的文化，这也许还可以理解。但是当他们声称，后现代这个定理反映了占优势地位的西方的模式的结束和向占据主导地位的东亚世界的过渡，这就出人意外了。在伊斯兰世界，这场有关后现代的辩论引起了巨大的兴趣，因为那儿的人把对西方的现代的片面性和畸形现象的批评理解为他们用以反对西方的'弹药'。"① 实际上，面对现代性问题，中国学者也有这样几种态度。第一，从所谓的民族性出发对现代性进行一分为二的取舍。第二，给中国社会补上现代性的一课。第三，视现代性为后殖民主义霸权加以拒斥。第四，把现代性当成生态破坏的祸首加以控诉。第五，跟着西方后现代批判现代性。其中也充满着地域性、民族性和意识形态性。

其实，关于现代性的地域性、民族性和意识形态性的表达，并不限定在非欧洲国家，即使在欧洲国家内部也有着这方面的明显的表现。迄今为止，人们对于后现代的争议很多。这些争议有关后现代的概念范畴，如什么是后现代，后现代与现代的关系等。也有关于后现代性质和种类的划分。其中对中国颇有影响的就是另类现代性（阿尔都塞）的说法。认为，后现代就是另类现代性，是对现代性的否定。这个另类现代性往往以两大世界的对立为起点，具有明显的民族性特点和国家意识形态的特点。按照这个观点，亚非拉欧美都有各自的现代性，伊斯兰世界、社会主义国家也都有各自的现代性，这种现代性都是与西方的现代性不同的，因而具有另类的属性。在阿尔都赛的眼中，毛泽东思想也是一种另类现代性，也具有后现代的特征。这样一

---

① ［德］沃尔夫冈·威尔施：《我们的后现代的现代·第五版前言》，洪天福译，商务印书馆2004年版，第3页。

来，另类现代性成了思想文化上不同国家意识、民族意识的表现，这跟原本是对于西方现代性的自反式思维不同，形成了他反和反他的思维模式，从而总是在与西方的对立中维护一种现成的意识形态。而事实上，亚非拉几大洲究竟在多大程度上具有西方意义上的现代性，却是不言自明的，更何况什么后现代性了。

所谓的欧美之外的另类现代性，是一个伪命题。这些欧美之外的国家和民族大都只是在享受着西方现代化带来的文明成果，尤其是资本扩张和技术进步带来的成果，而与科学、民主、法制、社会福利等现代性相比，尚有很大距离，还没有进入用后现代反思批判现代的历史阶段，因此，在非欧美国家并不存在另类的现代性，而是不具有现代性或不具足现代性。沃尔夫冈所说的东亚的、伊斯兰阿拉伯的对于现代性的理解是将现代性民族主义化了。这种民族主义化，或者在尽情享受现代化物质成果的同时类似中国宋明理学“坐在禅床上骂禅”；或者像中国晚清那种“中体西用”，只利用西方的科学技术来维护自己的统治，但却都忽视了西方现代化中现代性这一核心价值观对于现代社会的决定性因素。因此，阿尔都塞这种来自民族性的、地域性的、意识形态性的对于现代性的理解，所指涉的并非现代性的正品或另类，而是非现代性。这种非现代性往往打着革命、反对资产阶级等招牌，类似于后现代对于现代性的反动，但实质上由于其所反恰恰是现代性的核心价值观，因此，只能属于非现代性的对于现代性的反动。而后现代则属于现代性的对于现代性的自反。沃尔夫冈的著作《我们的后现代的现代》，认为后现代是现代的延续和对现代的自我反思、自我批判，实际上就有区隔真正的现代性与非现代性或所谓的另类现代性的意思。阿尔都塞的另类现代性由于缺乏现代性的基础，因而其“另类”也就不是现代性的另类了，而只能是非现代性。

当然，全球化也是现代性化而非简单的物质现代化的过程。这一过程包括对于全球范围内的不同体制的渗透和改造。事实上，随着全球化的推进，全球范围内，无论意识形态的对立多么严重，资本的逻

辑，正如詹姆逊所说的，统治了世界，技术的进步将人进一步异化。这一点，在苏联、东欧和中国都有最为明显的表现。资本和技术的全球化带来了现代性的普遍有效性。而立足于地方的或民族的意愿对于起源于西方启蒙时代的现代性的改造，或者所谓另类现代性的表达，并不能改变由于技术进步和资本控制而带来的对于民族文化和地方经验的冲击。即使在原教旨极端主义盛行的国家和地方，也是在拿着西方的现代化武器而在进行所谓的圣战。因此，“另类现代性”由于其非现代性属性而与真正的西方现代性相抵牾，只能借助非欧美国家的地域性和民族性而进行意识形态方面的抵御和斗争。但这种抵御和斗争也只能在西方现代性的场域中展开，因为欧美之外的许多国家尚未形成这种场域，因此难免隔空打牛。

由于无法摆脱对西方现代化成果即资本和技术的依赖，因此，所有欲与现代性划清界限的努力都不会产生实际的效果，只能产生一些意识形态领域的斗争。中国改革开放30多年来，就是沿着这样两条道路走。一方面，要实现四个现代化，要积极地吸收和借鉴全人类的优秀文明成果，甚至主要是吸收和借鉴西方的科技成果和管理方式、资本积累和运营方式；另一方面，是要防范和抵御西方现代性思潮的渗透和侵蚀。这就叫“两手抓，两手都要硬”。因此，在中国，西方现代性只是学术界讨论的一个话题，而非主流意识形态关注的问题，甚至现代性这一话题和术语都无法进入官方主流媒体。因此，现代性问题在中国，也如在其他国家和地区一样，只是一个意识形态范畴的问题，而非一个实在的经济问题或技术问题。事实上，即使在西方和美国，也没有听说哪个公司或哪个资本家是在用自我解构的方式在运营，也没有听说哪个科研集团在用后现代的方式去解构科学和技术。相反，他们仍然热衷于按照经济学规律去积累资本、运营资本并获取利润；仍然在按照科学研究的规则去发明和创造。因此，现代性是一个既与现代化紧密相连的属性，又是一个与经济基础和生产力发展游离的意识形态。

正是由于现代性的意识形态特征，导致了它必然会在全球化背景下形成巨大的思想空间。可以在现代性与非现代性之间，现代性与反现代性之间，现代性与后现代性之间，现代性与前现代性之间形成巨大的张力和众多的种类，会产生现代性地图。如西方现代性、美国的现代性、中国的现代性、日本的现代性、俄罗斯的现代性、东亚的现代性、伊斯兰的现代性、大洋洲的现代性和非洲、拉丁美洲的现代性。在如此众多的意识形态领域中，现代性既是对资本扩张、技术进步的记录，又是对各自理解、各自主张的现代性的表达。但是，无论这些理解和表达如何不同，都首先是思维方式的不同。如宗教国家要不要宗教世俗化，就不仅仅是土耳其要加入欧盟的问题，而是在现代化进程和全球化过程中的宗教地位问题；如中国要复兴传统文化，就有一个如何与现代性相衔接的问题，而非复古的问题。这些问题的出路在于你怎么想。是想全盘接受、全面西化，还是土洋结合，中体西用，还是只享受成果而不问精神。

别现代理论并不固守地域性、民族性和意识形态性所带来的对立性思维方式，而是秉持跨越式停顿的思维方式和科学、民主、自由的核心价值观，是对国家意志、地方利益、地方经验、地方表达的超越，是一种全球性思维和全球性策略，因而具有普适性。跨越式停顿这种思维方式的进步，在于跳出民族和意识形态对立而从新的时空观即后现代之后而不是现代之后去思考现代性问题，从而提出不同于所谓另类现代性的主张和主义。别现代主义综合了各种现代性，包括现代性的反面，因而具有综合创造性。它是一种吸收了前现代、现代、后现代的思想成果，而又别出一路、别出心裁的全新规程、全新战略、全新思维。唯其如此，才有可能成为后现代之后的思想引领者。

别现代的跨越式停顿有着独特性和超越性。别现代借鉴了禅宗的思想，但又超越了禅宗的思想。禅宗的顿悟之法受到现代主义的青睐，其“对法”颇具后现代的处事方式。慧能的“菩提本非树，明镜亦非台。本来无一物，何处惹尘埃”是对神秀的“身是菩提树，

心如明镜台。时时勤拂拭，莫使惹尘埃”的超越，就是釜底抽薪式的言语道断，是对本体的解构，是对话题的改造。这是顿悟禅法的精要，但也仅止于此。而别现代的跨越式停顿却在这种本体否定之后更加关注“百尺竿头，更进一步”的事，也就是关注“更进一步”之后的坠落和坠落之后的事；关注“将漆黑桶兜底打穿”之后的事。实质上，禅宗的“呵佛骂祖”与后现代的解构非常相似。可以说，后现代与禅宗思维方式如出一辙，但缺少禅宗的智慧。而别现代要跨越禅宗的思维，在“本来无一物”的本体否定之后，再来一次革命性的跨越式停顿。这就是“人不惹尘埃，尘埃自惹人。在下当是问，本来岂非物”“尘埃不惹人，人自惹尘埃。念念空空想，尘埃自何来”。别现代并不否定本体的存在，但不会拘泥于本体，而是跨越本体，在“离岸”中反观本体，重新思考那是无边的苦海还是设定的虚妄。

跨越式停顿作为别现代主义的思维方式，更具有策略性。跨越式停顿不仅可以改变对立的身份和地域性、民族性的立场，而且更重要的在于可以改变和制定规则。别现代跨越式停顿与意识形态的现代性不同，避开无端的争论，直指规则的制定。比如打篮球，前现代的思维方式是给有底的框中投球，投不中或投中了又弹出了不算。但投中了却得派人上去取，这样就要耽误很多时间，比赛会中断，影响比赛和观赏的兴趣。现代性的思维第一步是发明一台机器，代替人到球篮的上方取出篮球。这样虽然比人工快了许多，但比赛仍然要中断。第二步是改变规则将篮底打穿，球会自己掉下来，避免了派人上去或用机器上去取球影响比赛的尴尬。这样就形成了我们今天的比赛规程。后现代的思维是反其道而行之，前现代和现代的思维都是要把球投进去的，而后现代却要破坏这个“进去”的规程，要以球砸在篮板的中心而不能进球为目标，属于跟投进派对立的不进派或篮板派。而别现代另辟蹊径，跨越了前现代、现代和后现代的思维方式，虽然也要把篮球投进篮，但投进之后落地之前却又要这个球从篮中被击出去，

以投进与投出的合二为一为评判得最高倍分（可能是3分球的5倍）的标准。与投进派与不进派相比，是投出派。比较起来，现代思维较之前现代是一种伟大的进步，是百尺竿头和将桶底打穿了，后现代是一种刻意的反动，而别现代却是吸收继承了前现代、现代、后现代的积极成果的别出一路、别出心裁。其新就新在与前现代、现代、后现代的都有所不同，但又同时包含了前现代（进篮）、现代（穿篮）、后现代（不进篮）的积极成果。如吸收和继承前现代投进去取出来的创意及规程、现代的投进去不用取的创意和规程，后现代的不能投进去的创意和规程，而来一个投进去再投出去的创意和规程。投进去而又投出来的创意和规程，对于篮球运动员来说，是一次史无前例的尝试，将会改变目前篮球由于频繁进球而观众日趋减少并被足球赛吸走的趋势，但要求防守方运动员要有极速的反应能力、超常的弹跳能力和强大的击球能力。因此，别现代的要将投进去的球在落地前沿着篮筐击出去的创意和规程是一次革命性的变革，其先导是最为先进、最为高端，也最为有趣的思维方式，这就是跨越式停顿。通过不断地中断在某一个时期已被大家都认可的规则思路，进行变革，推进了比赛的发展。因此可以说，别现代首先是一场思维方式的革命。唯有这个思维方式的革命，才能引导新规则的制定和话语权的把握。但是，这个规则的制定是在共享、共赢的平台上进行的，因而取消了民族性身份和意识形态性立场，能够为大家所接受，而不是囿于意识形态的特立独行的另类主张。

别现代既是新的思维，也是新的战略，其实质就是创建规则，引领世界。创建规则，是在全球化背景下，在很高层次上和很高地位上才能做到的事。这个很高就是说，有很强的思维创新能力，有很远的战略眼光，有很大的精神凝聚功能。其道路有人跟随，其方式有人模仿，其经验有人推广。也就是说在整体上，或在某个局部上，达到了第一，产生了很大的影响力。当今中国之于全球，已经到了中国离不开世界，世界也离不开中国的地步，创建和制定规则，已有可能，也

有必要，也更有义务去进行规则的建构。在这个意义上说，别现代跨越式停顿的登场，适逢其时。

别现代是在对后现代之后的预设中制定规则，因此，特别需要思维的超前性、理论的前瞻性和规则的可行性。当然，别现代以制定规则为己任，但并不是盲目地制定具体的规则，相反，只是提供一个思路，制定一种战略，发明一种思想，其最主要的任务是启发别人去思考这个世界的规则制定。

从制定新规则的角度讲，别现代是新世纪的开创者和建设者，是新世纪的引领者。唯有一个新型、健康向上、组织有序、富于创新、不断进步、日趋强大的国家和民族，才会有这样的新思维，才配做新世纪新规则的制定者和新世纪的引领者。用在社会发展上，就是跨越后的停顿，是跨越式停顿。用在思想建构上，就是在中西马我之间游刃有余，在跨越中停顿，在停顿时跨越。跨越，是超常规发展，也是新常态；停顿，则是反常态，是新跨越。别现代，唯其是跨越的，它是超现代的；唯其是停顿的，它又是反思的，是建构的。超现代，不是不要现代，而是说它要比现代的思维更加进步，直接跨越了现代思维而进入了新的境界。停顿，也不是回归自然，而是暂时退回来重新凝聚能量，树立新的目标。因而跨越式停顿是超级目的与超级智慧的合一，是自由意志与客观规律的结合，是一种新的哲学境界。

第三节　跨越式停顿：停顿而非终结

跨越式停顿与西方流行的各种终结论有着本质的区别，但与跨越式发展相比，更是社会主义和资本主义兴亡更替的镜像。

美国历史学家佛朗西斯·福山（Francis Fukuyama）在其 1992 年出版的《历史的终结和最后之人》一书中预言，本世纪即 2000 年谢幕之时，将是资本主义凯旋之日。届时，西方民主制度全面胜利，引领世界进入至善至美之境。福山的预言即所谓的历史终结论实质上是

指社会主义制度、专制主义制度、政教合一制度及一切前现代制度的终结和后资本主义、民主人道主义的彻底胜利。在福山看来，所谓历史的终结只是所有不同于资本主义制度的社会的终结。对福山的预言，人们一般会重新拾起曾经有过的几个挑战。

首先是来自西方思想界的挑战。马克思主义经典作家对于社会发展阶段中社会主义战胜资本主义早有预言。还有西方马克思主义对资本主义制度对人的异化并将人变成“单向度”的人的现状（马尔库塞）的批判。最后是后现代主义者对资本主义现代性的批判，似乎都在警醒人们，资本主义不可能是大同世界的美好蓝图。

其次，来自中国现实的质疑。中国仍然在坚持走社会主义道路，经济保持了长期的中高速发展，繁荣昌盛，而且出现了在经济发展上领跑的趋势，福山的社会主义终结论与此现实南辕北辙。

但是，如果从跨越式发展和跨越式停顿相互对照的角度看，一些曾经在军事、技术、经济上都很强大的国家及其盟友会在一夜之间解体，恰恰是跨越式发展带来的必然结果。在前现代甚至是农奴制基础上的联盟国家，可能会在技术、经济、军事上实现蛙跳式跨越发展，赶超西方现代国家，但在政治制度、社会文明、自然生态方面，却由于缺乏社会主义核心价值观中的自由、民主、法制、平等、公正等社会主义的现代性，从而自行解体，归于失败。相反，汲取了国际共产主义运动经验教训的中国，却能在极“左”路线猖獗之时实现跨越式停顿，及时终止了那种将社会主义导向解体的巨大惯性，又能启动权力的自我约束机制，主张“将权力的老虎关进笼子”，向真正具足的现代性迈进，从而避免了重蹈苏联覆辙而走向民族的现代复兴之路。同样，资本主义垂而不死，就在于起始于资本主义原始积累期资本家知识分子的跨越式停顿，即对资本的血腥和贪婪的无止境的本质的认识，从而终止了资本血腥和贪婪的无止境的巨大惯性，从社会福利制度以及利润财富分配制度的建立入手，避免了资本主义制度的灭亡，并依然长期平稳地运行。

以道观之，历史终结论则可为不经之谈。别现代不相信背离现实的预言，也不按照社会制度和社会意识形态的对立来取舍并预言谁兴谁亡，而是在后现代终结的地方回望后现代的、现代的、前现代的历程，得出自己的结论。事实上，世界上的发达国家，公有制与私有制并存，政治民主与管理集中携手，往往是你中有我，我中有你。别现代秉持阴阳互根之道，相信，社会主义和资本主义是可以永远共生的不同制度，是阴中有阳，阳中有阴的大道运行。即使到了后后现代之后，这种现状依然如故。此所谓孤阴不生，独阳不长。资本主义与社会主义平行发展，但又相互牵连，相互补充，从而达到别现代主义的完善。但别现代主义从不认为会有社会历史的终结。所谓历史的终结只是自然史终结的结果。也就是人类被自然毁灭后，人类社会历史的自动终止。否则，就没有社会制度的终结，而只有社会制度的不断完善。在这个意义上，社会历史甚至不会终结于马克思主义经典理论所描述的共产主义社会。终结意味着熵增的最大阈值。

阴阳互根之道发展到今天已非中国哲学独有的思想，而成为全球共享话语，并首先在西方知识话语中得到了印证。荣格（Carl Gustav Jung）就认为，男性的内心都有一个女性化的自我形象，而女性则有一个男性化的自我形象。这就是男性的阴性基质（Anima）和女性的阳性基质（Animus）。这表明，男性有女性的一面，反之同理，女性也有男性的一面。这种阴性基质和阳性基质，就是内化了的、关于异性的想法。这也许是男女可以变性的理论根据。当然，阴中有阳，阳中有阴，并不能替代阴性或阳性本身具有的本体性和主导性。这里只存在交互性和异质性，不存在绝缘性和同质性。阴阳此消彼长，变化不已，就构成了事物的存在样态和运动本质。因此，福山的历史终结论亦即社会主义终结论并不符合阴阳互根并生之道。

历史终结论在西方由来已久。黑格尔的艺术终结论可谓历史终结论之鼻祖。他认为，随着哲学和理性的发达，在艺术发展的浪漫阶段结束之后，艺术最终会自我终结。黑格尔的艺术终结论影响很大，后

经当代美国哲学家丹托（Arthur C. Danto）的新的艺术终结论，似乎人类艺术真的就终结于1964年的某月某日了。尽管为艺术终结论辩护的论著非常之多，但现实并非如此。在广大的第三世界，艺术可谓欣欣向荣、蒸蒸日上。实际上，艺术之树常青，其永久的魅力即来自不断的跨越式停顿。但这种跨越式停顿不是终结艺术，相反，而是旧的艺术形式、艺术风格和艺术思潮被不知不觉地突然停顿，从而兴起了新的艺术形式、艺术风格和艺术思潮。时髦、流行、创新，作为艺术之树常青的必要条件，都是以跨越式停顿为前提的，符合艺术的随机发展规律。及时地运用跨越式停顿规律，主动停下来反思某些正在走红的艺术形式，客观估量其发展前景，做到未雨绸缪，及时转向，才有可能保持艺术在变异求新中的可持续发展，而不是一条道走到黑，等到被观众和市场抛弃了再去弥补。

虽然西方各种流行的终结论不一定靠谱，但确实是一个警示，这就是莫等闲，不要自以为自己具有全部的真理和所有的优点，因而故步自封。相反，如果固守一穷二白的社会主义理念，固守权力万能的社会制度观，这样的社会制度肯定难逃被历史终结的命运。相反，如果秉持别现代的跨越式停顿思维方式，那么，在发展中停顿，在停顿中反思，在反思中发展，在发展中跨越，又在跨越中停顿，如此循环往复，就能够保持清醒的头脑和健康的状态而获得可持续的发展。

跨越式停顿特别适合中国的国情。别现代主义是建立在现代性和现代化基础上的高度自觉的思想方式、价值取向和主义建构。它继承了前现代、现代和后现代的积极成果，而又超越这些阶段，达到一种最高的理想境界。跨越式停顿的思想产生在中国，有其现实的国情根据。中国的国情是，现代化水平不低，但现代性觉悟不高，也就是社会主义核心价值观中的科学、民主、自由的程度不高。中国在工业、农业、科技、国防方面都表现出很高的现代化水平。其稳居世界第二的国民经济总量和日趋强大的国防力量，都说明其现代化，尤其是物质现代化已经步入世界先进行列。但就管理水平和教育水平而言，中

国仍很落后。这种落后可被视为精神文明方面的落后。主要表现是现代意识不强，文明程度不高，学术思想欠发达，为人素质欠缺，封建意识浓厚。海外旅游中累累曝光的斗殴、辱骂、喧哗、吐痰、撒尿等“大国小民”现象，都是明证。还有官员腐败，门生政治，裙带关系，迷信风气盛行。官员、富商包二奶、养小三的问题也很突出。这些问题来自前现代的封建意识残余，但也不完全如此。造成目前中国现代化水平高而现代性差的另一个原因在于中国的跨越式发展，即在经济上、技术上的跨越和赶超，虽然经济实力和科技水平都上去了，但人们的思想意识、价值观念等并未与之同步发展。在这种情况下，也就是在中国高速现代化的过程中，亟须停一停反思自己的路径、目标、处境和前景。这种停一停并非停滞不前，而是自我反思，自我调节，自我更新，目的还在于两个文明的协调发展，构建一种健康的别样的现代性。这种别样的现代性既符合中国的国情，又能在现代、前现代、后现代的交错中保持积极向上、独立发展的态势，并对全球发展产生积极的影响。

第五章

别现代：哲学四边形与中西马我

——兼回应阿列西·艾尔雅维茨先生*

阿列西·艾尔雅维茨先生在欧洲的《哲学杂志》（*Filozofski vestnik*）上撰文《主义：从缺位到喧嚣？——评王建疆教授的〈主义的喧嚣与缺位——以中国美学为例〉》（*From Absence to Bustle? Some Comments to Jianjiang Wang's Article "The Bustle or the Absence of Zhuyi"*），对我同期发表在同一刊物上的英文文章《主义的喧嚣与缺位——以中国美学为例》① 进行评论。依艾尔雅维茨先生的说法，是为了便于形成全球范围内的学术对话和国际学术文化交流，构成共同的学术话语。他说："在过去，学术界常常在'文人共和国'② 内部构建沟通的桥梁，而如今我们没有理由不在更大规模的基础上再次实现这一理想。这种合作与交流的需要是各个国家、各种文化之间达到真正理解的一个必要的先决条件，也是把'他们'当成'我们'来

* 本章发表于《探索与争鸣》2016 年第 9 期，《社会科学文摘》2016 年第 6 期转载，《人大复印资料．美学》2017 年第 1 期转载。

① Wang Jianjiang, "The Bustle and the Absence of Zhuyi. The Example of Chinese Aesthetics", *Filozofski Vestinik*, Letnik, XXXⅦ, Stevilka 1, 2016.

② 艾尔雅维茨说："'文人共和国'是一个启蒙运动时期由谈话和争论组成的虚拟社群，包含了一些重要的学者和文艺界人士（即启蒙运动者），他们在 17 和 18 世纪的欧洲和美国共享知识，同时尊重彼此间语言和文化的差异。"见 Aleš Erjavec, Zhuyi, From Absence to Bustle? Some Comments to Jianjiang Wang's Article "The Bustle or the Absence of Zhuyi", *Journal of Art + Media Studies*, 2017, 13。

认识的任何努力尝试的一个基本特征。”① 由于作为前国际美协会主席的艾尔雅维茨先生是当今国际最著名的美学家之一，因此，很有必要对他进行回应，以便推动这个话题的进一步国际化深入研究。

第一节 哲学和美学上之“四边形”期许与“声音”尴尬

艾尔雅维茨先生首先认为我的文章具有普遍的国际意义。他说：“我认为西方过去和现在发生的一些事件和进程与中国发生的那些事件和进程虽然有差异，却在某种程度上也有相似之处。类似我们之间的这种对话将有助于避免和纠正一些在全球广泛流传的有关思想的共存性、相对重要性和创新性方面的错误和实践。”由于我所讲的“主义的喧嚣与缺位”现象曾经发生在欧洲、苏联、现在东欧和广大的第三世界，因而这个问题不仅仅是中国学术界的问题，而且也是全球性的问题。

艾尔雅维茨一边认为中国将突破理查德·舒斯特曼的哲学四帝国模式②，而形成世界哲学四边形（欧洲、美国、俄国、中国），这个四边形正是由于中国的加入而形成。他说：

> 在我看来，当代中国的主义、艺术和理论（涉及美学、哲学和人文学科）在许多方面都与西方目前或者近来的情形截然不同。如果说几十年前，西方的文化对抗和竞争主要出现在美国和欧洲（特别是法国）之间，那么现在这种两极的趋势已转变为一个四边（即美国、欧洲、中国与俄罗斯）的较量。我们仍然见证

---

① Aleš Erjavec, Zhuyi, From Absence to Bustle? Some Comments to Jianjiang Wang's Article "The Bustle or the Absence of Zhuyi", *Journal of Art + Media Studies*, 2017, 13.

② Richard Shusterman, Internationalism in Philosophy, *Metaphilosophy*, Vol. 28, No. 4, 1997.

> 着美国和欧洲文化的蓬勃发展，但是现在有一个全新的竞争者参与其中，它就是中国。曾有一段时间，人们认为这个新的竞争者似乎应该是苏联国家，但遗憾的是他们未能承担重任。①

艾尔雅维茨充满期许的评论文章，看起来平和，像在叙述一段事情，但这种叙事对我们来说却颇多启发。他所描述的“哲学帝国三剑客”——英美、法、德彼此在思想文化领域征战的历史，也是一幅“主义”争霸的世界地图，使人眼界大开。但是，艾尔雅维茨的问题却是尖锐的。

第一，法国人对抗美国人的大众文化用的是精英主义，这个精英主义中国有吗？

第二，可以作为主义武装的而非权力工具的马克思主义，中国有吗？

第三，在法国政府抵抗全球化——美国化的同时，众多的主义，诸如后现代主义、后结构主义等，以及众多的独立思想家，中国有吗？如果没有，中国如何在面对欧美文化冲击时挺立并自主呢？

第四，如果中国没有思想家，中国的主义建设是否会变成一种政治运动？

第五，而在此运动之后是否就有真正的主义建立起来呢？

艾尔雅维茨的问题是尖锐的，洞察力是深刻的。好像在他面前我们已无话可说，干着急，没办法，就只有像我在自己的文章里所说过的那样继续做西方主义的看客了！②

我不知道艾尔雅维茨这个四边形是否与GPS/伽利略/格罗拉斯/北斗四大卫星通信系统有关联，但艾尔雅维茨的这个四边形期许，由

---

① Aleš Erjavec, Zhuyi, From Absence to Bustle? Some Comments to Jianjiang Wang's Article "The Bustle or the Absence of Zhuyi", *Journal of Art + Media Studies*, 2017, 13.

② 参见王建疆《中国美学：主义的喧嚣与缺位——百年中国美学批判》，《探索与争鸣》2012年第2期。该文为《人大复印资料·美学》2012年第4期转载。

于连带着人与动物的区别，因而大有置人于动物界的嫌疑。他在文章的后半部分发挥了法国哲学家雅克·朗西埃（Jacques Rancière）对亚里士多德《政治学》一书中关于人与动物的区别在于语言/发言（speech）与声音（voice）的引述，并以此语言和声音的区别作为标准，将中国放在了声音——人与动物皆有、语言——人与动物两大系统相区别的考量中。艾尔雅维茨说：

> 所谓的“第三世界”再次从角逐中逃离并继续保持“沉默”，而中国正在努力获得一种“声音”，这种声音诠释了当代法国哲学家雅克·朗西埃的观点①。在《政治学》一书中，亚里士多德宣称人“是一种政治动物因为人是唯一具有语言的动物，语言能表达诸如公正或不公正等，然而动物所拥有的只是声音，声音仅能表达苦乐。然后整个问题就成了去了解谁拥有语言，谁仅仅拥有声音？”世界上许多国家，无论大小，都发现自己在美学、哲学和人文学科上处于与中国相似的境地，但它们之中努力发出自己声音的毕竟是少数。我认为王教授的文章是表达这种声音、使之为国内外所知晓的有力尝试。我相信这种姿态——获得声音——对任何成功的自立，因而对树立自己在世界上（和社会中）的地位有着极其重要的意义。②

但这种中国的“声音”按艾尔雅维茨的说法并非西方政治家和哲学家包括美学家所认可的“语言”，而只是“声音”，因而难免尴尬。但对于真正认识到中国现状的人来说，艾尔雅维茨不过就是说了一句大实话。为什么这么说呢？我在谈论主义的时候就说，一个民族，如

---

① Jacques Ranciere, *Aesthetics and Its Discontents*, trans. Steven Corcoran, London: Polity, 2009, p. 24.

② Aleš Erjavec, Zhuyi, From Absence to Bustle? Some Comments to Jianjiang Wang's Article “The Bustle or the Absence of Zhuyi”, *Journal of Art + Media Studies*, 2017, 13.

果没有形成自己的主义就不可能占领理论、思想、哲学的高峰，就不可能登上世界历史舞台[①]。而且我在另一篇正在讨论的《中国美学和文论上的“崇无”“尚有”和“待有”》一文中，明确提出中国美学和文论上最为迫切的问题，就是“待有”的问题。待有就是等待有。等待什么呢？等待属于中国式原创的主义[②]。对于我的主义观，学界有不同看法。王洪岳教授、夏中义教授分别对我的《中国美学：主义的喧嚣与缺位》和《中国美学和文论上的“崇无”“尚有”和“待有”》这两篇文章进行了学术批评[③]。但事实上，正如我在《思想欠发达时代的学术策略》中所说的那样，我们由于缺乏原创性的主义，因而尚处于思想欠发达国家之列[④]。我们不能为了所谓的民族感情而无视眼前欠发达的事实。

尽管艾尔雅维茨对中国有较深的了解，也曾参加中国学者主持的国家社科基金项目，而且他也在接着我的思路说话，表面上看起来似乎在认可并推动我的观点走向深入，但是，说实话，艾尔雅维茨的这篇评论我越看越沉重，因为他的论述，他的每一个例证似乎都在拷问着我：你提出要建主义，但你准备好了吗？你们中国要成为G4，成为所谓的四边形中的一边，那么，你们准备好了吗？艾尔雅维茨的这种拷问，实际上也是近几年来我在国内外的学术会议上屡屡遇到的。每当我就创建主义的问题发完言，就有与会代表关切地问我“你有主义吗？”“你的主义是什么？”作为长期的思考，也是为了免予尴尬，我只好抛出自己的主义——别现代主义，权当抛砖引玉了。

---

① 参见王建疆《中国美学：主义的喧嚣与缺位——百年中国美学批判》，《探索与争鸣》2012年第2期。该文为《人大复印资料·美学》2012年第4期转载。

② 王建疆：《中国美学和文论上的“崇无”“尚有”和“待有”》，《学术月刊》2015年第10期。该文为《人大复印资料·美学》2012年第12期转载。

③ 王洪岳：《精神建构的彷徨与出路——兼与王建疆先生商榷》，《探索与争鸣》2012年第4期。夏中义《学术史提问的方式——回应王建疆教授》，《学术月刊》2016年第6期。

④ 王建疆：《思想欠发达时代的学术策略》，《中国社会科学评价》2015年第4期。

第二节　空间并置中的别现代主义

为什么艾尔雅维茨认为中国哲学和美学目前还只有声音而无语言呢？主要原因还在于他尚未看到中国真正意义上的个人独创的主义。还有，他担忧，如果中国的学者开始建构主义，那么，这会不会是政党和政府主导的政治运动呢？也就是类似东欧小国社会主义“五年计划”式的“主义”建设运动呢？艾尔雅维茨说：

> 克罗地亚哲学家显然不想对几无所知的中世纪的克罗地亚哲学家的历史进行研究，而是想要研究德里达、拉康、利奥塔等。（于此，他们与他们的中国同道有几分相似）事实证明，在这种情况下，正如许多其他国家一样，来自政府或其机构的支持常常不能带来期望的结果，放手让研究者追求他们自身的优先项则更有效果。在某种程度上，这种差异像极了为自由市场生产和为五年计划生产的区别。在这类东欧小国，主义的诞生似乎主要来自于后者。

按照艾尔雅维茨的说法，这个“五年计划”式运动已在东欧民族主义复兴过程中的克罗地亚哲学闹剧中得到证实。因此，艾尔雅维茨对我的评论看似平易亲和，实则入木三分，是一种有条件的哲学“四边形”期许，是吊着胃口的期许。

在接下来的论述中，艾尔雅维茨进一步写道：

> 我们注意到“-ism”① 并不是“主义”这个术语的含义在西方语言中的完美呈现，尽管我同意王教授在西方也产生了与主义相

---

① “ism”是英语“主义”的后缀。

似的东西。或许诸如“movement”（“运动”）和“trend”（“趋势”）之类的词可能部分地适合于主义的翻译。

这里需要说明的是，艾尔雅维茨将我所说的主义的建设想象为社会主义国家“五年计划”，理解为运动，这显然是误解。这种误解既来自他本人对中国背景的有限了解，也基于他本人对我的文章的理解不够。我是这么说的：

我认为，首先应当注重具有个人原创和个性特点的哲学和美学思想的建设，而思想的建设首先是主义的建立。①

可见，艾尔雅维茨理解的主义与我有距离。我的主义就是具有引领性的思想和理论，是具有个性特点和民间色彩的学术主张，而非政党主导的政治运动和政治倾向。

当然，也许这种关于主义是不是政治运动和政治倾向以及国家规划的问题并不那么重要，关键要看你究竟有什么主义。

别现代（Bie-modern）和别现代主义（Bie-modernism）不仅是话语创新，而且也是思想创新、观念创新、理论创新。别现代的理论基础是时间的空间化，它的逻辑展开是发展的四阶段论。

（一）别现代的时间空间化理论

时间的空间化，在当今西方空间理论盛行之时，人们很容易将其与西方的空间理论混同，比如与列菲伏尔的空间理论、福柯的空间理论、戴维·哈维的空间理论相混同。但实际上，我讲的时间空间化并不是从西方空间理论中延伸出来的理论，也不是对西方空间理论的运

① Wang Jianjiang, “The Bustle and the Absence of Zhuyi. The Example of Chinese Aesthetics”, *Filozofski Vestinik*, Letnik, XXXVII, Stevilka 1, 2016.

用，而是对中国现实的概括。确切地说，是对中国社会形态和历史发展阶段的概括。

中国目前处于现代化的进程中，现代性的民主、法制、自由、和谐等作为社会主义核心价值观已经深入人心，但同时，前现代的封建意识和宗法制度的残余仍很有市场，而后现代的先锋艺术和解构主义文化也很盛行。这种现代、前现代、后现代交织在一起的时代特征，截然不同于西方断代式（如现代取代前现代，后现代超越现代）的社会形态和历史发展阶段，具有鲜明的时代特征。因此，别现代就是别现代，不是现代，也不是前现代，更不是后现代。

正是这种现代、前现代和后现代交集纠结的现状导致了时间的空间化或时代的空间化。这种时间的空间化不需要理论的推导，只需要对现实的认识和概括。因此，时间的空间化理论是不会从现有的西方理论中找到根据的。

20 世纪以来最重要的空间理论事件来自列斐伏尔的“空间生产”思想，导致地理空间和哲学空间概念的社会化，被称为“空间转向”，成为影响至今的空间理论研究的重要思想来源。但列菲伏尔所讲的资本主义的“空间生产”以及这种生产所构成的空间，如绝对空间、抽象空间、神圣空间、历史性空间、资本主义空间、身体空间、想象空间、矛盾性空间、差异性空间等，很难在中国的现实社会中找到对应。列斐伏尔还将空间化的历史过程概括为从自然状态的绝对的空间，中经埃及式的神庙与暴君统治国家的神圣空间和希腊式的城邦、罗马帝国的政治国家的历史性空间，到资本主义的财产的政治经济空间即抽象空间，再到当代全球化资本主义与地方化意义的对立的矛盾性空间，以及未来的差异性空间六个阶段，就与中国的空间现状更不搭界了。中国的社会形态要比列菲伏尔研究的法国这样的单一资本主义形态更为复杂。因此，法国乃至整个西方的空间理论都很难概括中国由不同时代、不同生产关系、不同意识形态的并置及其矛盾冲突所造成的复杂空间。

别现代的和谐共谋期、矛盾冲突期、和谐与冲突交织期、自我更新与超越期是列菲伏尔的空间理论中对于六个历史阶段的划分所不能概括的。

再就西方空间理论方面的另一位代表性人物福柯的理论而言，别现代的空间是时代的大空间，而福柯的空间是个人微空间。因此，福柯的空间理论不可能是别现代的立体的时代网状空间，而只能是对个人的压迫、规训及个体反抗的微空间。

总之，别现代时期是现代、前现代和后现代的并置和谐，这种社会形态和历史发展阶段与西方式的现代是对前现代的中断，后现代是对现代的中断的历史，以及福柯的历史中断论完全不同，因此，别现代的时间空间化就是一个立足于现实的独特的理论，而非西方理论的翻版。

总之，别现代的时间空间化与西方人文社科领域中的空间理论相比，具有时代的延续性而非中断性；具有来自对现实概括的直接性而非嫁接性。从这个意义上说，别现代理论最适应中国现实，是中国的空间理论。

（二）别现代的发展四阶段理论

生命体的活动和社会实践与时间关联在一起，就形成了生命的历史和人类社会的历史。中国有着至少三千年有文字记载的历史，这是常识。德国哲学家黑格尔说：

> 更令人惊叹的是，这个民族拥有自远古以来至少长达5千年前后相连、排列有序、有据可查的历史，记述详尽准确，与希腊史和罗马史不一样，它更为翔实可信。[①]

① ［德］黑格尔：《世界史哲学讲演录》，刘立群等译，商务印书馆2014年版，第114页。

但出乎人们意料的是，黑格尔接下来说：

> 在任何情况下，它都把自己的特性一直保持下来，因为它始终是独立的帝国。这样，它就是一个没有历史的帝国，只是自身平静地发展着，从来没有从外部被摧毁。其古老的原则没有被任何外来的原则所取代，因此说它是没有历史的。①

黑格尔在他的《历史哲学》《法哲学原理》《世界史哲学讲演录》等著作中，一再地强调中国的历史从本质上看是没有历史的，“是一种非历史的历史”②，它只是君主改朝换代、流氓轮流坐庄的一再重复而已，任何进步都不可能从中产生。而且由于在中国主观精神自由从未发生，因而真正的伦理、宗教、科学、学术、艺术都离中国很远③。国内哲学界一般认为，黑格尔是从他自己的逻辑体系来演绎中国历史的，从而用逻辑遮蔽了中国的历史。如果从历史事实看，中国古代的历史未尝不是黑格尔所描述的那样，虽然近现代的中国社会历史已经把黑格尔关于中国古代历史的观点抛在了后面。但是，若从时间的空间化上讲，当下这个由现代、前现代、后现代交集在一起的中国有无历史的进步呢？这是任何一个关于社会历史的理论都无法回避的。

与黑格尔相反的另一种新的中国历史哲学观值得注意。最近，中国社会科学院的赵汀阳先生在他的《天下主义的未来可能性——对当前一些质疑的回应》中说：“现代性的秩序虽然尚在现在进行

① ［德］黑格尔：《世界史哲学讲演录》，刘立群等译，商务印书馆2014年版，第114页。

② ［德］黑格尔：《历史哲学》，王造时译，上海书店出版社2001年版，第112页。

③ ［德］黑格尔：《世界史哲学讲演录》，刘立群等译，商务印书馆2014年版，第131—136页。

时，但作为一个‘问题’却已经属于现在完成时，就是说，现代性已经不再生长，是一个已经结束了的问题，已经成为历史学的对象，而不属于未来的问题。”① 如果我没理解错的话，中国应该已经是现代国家或者超现代国家了。现代性问题对中国已经不适应了。与黑格尔的中国历史停滞论相比，赵汀阳的论断显然是中国历史腾飞论了。但无论从中国的历史还是从中国的现实看问题，中国都不是没有历史的，也不是从历史中飞过去的。这里的关键在于中国的社会形态究竟是什么，这种社会形态的内在组织结构和动力结构是什么。

黑格尔的中国历史非历史论，如果就因为中国几千年的封建社会都在重复着同一个行为模式，循环运动，只有空间而无时间而言，似乎也能成立。但如果从今天回首历史，这种时代的空间凝聚早已解冻。但这种解冻并非我们已经跨越了现代而进入了后现代。相反，我们离真正的现代性还有距离，前现代还是我们今天社会的梦魇，时时在纠缠着我们，蒙蔽着我们，毒害着我们。我们今天的许多社会悲剧都有前现代思想和制度的影子。因此，并非现代性的问题已经过时，相反，正在困扰着我们。

别现代的时间空间化既非老黑格尔的历史停滞论，也非赵汀阳的历史飞越论所能解释的。因为，别现代有着自己来自社会现实的结构和功能。别现代主义的首要任务就是要展示现实社会的这种结构和功能。

黑格尔关于中国无历史的观点和赵汀阳的现代性终止的观点都涉及中国的历史和历史发展以及社会形态，因此直接关系到对当下中国的认识。若按中国无历史的说法，当今的中国仍处于前现代，与现代无关；而按现代已经成为历史的说法，中国已经走过了现代，而进入

① 赵汀阳：《天下主义的未来可能性——对当前一些质疑的回应》，《探索与争鸣》2016 年第 5 期。

了后现代或后后现代。但从中国的现实出发，这两种说法都是不符合中国的国情内容的。因此，寻找中国的国情内容就显得十分必要。所谓中国的国情内容并非抽象的某种主义，而是由具体的阶段和形态构成的具体存在。因此，别现代的具体内涵就存在于这种阶段和形态构成的具体存在中。

别现代主义并非止步于时间空间化，而且还有具体的内涵，这就是由现代、前现代、后现代之间的矛盾和斗争所导致的发展阶段论。别现代时期的主要问题是混杂中的错乱和多元中的对立，并明显地表现在社会生活的各个方面。因此，别现代主义认为，由于时间的空间化，即现代、前现代、后现代的空间并置，从而形成了现代、前现代和后现代既和谐共谋又内在冲突的张力结构。在这个张力结构中，和谐共谋期只是别现代的初始阶段，接着便是对立冲突阶段。由于现代与前现代之间在思想、制度方面天然的对立，和谐共谋总会随着社会矛盾的凸显而让位于对立冲突。但是在对立冲突期，由于健康社会的自我调节能力，也会出现对立冲突与和谐共谋并置的状态。这就如当今中国的医患冲突一样。首先是患者给医生志愿送红包，达到和谐共谋，接着，由于患者的经济负担加重，而对医生的期许又不断地归于失望，从而局势发生反转，这就是患者及其家人在肉体上伤害医生和护士，从而进入对立冲突期。但医患双方在对立冲突之后又会出现新的平衡，这就是新规约的出现，患者不再送红包（一种行贿的方式），医生不再收红包（一种受贿的方式），但也不敢再为牟利而过度治疗，从而达到医患关系的理性化常态。但光有这种和—斗—和还是不够的，因为这样就没有进步，就是“非历史的历史”。因此，觉悟者，尤其是管理阶层的觉悟者最早进行自我反思、自我更新、自我超越，从而进入一个新的管理层面，并将社会带到一个新的发展水平。这个过程就是自我更新超越期。自我更新超越期就是虚妄的现代性的终结和真正的别样现代性的生成。

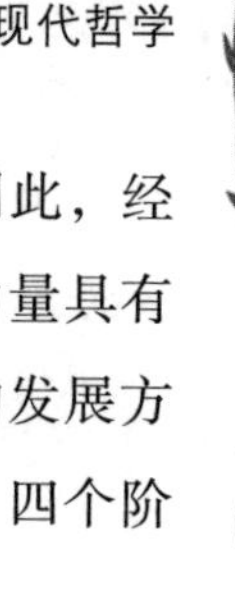

由于现代、前现代、后现代相互纠结，既和谐又对立，因此，经过矛盾和斗争在别现代时期会形成一种主导性的力量。这种力量具有权重的作用，可能是现代性，也可能是前现代性，因而社会的发展方向具有随机性。但社会发展和进步的总趋势不会改变，因此，四个阶段的理论仍然有效。

当然，别现代的四阶段论，即和谐共谋期、对立冲突期、对立冲突与和谐共谋并存期、自我更新超越期，前论已有详细的论述，这里只是说明别现代的发展理论不同于列斐伏尔的六阶段论，而且并非一个简单的口号，相反，是一个理论体系，是一种原创的思想，是一个原创的主义。

别现代主义不同于别现代，其思想主张是期许符合人类进步趋势的主导性力量的出现，通过社会的自我调节、自我更新、自我超越，更新别现代，超越别现代，终结别现代，具足别样现代性，从而进入更为理想的社会发展阶段。

回到艾尔雅维茨的评论上来，别现代理论的提出并非他所担忧的国家五年计划的产物，而是别现代理论创始人的个人研究成果。尽管别现代理论文章在发表时冠以国家社科基金项目阶段性成果，但事实上，别现代的首次提出，始于2014年第12期《探索与争鸣》上我的文章《别现代：主义的诉求与建构》，而我的国家社科基金项目“后现代语境中英雄空间的解构与建构问题研究”立项于2015年。该项目于2016年6月经国家社科基金办公室同意改名为“别现代时期的英雄空间解构与建构问题研究”，原因在于，经过研究，我们发现中国并未处于后现代语境中，而是处于别现代语境中。这里虽只有“后”与“别”的一字之差，但中国的社会形态和社会历史阶段的特征已然完全不同了。因此，别现代理论并非官方五年计划的产物，而纯粹是个人完全独立自由的创造，是在接受项目资助情况下的个人独创。事实上，提倡主义，是我自2012年起一贯的学术主张，已经发

表了数篇文章，并引起讨论①。别现代的提出只是我的关于主义的主张的践履，也可以被称为别现代主义。我想，别现代主义应该是对艾尔雅维茨及其国内外其他对中国哲学、美学、人文学科持疑论者的最好回答。

第三节　中西马我与悖论破题

艾尔雅维茨的世界哲学人文学科四边形论是对他曾经同意并引述过的理查德·舒斯特曼的哲学四帝国论，即英美哲学、欧洲大陆哲学、苏联哲学和远东哲学四个帝国概念的修正。用世界哲学四边形理论取代他曾经认同的世界哲学四帝国论，即用中国取代远东，这无疑会使中国的读者兴奋不已。但是，当我们看到艾尔雅维茨关于"语言"（speech）与"声音"（voice）的对比后，这种乐观的盲目性显而易见。艾尔雅维茨的行文风格很像庄子的先扬后抑。庄子说："山林与，皋壤与，使我欣欣然而乐与！"大家都很高兴，大自然的美啊！但是庄子笔锋一转，接着说："乐未毕也，哀又继之。哀乐之来，吾不能御，其去弗能止。悲夫，世人直为物逆旅耳！"（《知北游》）这段曾被广泛征引，用来赞美庄子是自然主义美学大宗师，但实际上讲的却不是自然的美，而是讲被外物异化了的人的逆旅之艰难和悲哀。当我们为艾尔雅维茨这个四边形期许而兴奋不已时，又被艾尔雅维茨

---

① 王建疆：《别现代：主义的诉求与建构》，《探索与争鸣》2014 年第 12 期，《人大复印资料·社会科学总论》2015 年第 2 期转载；《别现代：美学之外与后现代之后——对一种国际美学潮流的反动》，《上海师范大学学报》（哲学社会科学版）2015 年第 1 期，《社会科学报·学术文摘》2015 年 4 月 9 日第 3 版；《中国美学与文论上的崇无、尚有和待有》，《学术月刊》2015 年第 10 期，《人大复印资料·美学》2012 年第 12 期转载；《思想欠发达时代的学术策略》，《中国社会科学评论》2015 年第 4 期；《别现代：话语创新的背后》，《上海文化》2015 年第 12 期；《别现代：跨越式停顿》，《探索与争鸣》2015 年第 12 期，《人大复印资料·哲学原理》2016 年第 3 期转载，探索与争鸣编辑部全国征文讨论；《别现代：人生论美学的学科边界与内在根据》，《文艺理论研究》2016 年第 2 期。上述文章在学界均引起了广泛讨论。

泼了一桶冷水：你们只是在发声，还没有语言（发言）！

那我们到底是在发言还是在制造声音呢？我想，本文第二部分中我已经表达了自己的观点，我们不仅有声音，而且也有语言；不仅在发声，而且在发言了。但是，艾尔雅维茨的语言与声音区别论是怎么来的？追索这个这个问题，也许能够使我们的话题更加深入。

1997 年，艾尔雅维茨撰文讨论哲学的民族性和国际性问题，针对理查德·舒斯特曼的哲学帝国理论，结合斯洛文尼亚这样的小国的现实，提出了自己的观点。理查德·舒斯特曼的哲学帝国理论认为，世界上的哲学原理都来自哲学帝国，绝大多数的对于哲学帝国的趋附只能形成附属于哲学帝国的哲学学派①。艾尔雅维茨在接受这种观点的同时指出，小国哲学可以选择舒斯特曼的两条道路之外的第三条道路，这就是不依不靠独立发展，走自己的路，但同时保持与哲学帝国和哲学国际的交往②。艾尔雅维茨是这样说的，也是这样做的。除了他之外，还有他文中提到的他的同胞，斯洛文尼亚的大哲学家齐泽克。他们两位来自"小国""小文化"的哲学家和美学家，给我的启发蛮大的。正如傻大个打不过小精灵一样，一个经济大国未必就是哲学大国，更不一定成为哲学帝国；倾一国之力通过五年计划也未必就能产生哲学家，相反，可能由于来自权威性意识形态的规训，使得本该成为哲学家的也只能成为一个普通的论文发表者。哲学家首先是一个个我，是一个高度精神自由的个我。因此，我认为中国哲学、美学、人文学科要走的路既不是哲学帝国的振臂一呼集者如云，也不是哲学帝国外的对于哲学帝国的亦步亦趋，而是要走自己的路。但又与斯洛文尼亚的路不同，而是中西马我并存之路。中西马已经是中国文化传统、思想传统、哲学传统的固有成分，摆也摆脱不了的。但

① Richard Shusterman, Internationalism in Philosophy, *Metaphilosophy*, Vol. 28, No. 4, 1997.

② Aleš Erjavec, Philosophy: National and International, *Metaphilosophy*, Vol. 28, No. 4, 1997.

“我”的缺位尚待填补。在别现代主义看来，最关键的还是要看“我”，即作为个我的自己的原创力。因此，我强调哲学人文学科建构中的中西马我。艾尔雅维茨说：

> 过去十年，在一些场合我见证了中国美学家之间的争论，他们批评他们的同胞对西方思想不加批判地拿来，而没有提供一种中国化的替代性选择。这些批评旨在改变那些在他们看来是对西方理论、方法、主题不加批判的一味亲昵的做法。这些中国美学、哲学和人文学科的支持者，当然也是中国传统的支持者。他们认为正是西方美学、哲学和人文学科将中国的思想遮蔽，使之变得无关紧要。他们希望停止甚至扭转这一趋势，于是创造理论或者一组理论作为对当代中国和全球问题最原创的“中国”式的反应。接下来一个重要的问题就是这样的“中国”式理论到底背靠中国传统的哪个部分或哪种潮流？是儒家思想、新儒学、道家思想、马克思主义还是其他？于此，这个悖论的不育性显露无疑：对我而言所乐于见到的是，让所有这些理论在和谐或者冲突中共同存在，但同时，理论与文学和艺术就在传统与新的“外国”理论的对立中被内在地撕裂了。在这种情况下，除了斗争和缓慢的相互交流甚至同化之外，别无他法。在其他一些国家，这类困境呈现了不同的面貌：如在后殖民地国家，对抗常出现在殖民与后殖民话语和文化之间。由于中国不是殖民地，此外，在上个世纪的大部分时间里是马克思主义国家，因此，在殖民地获得的经验教训能否被大量用于讨论中国的问题？我不以为然，因为我对后殖民研究可以用于解释社会主义国家的发展表示怀疑①。

① Aleš Erjavec, Zhuyi, From Absence to Bustle? Some Comments to Jianjiang Wang's Article "The Bustle or the Absence of Zhuyi", *Journal of Art + Media Studies*, 2017, 13.

艾尔雅维茨评论的这种现象应该是当下中国哲学和美学的现状，而且依他的说法，目前没有更好的办法改变这种现状。但是，艾尔雅维茨的问题在于他只了解部分现状，而非所有现实，因而缺乏概括性。事实上，在中国哲学界已经对这种现状有了界分，这就是中西马①，即中国传统哲学和美学思想，西方哲学和美学思想，马克思主义哲学和美学思想。但随着一些新的具有原创性的个我的思想和观点的出现，这种界分正在被打破。这种被打破的突出点就是个人创造的而非所谓“五年计划”规划的学术和思想正在形成，我的别现代主义是，吴炫提出的否定主义美学，赵汀阳的新天下主义也是。因此，中国当下哲学的格局应该是中西马我格局，而非以前的中西马格局。由于中西马作为思想资源最终都要融合进个人思想家的思想和理论的创造中，思想创新、理论创新、哲学创新其本质仍是个我的，因而中西马我并提在中国也是水到渠成的。

别现代时期的主要问题之一是经济、军事、政治、外交的发达与思想的欠发达构成的矛盾。这种欠发达的主要表现是缺少主义。这种思想欠发达的观点不是对亚里士多德的声音论、德里达的中国无哲学论的背书和追随，而是基于基本的社会现实。如拙文《思想欠发达时代的学术策略》所揭示的那样，别现代是一个发展中的阶段。实际上舒斯特曼哲学帝国理论中没有中国哲学的地位的说法是老黑格尔思想的延续。同样的说法在德里达的中国无哲学论中得到了更为明显的表达，也引起过中国哲学界、思想界和学术界的很大反响。但不论是黑格尔，也不论是舒斯特曼还是德里达，他们的观点如果用在中国古代哲学的描述上就显然是错误的，将古代中国从哲学帝国排除也是不对的。仅就中国现代和当代哲学而言，熊十力、冯友兰、牟宗三、李泽厚都不能不被称为哲学家。尤其是李泽厚，也是得到欧美国家哲学

① 中西马的说法来自中国哲学界。如2014年12月在复旦大学举办的“第四届中哲、西哲、马哲专家论坛”就是这么称呼的。

界、思想界承认的哲学家和美学家。因此，说中国的思想欠发达现象，只是就经济的高速发展与哲学人文学科的相对滞后而言的，并非中国的哲学和思想就停顿了。当下中国，唾弃山寨，鼓励独创已蔚然成风，相信会在中西马之外更多的“我”的学说会破土而出。

艾尔雅维茨对我的评论的最大的启发是哲学、美学、人文学科上的世界主义与民族主义的悖论问题。

正题：真理是没有国界的，是没有民族性的，是世界的，因此，讲国家真理、民族真理是不成立的。

反题：在世界公民出现之前，真理都是在民族国家中产生的，没有民族性的真理又怎么能在民族中行走？

就艾尔雅维茨所举的法国文化与美国文化的竞争而言，如果真理是世界性的，那么，这种竞争还有什么必要？如果真理是民族的，那么，法国的思想为什么会在经过了与英美、德国的对抗和竞争后成为世界的思想呢？当然，任何悖论的深刻处就在于它摆脱了简单结论的武断。确实有不少人信奉没有论证的“越是民族的就越是世界的”这句话，并视之为箴言。但事实是这样的吗？我们看到过世界各地贫穷落后处于大山深处的弱小民族，他们除了被观光之外，其前现代的文明是具有世界意义的吗？因此，正如强调法兰西文化神圣性的法国思想那样，坚持民族主义未必就是与世界背道而驰，而那些追随哲学帝国的附庸国们鼓吹世界主义也未必就是真理在握。哲学是世界的还是民族的并不重要，重要的在于是否具有世界价值。所谓世界价值就是对人类具有普遍的意义。试想，如果法国人搞出的比美国人、德国人和俄国人多得多的思想和主义对人类世界没有任何价值，法国思想又怎能会被欧洲大陆哲学、英美哲学、中国哲学所接受呢？又怎么能够取代美国而成为世界哲学和思想的中心呢？因此，世界性与民族性的矛盾或悖论并非艾尔雅维茨所说的不育或不产，即生发不出什么问题来，相反，这一悖论，对当下中国哲学和美学乃至整个人文学科来说，是极具启发性的。其启发性就在于如何走出这个悖论。中国哲

学、中国美学是否能够发达起来，关键在于看你是用民族主义排外，还是在用普遍真理、普世价值表达一种具有民族性的思想。

在中西马我的格局中，在世界性与民族性的悖论中，没有必要搞中与西与马的对立，没有必要用中西马将我遮蔽掉、消灭掉，更没有必要搞混杂，而是要抛开这一悖论，抛开对立和混杂，突出中西马我中“我”的个性和原创性，只有这样，才能真正解决思想欠发达的问题，确立四边形的现状，否则，将永远陷入抽象的民族主义与世界主义之争而于事无补。设想如果法国不是在这半个多世纪以来出现了一大批独立的思想家，那么，法国人的民族主义又怎能转变为世界主义。因此，正如艾尔雅维茨所说，西方的、后殖民主义的种种路径并不适合于中国。中国的路我认为就在脚下，就在于依据中西马资源的个人独立的创造。

别现代时期是个多元混杂的时期，中西马我各领风骚。但别现代主义不同于别现代的混杂，而是主张纯一，这种纯一就是对别现代的主导而非被别现代所主导。坚持“我”的独创性，就不会像古罗马模仿古希腊，不会像亚非拉奥效仿某一个欧美发达国家那样失去主体性。事实上，在中国进行的马克思主义中国化和马克思主义大众化也就是与时俱进的有个我性和独创性的对马克思主义的发展。因此，我也期待着艾尔雅维茨提出的中国哲学在世界的四边形占位，但我首先认为，这个哲学四边形的形成和维护一定是超越了民族主义的，而非狭隘民族主义的。

针对狭隘民族主义，艾尔雅维茨提出了作为欧洲文化学术传统的“文人共和国”观念。“文人共和国”据我的理解就是宽容、开放、交流、相互尊重、求同存异，在国际化背景下思想交锋，价值共享。我们目前迫切需要打破在封闭的小圈子里独步六合的现状，更多地进入国际视野和世界哲学中去。

真正的大国容得下多元文化，容得下“文人共和国”，容得下别人对自己落后面的批评，鼓励思想创新、学术创新，因而容得下主义

的建构。大国不仅有文化的同化力，而且有自我调节、自我发展、自我更新的能力。立足于大国背景下的别现代主义，就是自我原创主义、自我调节主义、自我更新主义、自我超越主义和实事求是的对于核心价值观的兑现主义。

第二编

别现代美学

第一章

中国美学上主义的喧嚣与缺位*

1904 年王国维发表了《〈红楼梦〉评论》，研究“《红楼梦》之美学上之价值”，视《红楼梦》为“悲剧中的悲剧”①，从此拉开了中国现代美学的大幕。以往中国古代和近代的审美思想都被系统地整合到了“美学”的名下，中国美学由此诞生。于今走过 100 多年的中国美学，经历了产生、发展、变化的历史过程，取得了不小的成就，但问题也不少，其中学术思想欠发达的问题在美学上尤为突出，至今“是中国美学还是美学在中国”的问题还梦魇般地缠绕着中国美学界。反思这样的问题，我们发现，百年中国美学史的历史脉络中，曾经发生过的“主义”大讨论则最为引人注目。

第一节　美学上主义的喧嚣

中国现代美学从 20 世纪初产生后，由于其创始人王国维、蔡元培、鲁迅坚持了美学的“无用之用”的超功利原则，因而直到 1930 年，并未形成美学上的意识形态之争。1930 年以后出现了文艺有无

* 本章曾发表于《探索与争鸣》2012 年第 2 期，并为《人大复印资料·美学》2012 年第 7 期转载。

① 姚淦铭、王燕主编：《王国维文集》上册，中国文史出版社 2007 年版，第 11 页。

阶级性、是否超政治的论争。1940年蔡仪《新美学》的出版，被认为是意识形态美学的正式登场。有关文艺是否有阶级性，有关美学是功利性的还是超功利性的论争，一直延续到了50年代。

50年代的美学大讨论表面上看是“百家争鸣”，师生之间、专家学者与工农兵之间都可以互相批判。但这种批判从一开始就具有全国性的意识形态论争和阶级斗争的特点。首先，所有的美学问题都被冠以无产阶级或地主资产阶级的名分，美学具有了阶级性和阶级划分。其次，关于美的本质的讨论大多被定性为“唯心主义”的或“唯物主义”的，也有被定性为“客观主义”或“主观主义”的，从而中国美学有了清晰的意识形态分野。再次，这种美学的意识形态性总是跟美学的阶级划分紧密相连，如唯心主义美学被认为是地主资产阶级的思想表现，唯物主义美学则是无产阶级的思想表现。最后，由于这种阶级划分和意识形态对立，不少被划归为唯心主义美学的代表人物受到了政治上的牵连甚至人身方面的迫害。一场轰轰烈烈的美学大讨论，在造就了几位美学家和几个所谓的美学流派后，最后以政治思想斗争向新的阶段发展如反右、“文革”等而偃旗息鼓。

50年代的美学大讨论，形成了以吕荧、高尔泰为代表的主观唯心主义美学，以蔡仪为代表的客观唯物主义美学，以朱光潜为代表的二元论的主客观统一美学，以李泽厚为代表的实践美学。尽管有着过于鲜明的阶级斗争和政治思想斗争的色彩，但于美学而言，它在中国是史无前例的，以致学界冠以“五十年代美学大讨论”“中国美学四大派”等学术荣誉，庶几可以遮蔽那段被“左”倾思潮统摄的政治思想斗争历史。反观50年代的美学大讨论，其思想标记和逻辑脉络异常显著。这就是，50年代的美学大讨论不仅以“主义”来划分阵营、划分派别、划分思想，而且以“主义”来确立美学的进步性与落后性、革命性与反动性的。因此可以说，50年代的中国美学完全是主义的标榜和喧嚣。

主义是理论的升华，是思想的凝聚，是价值倾向的旗帜。但主义

是有层次之分的。主义也有自发的和原创的之分。如唯物主义和唯心主义就是自人类有了世界观，就自发地形成了，因此可以说是最原始、最普通、最初级的主义。而人类于近代所创建的主义，基本上都是自觉的、原创的、有针对性的因而是高级的主义。

50 年代美学大讨论中主义的喧嚣，实际上是在唯物主义和唯心主义的对立中发出的，具有原始性、普范性和低层次性，缺乏原创性。而且若按恩格斯关于唯心唯物的问题只在涉及世界观时才有意义、否则没有意义的说法，这种唯物与唯心的争论是否在美学层面上有效，值得怀疑。因此可以说，与近代西方以来的马克思主义、存在主义、实用主义、结构主义、科学主义等相比，1950 年的美学大讨论，处在主义的原始层面和初级层面上。在某种意义上说，只能称其为主义的喧嚣，而非主义的原创和建构。正因为这种主义的低端性，导致了 50 年代中国美学大讨论的以下几个特点。

第一，原初性。首先，从学科的升级换代上讲，20 世纪以来，西方美学发生了重大的历史转型。正如李斯托威尔（Listowel）《近代美学评述》所说，西方美学已从自上而下的形而上的美学向自下而上的形而下的美学转变。即从思辨的美学转向实验的、心理的、科学的、语言的美学。出现了许多新的思想、新的方法和新的流派，而中国美学仍然停留在美是主观的还是客观的问题上，而且以此为划分唯心主义美学和唯物主义美学的标准。其学术思想的落后性不言而喻。尤其是停留在世界观最基本问题上的美学讨论，层次不高，与当代西方美学之间至少有着半个世纪的代差。其次是研究内容的初级性，如对审美有无功利性这样的老问题不得其解，以功利满足或革命利益为美，完全无视审美的超功利的一面，从而导致好即美，有用即美，无产阶级的即美、地主资产阶级的即丑，唯物主义即美、唯心主义即丑等许多美学外行话语盛行。

第二，封闭性。20 世纪是西方各种思想繁荣，各种美学流派争相斗艳的时代，50 年代尤为突出。西方现代主义美学、西方马克思

主义美学于此时方兴未艾。但当时的中国由于政治上的极端封闭，与欧美国家隔离，远离西方思想和文化的主流。大陆很少出版西方的哲学和美学著作，美学研究者很难看到来自西方美学的著作。60年代中期由《哲学研究》编辑部编辑、上海人民出版社出版的《资产阶级哲学资料选辑》灰皮书和白皮书，也是以“内部读物”的形式在内部秘密交流的。这种现实反映在美学研究上，就是封闭导致的知识贫乏，大白话，说外行话，说别人说过的老掉牙的话。说是“大老粗”搞美学也不为过。这种封闭性表现得最为突出之处在于，固守唯物主义的藩篱，不敢越雷池半步，以美学的唯物主义为荣，以美学的唯心主义为耻，论者之间的相互攻击，实质上都在为维护自己是唯物主义者而展开。美学讨论的视域被封闭在了这种最为原始最为初级的主义之争中。

第三，政治化。美学的原理中存在着形式的无功利性和审美效用有功利性的悖论。康德最早说美是无目的的合目的。这一命题看似简单，实则成为美学的内行与外行的分界线。30年代起，有关文艺有无阶级性，文艺与政治的关系的讨论就已沸沸扬扬了。到了50年代，强调审美功利性的说法变本加厉，以阶级属性来为审美趣味划界，也为美学定性，表现出强烈的意识形态性和阶级斗争觉悟，从而把美学推上了政治斗争的轨道。美学大讨论中的有些学者就因为被指责为唯心主义美学而成了后来反右运动中的右派，受到了政治迫害。用政治干预学术，甚至代替学术，构成了那个时代美学的特色。

第四，议题短暂性。50年代美学大讨论的主义喧嚣，并没有成为80年代美学复兴时的主要话题。什么美是主观的或客观的，什么是主观唯心主义美学，什么又是客观唯物主义美学，等等，在过去争得死去活来的议题，在后来竟被人们看轻甚至忘记。从学术史的角度看，这些议题短暂而无长久的生命力。也可以说时过境迁，议题失效，缺少可持续性增长基因。

构成中国50年代美学特征的原因如下：一是中国现代美学从西

方移植，或借助于“日源新语”译介而来，是舶来品，因而先天不足。而现代美学的奠基人王国维、蔡元培、鲁迅等处在自辛亥革命开始的不断的革命运动中，其研究和理论建设时断时续，从而导致中国美学于先天不足之外发育不良。1930—1940 年的美学整体上不如现代文学那样受社会关注，因而美学的知识远未普及，年轻学子对美学的知识储备不够，学术视野不宽，思想准备不足，因而很容易被简单的意识形态之争和主义之争牵着鼻子走，其美学研究成了低层次主义论战的低层次学术成果。二是与西方隔绝，坐井观天，盲目自大，不知美学天地之广阔。尤其不知西方马克思主义美学的成就。也不知道现代西方美学的基本情况。因而闭门造车，独步六合。正如李泽厚在其《美学译文丛书序》中所说：“现在有许多爱好美学的青年人耗费了大量的精力和时间苦思冥想，创造庞大的体系，可是连基本的美学常识也没有。因此他们的体系或文章经常是空中楼阁，缺乏学术价值。这不能怪他们，因为他们根本不了解国外研究成果和水平。”李泽厚此话是在改革开放的 80 年代初讲的，而于 50 年代，中国美学的封闭与落后就可想而知了。三是以政治统治学术和学术争鸣，学术被狭隘功利化。审美的无功利性背后有着系统功利性。这就成了功利主义者要美学做政治工具的理由。

自 30 年代的文艺阶级性之争开始，到 40 年代毛泽东发表《在延安文艺座谈会上的讲话》，文艺的功用和美学的价值日益受到政党的重视。但不懂美学的人更容易把美学的潜在的对于系统的功利性或“无用之用”的“大用”变成狭隘的实用功利性，从而导致美学讨论的政治化。

第四，50 年代的美学大讨论既未衔接中国的美学思想传统，断了香火，又未与现实联系，缺了地气，成为“空中楼阁”。可以说，既不是中国的，又是无用的，因而 50 年代的争论议题到了 80 年代美学复兴时竟然不再有效，被人们搁置、遗忘或者回避了。

总之，由于 50 年代中国美学是在原初的主义之争中进行，因而

在主义喧嚣的背后却是主义的贫乏，这种主义的贫乏建基于知识的贫乏、思想的贫乏、学术的贫乏、学科的贫乏之上。

第二节　美学上主义的泛滥

80 年代改革开放，同时也迎来了中国美学的第二波热潮。但这次热潮与 50 年代的美学大讨论截然不同。首先是时代背景的不同。国门大开，思想解放，方法开禁，主义喧嚣，西学蜂拥，在打开的西方美学的宝库面前，应接不暇，中国美学只有顺从和追随，唯恐跟之不及。其次是没有形成 50 年代那样的美学大讨论，其议题分散。80 年代的中国美学不再延续 50 年代的议题，而是代之以全新的视野和全新的西方美学议题。但这些议题涉及面很广，有关于方法论的，有关于新观念的，还有关于技术应用的，当然也有关于美的本质的，但已被其他议题淹没。再次是西方的美学话语成了中国美学研究者的话语，中国美学患上了“失语症”。改革开放的结果是西方科技、文化、思想的大举进入。中国美学已经成为西方形形色色主义繁殖的土壤。尽管“反对精神污染”，加强社会主义精神文明建设等活动也抑制了极端的反社会主义主流价值观的倾向，但是，西方的主义入侵趋势并未得到抑制，反倒愈演愈烈。只要看一下那些冠以各种主义的西方美学著作的层出不穷的汉译和各个层次的学位论文中对西方美学中主义的竞相阐释，就知道这已经是无法阻挡的潮流。其结果是中国美学自身的特点被忽视，中国美学的多样性被遮蔽，直至中国究竟有无美学都受到了怀疑，中国与西方美学对话的前提正在消失。

20 世纪 80 年代西方美学涌入中国的最显著特征是主义的集约式轰炸。西方的美学尤其是近现代的西方美学，往往以“主义”冠名。虽然中国的美学思想源远流长，中国美学的内容非常丰富，但中国的美学思想自古以来几乎没有用主义冠名（只有道家被英译为 Daoism，儒家被译为 Confucianism），因此，在美学思想上并没有形成像西方美

学这样多的主义，只有现当代屈指可数的仍然是来自西方的马克思主义美学以及原始的唯物主义美学、唯心主义美学等，在这种情况下，所谓中国美学，已被这些空降的西方的主义所覆盖；所谓美学的多样性，似乎也只是西方美学上的众多主义的专利。西方的主义的美学潮水般涌入中国，不可能不对中国传统的美学思想和正统的意识形态造成冲击。西方的现代主义和后现代主义的美学思潮正在改造和塑造着中国人的审美观念、审美理想和艺术思维。这一点，只要我们看一下生活中追求当下享乐，文化上追求时髦新奇，艺术上注重过程，思想上玩弄解构，审美上只讲形式，就无一不能从西方美学的主义中找到出处。

相对于 50 年代中国美学大讨论中那几个原初的主义之争，80 年代以来美学上的主义泛滥成灾。但 80 年代以来的这些主义无一不是西方的。西方以主义为旗帜的美学在中国畅通无阻，如入无人之境，仿佛正在印证着全球化是美国化、西方化的预言。中国学者发出的在全球化背景下化全球的豪言壮语，不知何以为之。但我们听到更多的是中国美学患了“失语症”和只有“美学在中国”而无中国美学的悲鸣。西方的主义的美学之所以从 80 年代开始在中国泛滥，其主要原因在于以下几个方面。

第一，全球化的冲击。全球化曾被前美国国家安全助理布热津斯基认为是美国化。此语引起了包括法国在内欧洲国家的惊恐。事实上，全球化并非美国化，而是欧美文化率先主导世界经济和文化的发展方向，是资本的逻辑统治世界的开始。全球化来势之猛，也许是中国美学界所始料不及的。处在代差末端的中国美学在全球化背景下追随西方美学已成顺势之为。

第二，50 年代的美学大讨论由于其极强的政治化和原初性特点，其议题不仅不能延续下来，反而引起人们的反感。于是，80 年代伊始，人们带着期待和好奇的目光打量着西方美学和西方的自然科学。以至在 80 年代出现了美学文艺学的方法论热，成为第二次美学热的

一个重要的方面。但不久，随着方法论热带来的观念更新，唯心主义和唯物主义美学之争，在80年代的美学工作者看来就是一些政治化的议题，因而被抛弃，从而为西方主义的大举入侵留下了真空地带。

第三，真正能够抵御外来文化入侵的应该是本国的、本民族的文化。但就美学而言，50年代的美学大讨论并没有把五四以来已经被淡忘了的中国传统重新激活，并没有继承、发扬中国传统的审美文化，相反，在政治化的主义之争中，彻底割断了与中国传统的审美文化和美学思想的联系，从而两手空空，在面对西方的主义潮涌而入的时候不知所措，除了顺势之外，别无选择。

第四，与理论讨论的是理论，与思想对话的是思想，与主义抗衡的是主义。50年代中国的美学理论和美学思想，有其明显的局限性，不论是在方法上还是在观念上，也不论是在范畴上还是在体系上，都远远落后于西方。而于主义而言，实在不能说唯物主义、唯心主义是中国的主义。如此一来，我们在没有主义的情况下，又如何与西方的主义对话并进而平起平坐呢？与50年代相比，80年代以来的主义的喧嚣达到了无以复加的地步，甚至是泛滥成灾的地步，但仔细分析，这是两场完全不同的主义的喧嚣。50年代是中国人在中国的美学舞台上的唱着主义的喜剧、闹剧，而80年代却是西方人在中国的美学舞台上的独唱，而中国人只有当看客的份了。如果说，50年代中国美学表现为主义的喜剧和闹剧的话，那么，到了80年代及以后，这种主义的闹剧则表现为主义的悲剧：我们一贫如洗了！

第三节　美学上主义的缺位

与中国美学上主义的喧嚣和泛滥相对照的是中国美学上产生于本土的具有原创性的主义的缺位。我们没有在国际美学论坛上叫得响的属于中国人原创的美学上的主义，而且也无法拿着唯物主义美学到国际美学论坛上去讲，这就是我们中国的原创性的主义。造成这种尴尬

的主观方面的原因有二。第一，缺乏主义的意识。不知道任何理论包括美学理论发展的最高形态是主义和建立在主义基础上的学派。主义和学派是思想发展的最高境界。有些主义和学派是当下产生的。有些学派是在主义的影响下经过几代人才建立起来的。但无论如何，主义和流派是思想的里程碑，是一种学说、一种理论、一种思想能够独立于学术之林、思想之林的标志。缺乏这个标志，就缺乏必要的识别，就会被其他的思想整合，被其他流派淹没。我国春秋战国时期的百家争鸣，就在于有各种主义的竞相登台，互相砥砺，从而形成了思想的大繁荣、大发展，形成了中国历史上为后世难以企及的高峰。但当代学者，缺乏的恰恰就是这种创立主义的自觉意识，缺乏自成一家的雄心壮志，因而思想的火花没有燃起来，思想的境界没有升上去，最后只能是小打小闹，在自己营造的管锥之境中自我满足，而于思想的旗帜和主义的建立则从未进入其意识。第二，缺乏思想的独立性。盲目地顺从于现成的思想和业已僵化了的学科范式，或者把学术当成政治思想的附庸和工具，不敢独立思考，不敢出新，不敢创造，以为自己不赞成某种思想就是要远离它，或抵制它，而不是从对立面的思想中去学习方法。而对自己赞成的某种思想，就去崇拜它，顺从它，而不对它进行分析和批判，不是批判地继承，而是全盘接受，从而丧失了独立思考的能力。缺乏思想的独立，表现在许多地方，但有一点是一致的：如学习西方，就唯西方马首是瞻，唯西方主义是从。结果导致中国美学在替西方人背书，被西方倭化。如学古人，就以古人为完美无缺，视为圭臬，不予以批判。如说坚持马克思主义，就把它当成了教条，却不知道马克思主义的活的灵魂就是批判和创新。马克思主义就是批判地继承了人类最先进的思想并加以革命性的改造才形成的。而我们今天从事美学思想研究的人却以为马克思主义就是只能照搬的神圣律条，是不允许别人思考和反思的，是不允许别人建立学术上的主义的。这恰恰是有违马克思主义的批判精神的，是无助于思想的建设和发展的。

以上主观原因导致了个体对于主义创造的恐惧症。而造成美学上主义缺位的客观方面的原因有三：一是极“左”思潮的影响，禁锢了人们的思想。尤其是学术政治化，阶级斗争扩大化对知识分子的心理威慑和伤害，非一朝一夕就能消除。二是中国现代革命造成的与中国文化传统的疏离，不能从中国传统的优秀文化中汲取思想的精华，并将之作为当代美学思想建设的精神元素，因而在西方的主义蜂拥而来之际，找不到自己的立足地和出发点，无法与西方学者进行对话，从而成了无根的浮萍，遑论建立美学上的主义。三是学科化取代了思想建设。美学是门学科，但它是一门人文学科。人文学科不同于自然科学的地方在于其思想性和价值倾向性，其价值判断贯穿整个学科。50 年代和 80 年代以后，中国美学出现了两次主义的喧嚣。但进入 90 年代以后，中国美学舞台上全是西方美学上的主义在表演，而于中国美学，主义之争沉寂，而且根本上已被人们忘记了。而在同时，我们也确实看到了中国美学的繁荣，这就是学科建设的繁荣，如美学（分属哲学系）的、文艺美学（分属中文系）的博士学位点雨后春笋般地建立起来，美学的博士一批一批地毕业，美学的会议一个接着一个地开，美学的论文数以百计地发表，美学的专著数以十计地出版，美学的项目纵横交错，大有将稍有能力从事美学研究的人一网打尽的态势。中国美学的队伍也愈来愈庞大。2010 年第 18 届世界美学大会在北京大学召开，国际美协原有会员 600 多人，由于中国新会员的加入，使这次世界美学大会的参会会员猛增到了 1200 多人。但与中国军团的庞大不相一致的是，中国的美学家们并未提出令国际美学界瞩目的思想和观点，可以说规模之大和影响之小都是超乎想象的。因此可以说中国美学是繁荣了，但在这种繁荣的背后却是思想的贫乏、主义的缺位和学术泡沫鼓胀。还有就是项目代替学问、学科代替思想。其原因就在于项目化和学科化以金钱和现实的利益为引力，以数量为考评指标，已经给从事美学研究的人铺好了方便法门，人们可以不必冒险，不须通过深沉和痛苦的思考就能获得由数字考评带来的荣誉和

利益，从而使美学的思辨功能被缩小，美学的批判力被消解，美学的主义建设被抛到九霄云外。

以上客观原因导致了中国美学对于主义的集体失忆。主观原因和客观原因一起导致了不想去创造主义，不敢去创造主义，也创造不出主义的现状，使美学的思想性、原创性成为一句空话。

在全球化背景下，中国美学在与西方美学的对比中，不得不面临这样的问题，即什么是中国美学？是技术的美学、学科的美学、形态的美学，还是思想的美学、主义的美学？抑或五者俱全的美学？答案应该是不言自明的。因为任何学科首先在于它的学科性，以便成为人们研究和建设的对象；其次是它的形态性，以便与其他民族的美学有所区别；再次是它的技术性，以便对现实社会有所裨益。至于思想性，它是学科的灵魂，对于学科的精神武装和境界提升至关重要，人文学科如果缺少思想内容，则只剩下学科的空壳。而由思想基础上发展而来的主义，则是该学科屹立于世界民族之林的旗帜。德国美学就是因为有新老康德主义、新老黑格尔主义、新老马克思主义、新老叔本华主义、新老尼采主义、存在主义、怀疑主义而成为世界美学的制高点的。

在当今实施文化强国战略中的中国美学，应该有什么样的定位呢？我认为，文化大繁荣大发展需要哲学社会科学包括美学的大繁荣大发展。真善美历来被认为是人类知识体系和价值体系的三分天下。因此，文化强国中，注重中国美学思想的建设正当其时。真正繁荣和发展美学的要务在于学术上的主义并起，百家争鸣。也就是中国一贯提倡的“百花齐放”“百家争鸣”，以及“建立中国学派”的主张。

应该遵循增强补弱的原则，发展中国美学。所谓增强，就是发扬中华审美文化历史悠久、资源丰富、审美形态多样的优势，立足于中国美学历史和现状，挖掘、整理中国美学思想资源，建设中国美学思想体系，解决中国现实中的审美问题。所谓补弱，就是针对中国美学建设中主义缺位的弱点，有意识、自觉地提倡和加强美学上的主义建

设，创造出有民族特点、符合中国实际、有思想高度的中国美学的主义和美学流派。应该清醒地看到，面对中国的崛起，西方的各种声调并起。有的西方政要公开声称，中国永远不会成为强国，原因在于，中国只能向世界输出商品，而不能输出思想。这也就是我国目前面临的软实力短板。因此，提倡建立美学上的主义，大力提升中国美学的思想高度，增强主义的影响力，增加中国美学与西方美学对话的筹码，应该是当下中国美学的人文担当。

2009 年当我参加完在阿姆斯特丹举行的“全球美学对话”国际美学大会后，在法兰克福受到了歌德学院一位教授的接待。当我问他法兰克福有什么特产的时候，他说，有两样东西：一是欧元，一是法兰克福学派。欧洲中央银行就在法兰克福，欧元出自这个中央银行。法兰克福学派也被称为西方马克思主义学派，产生了数位学术巨匠。其主义和思想及其影响已呈高原高峰之势。

进而言之，不仅中国美学缺乏主义，而且中国哲学、中国伦理学，乃至整个中国思想界都缺乏学术上的主义。在文化强国的期盼中，我们没有自己的学术上的主义，又怎能跟西方的理论和思想对话？又怎能保卫文化安全呢？又怎么能够屹立于世界思想文化之林呢？

鉴于主义在学说中的至关重要性，又鉴于中国美学缺少主义，我在 2011 年 12 月海口“中国哲学论坛”上呼吁要有强烈的主义意识，要创建中国本土的主义。但这个主义已不再是原初形态的唯物主义和唯心主义，也不是社会形态的社会主义、资本主义。因为这些主义中的唯物主义和唯心主义或如恩格斯所说，仅限于世界观基本问题而对美学无效或如给美学贴社会主义和资本主义的标签而与美学无关。

常言道，伟大的时代呼唤伟大的思想家和学术巨匠。但伟大的思想家和学术巨匠并不仅仅是观点创新、学科创新。仅有这些还远远不够，因为还没有达到主义的高度。建构中国本土的思想，就从学术思想上主义的提倡和建构开始吧。

第二章

中国美学：主义的缺位与重建

——兼回应王洪岳先生[*]

王洪岳教授《精神建构的彷徨与出路——兼与王建疆先生商榷》① 一文，对笔者《中国美学：主义的喧嚣与缺位——百年中国美学批判》② 一文提出批评。在笔者的学术生涯中，主动与笔者商榷的已有数位。20 多年前笔者发表了自己的硕士学位论文《自我调节与审美经验》③，受到本教研室一位同事《美学拒绝“自我调节”概念》④ 一文的批判。这次王洪岳教授先肯定笔者关于中国美学存在着主义的喧嚣和主义的缺位的基本观点，甚至还有些许溢美之词，然后加以批评。这样一来，笔者就遇到了两种商榷的方式：一是针锋相对，全盘否定的；一是说你的文章表面上还行，实质上是有问题的。可以说，时隔二十年，不同的学者，不同的话题，境界也有不同。但于笔者而言，不管哪种商榷方式，都有利于笔者进一步思考我所引起的话题，值得感谢。

---

* 本章部分内容曾发表于《探索与争鸣》2012 年第 7 期。

① 王洪岳：《精神建构的彷徨与出路——兼与王建疆先生商榷》，《探索与争鸣》2012 年第 4 期。

② 王建疆：《中国美学：主义的缺位与重建——百年中国美学批判》，《探索与争鸣》2012 年第 2 期。

③ 王建疆：《自我调节与审美经验》，《西北师范大学学报》1990 年第 4 期。

④ 叶知秋：《美学拒绝“自我调节”概念》，《新华文摘》1991 年第 11 期。

第一节　中国美学上的主义话题才刚刚开始

王洪岳教授认为，我关于中国美学在主义的喧嚣中缺乏自己的主义的论断是正确的，关于这种主义的喧嚣和缺失的原因的分析也是“抓住了当代中国美学的要害”。“但是，对于思想为什么缺失，如何补救的问题，他（王建疆）开出的药方却是（一）从中国传统文化中吸取营养，‘立足于中国美学历史和现状，挖掘、整理中国美学思想资源，建设中国美学思想体系，解决中国现实中的审美问题’。（二）创建中国本土的主义，也就是要超越观点创新、学科体系创新的层次而达到主义的高度。笔者认为，这种观点并不能开创出新的具有原创性的中国美学。相反，可能重陷于百年中国美学话语的喧嚣、泛滥，其结果仍然是美学原创性的缺失。”① 但为什么呢？我未能从王洪岳的文章中找到直接的、明确的答案，我所能看到的解释是，王洪岳认为，我对“中国传统文化的解释”是错误的，而德国美学对于主义和思想的建构是成功的。于是，我一头雾水。至于说到什么我的“药方”适得其反地使中国美学上的主义建构陷入喧嚣和泛滥，就更不知其所云了。

因此，面对王洪岳针对我“开出的药方”的诘难，这里有几个问题需要说明。

1. 我对中国传统文化的解释是错误的吗？

王洪岳在立论伊始就认为我对中国传统文化的解释是错误的。他说：“对于何谓中国传统文化？王建疆并没有给出一个明确的界定。他甚至把五四以来的传统称之为‘传统文化’。而五四以来的新文化恰恰是与传统文化背道而驰的，特别是五四时期和 80 年代启蒙主义

---

① 王洪岳：《精神建构的彷徨与出路——兼与王建疆先生商榷》，《探索与争鸣》2012 年第 4 期。

为主调的文化。而传统文化和文化传统不同，五四以来的文化一般学人认为是一种文化传统，包括意识形态化的政治文化。五四以来的中国传统文化或曰文化传统及其中生长的美学因为带有某种意识形态意味，因而恰恰是王建疆要抛弃和批判的对象。那么汲取这种传统文化不是陷入自己所反思和批判的对象之中吗？”①

但我的原文是这样写的：“真正能够抵御外来文化入侵的应该是本国的、本民族的文化。但就美学而言，50年代的美学大讨论并没有把五四以来已经被淡忘了的中国传统重新激活，并没有继承、发扬中国传统的审美文化，相反，在政治化的主义之争中，彻底割断了与中国传统的审美文化和美学思想的联系，从而两手空空，在面对西方的主义潮涌而入的时候不知所措，除了顺势之外，别无选择。”② 两相对比，显然是王洪岳教授误读了我的原文。可能是忽略了我的“五四以来已经被淡忘了的”这段限定语，因此做了完全相反的理解，误认为我把五四以来的中国文化作为中国传统文化，从而得出了我的论点“可能重陷于百年中国美学话语的喧嚣、泛滥，其结果仍然是美学原创性的缺失”的莫名其妙的结论。

2. 创建中国本土的主义，是不是就“不能开创出新的具有原创性的中国美学”？是不是就“可能重陷于百年中国美学话语的喧嚣、泛滥”？

拙文《中国美学：主义的喧嚣与缺位》中的核心观点就是要创建中国本土的主义，而非西方的主义，也不是西方化了的主义。而与拙文相反，王洪岳的文章在并没有摆出充足理由的情况下，批评我的这一基本观点，并从所谓的“美学的本体”——“人本身的解放和自由”出发，大量列举西方美学尤其是西方美学思想中所谓的“主体

① 王洪岳：《精神建构的彷徨与出路——兼与王建疆先生商榷》，《探索与争鸣》2012年第4期。

② 王建疆：《中国美学：主义的缺位与重建——百年中国美学批判》，《探索与争鸣》2012年第2期。

性美学思想”，来批评中国美学中以儒、道、屈骚和佛禅为代表的美学流派的非主体性，批评当代美学中的反主体性美学。但这里的问题在于，创建中国本土的主义是否有错？创建中国本土的主义是否就一定要将中国的美学思想纳入德国古典美学的框架？是否一定要中国的思想皈依于一个大一统的源自德国人的“主体性美学”呢？

实际上，立足于本土，吸纳外来文化的精华，创建自己的教义和思想，使外来文化中国化，这在中国不乏成功的例证。最典型的就是佛教的中国化，包括中国禅宗的诞生和喇嘛教的形成。因此，创建中国本土的主义，包括创建中国本土的美学上的主义，并不意味着与吸收和借鉴西方的思想和文化对立起来，更不能说因此就没有原创性。难道只有将自己视为无主体、无本位的“无名”之状，完全委身于外来文化和思想，由着西方的思想和文化主导我们的文化建设、思想建设、美学建设，才能有原创性吗？

3. 主义的建立是否只需要精神批判？

人类的思想史告诉我们，主义的建立离不开批判，但仅有批判是建立不起美学的。不破不立，但破未必就有立在其中。关键在于破什么、立什么，目标要找准。否则，破掉了不该破的，立了不该立的，就可能出现灾难。“文革”中的“破四旧立四新”便是一例。同样，以主体性为最高标准，破掉了不符合主体性标准的中国美学，而树起了西方的主体性美学，那我们的美学除了洋化和奴化外，还有什么希望？

王洪岳的批判精神是值得充分肯定的。这也是我在《我们缺少一个什么样的审美》① 一文中所表达过的。我不仅批评过当代审美的商品化、伪饰化倾向，而且对西方所谓的“审美拯救论”都提出过质疑和批判。但是，光有民族精神的批判和民族精神的建立还是远远不

① 王建疆：《我们缺少一个什么样的审美》，《学术月刊》2008 年第 5 期，《新华文摘》2008 年第 19 期，《人大复印资料 · 美学》2008 年第 10 期转载。

够的。因为，美学不是政治伦理学，它虽然有着道德的内涵，有着对于功利性与非功利性的辩证联系，有着对于自由和解放的吁求，但美学更有自律性。除了精神内涵之外，还有审美形态、审美形式、审美风格、审美经验、审美心理等。其领域广大非一种精神能够统摄、涵盖。那种将美学问题政治伦理化、意识形态化、精神一统化的做法，恰好违背了美学的自律，也有违于美学作为人文学科的多样化原则。应该明确，美学上的主义并非意识形态化了的主义，而首先是学科上的主义。这是由美学的无功利性—功利性自律所决定的。因此，美学上的主义的建立就不仅仅是能够通过精神批判完成的。除了精神批判，还应该有本土观念、民族情怀、学科意识、审美规律等的影响和制约，是多种因素的凝聚，而不是单一元素的运行。在百年中国美学发展上后半段出现的一大问题却恰恰就是这种思维的狭隘化，即只围绕着政治—伦理展开价值判断和精神批判，而不注意精神批判之外的多因素的协调，尤其是忽视了中国审美形态的多样性，其结果是本土美学的发展被某种外来的具有强势话语的主义所统摄、所同化，最后只能导致中国美学为西方的主义背书的结局。

4. 美学上的主义是一元的还是多元的?

美学的多样性决定了美学上的主义的多元性。美学上的主义是分层次的。我们这个时代的美学缺少什么样的主义是亟须搞清楚的问题。我们不必重复历史，也不应效仿洋人，只能建立属于我们这个时代的、独立原创的主义。虽然，凡是变革社会、改造社会的主义的创建来自现实需要，来自改造世界、创造世界的精神“冲动”。但学科发展中的主义建设却未必能与其等而论之。事实上，美学上的主义有相当一部分来自对美学本体和自律的深刻认识，并不一定与改造世界、批判社会的冲动相联系。如形式主义美学、经验主义美学、结构主义美学等。近代以降，美学已有科学主义和人文主义之分。因此，美学上的主义的建构空间是广大的，可能性是众多的，不一定囿于社会批判的主体性美学一隅。百年中国美学之一弊却恰恰在于赋予了美

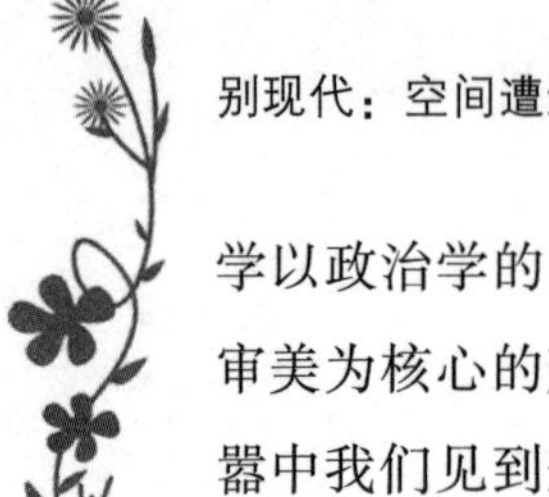

学以政治学的、经济学的、伦理学的改造社会的重任，而于美学的以审美为核心的建构却被忽视了。这在20世纪美学大讨论中主义的喧嚣中我们见到过，于80年代以来的美学研究中也不绝于耳。这种过分功利化的美学，在提倡社会担当和精神批判的同时，也使建立在无目的而合目的即功利性与非功利性悖论基础上的美学面临功能越界的尴尬，同时也导致了美学的单一化。因此，从多维、多元的角度去建立中国美学上的主义就尤为必要。

5. 究竟什么才算得上主义？

主义是思想的集大成，是思想的旗帜或识别标志的冠名。意识转变为看法，看法形成了观点，观点上升为思想，思想提炼出理论，理论凝聚、升华，被冠名后方可以成为主义。这是人类认识的一般规律，也是主义产生的一般路径。因此，主义并非一般的论点，也不是一般的思想和一般的理论，而是能够统摄和指导思想和理论建设，并对现实产生影响的精神指导。

真正的主义并不是空架子，也不是一个框，什么东西都可以装，相反，主义具有价值倾向和识别标志。是所指，而非能指，因此拒绝含糊。是边界，具有排他性，因此旗帜鲜明，如解构主义之于结构主义，资本主义之于封建主义，后现代主义之于现代主义，等等。因此，主义的问题不是有了观点、有了理论、有了思想、有了深沉就可以了，还远远不够！因为主义是思想的升华、凝聚，是价值倾向的标杆。对于建立在审美个性和思辨精神基础上的美学来说，必须有鲜明的价值倾向性和识别标志性。而且只有形成了主义，才可以建立起立于世界人文学科之林的美学。

主义具有统摄性。所谓的“大而化之”用在主义上是最恰当不过的。“大”指其涵盖性，“化”言其同化性和统摄力，能将一个理论体系或思想体系统摄在一面旗帜下，思想和理论被这个主义所“化”。这符合《孟子·尽心下》中的原意，与今天使用意义上的不谨慎行事并非一回事。

真正的主义除有内容外，还需有冠名。或以主观倾向冠名，如唯物主义、唯心主义；或以内在特质冠名，如结构主义、解构主义、社会主义、资本主义；或以时间冠名，如古典主义、新古典主义，现代主义、后现代主义；或以人名冠名，如马克思主义、达尔文主义；等等。时下中国美学中的“论……”或“……论”或“……学”，就都不是主义。不仅思想高度、原创功能、理论体系、旗帜特性没有达到主义应有的高度，而且在冠名上也不具备。但冠名并非可以任意而为的事，没有主义的内涵，又怎么去标榜主义呢？这大概也是王洪岳所说的当今中国学者在主义问题上的“彷徨、畏葸”的原因吧。

总之，关于美学上的主义的问题，我还是坚持认为，在主义的喧嚣中，我们恰恰缺少的是具有美学多样性和主义多元化背景下的中国气派、中国特质的当代中国美学上的主义，而不是已经甚嚣尘上的西方的主义。

第二节　中国美学：重建的可能性

我为什么一再强调中国美学需要本土的主义建设呢？关键在于认为，主义是理论的升华，是思想的凝聚，是价值取向的标杆。一种美学，甚至一个美学流派，如果还没有上升到主义的高度，那么，它是很难立足于世界人文之林的。而百年来中国美学仍然在“中国美学还是美学在中国”的质疑中爬行，其原因之一就在于任凭西方的主义在中国学术的舞台上喧嚣、泛滥，而我们只有当看客的份儿。当文化强国的历史使命落在了当代中国学者肩上的时候，如果还没有主义的意识高度，那么，我们的人文学科将永远成为西方政要们所预言的中国不能输出思想的见证，永远在精神层面上蜗居。因此，应该大张旗鼓地在学术研究和学科建设中提倡主义的建设，从目前的学术观点创新上升到学术研究上主义的创新；从对西方美学研究的创新，转换到民族美学主义上的建构。这是因为，观点的创新固然重要，但也是对大

学本科学士论文的要求；而学术研究上主义的创新，却是对超一流伟大思想家的要求。最早译介和研究其他民族文化中的主义的学者，自然具有新颖性，但他所研究的主义毕竟不是中国的，因而他的创新性是有限的、是有时间效应的，而且是很容易被超越的。因此，我是在文化强国的高度上，是在立于世界人文之林的高度上提倡中国美学创建主义的。而且我认为，只有这种对中国美学主义建构的必要性的充分认识，才是我们创建中国美学上的主义的动力源。

除了以上所讲建立中国美学上的主义的必要性，这里还需要讲一下在当前形势下创建中国美学上的主义的可能性。

我认为，当前创建中国美学上的主义，不仅必要，而且可能。理由如下：

第一，时代的呼唤。常言道，伟大的时代呼唤伟大的思想家和学术巨匠。从 1840 年鸦片战争开始，中国沦为殖民地、半殖民地，民族处于危亡时期，文化处于危机状态，直到 1949 年新中国成立，中国人民从此站了起来。但由于中国现代文化发展的特殊轨迹，中国现代文化并没有随着中国人民的站起来而立于世界之林。相反，随着“文革”劫难，中华文化遭到了前所未有的破坏。进入新时期以来，我国在经济上、科技上都取得了举世瞩目的成就。20 世纪 70 年代的西方思想家就已看到了中国这一东方巨龙苏醒、腾飞的趋势，预言 21 世纪是中华文化全面复兴的时代。这样一个千载难逢的伟大时代，必然呼唤伟大的思想家和学术巨匠，呼唤学术上的主义的开创者。

中华文化的全面复兴，首先离不开经济的发展和科技的进步，但仅有经济的发展和科技的进步是远远不够的。如果一个民族只能向国外输出商品和劳力，而不能输出思想，相反，只能接受和传播西方的思想和文化，那么，这个民族的文化复兴就只能是一句空话。而要达到向西方输出自己的思想的高度，就首先要求具有本民族的、本土的思想、理论和主义。而我们强调主义在文化复兴中的作用，就在于主义是理论的升华，是思想的统摄，是价值取向的标杆。只有主义才能构成思想的识别标志，才能与西方的思想对话，才能自立于世界文化之林。没有主义，仅有观点，是达不到输出思想，与西方对话的高度的。因此，在一个伟大的时代，美学上主义的创建应运而生，势在必行。

第二，文化建设的需要。我们必须看到，中国在经济和科技空前繁荣的同时，文化的发展相对滞后，表现在文化事业上道德建设与物质发达之间的不协调，精神萎靡，道德滑坡，重商主义和拜金主义盛行。本来是作为自由和解放象征的审美，也在图像增殖时代被商品化和伪饰化所主宰，成了资本扩张和商业逐利的工具。所谓的“商品美学”“美女经济学”大行其道，助推着思想的堕落和精神的蜕变。这在一个有着几千年文明教化，秉持人生修养和人生境界，有着内审美传统的中国，无疑是一个时代性的困惑。

面对商业时代审美的时代性困惑，西方的审美主义者开出了“审美拯救”的药方，但在一个审美也被异化，即审美商品化和伪饰化了的时代，所谓的审美拯救，无异于将带着病毒的血液输进患者的身体。因此，建构有着优秀民族文化传统和自由解放精神的美学上的主义，无疑是当前文化建设的需要。

文化强国需要哲学社会科学的大繁荣、大发展。而哲学的大繁荣、大发展，少不了美学的大繁荣、大发展。而美学的大繁荣、大发展，又怎能离开主义的建构？

第三，中国学者的学术素养已经具备。与20世纪30年代那些具有家学渊源，同时又留洋归来的学者相比，当代学者无论在国学素养还是在西学基础方面，都与之相去甚远。但新中国成立之后的当代学者，尤其是40后、50后、60后学者，却有着为新中国成立成长起来的学者所不曾有的对于中国现状的深刻认识，有着遭遇极“左”思潮泛滥却能意志弥坚的学术素养，更有着改革开放以来的思想解放和全球化背景下的世界眼光，既接受了现代西方的学术规范，又能在中国的现实中迸发出思想的灵感，因而其学术素质得到了迅速提高，其

学术创造力空前发达。这也就是中国美学界除了朱光潜、宗白华这些30年代成名的美学大师之外，还有50年代成长起来的李泽厚与之比肩的缘故。而且就目前李泽厚在国际美学上取得的声望而言，已是青出于蓝而胜于蓝。

李泽厚虽然还只是个案，但却说明当代中国美学学者的学术素养具有创建中国美学上的主义的潜能。剩下的就是如何激活这种潜能的问题了。

第四，知己知彼，中国学者有着比较优势。西学东渐以来，中国学者跟着西方走，学习西方，甚至唯西方马首是瞻。但这只是问题的一方面。另一方面，中国学者在向西方学习的过程中，具有了西方学者不曾具备的知识优势，这就是中西贯通的优势，或中西马我对西马我的优势。由于语言上的差异和语言习得能力的不同，中国学者更容易掌握以英语为代表的外语，从而最大可能地了解西方的知识、学问和主义。加上对于本民族文化的与生俱来的亲和，中国学者很容易做到知己知彼。而西方学者掌握汉语的困难程度远较中国学者掌握西语的程度高。再加上19世纪以来的西学东渐和西方话语霸权，最终导致了西方学者由于轻视中国文化而对于中国文化知识的相对匮乏甚至无知。在美学方面，西方的不少美学家还自以为美学是西方的专利，似乎只有美学在中国，而无中国美学。中西方学者这种在彼此了解方面的不对称、不平衡，最终可能导致中国学者在知识方面的优势向学术方面的优势的突然转变。饱受西方主义浸染和洗礼的中国美学，也极有可能在这种历史性的转变过程中，用西方学术界建构主义的路数来建立自己的主义。

第五，与知识上、学术上、主义上的知己知彼相连，中国学者应该有着后发优势。“后发优势”一词来自经济学。说的是经济上落后的国家和地区，由于省略或跨越了经济发达国家和地区已经走过的路程，因而获得了成本优势和时间优势，有可能超越经济发达国家和地区。中国经济奇迹就是一个明证。中国的美学工作者，完全有可能看

着西方美学在中国学术舞台上尽情地表演，然后汲取其精华，剔除其糟粕，根据中国的实际和美学发展的需求而进行主义的建构，后来居上。西方美学在主义上的一统天下，很有可能在中国式主义诞生的当下坍塌。原因就在于中国式主义是在西方式主义基础上诞生的具有中国风格和中国气派的主义，它跨越了西方主义的喧嚣，而在中西交汇中直达学术的顶端。当然，我们这里所讲的后发优势也是有条件的，也是需要时间酝酿的，并非一蹴而就的。但是，后来者居上，实现跨越是已被历史所证明了的一条规律。

第六，当代中国美学已经开始走向世界。2010 年第二版的《诺顿理论和批评选集》收入 148 位著者的 185 篇作品，始于古希腊的高尔吉亚、柏拉图、亚里士多德，终于美国女学者朱迪丝，被称为“最全面深广”“最丰富多彩”的权威选本，将成为全球理论与批评的“黄金标准”。选本中的美学一类最引人注目。此类仅收入 13 位学者，包括休谟、康德、莱辛、席勒、黑格尔等，李泽厚是其中唯一的非西方现当代哲学家。在著者评介中，编者称：“李泽厚是当代中国学术界的一个奇观！他所发展的精致复杂、范围宽广的美学理论持续地值得注意，特别是其中关于‘原始积淀’的独创性论述。”与此同时，刘再复出版了《李泽厚美学概论》，对李泽厚美学体系进行了全面深刻的总结、概述与评价，其中不少看法与诺顿文集的编者不谋而合，从而共同代表了中西学界的权威性评判。当然，众所周知，李泽厚本人也因其在哲学和美学上的贡献早在 20 世纪 80 年代就成为著名的法国国际哲学院院士。李泽厚的美学虽然没有达到主义的高度，但是，他的国际影响说明，当代中国美学已经开始走向世界，这为中国美学上主义的建立至少打下了信心和能力的良好基础。

第七，也是最重要的，中国学者的主义意识已经觉醒。我在提倡美学上的主义时，遇到了同行们三种不同的反应。第一种属于畏惧派。他们认为，中国美学确实需要主义，但主义的话题太敏感了，不敢谈论，怕引火烧身。第二种是观望派。他们认为，你提出主义，那

你建立了什么主义先拿出来看看再说。第三种是王洪岳的激进派观点，他肯定主义建构的必要性，但又认为，主义的建立来自精神批判和冲动，其思想源泉在于西方的主体性美学。但无论如何，中国美学建立主义的问题还是得到了多数人的理解，说明主义的意识正在觉醒。正是这种觉醒，构成了我们建立中国美学上的主义的必要前提，有了这个前提，主义的建立将成为美学研究者们自觉的行动。

总之，中国美学上的主义的建构不仅是非常必要的，而且是完全可能的，我们应该积极地投身到美学上的主义的建设中去。

第三节　中国美学：重建的路径

在我们论述了在美学上创建主义的必要性和可能性之后，我们还需明确建立中国美学上的主义的路径。

王洪岳教授在否定了我的有关从中国传统文化中汲取营养，创建中国本土的主义的说法或“药方”后，开出了自己的药方。这就是建立以德国主体性美学为灵魂支柱的批判美学，以及在批判中建立非美主义和反美主义的美学。

王洪岳教授在以主体性美学思想为指导的美学精神批判中，津津乐道于对丑、不美等所谓的审美形态的赞美。他说：

> 90年代以来，我们民族的精神状态大致经历过激进、恐怖、无望、无奈，后来趋于恶心、呕吐、平缓、烦恼、局促、窘迫、逍遥、期盼等情感形态，仍然被主流意识形态所重塑，从而形成了对于金钱、物欲、性爱乃至性本身的狂热追逐，最终积淀凝缩成为诸多新的美学范畴和艺术审美形态，如：（审）丑（又可分为混乱、造作、僵化等亚范畴）、不美（正常，又可分为陈旧、残缺和平庸等亚范畴）（丑和不美及其亚范畴为吴炫的划分）、荒诞（其形式体现为怪诞）、悖谬、喜剧（是一种往往和反讽结

合在一起的喜）、滑稽、反讽、戏仿、媚世（媚俗 kitsch）和堪鄙（坎普 camp）（媚世和堪鄙两个美学范畴由张法最早集中论述）等，一改往昔美学沉醉于优美、崇高、壮美、和谐、悲剧、古雅、意境等范畴和类型的状况。能够直面这些远非悦耳悦目、悦心悦意、悦神悦志的美学范畴或类型，在当下美学建构中是一种难能可贵的学术的或生存的勇气。①

我并不反对审美形态的发展和流变，也不否定丑在美学上的意义。但是，我始终认为，美学范畴是有边界的，审美首先是价值选择。如果不加分析地把丑和不美都视为“新的美学范畴和艺术审美形态”，那我们的审美还有什么意义？以这种丑的、不美的形态为美学的内容，会给美学带来什么？

王洪岳教授主张回归“美学的本真”，但什么才是美学的本真呢？还是再看看他的以下说法：

因此，我理解和阐释的当代中国美学应该是通过对现实感性世界和审美艺术感性世界的批判，去发现在这种批判和否定中的美，或者发现美作为对现实与感性的否定性的形式存在。因此，那些原本在当代中国美学著作中被忽视或无一席之地的，同时又真实反映了当代中国人精神生存状态的概念或范畴、类型，如上面提到的丑、荒诞、恐怖，恶心、反讽、媚俗，残缺、造作、僵化等，经过美学的甄别和批判，就能够堂而皇之地进入美学的殿堂，美学便摆脱了回避或无视这些新概念范畴的尴尬境地，也就摆脱了对意识形态的依附或纠缠状况，能够独立而坦然地面对或创造自己的此在的本真世界，进而成为具有鲜明时代特征的人文

① 王洪岳：《精神建构的彷徨与出路——兼与王建疆先生商榷》，《探索与争鸣》2012年第4期。

精神的思想体系。①

王洪岳教授直言不讳地要把丑、荒诞、恐怖，恶心、反讽、媚俗，残缺、造作、僵化等这些非美的因素作为对现实感性世界和审美艺术世界的“否定性的形式存在”，再经过美学的批判，使之“堂而皇之地进入美学的殿堂”，从而创造“本真世界”，回归“美学的本真”。但这样一来，美、崇高、平和、愉悦、高雅、完美、自然、生动等这些美的因素又将被置于何地？王洪岳讲美学的建构需要“冲动”，但为何而冲动？因为冲动就可以不论审美的性质甚至颠倒美丑吗？这种颠倒了美丑的非美主义和反美主义的美学就是“本真的美学”吗？

尽管王洪岳教授对我的有关建立中国美学上的主义的提法不以为然，甚至认为，我的有关从中国传统文化中汲取营养，创建中国本土主义的说法，“不仅不能开创出新的具有原创性的中国美学。相反，可能重陷于百年中国美学话语的喧嚣、泛滥，其结果仍然是美学原创性的缺失”。但是，我仍然坚持认为，当代中国美学上主义的建立，离不开从中国传统文化中汲取营养，离不开本土意识。原因即在于，当代中国美学缺少主义，亟须建立主义，但建设主义的思想资源却就在本土文化中。因此，我认为，建立中国式主义，以下的几条路径是不能缺少的。

1. 对中国古代“家”和“教”思想的提炼与改造。

中国古代思想的集大成者或被称为家，或被称作教。有的同时兼有家和教的冠名。如道家、道教，佛家、佛教，儒家、儒教等。就思想的知识形态和价值形态而言，家与教并无大的区别。但在精神维度上，教追求彼岸世界的理想状态，而家却未必。儒家的“不知生，焉

---

① 王洪岳：《精神建构的彷徨与出路——兼与王建疆先生商榷》，《探索与争鸣》2012年第4期。

知死”就是最好的说明。中国古代美学思想上的主义被称作“家”，是思想家思想体系中的一个重要方面，但却以非自觉的方式蛰伏着，只是到了近代美学学科创建后才苏醒。但无论如何，中国古代有美学思想，有美学上的主义，也有美学上的家，这是西方美学界承认的。因此，当代中国美学上的主义重建，首先应该继承和发展中国古代的美学思想，在此基础上创建具有民族特色的中国美学上的主义。在这方面，新儒家、新道家堪称楷模。只不过新儒家和新道家的美学思想还停留在有观点、有思想，但尚未形成理论，更未能上升到主义的阶段。因此，今天的美学建设，可以搞新儒家主义美学，新道家主义美学，甚至新庄子主义美学。实际上，庄子的思想在今天看来一点也不过时，如解构主义、生成主义等，都是美学上重要的思想，但早在庄子那里就有了典型形态。因此，新庄子主义就是涵盖了解构主义和生成主义，同时又是地道的中国气派的以个人冠名的中国式主义。

实际上，我们当代美学中的不少“论”，都是可以从中国古代家和教的思想中提炼改造成为主义的。如源自西方生态学或生态主义的生态论美学，就可以从中国的天人合一思想中概括为“和合主义”①美学的。这个和合主义不仅在思想产生的年代久远上，在对古代中国文化的影响和贡献上为生态主义所不及，而且就其天地人“三才”合一的思维方式的一以贯之性来说，也要比生态主义对于主体性哲学的反拨来得彻底。和合主义是在道的高度上讲世界和谐的，因而其涵盖性和统摄力是生态主义所无法比拟的。再加上和合主义的民族文化背景，其特定内涵决定了它的中国特质和中国气派。

再如“实践”一词，在中国传统文化的语境中应该是“修养”。这个修养包含了实践，但其外延要比实践大得多。主要还包括人的身心一体的修炼。这一点，哲学家张岱年先生曾有过精辟的论述。他说：“此处所谓实践，指传统哲学中的所谓实践，即个人日常生活，

① 参见张立文《和合学》，中国人民大学出版社2006年版。

与辩证唯物论所谓社会实践不是一个意义。”① 因此，完全有可能从实践美学中分化出一个修养主义美学②来。按牟宗三的说法，修养是中国文化与基督教文化的本质差别③。同时，中国人的修养历来是内外兼顾，身心一体的。这一点有着为西方的哲学家所难以企及的境界。近年来有学者极力推崇舒斯特曼的身体美学，如果将其放在中国的修养主义美学面前，无论在思想的广博深刻还是在历史久远上都会相形见绌的。

总之，从中国古代传统文化中汲取思想营养来建构当代美学上的主义，并不是一个简单的意识形态之争，而是一个对传统文化再学习、再认识的问题，唯有这种对本民族文化的博大精深有所认识，才能创建有根有源的美学上的主义。否则，只会在断了香火的文化氛围中当西方主义的看客了。

2. 对信息时代的感受和认识，使另一个世界的理念在非彼岸状态下再生。

另一个世界的理论使得另类世界主义的诞生已经成为可能。原本是死后在天国见到上帝或达彼净土的另一个虚幻的审美世界，在信息时代再生为一个此岸的虚拟的审美世界。如果说，宗教的另一个世界理论，还是一种虚无的诱惑，那么，网络的另类世界，已经极大地拓展了人们的世界，并冲击着人类已有的世界观和价值观，使得另类思想和另类主义的建立成为这个时段的特点。在图像增殖的现实中，在微博虚拟的世界里，人们对于网络审美的另类现象，已经从吃惊、嘲笑，成功地过渡到了认同和参与。从而审美的方式正在发生着变革，与之而来的是审美观念的变化，以及美学思想的发展，为另类主义美学的诞生进行着精神的铺垫。

---

① 张岱年：《中国哲学大纲》，中国社会科学出版社 1982 年版，第 6 页。

② 参见王建疆《修养·境界·审美——儒道释修养美学解读》，中国社会科学出版社 2003 年版，2009 年重印。

③ 参见牟宗三《中国哲学的性质》一书。

3. 对现实吁求的关注与回应，应该成为主义建构的思想源泉。

前述李泽厚美学已达到了中国美学前所未有的高度，但其不足仍在于未能将其创立的17个范畴进一步提炼和升华，从中提炼出一个主义来。也许他在等待后人给予“李泽厚主义”的冠名吧。尽管有人说：“在20世纪的中国美学发展史上，李泽厚是一个创造了独特命题和一整套美学语汇的唯一学者，也是一个真正具有美学体系的美学家。”① 当然这里的“唯一”未免夸张，而且就目前而言，他的美学仍然缺乏主义却是事实。这一点可能会限制他的可识别性和成就的高度。因为，前引《诺顿理论和批评选集》中受到最高评价的积淀说，并未能与他的情本体说、乐感文化说等一起凝聚为一个主义。也许，李泽厚那些虽源自中国审美文化但又借助西方化表达的美学范畴，如果能够与中国现实的吁求相结合，则可能有较多鲜活的本土特征。要用西方的术语表达中国的思想，这似乎是一个难题，但只有破解了这一难题，中国美学才会中国化。这一点，从孙中山、毛泽东等伟人的立足于解决当下中国现实问题的主义建构和思想表达中有许多珍贵的启发，值得借鉴和学习。

4. 将精神抽象化，将思想冠名化。

精神表面上看起来就是那么一股子劲，是一种力量。但在这股力量的背后却是一种鲜明的价值观和强烈的主观意志。因此，从某种意义上讲，主义也是一种精神。但作为主义的精神却必须是抽象化了的精神，而非具象化的表现。现实中媒体塑造了过多的精神要人们学习，其结果是精神被具象化后太多太烂太俗，人们已经无所适从。因此，与主义相联系的精神必须是抽象化了，是思想的凝聚。但思想要想达到主义的高度，却必须经过冠名。科学和技术上的发明都有个人冠名。有些国家的提案和法案也有个人冠名。冠名制的背后就是对个人知识产权和原创性的充分尊重，也是一种真正有效的对于原创性的

① 刘再复：《李泽厚美学概论》，生活·读书·新知三联书店2009年版，第76页。

保护和鼓励机制。思想只有被冠名后方有明确而集中的含义，从而具有很强的识别功能。否则，絮絮叨叨，不知所云。中国美学在论述方面并不差，但在精神的抽象和思想的冠名方面似乎尚未形成习惯，这无疑会妨碍主义的创建。但是，主义的被冠名与生造名词和概念并无关系。因为，主义来自思想的理论化，并在思想的理论化的基础上进一步抽象化、冠名化、标杆化，而生造几个词的做法是连观点表达都成问题的，又有何资格谈论主义的建立？

与西方的主义相对应的是，在中国古代并没有“主义”一词，有的只是“家”。但自战国百家争鸣以来，中国历史上很少再有主义出现。到了20世纪30年代，才又出现了新儒家和新道家。但新儒家和新道家并不涉及美学上的主义问题。中国美学上主义的缺位，与中国美学110多年的历史极不相称。原因在哪里？并非一言能够回答。但缺乏冠名意识，也不失其为原因之一。因此，创建主义，应该与冠名同行。

总之，中国美学的主义重建问题，除了必要性和可能性外，还有一个路径的问题。中国美学在主义喧嚣的同时本土主义缺位，反映了中国美学学科发育尚欠成熟，原创能力尚待整体提高的现实。我们应该面对这些现实，积极探寻中国美学上主义建设的最佳路径。

第三章

别现代：中国美学和文论上的“崇无”“尚有”与“待有”*

中国美学和文论上的关乎自身存在的大问题是尚有论与崇无论的争论。崇无论表现在两个方面。一是认为中国没有中国美学，只有“西方美学在中国”。二是认为中国文论患上了“失语症”，无法独立存在。而尚有论则相反，认为中国古代美学和文论都有自己的体系，而且当代中国文论和美学取得了辉煌的成就。而待有论却是对崇无论和尚有论的超越，是对我们尚缺什么以及期待有什么的思考，名之曰“待有”即期待有。

第一节　被崇无论笼罩着的中国美学和文论

（一）对中国古代美学和文论的否定

中国学术自从有了“美学”和“文艺理论”术语，就一直存在着一个或明或暗、或直接或间接地被逐级否定、逐时代否定的崇无论传统。

最早对中国古代美学进行否定的是被称为“中国美学第一人”的王国维。1904 年，王国维在《孔子之美育主义》中写道：“呜呼！我

* 本章部分内容发表于《学术月刊》2015 年第 10 期，并为《人大复印资料·美学》2016 年第 1 期转载。

中国非美术之国也！一切学业，以利用之大宗旨贯注之。治一学，必质其有益与否。美之为物，为世人所不顾久矣！故我国建筑、雕刻之术，无可言者。"①

1931—1934 年，老舍在《文学概论讲义》上提出："在中国文论诗话里便找不出一条明白合理的文学界说。"②

1942 年，朱光潜在《诗论》中提出："中国向来有诗话而无诗学，刘勰的《文心雕龙》条理虽缜密，所谈的不限于诗。诗话大半是偶感随笔，信手拈来，片言中肯，简练亲切，是其所长；但是它的短处在零乱琐碎，不成系统，有时偏重主观，有时过信传统，缺乏科学的精神和方法。"③

1987 年，杜卫在《电影艺术》上发表《当代中国美学在呼唤——告别古代》认为："'告别古代'是我国当前思想文化艺术界的一个中心命题。"④

1989 年，周来祥、陈炎在《文学评论》上发表《从中西美学的不同形态看美学的历史与未来》，认为："不可否认，中国古代美学有着直至今天仍不失其光辉灿烂的思想和丰富多彩的内容，包含着我们东方民族特有的智慧和独特的感受；然而同样不可否认的是，从总体上讲，中国古代美学尚处在一种前近代科学的经验形态。得出这一结论的根据主要有三点：一是缺乏严格的美学范畴，二是缺乏严密的论证手段，三是缺乏严整的理论体系。"⑤

相比之下，吴炫的对中国古代美学和文论的否定则是一种"否定主义"的否定。他认为，中国文化存在着一种传统的虚无

---

① 姚金铭、王燕主编：《王国维文集》下册，中国文史出版社 1997 年版，第 94 页。

② 老舍：《文学概论讲义·引言》，复旦大学出版社 2004 年版，第 1 页。

③ 朱光潜：《诗论》，北京出版社 2005 年版，第 1 页。

④ 杜卫：《当代中国美学在呼唤——告别古代》，《电影艺术》1987 年第 2 期。

⑤ 周来祥、陈炎：《从中西美学的不同形态看美学的历史与未来》，《文学评论》1989 年第 3 期。

主义。[①] 还认为，中国传统文化的精华是一些“碎片”。[②]

（二）对现代中国美学和文论的否定

肇始于王国维的以上这种对中国古代美学的否定，很快就延伸到了对中国现代美学的否定。

接着王国维否定论的是被称为“第一个为中国现代美学大张旗鼓的人”的蔡元培，他于1923年写了《五十年来中国之哲学》[③] 的文章，认为，由于近五十年缺乏中国人独创的哲学，因此，“五十年来的中国之哲学一语，实在不能成立”。这里的“哲学”自然应该包括具有学科形态的美学。因为早在1901蔡元培的《哲学总论》[④] 一书中已经提出“审美学论情感之用”“美育者教情感之应用是也”。可见，蔡元培知道美学的哲学归属，却否定现代中国的哲学和美学。因此可以说，王国维否定中国古代美学思想的存在，蔡元培则否定中国现代美学学科的存在，这种否定甚至否定了王国维和蔡元培自己所从事的具有开创意义的美学研究。

1988年，张首映在《批评家》上发表《处于“前美学”阶段的中国现代美学》[⑤] 认为：20世纪的中国美学仍处于“前美学”阶段。中国现代美学缺乏哲学，混同于文艺理论，又“失落了研究人生和人

---

① 2004年，吴炫在《河北学刊》上发表《“否定”何以成为“本体”》，认为：“我的看法是：西方的本体论和中国传统的本根论都有不适应中国当代文化建设需求的地方，但我们也不能步西方非理性主义的‘反本体论’思潮之后尘，倡导美学或本体论美学的取消，因为这很容易衔接上中国‘只可意会，不可言传’的美学传统、模糊哲学与感悟方法，也容易回归中国传统的虚无主义。”《河北学刊》2004年第2期。

② 1996年，吴炫在《书屋》上发表《“批判与继承”质疑》，认为：“所以我们用什么样的文化结构来统摄碎片般的传统文化‘精华’，用什么样的方法来处理、调配必定会发生冲突的中西方思想的‘精华’，将是‘批判与继承’这种思维方式所无法面对的。”《书屋》1996年第2期。

③ 中国蔡元培研究会编：《蔡元培全集》第5卷，浙江教育出版社1997年版，第137页。

④ 中国蔡元培研究会编：《蔡元培全集》第1卷，浙江教育出版社1997年版，第355页。

⑤ 张首映：《处于“前美学”阶段的中国现代美学》，《批评家》1988年第5期。

生审美化的道路和目的”。中国现代美学介绍多于研究，参照多于建树，评述多于哲学构思，外来知识多于内心体验，阐释印证多于真知灼见，致使中国现代美学几乎没有提出一个对世界上这门学科的崭新而有推动力的问题或一种论证方法。

1991 年，朱辉军在《福建论坛》上发表《当代中国美学往何处去》，认为：“首先，20 世纪以来的中国美学始终没有出现具有世界影响的、独创的、站在学科最前沿的美学思想。第一次高潮追随西方，第二次高潮师承苏联，第三次高潮又回溯西方；历史画了一个圆圈，几乎又回到了起点。我们没有‘艺术即直觉’（克罗齐）、‘美是生活’（车尔尼雪夫斯基）、‘有意味的形式’（贝尔）等影响一代美学研究的思想，而只有对别人的思想的阐释与解说。”“其次，与此相关，是 20 世纪以来的中国美学没有划时代的美学著作。”①

1997 年，唐龙、邱紫华在《孝感师专学报》上发表《二十世纪中国美学研究的困惑与选择》，认为：“毫不夸张地说，西方美学史上的各种美学观点、思潮都在 20 世纪中国美学研究中留下了自己的足迹。首先，西方美学的制导地位表现在中国美学研究所引进的基本理论和权力话语方面。”“其次，西方美学的制导地位表现在所运用的基本学说、原理、命题方面。”“它在相当程度上确立了以西方美学为中心的价值标准，在有意无意之中排挤了中国传统的尤其是有独特理论价值的美学理论。”②

1999 年，仪平策在《山东大学学报》上发表《论西方美学在 20 世纪中国文化语境中的学术地位、价值和意义》，认为：“20 世纪的中国美学史，总体上是以西方美学为推力、为主导、为中心的历史。”③

---

① 朱辉军：《当代中国美学往何处去》，《福建论坛》（人文社会科学版）1991 年第 1 期。

② 唐龙、邱紫华：《二十世纪中国美学研究的困惑与选择》，《孝感学院学报》1997 年第 4 期。

③ 仪平策：《论西方美学在 20 世纪中国文化语境中的学术地位、价值和意义》，《山东大学学报》（哲学社会科学版）1999 年第 4 期。

1999年，张道一在《东南大学学报》上发表《中国美学站起来》，认为："中国的艺术发展有着数千年的历史，其中蕴含的美学思想博大精深。然而，作为专门的美学研究，我国则落后了几个世纪。"①

2009年，罗钢在《文史哲》上发表《本与末——王国维"境界说"与中国古代诗学传统关系的再思考》②，认为：王国维把自己提出的"境界"与中国古代的"兴趣""神韵"之间的关系描绘为"本"与"末"的关系，近百年来，这个观点几乎已成为学术界的一种共识。实际上，王国维的"境界说"来源于以叔本华"直观说"为代表的西方美学传统，而"兴趣说""神韵说"植根于中国古代"比兴"的诗学原则，二者之间并不存在一种"本""末"的关系，王国维的"本末说"本身恰恰是近代东西方不平等文化关系的一种历史写照。由于王国维始终坚持认为，他提出的境界说远远高于兴趣说和神韵说，是中国诗学的根本，因此，对王国维境界说的否定，无异于彻底否定了王国维美学思想的中国血统和原创意义，他的"中国美学第一人"的桂冠已岌岌可危。

（三）对当代中国美学和文论的否定

在否定中国古代美学和中国现代美学存在的基础上，又有美学研究者提出了中国当代也没有美学的说法。

1995年，孙津在《文艺争鸣》上发表《世纪末的隆重话题》，提出："中国没有理论，这是我想说的，至少现在是这样。当我们要用理论来讲话时，想一想，举凡能够有真实含义的或者说能够通行使用的概念和范畴，到底有几多不是充分洋化了的（就算不是直接抄

① 张道一：《中国美学站起来》，《东南大学学报》（哲学社会科学版）1999年第1期。

② 罗钢：《本与末——王国维"境界说"与中国古代诗学传统关系的再思考》，《文史哲》2009年第1期。

来）。如果用人家的语言来言语，什么东西可以算得上中国自己的呢？”①

2000年，郑元者在《马克思主义美学研究》上发表《当代中国美学的四大遗憾》，认为：“在很长一段时期内，当代中国美学却缺乏元美学这一研究层次。”②

2007年，桑农在《思想战线》上发表《中国美学研究的当代走向》，认为：“严格意义讲，中国历史上并不存在作为一门科学的美学。中国美学史的研究，实际上也是对传统美学思想的清理。这些思想，散见于中国哲人的思考和艺术家的经验之谈里，因为可以纳入西方美学的学术视野，被我们挑出来予以历史的关照。中国丰富的传统美学思想，被肢解和整合到西方理论体系的框架之中。西方提供理论，中国提供例证。如此完成的中国美学史写作，在今天看来，无疑是西方中心主义的产物，是西方美学的翻版。”③

高建平在2007年第5期的《学术月刊》上发表的《文化多样性与中国美学的建构》一文指出：“中国古典美学也只是一些‘美学思想’而已。由他们所构成的中国美学史，只是中国美学的史前史。只有现代‘中国美学’，才是严格意义上的‘中国美学’。”但是，“在中国，人们在很长时间里已经习惯了一个等式，即中国等于古代，西方等于现代。这种等式将一种空间上的关系变成了一种时间上的关系。他们在写作名叫‘中国美学史’的著作时，所涉及的都是20世纪以前的中国美学。对于20世纪的中国美学，他们必须给另一个名称，例如，称它们为‘现代中国美学’但是，这种现代中国美学不仅在国际美学界很少受到关注，即使在中国，许多学者也对此信心不

---

① 孙津：《世纪末的隆重话题》，《文艺争鸣》1995年第1期。

② 郑元者：《当代中国美学的四大遗憾》，《马克思主义美学研究》第3辑，2000年第4期。

③ 桑农：《中国美学研究的当代走向》，《思想战线》2007年第2期。

足”①。

2002年笔者参加了在中国社会科学院学术会堂举行的一次国际美学大会。会上关于“是中国美学还是美学在中国”的问题，引起关注。实际上，这个问题是对我国哲学界探讨中国哲学是否“合法”的命题即“中国的哲学”与“哲学在中国”②的自然延伸。而中国哲学的合法性问题在蔡元培之后也成了著名的金岳霖之问③，即质疑究竟是中国哲学的历史，还是外来哲学在中国流行传播的历史。实质上都是在探讨有无中国哲学包括有无中国美学的问题。

（四）中国文论的“失语症”

在当代中国，与这种“很少受到关注”且“信心不足”的中国当代美学相同的是中国文论的“失语症”。

1995年，曹顺庆在《东方丛刊》上发表《21世纪中国文化发展战略与重建中国文论话语》，提出：“中国现当代文化基本上是借用西方的理论话语，而没有自己的话语，或者说没有属于自己的一套文化（包括哲学、文学理论、历史理论等）表达、沟通（交流）和解读的理论和方法。”“在话语系统上，现当代中国学者基本上认同西方话语，离中国传统话语已经十分遥远，近乎断根，患上了极为严重的失语症！这种失语症，是文化的病态现象。”④

1996年，季羡林在《文学评论》上发表《门外中外文论絮语》：“西方文艺理论体系……主宰着当今世界上的文艺理论走向，大有独

① 高建平：《全球化背景下的中国美学》，《民族艺术研究》2004年第1期。

② 郑家栋：《“中国哲学”的“合法性”问题》，《中国哲学年鉴》2001年号；郑家栋：《“合法性”概念及其他》，《哲学动态》2004年第6期。

③ 1930年金岳霖在冯友兰《中国哲学史》《审查报告》上册中提出：“所谓中国哲学史是中国哲学的史呢？还是在中国的哲学史呢？”《金岳霖文集》第1卷，甘肃人民出版社1995年版，第627页。

④ 曹顺庆：《21世纪中国文化发展战略与重建中国文论话语》，《东方丛刊》1995年第3辑，广西师范大学出版社1995年版。

领风骚之势。新异理论，日新月异，令人目眩心悸。东方学人，邯郸学步，而又步履维艰。西方文艺理论，真仿佛成了天之骄子了。”“反观我们东方国家，在文艺理论方面噤若寒蝉，在近代没有一个人创立出什么比较有影响的文艺理论体系，王国维也许是个例外。没有一本文艺理论著作传入西方，起了影响，引起轰动。①

1997 年，陈洪、沈立岩在《文学评论》上发表《也谈中国文论的“失语”与“话语重建”》：“‘失语’是一种文化上的病态，主要表现为当代中国文论完全没有自己的范畴、概念、原理和标准，没有自己的体系，也就是没有自己的话语，每当我们开口言说的时候，使用的全是别人也就是西方的词汇和语法；而且这一情形由来已久，溯其源头乃是‘五四’新文化运动。”②

2001 年翁礼明在《海南大学学报》上发表《疏离与倒置——对 20 世纪中国文论与文学的反思》，提出：导致了文学理论和文学创作的基本样态都是“舶来之物”，文学理论一开始就不是对文学创作经验的提炼、概括和总结，文学创作从观念、方法、风格、文本形式等基本质态，都是随着西学知识谱系的横移而从西方直接移植过来的；而文学理论又不是对这些新兴文学样态进行理论化的过程，同样是直接从西方的哲学、美学、文学理论中直接移植过来的。③

2004 年，蒋凡、羊列荣在《文艺理论研究》上发表《从“体系”的眼光看中国传统文论和文学批评》：“中国文论的‘现代转型’仍然是一次‘西方化’的历程。”④

中国美学和文论上的崇无论不仅使美学和文论上的“中国”一词

---

① 季羡林：《门外中外文论絮语》，《文学评论》1996 年第 6 期。

② 陈洪、沈立岩：《也谈中国文论的“失语”与“话语重建”》，《文学评论》1997 年第 3 期。

③ 翁礼明：《疏离与倒置——对 20 世纪中国文论与文学的反思》，《海南大学学报》（人文社会科学版）2001 年第 4 期。

④ 蒋凡、羊列荣：《从“体系”的眼光看中国传统文论和文学批评》，《文艺理论研究》2004 年第 3 期。

变得缥缈虚无，而且还使中国现有文化和学术的价值也变得疑窦丛生，其直接结果是消解了国内外美学界和文论界对中国美学和文论的研究兴趣，有可能使中国美学和文论彻底地边缘化。

第二节 尚有论对崇无论的批判及其自身缺陷分析

（一）受到挑战的中国美学和文论上的崇无论

中国美学和文论上的崇无论、“失语症”论并非没有遭到质疑，而是相反，遇到了激烈的反对。

董学文 1998 年在《北京大学学报》上发表《中国现代文学理论进程思考》[①]，认为“文论失语症”只是一种偏激的义愤之论，若以此来描绘和概括 21 世纪特别是现当代中国文学理论界的总体状况，认为现当代中国文学根本“没有自己的理论，没有自己的声音”因而主张要“重建中国文论话语”，是严重片面的、失真的。他认为这种提法的根本弱点和致命错误在于无视和否认了马克思主义文学理论在传播、发展及其与中国社会和文学实践结合过程中已经形成的本土化（民族化）特色的完整系统的合理性，全盘否定了近一个世纪以来中国文学理论建设做出的成绩。

熊元良 2003 年在《中国比较文学》上发表《文论“失语症”：历史的错位与理论的迷误》[②]，认为“失语症”论调在“文化复仇”情绪的支配下导致了理论偏失和内在悖论。“失语症”脱离了现实历史语境，在所谓“生存论”层面上存在“直接把古典当现代”的历史错位，在所谓的“话语重建”的“话语学”层面上同样矛盾处处，

---

① 董学文：《中国现代文学理论进程思考》，《北京大学学报》1998 年第 2 期。

② 熊元良：《文论“失语症”：历史的错位与理论的迷误》，《中国比较文学》2003 年第 2 期。

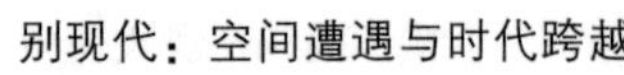

悖论多多。这些矛盾和悖论使得“失语症”论者不知不觉地滑入了中西之争的怪圈。之所以会出现这种情况，是由于“失语症”论者那种“欲与西方试比高”的“权力意志”所导致的结果。

蒋寅在《古典文学研究三“执”》[①] 和《如何面对古典诗学的遗产》[②] 中认为“失语症”这一命题难以成立，所谓古代文论的现代转向也让人难以理解：“然而在我看来，与‘失语’说一样，也属于对理论前提未加反思就率尔提出的一个虚假命题。”是西方理论介入下的浮躁。

南帆在《文学观念与文学理论资源》中指出：“人们没有理由任意将‘本土理论’偷换为‘传统理论’——本土与异域、古代与现代两对矛盾相互重叠的时候，这样的偷换尤其容易发生”，“本土理论既包含了传统理论的承传，也包含了异域理论的移植”，“异域理论的运用不能一概称之为‘失语’”[③]。

但与这些质疑和挑战相比，中国文论界和美学界出版了三本具有建设性的专著。一本是童庆炳的《中国古代文论的现代意义》[④]，一本是朱立元的《新时期以来文学理论和批评发展概况的调查报告》[⑤]，一本是张法的《中国美学史上的体系性著作研究》[⑥]，这三部专著都是崇有的，都认为中国美学和文论是有自己的体现的，而且取得了巨大的成就。

童庆炳的这部著作的中篇是《中国古代文论十大家读解》，指出，刘勰“撰写出中国第一部体系恢宏、逻辑严密、观点深刻的文论著

---

① 蒋寅：《古典文学研究三“执”》，《社会科学管理与评论》2007 年第 3 期。

② 蒋寅：《如何面对古典诗学的遗产》，《粤海风》2002 年第 1 期。

③ 南帆：《文学观念与文学理论资源》，《思想文综》第 5 期，中国社会科学出版社 2000 年版，第 256、257 页。

④ 童庆炳：《中国古代文论的现代意义》，北京师范大学出版社 2001 年版。

⑤ 朱立元：《新时期以来文学理论和批评发展概况的调查报告》，春风文艺出版社 2006 年版。

⑥ 张法：《中国美学史上的体系性著作研究》，北京大学出版社 2008 年版。

作”[1]。王国维“实际上，他的文艺思想是有体系的”[2]。这无疑是对前述王国维、朱光潜、老舍等前辈学者的崇无论的否定。

朱立元的调查报告在第三部分《调研的初步结论》中的第一个结论是“新时期以来我国文艺学取得了前所未有的伟大成就，必须予以充分估计”。[3] 这无疑是在对新时期以来中国文艺学现状进行充分肯定的同时，对中国美学崇无论和文论失语症论的直接否定。

张法在他的《中国美学史上的体系性著作研究》一书中，不仅详细列举和论证了从先秦到晚清中国美学史上有体系的13本著作，包括《礼记·乐记》《诗大序》《文心雕龙》《二十四诗品》《林泉高致》《园冶》《溪山琴况》《画语录》《〈水浒传〉评点》《原诗》《闲情偶寄》《艺概》《人间词话》等，而且更重要的在于第一次对中西美学著作体系性的特征进行了比较，在指出西方概念的实体性、单一性、抽象性、逻辑性、认知性的同时，揭示了中国美学概念的张力性、概念间关系的互动性、概念与实例的互证性、虚实相生的体系结构、阅读的体悟性五大特征，并以此来确证中国美学的体系性。这种对中国文本的实证分析，是尚有论对崇无论的一种整体性否定。

如果说，童庆炳、朱立元、张法的尚有论肯定了中国美学和文论的有，并在某种意义上点赞了这种有，从而撼动了中国美学和文论崇无论的基础，那么李泽厚的出现，则为这种崇有论提供了直接的支持。

2010年第二版的美国《诺顿理论和批评选集》收入148位著者的185篇作品，李泽厚忝列其中，成为与包括休谟、康德、莱辛、席勒、黑格尔等在内的13位入选美学家。[4]

---

① 张法：《中国美学史上的体系性著作研究》，北京大学出版社2008年版，第137页。

② 同上书，第287页。

③ 朱立元：《新时期以来文学理论和批评发展概况的调查报告》，春风文艺出版社2006年版，第216页。

④ 贾晋华：《走进世界的李泽厚》，《读书》2010年第11期。

在尚有论看来，除了李泽厚，还有一大批老一辈美学家、文论家的美学研究和文艺理论研究也都有极强的原创性和中国特色，也都没有失语，相反，成了中国美学和文论的标杆。梁启超、鲁迅的小说理论，王国维、蔡元培的美学思想，冯友兰的人生境界说，钱锺书的谈艺语录，宗白华的中国意境美学，李泽厚的美学体系，蒋孔阳的美学新论，新儒家、新道家的思想流派等，不仅继承和发扬了中国美学思想，而且在他们的影响下形成了中国文艺学、美学、哲学的新传统。因此，所谓的失语症并无长久的绝对的意义，可能针对某一时期的某些学者是有效的，而针对一个历史时期有成就的美学家和文艺理论家而言，就是无效的。

另外，在我国当代一些重要的美学教科书中，中国审美形态的总结和概述正在逐步增加，一改两千年前凡论审美形态就是西方的悲剧、崇高、喜剧、荒诞、滑稽的写法，中国的中和、气韵、意境、神妙、阴柔与阳刚、空灵、飘逸等已进入了当代中国美学的教科书中，与西方的审美形态分庭抗礼，在中西审美形态的对比中，显示中国美学的特性①。

因此可以说，与中国美学和文论上的崇无论形成强烈对比的中国美学和文论的实绩，正好构成了尚有论对崇无论的挑战。

但问题的核心不在于尚有论如何驳倒崇无论，而在于“中国美学还是美学在中国”的疑问并没有因为尚有论的存在而消除，相反，依然存在。也就是说，尚有论所言中国美学千好万好，但真正独创而又对世界美学发生影响的地方在哪里？换言之，中国美学的有无问题在全球化背景下已不再是一个封闭的自说自话的问题，而是一个需要在

① 朱立元《美学》在“中国审美形态”专章中论述了中和、气韵、意境三种中国的审美形态范畴（朱立元主编：《美学》，高等教育出版社2001年版）。王建疆在《审美学教程》中新增了神妙、阴柔与阳刚等中国的审美形态范畴（王建疆主编：《审美学教程》，复旦大学出版社2007年版）。叶朗《美学原理》中论述了顿挫、飘逸、空灵三种中国的审美形态范畴（叶朗：《美学原理》，北京大学出版社2009年版）。

全球化背景下加以考量的问题，是一个需要国际认同的问题。因此，中国美学如果止步于尚有论的有而故步自封，其对中国美学的走向世界就像崇无论的无一样产生不良影响。因此，在否定崇无论之后，尚有论还需进一步提升自己，将中国美学的“有”变成大，把大变成强，把地域变成全球，把国家的变成国际的。而要做到这一点，尚有论对中国美学的已有体系和当代中国美学成就的自我反思就不可或缺。只有通过自我反思，在与西方美学的比较中，才能发现自身的不足和缺陷，才有可能在有的基础上进步。而要自我反思，对于中国美学崇无和尚有现象后面的成因的探讨就尤为重要和必要。

（二）中国美学和文论上的崇无论和尚有论的成因分析

1. 中国美学和文论上的崇无论的成因很多，但大致不出主观与客观两个方面。

（1）主观原因。

首先，未能深究悖论并跳出悖论。中国是论文大国，也是美学大国。“为美学的美学”制造了太多的美学著作和美学论文。其悖论在于，在一个有过数次“美学热”的中国，并没有中国美学，却只有美学在中国，从而形成了一种背反的中国美学。但崇无论者并未深究这一悖论的成因，从一个更高的高度去看中国美学的虚无与实有的问题，而是顺从了没有中国美学只有美学在中国的悖论。

其次，来自对中国审美形态多样性和独一无二性及其对中国审美形态研究的忽视。中国的审美形态无论在数量上还是在独特性上，都有着为西方审美形态所不及的地方。往往是古代西方有的审美形态，中国古代也有，如优美、滑稽、喜剧等，凡现代西方有的审美形态，中国现当代也都有，如悲剧、荒诞、丑陋等，但相反，中国有的审美形态，西方过去没有，现在也没有，如气韵、意境、空灵、飘逸、沉郁、阴柔与阳刚等，显示了中国审美形态的多样性和独一无二性。中国美学崇无论者无视中国审美形态的如此多样性和如此独一无二性，

也无视众多对于这种多样性和独一无二性的大量的、长期的研究成果，而是完全按着西方美学的理论框架来看中国的美学研究，最后得出了没有中国美学，只有西方美学在中国的崇无论。

最后，从“拿来主义”看问题，误以为一切都是拿来的，从而遮蔽了中国美学和文论的研究成果。中国美学和文论确实在相当长的时间里对西方的美学理论和文学理论、艺术理论，不加选择地介绍、贩卖，并用西方的理论来套中国的现实，或用中国的例证去证明西方的正确，缺少怀疑与批判精神，形成了唯西方理论马首是瞻的思维惯性，造成了以拿来的代替自己的后果。但是，这种情况并不能遮蔽中国古代美学和古代文论形成的历史。中国古代的美学家和文论家都是从具体的诗词、小说、园林、绘画、音乐、文体等具体审美对象开始研究美学问题的，而不是从什么主义中直接推演出美学思想来。文论的情况更是如此，都是从创作、作品、体裁、接受等具体问题开始研究的。但拿来主义习惯于拿来，以为自己的也是拿来的，从而形成了自我遮蔽，导致崇无论。

（2）客观原因。

首先，古今语境转换方面的困难。1962 年，郭绍虞在《光明日报》上发表《关于〈沧浪诗话〉讨论的补充意见》，提出：“用外来术语来说明中国学术思想上的问题，总有些距离，不会完全合适的。问题就在产生这些术语的历史环境并不与中国的历史环境完全相适合。”① 这里涉及的就是中国古代美学和古代文论的当代语境问题。实际上这里有个难题，即现代语境未必能够真实地凸显中国古代的学术思想，但离开了现代语境，古代学术思想将变得无法理解，会产生一种真正的失语症。在这种不得不为的困难面前，在古今思想的差距面前，很容易滋生当代中国古代美学和文论研究是否失真的疑问，进

---

① 郭绍虞：《关于〈沧浪诗话〉讨论的补充意见》，《光明日报》1962 年 9 月 12 日第 4 版。

而否定当代研究的合法性。

1995 年，牟世金在其著作《文心雕龙研究》中提道："把古人的理论分割开，而按现代理论的框框对号入座，这种方法是轻而易举的，但不仅意义不大，还有碍于认识刘勰自己的理论原貌和特点，自然更谈不到研究的深入和发展。"① 这是以现代表达古代的困惑。

1999 年，张少康在《文艺研究》上发表《古文论研究杂识》②，主张"以一种平常心来对待古代文论"，"不汲汲于用"，由于古代文论的"术语和范畴适用说明古代文学的特点"，"语境的丧失使得古文论无法用以评说今日之文学"。但是否都如此，恐须具体对待。

以上说法都是有关中国古代文论的现代研究所遇到的问题，是一个古今术语不对等、不匹配的问题。

1999 年，余虹在其著作《中国文论与西方诗学》中提出："'中国古代文学理论史'的写作在既有的现代汉语语境中至少会造成双重假象：其一，仿佛中国古代有一种'文学理论'，即有一种西方式的文学意识和理论，这种意识和理论可以从古代文论、诗论、词论、曲论、小说论中抽取出来；其二，仿佛古代汉语中的文学一词与现代汉语中的文学一词有某种渊源关系，仿佛后者的语义是从前者派生出来的。""我们有权借用今天的概念意识去有选择地书写过去的言述艺术史，但我们无权将某种古人没有的意识强加给古人。"③

但如何才能做到恰如其分地转述和阐释中国古代美学和古代文论，克服由于古今语境的不同所带来的困难，实在是一个难题，在这种情况下，中国美学和文论的研究很可能因为西方美学和西方文论话语在中国的通行，而给崇无论者提供了支持。

其次，学科与思想结合时的错位。人文学科的学科标准往往会与

---

① 牟世金：《文心雕龙研究》，人民文学出版社 1995 年版。

② 张少康：《古代文论研究杂识》，《文艺研究》1999 年第 3 期。

③ 余虹：《中国文论与西方诗学》，生活·读书·新知三联书店 1999 年版，第 64、66 页。

思想标准相关，但学科的标准不同于思想的标准。学科的标准具有当下确定的特点，即以研究对象和命名来确定该学科的成立。而思想的标准与学科的当下确认不同，往往具有“追认”的特点，即在一种学科之下，回溯这一学科产生的思想轨迹，从而形成这一学科的历史时期划分。如古代美学思想史、近代美学思想史、现代美学思想史等，其实都是后来追加的。因为在古代连“美学”都没有，哪有什么古代美学思想史呢？只有在学科的名分下，相关思想才能得到有效的、系统的整合。因此，在学术研究上应该坚持学科性与思想性统一而学科性优先的原则。

但思想的标准与学科的标准的统一却是一件困难的事。因为，从学科意义上讲，新的学科更加注重学术上的新，而非思想上的新。如被尊称为“美学之父”的德国美学家鲍姆嘉通的“Asthetik”或英译“Aesthetics”就主要是“美学”作为学科的诞生，而非新思想的诞生，因为有关美学的思想尤其是注重审美感性的思想早在人类的轴心时代就已经形成。可以说，鲍姆嘉通的主要贡献是在美学学科上的界定，而不是在美学思想上的创新上。人们在研究德国美学思想史时发现，康德、谢林、席勒、黑格尔等一大批美学家使得鲍姆嘉通黯然无光，原因即在于思想与学科有联系的同时毕竟有区别：有时是学科凸显而思想淡出，有时却是思想盛行而学科淡化。思想往往是自己的，但学科却可能是引进或移植别人的。这样一来，中国的美学思想和文艺思想，往往而且必须装在西方的“美学”学科的框架内，否则，中国的文艺思想和美学思想本身就会形成表述上的失语。但用西方的学科来表述中国的思想，难免造成“中国的”被西方所统摄、所同化的另一种“失语”假象。这就是中西文化交流中必然出现的思想与学科错位的现象。在这种错位中，会出现“以西释中”和“以中释西”两种不同情况。但究竟出现哪种情况，其“关键仍在于看是要解决谁的问题，而不在于用谁的语词。以西语为用，以中论为体，

仍是体用结合，洋为中用”①。这就如同用马克思主义解决中国的问题，从而形成毛泽东思想一样。相反，脱离中国的实际和问题，以西论为体，以汉语为用，仍然是中为洋用，以中释西。

尽管中国美学和文论中的崇无论难以坐实，但这种基于以上客观原因的崇无论却与目前流行的中国历史虚无主义和中国文化虚无主义并无直接的必然的联系。其原因就在于历史文化虚无主义来自对中国历史和文化价值的否定，而中国美学和文论上的虚无论只来自古今语境的错位和学科与思想的错位，是一个认识问题，有恨铁不成钢而非“文化复仇”的情绪，亦非否定中国文化的价值诉求，更不能说什么否定了主流意识形态。

2. 尚有论产生的原因

首先，来自对中国美学和文论研究现状的乐观。本来，中国当代美学和文论研究在畸形发展。一方面，中国美学已经走向世界，有了国际影响的美学家；另一方面，中国美学却是世界美学垃圾的制造大国。其特点之一是跟着西方的“主义”任意嫁接美学和文论，如自然主义美学、感伤主义美学、表现主义美学、直觉主义美学、心理现实主义美学、科学主义美学、形式主义美学、结构主义美学、后结构主义美学、经验主义美学、实用主义美学、女权主义美学、后殖民主义美学、西方马克思主义美学等，都成了当代中国美学和文论论著中具有制导性的主体关键词，使中国美学的研究成了西方美学思想或主义的注脚。其特点之二就是按行业来任意命名美学，如农业美学、工业美学、商业美学、军事美学、医疗美学、技术美学等，致使“美学”一词泛滥成灾，有一种行业就有一种美学，而于学术的原创和思想的发展却异常贫乏，是一种虚胀，因而很难得到国际美学的认同。正是未能识破这种畸形发展，从而为中国美学尚有论者提供了判定的

① 参见王建疆《反思全球化背景下的“传统”和“话语霸权”》，《学术月刊》2006年第11期。

依据。这个依据并不全面，也不正确，是一个片面的、畸形的依据。但正是这个片面的、畸形的依据却导致了尚有论对中国美学现状的误判，当代美学和文论所急需的独创性美学原理和美学范畴却被遮蔽了，从而产生盲目的乐观。

其次，对中国古代美学和文论的体系及其在当代的生发性认识不足。中国古代美学和文论理性逻辑和形式逻辑两个方面都有欠缺，从而影响到与国际哲学、理论的交流沟通和通约。中国古代美学和文论如何走向世界的问题并不是语言转换问题，而是范畴体系与逻辑架构的问题。许多只有论断而无论据和论证的表达，很难得到以逻辑见长的西方学者的理解和接受。如果看不到这一缺陷，只是肯定中国美学的和文论的体系之有，对于中国美学和文论的发展来说并无裨益，相反还会造成自我满足的感觉。另外，中国古代美学和文论受其汉语表达和逻辑架构的限制，在当代很难生发出新的理论，也很难与西方理论对接、交流，从而影响到中国美学和文论虽然有但难以产生国际影响。

总之，中国美学和文论中的崇无和尚有之争是一个历史上延续下来的问题。无视这个问题，就等于回避美学和文论上的重大问题，无益于美学和文论的发展。但囿于这个问题，也不会产生更大的学术价值，因为很显然，有会怎么样？没有又会怎么样？因此，中国美学和文论的有无之争是一定要被超越的。唯其被超越，才能有中国美学和文论的本真存在，才会有中国美学和文论的走向世界。

第三节　走出有无之争：寻找中国美学和文论之“待有”

中国美学和文论中的崇无与尚有之争，表面上看是一个最为原初的有和无的问题，但实质上它所反映的却是对自身独立性的焦虑和对发展的渴望。但在悲观的崇无论笼罩下的中国美学和文论，很难谈到

发展，顶多只有焦虑而已。

但是，乐观的尚有论是否就值得乐观？中国古代是否就有得到世界承认的美学体系和文论体系？如果有，那么，为什么还会出现崇无论呢？“是中国美学还是美学在中国”的疑问为什么至今不绝于耳呢？看来，问题并非崇无或尚有那么简单，需要我们进一步深思。

尽管崇无论与尚有论针锋相对，但其存在的意义是超越了选边站的。因为，绝对的有正如绝对的无一样，并不符合中国美学和文论的实际。事实上，要证明中国美学和文论的无，要比证明中国美学和文论的有更难。你说只有西方美学在中国而没有中国美学，那么，李泽厚美学不是中国美学吗？所以，绝对的崇无论很难立足。但是，当你轻而易举地证明了中国美学和文论的有之时，问题接踵而至，即中国有自己的美学和自己的文论又能怎样？还不是在世界上没有得到承认，没有地位吗？因此我认为，较之中国美学和文论上的崇无与尚有之争，更为重要的是：中国美学和文论除此有无之外，是否还有一个“待有”的问题？所谓的“待有”，就是尚未有，但不同于没有，而是在跟别人相比较时，看看我们还缺少什么，而非我们已经有什么。已有和没有都是已然的事，是历时形态的，而待有或期待有却立足于比较，指向未来，是共时性态的。走出崇无尚有论之后，就不该满足于实有或已有，而是要探究待有，即我们还缺什么。只有把待有的问题搞清楚了，才能找到中国美学和文论的当代坐标，在全球化背景下确立自己的位置，否则，囿于有无虚实之辩，将不会产生更有价值的成果，更谈不上对未来发展的预判和对策。正是基于对待有的关注，我认为，中国美学和文论在超越崇无尚有之后，应该首先面对以下几个“待有”的问题。

我们缺少什么样的美学？

中国美学从未像今天这样处于繁华后面的贫瘠。一方面，中国当代的美学急剧膨胀，有一种行业就有一种美学，几乎无一遗漏；但另一方面，我们缺少原创性的美学原理，尤其是美学上的主义。相比之

下，我们今天中国的美学研究，都笼罩在西方诸多的主义之下。如存在主义美学、结构主义美学、解构主义美学、现代主义美学、后现代主义美学、后殖民主义美学、女权主义美学等。当代中国的美学研究已经成了西方五花八门的主义的试验场、展览室、大舞台。而真正属于中国人的主义却很难见到。我们虽然也有不少有成就的美学家和文论家，如宗白华、李泽厚、蒋孔阳等，但有多少原创性的原理在国际上产生影响呢？还有就是中国美学家们近几年来对诸多中国审美形态范畴的提炼并被写入教科书，从而拓展了中国美学的研究领域，但又有哪一条是得到西方美学界承认的？因此，与西方相比，中国美学和问题尚未占据学科的制高点。关键在于缺乏原创性的主义。这一点就连李泽厚也不例外。西方的主义喧嚣，而我们只是看客。没有主义的美学就只能跟着别人走，被别人的主义和思想所统摄、所遮蔽。美学原理需要多维的深层次的建构，特别需要主义的统摄和引导，这种主义就是美学中的哲学思想和哲学方法，也是多种专业学说和理论的思想武装。而这一点恰好是我们的短板，是我们的未有和待有。因此，中国美学目前的第一未有和待有就是主义的缺失和主义的建构。

我们缺少什么样的文论？

与美学的原创相比，中国文论的原创程度更加低下，这也是失语症论者首先发难的地方。朱立元先生《新时期以来文学理论和批评发展概况的调查报告》是他主持的教育部重大攻关项目“马克思主义文艺理论中国化研究”的阶段性成果，该成果客观地、全面系统地总结了新时期以来中国文艺理论和批评的发展概况，对新时期以来的文艺学和美学研究成果予以高度的评价。但就是在这份调查报告中，我们仍能发现中国美学和文艺学之待有。这就是尽管新时期中国美学和文论研究空前繁荣，成绩斐然，但历数家珍，却很难发现我们在文艺理论方面有多少原创性的东西。

原创是什么？是填补空白吗？是，也不是。关键看你填补什么空白。如掀起一场讨论，增设一个博士点，对没有多大价值无人问津的

文本进行研究等，这在特定的情境下是填补了空白。但是，这种填补空白与学术的原创没有必然联系，相反，有时是对无价值对象的投机取巧。事实上，真正的原创首先表现在次级核心范畴群的发现和建立上，如西方经典的剩余价值说、生物进化论、潜意识原理、心理距离说、移情说等，中国美学家的积淀说、多层累突创说、审美调节机制说等，而不是作为学术研究和组织建设的一系列活动。而恰恰这一点我们不会轻易地从当代中国文论中找到。如果连基本的次级核心范畴群都没有建立起来，又怎么可能去建立自己的文论上的主义呢？因此，缺乏次级核心范畴群的当代中国文论，首先应该面对这种待有。

面对以上这些“待有”，应着重解决以下几个问题。

1. 中国式主义的建构及原创性问题。

主义是理论的升华，是精神的凝聚，是思想的指南。美学、文艺学的发展必然呼唤有独特理论建构和思想深度的学派。而学派建立的最终形态或高级形态乃是主义的形成。主义是最具有原创性的，是在思想之林中独步的，而不是藤缠树般纠结不清、似是而非的。中国美学和文论只有形成自己建立在“百家争鸣”基础上的主义时，才能形成与西方对话、交流的思想体系，才能促成真正意义上的中国审美文化的复兴和完全意义上的走向世界。当然，我们应该提倡高端原创，即主义的原创、原理的原创和范畴的原创，而不是那些投机取巧式的“填补空白”的原创，因为许多与某某行业挂钩的某某美学已经被证明是圈地式的名分之争，而无美学的原创之实。

2. 从中国实际出发，创建次级核心范畴群和体系的问题。

次级核心范畴是理论体系建构的关键。王国维提出了 29 个具有中西合璧特征的美学范畴，包括审美形态范畴，这为他“中国美学第一人”的地位奠定了基础。王国维这些美学范畴是源于中国古代诗学又超越了中国古代诗学的，如“有我之境”“无我之境”“造境”“写境”“隔与不隔”“古雅”“眩惑”等。尽管王国维的境界说被有的学者认为是西方的血统，但除了境界，还有 28 个范畴，是否都是

西方血统？有待系统考察。但这种创建次级核心范畴的努力还是需要大力提倡的。李泽厚创立了 17 个美学范畴，如积淀说、乐感说、情本体说、儒道互补、美感二重性、美感三层次说等，从而使他自己的美学以体系的形式跻身于世界美学之林。因此，一定要从中国美学实际出发，而非从西方的主义出发。切勿上了西方人的反本质主义、解构主义、否定主义、怀疑主义的当，诸如什么不要体系，不要本质或本体等。实际上，西方的这些反体系论者都有自己的体系，主义突出，思想脉络明确，俨然一体，而非碎片。再者，对中国美学和文论来说，不是体系多了，相反，是体系少了。体系是理论的完整形态，体系是思维的必然归宿，体系也是最好的识别标志。因此，走出崇无论的中国美学和文论，面对当前之“待有”，应该摆脱后现代解构思潮的影响，注意从中国实际出发，从创建次级核心范畴开始建立自己的理论体系。

3. 学术清理问题。

美学界近几年不少学者呼吁对百年学案的清理。也许这种学术清理，能够使我们更清晰地看到中国美学和文论在中西交流过程中的生成和发展以及功过是非，明辨其中的虚无与实有及其待有，从而总结经验，吸取教训，避免粗放，走向精确，使学术的发展精益求精，达到同时期国际学术水平。

以上三个问题并非中国美学和文论的所有问题，而是在当下迫切需要解决的问题。这些问题首先涉及的是中国美学和文论是否具有识别性和统摄性的问题。所谓识别性，就是地道的中国美学和文论，而非西方美学和文论在中国。所谓统摄性，就是理论的涵盖性和主义对于思想的驾驭能力。如果美学和文论缺乏识别性和统摄性，就会要么跟着别人走，要么成为散状物，凝聚不成一个强有力的思想，不具有识别标志，遑论影响力。其次，主义和范畴的问题涉及同化力和创造力的问题，也是当代中国美学和文论孜孜以求的目标。在历次人类文化的复兴过程中，哲学、美学在彰显自己的识别性和统摄性的同时，

就像它们自身业已显示的那样，必然具有影响力，进而产生同化力。近代世界史上对人类进步产生了重大影响的人文思想，无非主义和次级核心范畴，正是这些主义和范畴征服了人们的思想，产生了社会进步的动力。而思想的同化力首先来自于思想的具有知识产权的创造力，来自于它的原创性。正是在这个意义上，我们不遗余力地要超越崇无论和尚有论，提倡待有论，就是要有一个明确的追求目标，为此而不惜“众里寻他千百度”。最后，学术的清理，是发挥史鉴的功能，总结经验，汲取教训，从而使当下的及至未来的美学和文论研究少走弯路。

总之，待有论就是立足于中国美学和文论的实际，把自己置身于全球美学和文论的语境中，反省教训，总结经验，发现差距和缺失，找到需求点，有针对性地进行中国美学和文论的建构，使中国美学和文论进入一个新的境界。

第四章

别现代：主义的问题与问题的主义

——兼回应夏中义先生*

近来，夏中义先生在他的《学术史提问与“新世代”焦虑——兼回应王建疆教授》[①]（以下简称《焦虑》）一文中对我的《中国美学和文论上的“崇无”和“尚有”与“待有”》一文[②]以及我关于主义建构和别现代主张的系列论文提出批评，断言我提出的“主义”和别现代理论“完了”。最后，夏先生以钱锺书学案为例告诉我们要走一条朴学的道路。夏中义先生素以思想的启蒙和对民国以来学案的清理著称，故对其观点不得不予以重视。

第一节 对朴学及其学案派的诊断

对我提出的中国学术一方面是主义的喧嚣另一方面却是主义的缺失的悖论以及别现代理论做过批评的不止夏中义先生一人。2012 年就有王洪岳先生撰文与我商榷[③]，2015 年有陶国山先生的批

---

* 本章曾发表于《上海师范大学学报》（哲学社会科学版）2017 年第 1 期。

① 夏中义：《学术史提问与“新世代”焦虑——兼回应王建疆教授》，《学术月刊》2016 年第 6 期。

② 王建疆：《中国美学和文论上的“崇无”和“尚有”与“待有”》，《学术月刊》2015 年第 10 期。

③ 王洪岳：《精神建构的彷徨与出路——兼与王建疆先生商榷》，《探索与争鸣》2012 年第 4 期。

评文章[①]。而且这一学术讨论已经进入国际视野。著名美学家阿列西·艾尔雅维茨对我发表在欧洲《哲学杂志》上的关于主义的英语文章[②]进行评论[③]，还有几位外国学者正在撰文跟进讨论。艾尔雅维茨针对我提出的主义的问题指出："我认为西方过去和现在发生的一些事件和进程与中国发生的那些事件和进程虽然有差异，却在某种程度上也有相似之处。类似我们之间的这种对话将有助于避免和纠正一些在全球广泛流传的有关思想的共存性、相对重要性和创新性方面的错误和实践。"[④] 于此，这个"主义"的讨论已不再仅仅是中国的，也是世界的了。夏中义先生在人文思想和文艺理论研究之域倡导朴学，并身体力行，做了许多民国以来大学者的学案，这在大学隐匿、小学盛行的当下格外引人注目。而且更重要的是夏中义先生已将自己对学案的分析上升到学风、方法和气度上。如《"百年学案"：学风、方法与气度》一文所示：

> 本文旨在论述20世纪中国文艺理论史案（简称"百年学案"）研究的若干现象：一曰学风，若无朴学学风，"百年学案"探索难以为继；二曰方法，"文献———发生学"方法作为"百年学案"赖以深化的思维规程，可谓是朴学学风的当代演示；三曰气度，朴学学风源自学人气度，该气度以学者有否"学术史"意识乃至"学派"建设意向为标识。[⑤]

---

① 陶国山：《美学的"家族相似"与回归》，《上海大学学报》（社会科学版）2015年第4期。

② Wang Jianjiang, "The Bustle and the Absence of Zhuyi. The Example of Chinese Aesthetics" *Filozofski Vestinik*, Letnik, XXXVII, 2016.

③ Aleš Erjavec, Zhuyi, From Absence to Bustle? Some Comments to Jianjiang Wang's Article "The Bustle or the Absence of Zhuyi", *Journal of Art + Media Studies*, 2017, 13.

④ Ibid.

⑤ 夏中义：《"百年学案"：学风、方法与气度》，《文艺研究》2006年第8期。

显然，夏中义先生把朴学看得很高，它已经成了文艺理论史写作的基石。

朴学，这个现代学术中的低频词，往往会因为人们不了解它的文献学和小学的含义而令人肃然起敬。但说白了，朴学就是一种前现代最原始、最朴素也最简单的国学方法。包括经典考证梳理、声韵训诂之学、文章学等传统国学范畴。但夏氏朴学并非经典意义上的朴学，即汉学、宋学和清代小学，而是个性化的朴学。因为夏中义先生在《焦虑》一文的“内容提要”部分明确地指出：“要多研究‘问题’，少谈‘主义’。”而且，从夏中义先生行文中对于主义的嘲弄和揶揄，不难看出这是一种专与主义“过不去”的朴学。

朴学，既要突出学案，又要否定主义，在此一身二能的要求下能否胜任，是否有必要，它到底引出了什么问题，就值得关注。顺着夏中义先生要有抓手和“把柄”的“诊断”思路，在表达我们的观点前还是用他的诊断法先来诊断一下他自己的这种朴学吧。

夏氏朴学主要依据文献资料对思想史进行“文献发生学”研究，整理出思想史和思想者个人的谱系来。其中有两个给我印象最深的学案，一是对陈寅恪、吴昌硕思想之祖的考证，一是对钱锺书入列美学先人祠的谱系的确立。

其于2014年发表的《自由观念的中国面孔———论陈寅恪、吴昌硕对陶渊明的思想认祖》中声称：

> 远在“五四”新文化启蒙之前，中国面孔的自由观念早在儒生—知识者群落流播甚久。若以1919年“五四”为时间下限，则从陶潜（369—427）算起，它已流传近1500年；从苏轼（1013—1101）算起，它已流传900年；从龚自珍（1792—1841）算起，它已流传70年；从吴昌硕（1844—1927）算起，它已流传25年；从王国维（1877—1927）算起，它已流传15年。换言之，中国面孔的自由观念在“五四”之前，已如渴望燃烧的千年

干柴堆得神州遍野皆是。”①

此文在夏先生诸多的学案文章中颇有分量，它梳理了中国自由观念的源头和流别，意义兼及学术和思想两个方面。但是，这里至少有三个问题需要夏氏朴学的自我“证伪”。

问题一，自由观念的界定是否清楚？将陈寅恪的自由思想之祖定为陶渊明，并进一步将这一个案的结论扩大到整个中国自由观念的历史，似乎中国的自由观念的祖先就是陶渊明了。尽管夏文着力辨析的是“中国面孔”的自由观与西方自由观的不同，但是，中国的自由观的实质是什么，却未见详论。记得胡适说过：

> 在欧洲文字里，“自由”含有“解放”之意，是从外力制裁之下解放出来，才能“自己做主”。在中国古代思想里，“自由”就等于自然，“自然”是“自己如此”，“自由”是“由于自己”，都有不由于外力拘束的意识。陶渊明的诗：“久在樊笼里，复得返自然”，这里“自然”二字可以说完全同“自由”一样。②

这里的问题在于：胡适的说法是否周全？陶渊明的自由观有多大的涵盖性？如果这些问题不清楚，“中国面孔”的自由如何落地？

问题二，自由观念的源头清楚吗？夏文认为，“中国自由观念的面孔”之祖先是陶潜，如说：

> 这就是说，陈对陶的“自由思想”认祖，……而不像上古隐士仅仅飘逸在零星传说中。更重要的是，完全可把陶的诗文编年

① 夏中义：《自由观念的中国面孔——论陈寅恪、吴昌硕对陶渊明的思想认祖》，《探索与争鸣》2014 年第 8 期。

② 俞吾金编选：《胡适文集》，上海远东出版社 1995 年版，第 385 页。

史读作陶诗性地展示其一辈子追求的心灵受难史，而不像庄子思绪雄放得像鲲鹏高举，却老让后世吃不准他究竟是人还是仙，他能否永远站在云端，不食人间烟火。①

显然，夏文在用排除法排除了“经虚涉旷”的庄子及“魏晋风度”的“竹林七贤”，从而得出结论：

其一，拟与“五四精神”通约的陈寅恪的“独立、自由”，与其说源自西方自由主义（查无实据），毋宁说中国面孔的自由观念本有其绵延千年的人文血脉，此即“陶潜→苏轼→龚自珍→吴昌硕→王国维→陈寅恪”。②

但我们不禁要问，中国的自由思想的历史就这么短暂吗？胡适说过：

我们思想史的第一个开山时代，就是春秋战国时代——就有争取思想自由的意义。③

老子庄子对于社会的批判自不在话下，就连主张“克己复礼”的孔子，其最能彰显其精神境界的“曾点气象”“孔颜乐处”，又怎么不是自由的思想呢？，由此，中国的自由思想，到底是2500年前还是1500年前，这里有1000年的距离呀！

问题三，“自由”的中国语源或辞源清楚吗？“自由”一词汉代已经出现，郑玄注《礼记·少仪》“请见不请退”云：“去止不敢自

① 夏中义：《自由观念的中国面孔——论陈寅恪、吴昌硕对陶渊明的思想认祖》，《探索与争鸣》2014年第8期。

② 同上。

③ 俞吾金编选：《胡适文集》，上海远东出版社1995年版，第386页。

由”（［唐］孔颖达等正义：《礼记正义》，卷三十五），已经超出了胡适所谓自然的意思。在唐代更有了独立自主和解放的意思。唐代百丈怀海禅师问：“‘如何得自由分？’”其师马祖道一答曰：“能照破一切有无诸境，是金刚慧。即有自由独立分。”① 而百丈怀海的“放出沩山水牯牛，无人坚执绳鼻头。绿杨芳草春风岸，横卧高眠得自由”。禅诗更是传世之作。百丈怀海以立《百丈清规》也就是禅宗的规矩和法度而闻名于世，其“自由独立”就是禅宗人追求的身心两方面的彻底解放。这里对于“自由”的引述如果进一步概括分类，是可以由此而见出中国古代自由思想的多种含义及其谱系的，既非胡适所说的仅仅为自然，也非与西方自由观不可通约。

其实，早在与夏中义先生商榷之前，我已经对相关学科领域的朴学及其学案有过大致的了解，并提出了自己的看法。如在 2014 年我就美学文献整理问题撰文认为，美学文献不同于一般的古典文献，而是以理论和识见对于原始材料的发现、概括、提炼、整理的结果。这一看法并非凭空而论，是基于当代中国美学史整理和美学建构出现的问题和教训而进行的总结②。事实上，朴学在中国哲学、美学的运用方面也出来不少的问题。不顾思想流传而将朴学放大，遂致思想被否认的学案比比皆是，如著名文献学家高明的《老子帛书校注》中关于老子“无为而无不为”这一名句的真伪问题的论断，就是以朴学诊断哲学思想和美学思想的败笔③。著名历史学家钱穆的《庄老通辨》以庄子为“中国道家思想的开山大宗师”，也是考证错误的结果。美学方面完全以“美”字来取舍美学史材料，写成的美学简史，

① （宋）普济：《五灯会元，百丈怀海禅师》，苏渊雷点校，中华书局 1984 年版，第 135 页。

② 王建疆：《中国美学文献整理的方法论原则新探》，《四川师范大学学报》2014 年第 5 期。

③ 高明认为：“‘无为而无不为’本不出于《老子》，它是汉初黄老学派之产物。”（高明：《帛书老子校注・序》，中华书局 1996 年版，第 5 页）但郭店楚简《老子》中就有“无为而无不为”句。

结果恰好错过了中国古代“道”“气”“象”“妙”等涵盖面更大、影响更深远的美学范畴①。还有通过考证，得出王国维境界说来自德国美学的结论②，等等，都是朴学自我暴露的问题，而非对问题的解决。可以说，朴学这一产生于前现代的治学方法，固然仍有其可信度和可行性，但其可信度和可行度并不是无限的，而是有限的。若以其有限而达无限，殆矣。通过对夏氏朴学的学习和研究，我的疑问在于，朴学也好，夏氏朴学也好，这种长于文献整理和考证的方法，在哲学思辨和美学理论建构的跨界使用中会不会留下与专业方圆不周、相互龃龉的缺憾？因此，将朴学作为思想建构、理论创新时的辅助工具未为不可，但将其放大为思想建设和理论创新本身，甚至以朴学或几个“学案”来替代学术或主义的建构，则既有僭越之嫌，也恐力不从心。

中国的学术也同中国的政治一样忽左忽右。要不就跟着西方走，唯西方马首是瞻，对传统的国学不屑一顾；要不就盲目排外，以国粹、国学为全世界唯一之宝。夏先生对主义论的责难大概不出朴学国粹之右，是只见小学不见大学的普遍国情的集中表达。在一个缺乏主义因而需要主义的建构的国度里，在主义的建构过程中，有时也可能需要文献考证的朴学支持，但文献考证的朴学并不能替代主义的建构。以自己没有主义甚至不可能有主义而用文献学的方法或朴学的方法否定主义和主义的建构，恰恰是忽略了现实中对于思想、理论和主义的急需。

第二节　主义的问题与问题的主义

夏氏朴学对主义的批判是严厉的，但波及未免太广。夏文：

① 叶朗对这种普遍现象进行了纠正。参见叶朗《中国美学史大纲》，上海人民出版社1985年版，第24页。

② 罗钢：《意境说是德国美学的中国变体》，《南京大学学报》（哲学、人文科学、社会科学版）2011年第5期。

> 这就意味着，当建疆踌躇满怀地放言：“主义是理论的升华，是精神的凝聚，是思想的指南和行动的纲领”，完了，此“主义”可以是非学术辞典中的大词，然它肯定成不了美学“概念”。因为美学作为对非功利的审美经验的知性提纯，它无心也无力诉诸“行动”，更扯不上“行动纲领”。①

实际上，不论是大词还是小词，就主义的共同功能而言，如何就不是思想的指南，如何就不是理论的升华，如何就不是精神的凝聚，如何就不是行动的纲领？难道主义就是一个故事，是一段美妙得生花的文字？中国文艺界和美学界流行多年的现实主义、浪漫主义、现代主义、后现代主义等，哪个不具有引导、指导和方法、路径的功能？甚至像过程主义、超现实主义、建构主义、解构主义，就是美术的、建筑的也是美学的行动纲领。再就举国体制的“走社会主义道路”，不也是理论表述、思想指导、行动指南和口号方式吗？遗憾的是，夏氏朴学并未对此关键之处予以辨析，而只是一句“完了”做了断状。

夏氏朴学之针对所向在于主义。文章伊始就批评所谓的“学术民族主义”，似乎民族、国家这些概念在夏先生那里已经过时，不该存有。但令人疑惑的是，夏中义先生的文章屡屡以“中国”命题，如《自由观念的中国面孔》云云，可见他是讲国家，也讲主义的。

但夏中义先生对别人讲的主义的否定是坚决的。如说：

> 只要人性的幽暗总有上帝之光照不到的角落，慎重的学术史论就绝不应把一个民族国家的美学史福祉全寄托给不靠谱的“主义”，它往往是水货，却听上去很美。当朴质的史实一次次地把建疆所“待有”的那块“主义”水晶里的水挤干，建疆还愿继

① 罗钢：《意境说是德国美学的中国变体》，《南京大学学报》（哲学、人文科学、社会科学版）2011 年第 5 期。

续梦想“主义”会像圣诞老人那般承诺给他一堆优质“理论（体系）”么？[①]

显然，夏文一是认为，主义是空的，经不起证伪的。二是认为，主义无什么用处。三是最根本的，主义的建构与其朴学不相容，所以必欲排除而后快。为此，有必要重新考察主义。

主义有层次之分，有大小之辨，有古今之差异，有自觉与非自觉之别，主义也有或偏于理论、或偏于实践的不同，除此之外，主义还有对专业的适用与不适用的问题。主义有以概念命名的，也有以人名命名的。但无论如何，主义首先必须是原创的、独一无二的。在西方，尽管主义的构成五花八门，但有一点却是共同的，这就是：主义是道路，主义是标杆，主义是指南，主义是统摄。在人类自觉且发达的时代，人们的思想和行动，不管习惯还是不习惯，承认还是不承认，都摆脱不了主义的统摄和制约。就说夏氏朴学吧，尽管对主义嗤之以鼻，但朴学之朴，不就是一种治学的方法和路径，是一种治学的主张和思想并从而走过的一条道路吗？如果将这种主张和思想及其道路凸现出来，作为自觉的行动纲领，不就是朴学主义吗？但遗憾的是，夏氏朴学却并没有这样的主义意识。因此，对于被笼罩在社会主义的光环下却不敢称谓自己也有主义的中国学人而言，忌惮主义实在是一个悲剧。

百年中国美学中最大的教训就是主义的喧嚣与主义的缺失并置[②]。说主义的喧嚣，就在于50年代的美学大讨论都是围绕着唯物主义、唯心主义或主观主义、客观主义展开的，80年代以后的中国美学研究包括大学生、硕士生、博士生所写的美学文艺学论文无不笼罩在西

---

① 夏中义：《学术史提问与“新世代”焦虑——兼回应王建疆教授》，《学术月刊》2016年第6期。

② 王建疆：《中国美学：主义的喧嚣与缺位》，《探索与争鸣》2012年第2期。

方的主义之下，用中国的材料论证西方的主义，但却没有中国人独创的主义，因此，主义的喧嚣是西方的主义在中国的喧嚣，主义的缺位却是中国人独享的悲剧。造成这种现状的原因在于，我们没有自觉的原创的高层次的主义意识和主义概念，因此，要不就是捡起唯物主义、唯心主义这两面与美学无关的旧旗摇动呐喊，要不就是为西方的主义支场子，替西方的主义背书。

我之所以强调主义，是因为有主义的理论建构和思想表达，是涵盖性很强的概念，如无主义的表达，很难达到高度。在当代中国的美学研究中，以某某说，某某学命名的新成果不时可以见到，但以主义命名的却很少见到。有主义的某某说、某某学跟无主义的某某学、某某说之间还是有层次之别的。我曾经有过一个美学史的提问，这就是：怎样才能成为一位美学家?[①] 我的答案是美学家的最基本要求在于提出了独创性的次级核心范畴并产生了影响。如李普斯、古鲁斯的移情说，布洛的心理距离说等。但要成为一流的美学家，仅仅提出一些原创性的次级核心范畴远远不够。还应该有主义以及在主义的旗帜下形成的流派。[②] 事实上，马克思主义、存在主义、西方马克思主义、现代主义、后现代主义虽然不是关于美学的专论，但美学的问题，文艺的问题，文化的问题，甚至宗教的、政治的、伦理的、经济的、历史学的问题，没有哪个学科能够逃离这些主义的制约。也就是说，真正有影响力的主义，实质上就是哲学。就美学学科而言，它是专业的、有技术因素（如审美心理学、实用美学）的，但美学之所以为美学，除了专业技术，还有思想，这些思想渗透在专业技术中，并无时无处不在制约着美学的专业技术。在这种专业技术和思想并置的情况下，大的思想，涵盖面广的思想，统摄力强的思想，尤其是经过理论抽象凝聚为主义的思想，就有更大的影响美学发展的统计优势。这

① 王建疆：《怎样才能成为一名美学家》，《南方文坛》2014 年第 2 期。

② 王建疆：《中国美学：主义的喧嚣与缺失》，《探索与争鸣》2012 年第 2 期。

也是美学界尊重美学专家，但更崇拜美学思想家的原因。

主义除了以上特点外，还有一个适用不适用的问题。没有主义，会缺少主心骨，但盲目地尊奉主义，也会出问题。但这个问题并非主义本身的问题，而是选择和应用主义的问题，就如吃饭是生存的必需，因而没有问题，但吃什么，怎么吃，以及吃出了问题，就与吃不吃饭本身无关，而是怎么吃，怎么选的问题。主义的反对派往往将这两个概念用混了，从而出现一概否定主义的冲动。近百年前，胡适对于自己的“多研究些问题，少谈些主义”的主张的修改，就是对这个问题上自己的偏执之见矫正的结果。

胡适于1919年7月《每周评论》第31号上发表了《多研究些问题，少谈些“主义”!》这篇影响至今的文章，但很快就分别引起了蓝志先、李大钊的撰文批评。蓝和李都认为胡适的少谈些主义论，夸大了主义的危险，而且是倒果为因，把主义本身与对主义的错用混淆了，因而因噎废食。作为讨论结果，胡适最后对自己的观点进行了调整，即把先前主张的“多研究些问题，少谈些‘主义’”改成了“多研究些具体的问题，少谈些抽象的主义”①。这里新加上去的“具体”和“抽象”的限定，说明胡适这样一位大学者并非一味地反对谈论主义，而是反对那些国人未必搞得清的抽象的因而与我们的现实联系不起来的主义。事实上，胡适的《演化论与存疑主义》《问题与主义》《易卜生主义》《非个人主义的新生活》《自由主义》等，都是关于主义的重要论文。因此，从少谈些主义到少谈些抽象的主义这种看似小小的变化，却不仅是胡适思维的深化，而且是胡适观点的公允。然而，时至今日，中国的学者们还在不假思索地套用胡适本人未曾修正过的观点，而不顾胡适本人已经修订过的新观点，不亦过乎？

① 胡适：《问题与主义》，见《胡适自选集》，安徽人民出版社2013年版，第23—37页。

中国的问题与主义之争有百年之久，说明这个“主义”出了问题。出了问题就该解决问题。如何解决？依据什么方法和路径解决？解决的目标是什么？如何勘验是否解决？对这一系列主义的问题的回答，无疑又会形成新的不同的主义，如新胡适主义、修正主义、问题主义等。这就是从问题中产生主义，这就是问题与主义的辩证法，而不是问题对主义的排除法，也不是问题对主义的兼并法。问题与主义是天生的孪生子，一个离不开一个，离开了就会有麻烦。从胡适开始的问题与主义的纷争，不断地被中国学界提起，但主义的问题总是被人们搁置，这只能说明中国学界的浅尝辄止、一知半解，更重要的在于缺少修正和创新，从而胡适成了我们搞不出主义也从未想着搞主义的借口。这一点对于撰写了十数篇有关“主义”的胡适来说，如其泉下有知又该作何感想？

中国的学者忌谈主义，表面上看是胡适的影响，实际上原因复杂得多，也深刻得多，我已有专文讨论过了①，这里不赘。但有一点可以肯定，随着时代对哲学和思想建设的吁求，该是将主义的问题变成问题的主义，从而形成有个性、有特点、原创的不同层面、不同领域的主义的时候了。

夏中义先生大量列举我的“别现代”的论文，的确有将之视为主义的意思，若有人称之为别现代主义，也未为不可。事实上，我已经在拙文《别现代：话语创新的背后》中做了如下表述：

> 别现代的提出始于对思想欠发达国家现状的忧虑，力图在全球化背景下建立中国语境，摆脱思想欠发达国家的尴尬。别现代首先是对社会形态和历史阶段的认识和把握，是对前现代、现代、后现代三种情况并存的社会结构和时代特征的认识和把握。别现代是由多种社会形态交织、矛盾、互补所构成的张力性结

① 王建疆：《思想欠发达时代的学术策略》，《中国社会科学评论》2015 年第 4 期。

构。其中充满着随机选择性和结果的难以预测性。建立在别现代基础上的别现代主义则是对别现代的价值倾向，是对别现代的统御，目的在于超越别现代，达到更为理想的存在状态，进入更高的发展境界。①

应该说，别现代是从主义的问题即“待有”出发，结合中国的现实建构问题的主义，是对特定社会形态和历史阶段的实际概括。别现代并非主义的空谈，而有具体的内涵。随着研究的深入，别现代的具体内涵会更多地展示出来。

第三节　对“美学先人祠”的诊断

“别现代”并不贬低朴学，也不是登高振臂之为，其话语创新的背后是对中国社会形态和社会历史阶段的考察和解构主义、语义分析方法的运用。“别”的挖掘和使用就是语义分析、语义否定、语义清理的结果，但它不是不要现代性，不是告别现代性，而是说，别现代就不是严格意义上的现代。别现代也不是要解构现代性，相反，别现代兼具解构与建构的功能。“别”虽具法国解构主义大师德里达“延异”（différance）之妙，但不同处却在于“别”有着中华文化之根，而 différance 却是一个生造的词。别现代的“别”，兼具“不要”“告别”“另外”“别扭”“错别”“别车”等古今含义，但又都不是这些含义中的某一个。由于我们处于现代、前现代、后现代交集纠葛的时代，既有现代、前现代、后现代的元素，又不能简单地将其归结为现代或前现代或后现代。就好像一个人，一只脚站在了现代的楼梯上，另一只脚却还在前现代的泥潭中，同时又抱着后现代的大腿。因此，用“别现代”就最为“神似”地概括了这一时代的总体特征。别现

① 王建疆：《别现代：话语创新的背后》，《上海文化》2015 年第 12 期。

代是在解构"现代性""复杂现代性"[①]"可选择的现代性"（alternative modernity）[②]"另类现代性"（alternative modernity）[③]基础上的建构。别现代不认为我们只有唯一的现代性，而是同时存在着后现代性和前现代性。"别现代"之所以能够成为热词，就在于它与它所概括的社会现实形态和社会历史阶段的特征能够天衣无缝地吻合起来；能够概括而又巧妙地表达对于社会形态和历史发展阶段的看法和思想；能够使人过目不忘。从这个意义上说，至少在哲学和美学领域，思辨的方法、分析哲学的方法，在思想和哲学建构方面，至少有着为传统的朴学方法难以企及的地方。

夏中义先生提倡朴学，贬低主义的一个抓手就是将我国著名的文学家钱锺书供在了美学的"先人祠"。但于我看来，需要朴学力主的"证伪"。首先要问的是，为什么没有宗白华的地位？其次要问的是，先人祠入选的标准是什么？却未见夏中义先生的详论。

夏中义先生对于中国美学先人祠的排序是：

> 纵览20世纪以来的中国美学（文论）历程，此"新世代"拟排位"第五代"。这就是说，在"新世代"尚未被纳入美学"先人祠"之前，此"先人祠"已将各代最具标志性的"本纪"级人物，按辈分排序如下：第一代王国维（1877—1927）→第二代朱光潜（1897—1986）→第三代钱锺书（1910—1998）（→第四代李泽厚（1930—）。"新世代"人氏若亦想留名青史，请拨冗追忆哲贤当年是以何"角色自期"来兼济使命，又是在怎样融贯中西文化的视界中，令其学思巍然而成中华美学（文论）的断

---

① 汪行福：《"复杂现代性"框架下的核心价值建构》，《中国社会科学》2013年第7期。

② ［美］安德鲁·芬伯格：《可选择的现代性》，陆俊等译，中国社会科学出版社2003年版。

③ 刘康：《毛泽东和阿尔都塞的遗产：辩证法的问题式——另类现代性以及文化革命》，田立新译，《湖南科技大学学报》（社会科学版）2005年第6期。

代性峰值，至今让海内外仰慕不已。

这里对中国美学充满了赞誉、期许，着实令人感动。但是，钱锺书是怎样进入美学先人祠的呢？请看下面对《管锥编》的评论：

> 于是读者惊讶，邀法国斯泰尔夫人来附和《毛诗正义》，让英国詹姆士、伍尔芙来牵手《楚辞·九章》，此类天方夜谭式的奇观在钱的笔下，竟显得如此自然近乎天籁。这般精巧、精湛、精美、精妙地熔古今中外于一炉的中国美学（文论），海内外谁会不翘大拇指情不自禁地赞叹且致敬呢？

钱锺书先生的故事我们听得多了，但夏中义先生这段描述还是蛮有意思的，读起来很痛快。但痛快之余却很痛苦。当人们对伟大思想的期许被文学修辞所代替，当翘起的大拇指对着一个书篓子的时候，那么，尚处于思想欠发达而又不甘于欠发达而努力赶超世界先进水平的国家①，它还有希望吗？

学术研究是不能以个人的偏好来代替学术通则的。夏先生极力赞美的钱锺书的家训——“默存”，虽然是一个成功的个案，但绝不是具有普遍意义的理想的治学之境。早在960多年前的范仲淹就提出了“宁鸣而死，不默而生”的主张，应该是中国思想史上政治讽谏自由观的诗意化表达，是一种有着社会担当的表达方式或更准确地说，是一种鸣放方式。因此，钱锺书的“默存”就中国传统来说，仅具有个我性，而无普遍性。而且就美学和人文学科的使命而言，范仲淹与其自由主张相联系的“先天下之忧而忧，后天下之乐而乐”，无疑其境界远在钱锺书之上。如不顾及这些事实，而囿于一隅，难免影响其学说的普适性。退一步讲，就如夏中义先生所说，思想家的历史责任

① 王建疆：《思想欠发达时代的学术策略》，《中国社会科学评价》2015年第4期。

在于“提出并回答时代的重大命题”① 而论，如果按钱锺书先生的家训都“默存”了，还怎么提出并回答时代的重大命题呢？再说，中国几代学者所盼望、所梦想的是什么？不就是“百家争鸣”吗？如都默存了，还鸣什么？还有学术和思想的存在和发展吗？我不否认作为个案，陈寅恪的独立人格，钱锺书的知识都有不可否认的价值，但就学术的通则而言，并无普遍意义。其学案的发微也就是对于历史的回顾，对于教训的汲取，但他们不可能成为学问的楷模。因为现时代不仅是信息时代而且是信息爆炸的时代了，知识的适用性已居首位。夏中义先生推崇默存，但自己并不默存，努力建构属于个人风格的夏氏朴学，以朴学发微思想，才有今日之成就。因此，按照夏氏朴学诊断法，我的诊断是：

诊断结果一：大师可以学也可以不学，那要看学习者自我的选择，而非外在的派定。在学术民主时代，任何强以大师的道路为别人的道路，以大师模式为别人的模式的主张和做法，都是对大师的误读，甚至是解构而非建构。

诊断结果二：把钱锺书先生从“美学的先人祠”中请出去。原因很简单，虽然钱锺书先生是一个了不起的文学家和兼通中外文献学的大师，但于美学而言，并没有比较系统的理论，也没有美学的主张，没有美学的次级核心范畴，或许也有一些美学观点和美学主张，我们都曾遇到过，但都掩埋在他的大量的中外文献对举中，缺乏理论所必需的明晰性、抽象性、思辨性、论断性和逻辑性。另外，中国美学界除了夏先生，会有多少人称钱锺书为美学家的？

诊断结果三：夏先生列举的钱锺书大师楷模，于文献学而言自有意义，但于美学而言，似无关系。不仅没有关系，而且只能显示“思想欠发达”的片段。在一篇讨论重大理论问题，甚至是主义的问题

---

① 夏中义：《思想家的历史责任：提出并回答时代重大命题——答〈探索与争鸣〉记者问》，《探索与争鸣》2014 年第 3 期。

时，却将理论降为故事，将思想稀释于赞许，其理论的逻辑性在哪里，思想的思辨性又在哪里？

诊断结果四：美学的哲学根源决定了它永远无法脱离形而上学思辨和主义的建构。欲提出和解决重大社会问题者，不去砥砺思想、扩展视野、提高境界，而是一股脑儿地钻进个人风格极浓的朴学中“默存”起来，却又反对主义的建构，这岂不与思想的建构愈行愈远？

总体结论是：第一步，重新回到胡适矫正过的问题与主义上来，这就是“多研究些具体的问题，少谈些抽象的主义”而非“多研究些问题，少谈些主义”。第二步，“多研究一些具体的问题，大胆地谈论一些具体的主义”。第三步，“多研究一些问题，多建立一些主义”。第四步，“从主义的问题中建立起问题的主义”。

当此思想欠发达时代小学盛行、大道隐匿之时，不啻于中国美学和文论，中国的哲学、人文学科、社会科学，中国的学术、思想、理论中到底缺少什么，我们的“待有”是什么，这难道还不是一个值得思考的问题吗？

第五章

别现代：美学之外与后现代之后

——对威尔施·沃尔夫冈引领的一种国际美学潮流的反动*

美学在中国，近年来应和着一些西方美学家提出的命题而讨论所谓的“回潮”或“回归”现象。2014 年 6 月在华东师大王元化档案馆召开的上海市高校文艺理论界美学研讨会就以“美的回潮”为主题展开讨论。“美的回潮”（Return of Beauty）是德国美学家沃尔夫冈·威尔施发表在中国一家学术杂志上的英文论文①。这篇文章是针对 2005 年德国柏林举行的“国际美节”对美的回潮/回归的讨论而发的。沃尔夫冈·威尔施曾因其《重构美学》一书中“日常生活审美化”的命题而在中国美学界引起过热烈而又长久的讨论。而他于 2013 年波兰克拉科夫市由亚格龙尼安大学主办的第十九届世界美学大会上宣读的 *Aesthetics Beyond Aesthetics*② 即“美学在美学之外”一文，也在中国引起了积极反响，尤其是受到 2013 年新当选的国际美协主席、中国社会科学院高建平先生的大力推介。高建平发表了数篇文章包括 2014 年发表的

---

* 本章曾发表于《上海师范大学学报》（哲学社会科学版）2015 年第 1 期，并为《社会科学报》转载。

① 沃尔夫冈·威尔施：《美的回潮?》（*The Return of Beauty*?），《文艺理论研究》2013 年第 1 期。

② Wolfgang Welsch, *Aesthetics Beyond Aesthetics*, book of abstracts, 19th International Congress of Aesthetics, Krakow 2013 Poland, www. ica2013. pl.

《美学的超越与回归》[①]，系统地阐发了“美学之外”的“超越”和“美学回归”的命题，使美学的回潮或回归成为中国美学界关注的问题。虽然沃尔夫冈·威尔施的美学的“回潮”（return）是指一种现象，即美学由冷变热，由较少人关注而变得有更多人关注了，高建平的美学“回归”（return）指的是一种研究方法、一种研究倾向和学术趋势，即美学要回归到美学之外的自然和社会生活中去，但后者却正好是沃尔夫冈·威尔施所讲的“transcend”（超越）和“beyond”（超越）的主题，因此，他们在精神实质上没有什么不同，相反，是一脉相承。对这些具有国际性倾向和主导性的热门话题展开讨论，对于时下不是那么景气的美学研究来说也许不无裨益。

第一节 “美学之外”的“回归”

一种研究既在对象之内又在对象之外，这在当代应该是一种具有普遍性的方法。其主要功用在于突破专业视障，获得灵感，另辟蹊径。现代自然科学、社会科学和人文学科研究的很多成就就来自突破已有研究对象和固有研究方法的跨学科联合攻关。中国古代著名诗人陆游早就有“功夫在诗外”[②] 的说法。都是一种跳出三界看三界的智慧。沃尔夫冈·威尔施的“在美学之外”，指的正是这种方法论智慧或他自诩的“新美学实践或战略”[③]。

沃尔夫冈·威尔施在《美学超出美学之外》中认为：“早在 1995 年，我就提出美学的原理应该超越狭隘的艺术框架，而走向反映艺术之外的审美现象，即要有在科学中、在政治中、在经济中、在设计中、在生态中、在生活世界中的美学，一个主要的论据是，美学自身

---

① 高建平：《美学的超越与回归》，《上海大学学报》2014 年第 1 期。

② 陆游：《示子遹》，《剑南诗稿》卷七十八。

③ Wolfgang Welsch, *Aesthetics Beyond Aesthetics*, book of abstracts, 19th International Congress of Aesthetics, Krakow 2013 Poland, www. ica2013. pl.

特别是在现代早已经超越了狭隘的艺术框架并与艺术之外的现实相联系并建立了娱乐关系，如与政治、现实世界等的联系。同时，对我来说，艺术和艺术家们已经朝着这个娱乐的方向前进了。今天，不仅美学超出以艺术为中心的美学的限制这种转变是非常明显的，而且，艺术本身也已超出了自治艺术的金丝笼而走向具有决定性意义的审美实践。"① 沃尔夫冈沿着这个美学在美学之外的思路，进一步提出了"艺术超出艺术之外"（Art today is art beyond art, i. e. Beyond autonomist art）尤其是超出自治主义艺术之外的观点。②

从沃尔夫冈·威尔施以上的超越论看，已不仅仅是一种方法论，而是一种建立新实践美学的战略。正如他于 1997 年出版的 *Undoing Aesthetics*③（陆扬、张岩冰译为《重构美学》）④ 一书的题目用了"undoing"这个英文词来加以表述的那样，目的就在于要为美学解套，要突破美学的界限，超出美学的范围。他说："我们不能再做艺术本质论的囚徒。但是它可能会进一步证明，突破这整个框架，即美学与艺术论的传统等式，甚为必要。艺术论内在的多元化，即由艺术单一的概念性分析转变为对艺术的不同类型、范式和观念的分析，应该补充以美学外在层面上的多元化，将其学科领域扩大至超艺术的问题上来。"⑤ 可见，undo 的实质，在沃尔夫冈·威尔施那里就是突破美学和艺术的原有框架，实现超越，实现"多元化"。

高建平沿着沃尔夫冈·威尔施的这种超越论进一步提出了"杂美学"式的"回归"（return）⑥ 论。他说："美学的超越不是追求一种

---

① Wolfgang Welsch, *Aesthetics Beyond Aesthetics*, book of abstracts, 19th International Congress of Aesthetics, Krakow 2013 Poland, www. ica2013. pl

② Ibid.

③ Wolfgang Welsh, *Undoing Aesthetics*, Sage Publication Ltd. , 1997.

④ 沃尔夫冈·威尔施：《重构美学》，陆扬、张岩冰译，上海译文出版社 2002 年版。

⑤ 同上书，第 108 页。

⑥ 参见高建平《美学的超越与回归》中的英文提要 *The Transcendence and Return of Aesthetics*，《上海大学学报》2014 年第 1 期。

超越性，而是超出传统美学，关注生活实践、环境生态以及社会文化。超越美学，不是美学的提‘纯’，而是‘杂’，成为‘杂美学’。”① 这种杂美学，也就是美学超越传统之后的回归，是一种新美学的建立。他说：“在当代社会，图像泛滥，消费文化主导，艺术和审美都发生着深刻的变化。在这种情况下，我们需要美学的回归。这种回归，不是重回传统美学，而是创造新美学。新美学要创新阐释艺术的功能，要重新定义审美在生活中的意义，也要重新建构自然环境、社会文化等各个领域的美学。”进而言之，“这种‘杂美学’的第一要义，当然是要走出传统美学的边界。从这个意义上讲，我们首先要做的，是说明这种美学不是什么。当沃尔夫冈·韦尔施说要‘undoing aesthetics’之时，他说的是要对既有的 aesthetics 做 undo 的工作。具体说来，要走出一些美学的基本前提”。可见，建立突破传统的思辨美学的新实践美学，是国际美学界不少人的共识。

高建平进一步指出，这种回归论实际上也是近年来国际美学界的一种倾向：“这是对美学复兴的呼唤，也是对正在出现的现实过程和学术发展趋势的描述。”其实，在我看来，这种来自欧洲美学的回归论，就是一种新实践美学，其进一步的表述应该是“美学要行动”。2013 年在波兰召开的第十九届世界美学大会的主题就是“行动中的美学”或“美学在行动”（Aesthetics in action），强调关注美学在社会生活中的作用，要美学有所作为、有所行动。

但是，这场由沃尔夫冈·威尔施打头，在国际上蓬勃兴起的超越论美学或新实践美学，或杂美学，或行动美学，或回归美学，却面临这样的难题。

1. 在美学之外，仍无法消除美学在“回归自然和社会生活”的过程中学与用二者难以兼得的难题。美学之“学”，就是“问”与“答”，就是问题之思，是概括总结、阐释、论证，都是思辨的过程，

---

① 高建平：《美学的超越与回归》，《上海大学学报》2014 年第 1 期。

是理论产生的过程。而美学之用却是要应用，要行动。但在行动中的美学却不得不脱离原理层面的问、答、思，在应用的层面上，跟一般的创造、设计、规划、鉴赏、批评等无大的区别。它可能就是剧情，也可能是表演，是对剧情和表演的鉴赏和评判，也可能是行为艺术，是健美和美容、文身，也可能就是装饰，是规划和设计，但都不是美学之所以为美学的理论研究。

因此，美学回归社会和自然的行动一直面对这样的悖论，纯粹无为的理论思辨的美学，除了在大学里为个人晋升职称和争取奖金外，对社会一无用处。因此，在频繁举行的美女选秀，歌王选秀、美术会展、设计大赛等活动中，从未见到所谓的美学家评委的身影，美学家已成为无用之人。尽管“美学”和“审美”这些词都被用在了发廊和洗脚店的门牌上用以招揽顾客，但美学家们却黯然出局，并被人们忘记。但另一方面，美学一旦脱离了问答思而进入实践层面，就只是美学的应用，而非美学研究。现代社会的细致分工，已经导致理论研究与技术应用的分离，那种既搞理论又搞应用的全能型专门人才已是凤毛麟角。尽管现实的需要呼吁美学要实践、要行动，呼吁美学家要行动起来，但是，一旦遇到专业的艺术领域和专业的规划、设计、展现领域以及与之相伴的技术领域，美学家们能否胜任，能否行动，就成了问题。面对具体领域、具体问题，绝大多数美学家只能是浅尝辄止，不会有大的作为。否则，社会中涉及美学元素的机构、组织、活动，岂非成了美学家的天下，而专业的艺术家、设计师、创意大师岂不都要失业了？

所谓美学要回归社会生活实践中去，回归行动中去，实质上还是回到艺术家和工程师、技术员的领地去，而非美学家的领地。如此一来，所谓的美学在行动，实际上只是美学被行动而已。当代流行的概念艺术、装置艺术为了证明一种美学观念，或者为了反对一种美学思想而从事的创作过程，实质上都是美学观念被艺术家图解了、行动了，而非相反。在这种情况下，美学成了艺术家手中的工具，或者成

了玩物。如建筑上的将整个大楼装饰成底朝天，在单杠上挂一条铁索等，就是为了反对对称、和谐的美学观念，就是为了表现反运动的美学思想。

因此，超越美学理论和美学思辨，在美学之外，美学回归、美学在行动中、新实践美学、杂美学等，虽然听起来新颖，也不乏一种探索，但在具体的实践中，美学之内也好，美学之外也好，都无法克服美学有用无学与有学无用的悖论，因而只是一厢情愿。

2. 美学超出美学之外的首倡者沃尔夫冈·威尔施认为，美学之所以要超出美学之外，就在于经典美学基于狭隘的艺术论。但是，我认为沃尔夫冈的这种观点似是而非。众所周知，把美学建立在艺术论基础上，的确是黑格尔的功绩，他把美学称为艺术哲学。谢林也是这样的主张。乃至鲍桑葵的美学史，塔塔尔凯维奇的美学史也都以艺术论展开。但沃尔夫冈却忽视了一个西方美学史上的重要事实，这就是，席勒美学从艺术走向了社会生活和审美教育。而近代美学之父康德则很少谈艺术，也从未有过美学是关于艺术的哲学的说法。但就经典美学的影响力而言，康德的美学属于纯粹美学原理，是横跨自然、生活、伦理、艺术的具有最大统摄性的大美学，而非艺术论的小美学。因此，所谓的超越论，只是一个基于以偏概全的不周全的说法。其基础不是整个美学，也不是德国古典美学，而只是德国古典美学中的艺术论美学。因此，这一狭小的基座是否能撑得起对整个古典美学的否定就不是没有问题。事实上，美学原理从来就不局限于艺术论，艺术至今也不只是纯艺术，而且越来越不是了。因此，超越什么的问题，需要首先选准对象，而非盲目的一概而论。

如果把超出纯艺术之外、超出传统的经典美学之外、从纯粹美学到杂美学，要美学回到自然和社会生活中，视为美学的回归，似乎词不达意。我们不禁要再问一遍，这种美学是在回归吗？实际上，所谓回归，是一个有方向的动词，是一种可逆的行为方式。但是，可逆，是有条件的。璞散之为器，但器碎不能为璞。因此，杂美学也好，回

归也好，实质上都如美学之外的论者所说，是要超越欧洲 18、19 世纪以来建立在人文理性基础上的美学思想，把审美从无功利、超概念的定理中放逐出去，而代之以功利主义的、感官解放的后现代美学。这显然是反传统美学，是超出，而非回归。再说，如果美学放弃了基本理论而落入自然和生活中，那么，美学是否还有存在的必要？事实上，沃尔夫冈·威尔施回归论的核心就是要借突破学科边界而否定 18、19 世纪以来建立在人文理性基础上的美学思想，是后现代在否定工具理性的同时殃及人文理性，这是美学的倒退而非回归，更非创新。这种否定人文理性的后现代美学是否能提供美学之外的出路？我看未必。美学作为人文学科，一旦脱离了人文理性，就必然会成为杂乱无章的感官膨胀、欲念滋生的非理性美学①。

杂美学取代纯粹美学，感性美学取代理性美学，表面上看是后现代美学的胜利，但这种在美学之外的胜利，并不能提升美学作为人文学科的精神品质，相反，很有可能导致美学的非学理化，同时，也会导致如沃尔夫冈所说的②，当代艺术家谈艺术无疑是在谈美学，这种僭越所造成的艺术的学理化。以上两种由于僭越而带来的可能性后果对美学研究和艺术家创作来说，都不是什么好事。

事实上，所谓的“杂美学”，在当代中国不是没有，而是泛滥成灾，到了几乎只要是一种行业就有一种美学的地步。如工业美学、农业美学、医疗美学、整容美学、养生美学、军事美学、战争美学、格斗美学、暴力美学、教育美学、科学美学、体育美学、运动美学、经济美学、证券美学、商业美学、美女经济学等，不一而足。在一种繁荣的假象背后却是美学内涵的缺失，徒有美学之名，而无美学之实。

---

① 参见朱立元《对西方后现代主义文论消极影响的反思性批判》，《文艺研究》2014 年第 1 期。

② 沃尔夫冈·威尔施：“Many contemporary artists, when speaking of their work, prefer to talk about aesthetics, not about art.”（当代许多的艺术家，当他们谈及艺术作品时，与其说是在谈艺术，还不如说是在谈美学）见 Wolfgang Welsch, *Aesthetics Beyond Aesthetics*, book of abstracts, 19th International Congress of Aesthetics, Krakow 2013 Poland, www. ica2013. pl.

它们是地道的杂美学，却既不能提出新颖的美学观点，又不能解决行业内的美学问题，只是美学与行业名称的黏合而已。这样的杂美学只能制造虚假的中国美学繁荣现象，却永远无法进入美学的殿堂。这种没有内涵的、圈地式的美学，虽然杂色斑斓，但于美学的发展有害无利，很有可能引起人们学术思想上的茫然和对美学的失望[①]。

3. 所谓的“回归就是创新”，令人费解。既然是创新，为何又要回归？回归（return）是回去的意思。创新是向前的意思，二者泾渭分明。如果按回归生活就是创新的说法，则不可能再有创新。众所周知，19 世纪法国思想家卢梭早就有了回归自然的思想，19 世纪俄国美学家车尔尼雪夫斯基早有“美是生活”的命题，虽然这些思想并非最先进的唯物主义思想，但却早已将美学植根于自然和社会生活的土壤中。再如果按美学的分工或学科分化而言，20 世纪初英国的工业工艺设计理念深入人心，1919 年德国的包豪斯艺术设计学校成立，伴随工业设计和建筑设计而生的实用美学或应用美学早就在工业生产、城市建筑和日常生活中被娴熟地应用了，而且，实用美学代表了科技、生产、艺术相融合的发展方向[②]。实用美学在中国也已受到重视。20 世纪 90 年代李泽厚先生就指出：技术设计的美学要比哲学的美学和文艺美学更重要，“因为它是关系到广大人民物质生活和精神生活的大问题”，技术美“是社会美的核心和基础，它比自然美、艺术美重要得多”[③]。传统的经典美学理论在发展的过程中，并没有完全与审美实践脱节，相反，其结合日趋紧密。因此，Aesthetics Beyond Aesthetics 中文译名作为一个命题，要美学舍弃了它的理论传统而回归生活、回归社会、走向实践，有多少新意？又有多大的必要？再就这一命题的实质而言，这种超越传统美学的回归，实际上是要美学行

---

① 王建疆：《当代中国美学评析》，《学术论坛》1994 年第 4 期。

② 参见凌继尧《美学十五讲》第十讲，北京大学出版社 2003 年版。又见徐恒醇《设计美学》第四章“审美范畴论”之第二节“技术美”，清华大学出版社 2006 年版。

③ 李泽厚：《走我自己的路》，安徽文艺出版社 1994 年版，第 620 页。

动，而完全舍弃理论建设的“行动”，是要美学家们舍其长而用其短，势必造成适得其反的效果，搞不好就会邯郸学步。

“美学之外”的命题意在美学要另辟蹊径，不妨被视为开出的一剂挽回美学颓势的药方。当前美学的困境来自上不能以理论的信誉和逻辑的力量使学者们保持对于所谓“第一哲学”的信服，下又不能解决日常生活中的问题，成为不上不下的“无用”之学。2013 年的世界美学大会“美学在行动”在征稿之初就显示了这种尴尬。以至于第十八届国际美协主席柯提斯·卡特（Curtis Carter）在会前致全体美学会会员的信中辩解道：美学在行动，并非要美学家们都到大街上去，到舞台上去，到实验室去，到生产车间去，而是要大家关注当下的艺术和审美活动。[①] 但当他讲到“关注”时，已与他先前所说的“行动”不搭界了。

总之，我认为，超越美学也好，回归美学也好，杂美学也好，行动美学也好，也不论美学能否行动，美学是否就要在美学之外，也不论后现代主义思潮到底对中国产生了什么样的影响，这种立足于后现代语境的探讨都在为美学走出困境而努力着，值得尊重，也值得关注。但问题在于，这种企图通过超越经典美学理论和思辨传统而摆脱困境的努力是否路径正确，是否就是必然有效的，是否符合中国的美学实际，值得我们思考。

第二节　后现代之后将会是什么图景

后现代主义是一种影响至深至广的思潮，其对中国美学的影响正面与反面并存。就其正面影响而言，其反工具理性、反权威、去中心、终

① Newsletter：IAA 19th International Aesthetics Congress，“What might Aesthetics in action mean? It is not a call to abandon research and teaching and turn to the streets. Rather it is to take stock of what we can do in making sure to investigate opportunities to connect aesthetics to other aspects of understanding and action in the world. ”

止宏大叙事、解构现成的思想，就有批判性、反思性的启迪，促使中国美学走向开放的多元的发展道路，带来各种美学观点应运而生，不拘一格。实践论美学与后实践美学的论辩就是超出实践真理观信仰而专注学术的突出的一例。其反本质的思想方法，冲击着20世纪50年代以来形成的美学形而上学思维定式，帮助美学家摆脱了美学归属于唯心主义还是唯物主义的束缚，也不再恪守实践的神圣性，走向了更具有符合美学实际和现代价值的学科建设上。后现代带来的思想解放，也使中国美学具有了国际眼光，并积极寻求与西方美学的对话，如参加艺术终结论和生态美学、身体美学方面的国际性学术讨论等①。

本文提及的美学回潮、回归说，正好体现了一种后现代思潮。当然，在思想上的反本质、去中心、解构经典之外，后现代还有一种回到社会生活，回到原初的倾向，与资本主义现代性相对抗，与一些陈旧无用的所谓经典相反动，与艺术的伪装和美学的矫饰相抵触，都具有积极的方面。美国雕塑家基顿·韦恩来到中国甘肃秦安县这一人类第一个地表建筑的诞生地——大地湾文化遗址所在地，烧制了很多陶碗、陶盘和陶罐送给农村人，并声称这就是后现代艺术。虽然老乡们也很感动，但最感到震撼的却是美术学院的师生们：原来时髦的、高深莫测的后现代就是这么回事！后现代的回归性的确具有质朴的、原生态的、大众的属性，用在中国抵挡由福尔马林、过氧化氢、三聚氰胺、苏丹红、瘦肉精、敌敌畏等无数化学专利品伪饰起来的非常具有审美视觉效果的有毒食品，也就是拔掉美学帮凶的外衣，复原一个安全卫生的世界，也具有实在可行的效果。

但是，后现代美学理论的否定性、回归性，除了积极意义外，也有不少弊端②。尤其是其身在其中而又反对自身的做法，显得相互矛

---

① 参见朱立元《试论后现代主义文论思潮在当代中国的积极影响》，《上海大学学报》（社会科学版）2014年第1期。

② 参见朱立元《对西方后现代主义文论消极影响的反思性批判》，《文艺研究》2014年第1期。

盾和相互对立。如在理论方面，极力夸大艺术与美无关的思想①，而遮蔽艺术也与美学密切相关的现实，就很容易动摇人们对于美学的信心。更有甚者，如果按丹徒的新艺术终结论，艺术已经终结于1964年的某个月某一天了，那么，艺术都终结了，还有什么必要讨论艺术以及文艺美学？同样，在艺术创作上，打着回归原生态的旗号，裸露身体的诱惑，表现性交、暴力等原始本能，这些后现代的艺术，就一直为人们所诟病。

否定艺术、否定经典美学、解构崇高、反宏大叙事、反对阐释等，完全是一种后现代去中心、非本质思想和方法的体现，表现出后现代主义解构传统美学的策略。但作为一个美学研究者，在大潮涌起之时，还是应该保持自己独立的判断，对后现代主义美学保持冷静的分析。尤其是在对待经典美学原理的问题上，更应该做联系实际的分析。事实上，经典美学原理，尤其是康德建立在二律背反基础上的美学原理，至今仍然有着涵盖古今、统摄审美理论、影响审美实践的功能。比如，被后现代美学所诟病的审美无功利理论，就是康德美学的精髓。其博大深刻之处在于它同时含摄了审美在现象上和在本质上不同的功利特点。这就是，审美是无功利的功利，是无目的而合乎目的。即所谓的表面无功利，而根子里是功利的。这一二律背反同时涉及了美的系统功利性和个体功利性、审美的表面无功利性和本质功利性以及审美中功利的隐蔽性特点、二重性特点、系统性特点和生成性特点，这要比绝对的审美无功利论和审美就是为了功利的主张无论在思辨的深刻程度上，还是在与审美现实的接近上，在审美实践的谋略上，都要深刻得多、全面得多、辩证得多、合理得多、高明得多。因此，在后现代美学企图借助解构狭隘艺术论美学的藩篱而否定整个经典美学，解构经典美学的同时，后现代美学自身的合理性同样应该受

---

① 沃尔夫冈·威尔施：《美的回潮？》（*The Return of Beauty*?），《文艺理论研究》2013年第1期。

到审视和质疑，甚至首先应该受到分析和批判。在肯定后现代美学对当代美学的贡献的同时，对其极端性、盲目性和危害性，都应该有个清醒的认识。只有这样，才能在创新和守正之间保持理性的维度和必要的张力。

在反思后现代美学思潮的时候，除了首先面对后现代的合法性之外，还有一个后现代的持久性问题，也就是说，后现代会永远无休止地“后”下去吗？

沃尔夫冈·威尔施的美学在美学之外的理论来自后现代对于启蒙时代康德、黑格尔建立起来的美学法则的解构和对艺术原理的背弃。后现代以所谓的审美现代性否定现代主义的工具理性，包括自启蒙时代以来的理性主义，通过反对无功利论正在将经典美学打入无本质的地狱。人类以往苦心经营建构起来的美学大厦将在后现代无本质、无中心、无权威的三无论证中走向末路。但后现代在否定了现代，又否定了古代和古典之后，就会独步六合，成为永生不败吗？我看未必。借助歌德的说法，任何理论都是灰色的，生命之树长青。后现代也不会因为否定了现代和古典就从此而青春永驻了。相反，后现代自身也难逃被解构和被“后掉”的命运。

1. 后现代必然导致后后现代，原因有三。

一是时间之矢的不可逆，今天的后现代，在未来必然成为现代的一部分，不可能是永远的后现代。“现代”这个词本身就是生成性概念，在中世纪的教会中就已产生。当今世纪的现代，几个世纪之后必然成为近代。后现代是不可能永远后下去的。

二是后现代来自现代主义的自反式思维和自反式运动。后现代的无本质、非理性、无中心、无权威、不可阐释的信念，殃及后现代自身存在的稳定性和凝聚态。因此，后现代虽然是一道亮丽的风景线，但这道风景线由于自身的不确定性和离散性，总有退去的时候。后现代必然会被来自自己思想内部的革命性因素“后掉”，就如现代被后现代“后掉”一样。事实上，在后现代时期，后后现代已经悄然兴

起。这一基于人类语言表达局限的新词，的确昭示了后现代的好景不长。

三是按辩证法规则，事物的发展不是直线运动的，而是在正反作用中前进。后现代只是历史进程中的一环，而非终极的形态。如果把“后”作为一种超越，那么，后现代将必然会在否定之否定中被超越、被“后”掉。

2. 后现代主义是思想玩家们的舞台，但也是这些玩家们自我终结的场所。说他们是玩家，就在于后现代的思想家们各自制定规则又同时否定规则，消解意义但又彰显意义。就如后现代行为艺术家那样，一方面解构现有的伦理道德和艺术规范；但另一方面又极力通过媒体放大各种惊世骇俗的挑战伦理和艺术规则的艺术事件。玩家们虽然玩得开心，但无限制地解构和消解意义，也使他们的所作所为日趋无意义，日趋游戏化。因此，可以预言，极端的后现代之后将是西西弗的隐喻现实化之时。到那时，思想玩家将为玩思想付出终身徒劳无功的代价。丹徒关于艺术终结于1964年的某一天的终结论被终结了。原因在于艺术没有终结，而是在蓬勃地发展，而且也不可能终结，相反，所有关于艺术终结的预言、判定、理论不管在逻辑游戏中如何游刃有余但都已被证明是远离事实的臆说。美学家和文艺理论家在玩艺术终结论的过程中自我陶醉，却将自己的理论终结。

3. 如果继续沿着西方后现代的惯性前行，那么，后现代之后将是美学的无厘头时代，也就是德勒兹所谓的千高原比喻、块茎理论欢呼胜利的时代。利奥塔的结束宏大叙事论和反崇高论在将古典主义和现代主义摧毁的同时，也使后现代之后的美学变得无足轻重，出现普利高津描述的混沌时代。因此，后现代之后应该是摆在我们面前的一个值得重视的问题。

美学作为理论，作为思想，应该有理论和思想的预见性。要像处在19世纪的马克思思考和预测世界文学的来临那样，要在前现代中思考现代，在现代中思考后现代，在后现代中回望、审视现代、前现

代，同时思考后后现代。只有这样，才有可能保持思想独立和理论创新。否则，只能被动地应付，盲目地顺从。

在当今美学回潮/回归之际，超越以往的顺习而为，借他山之石在后现代美学之外思考后现代美学；在美学回归生活之际，恢复美学的思想的和理论的建设；在美学趋杂之时，把握美学的纯粹。这种貌似“反其道而行之”的后现代思维方式，实际上正是在后现代的离散状态中，吸收其否定之功力以为守正之用，凝聚其超越之能量而为发展之需。

第三节　中国美学的别现代

我这里用“中国美学”这样一个在有些西方学者眼里极具民族主义（我们叫它爱国主义）色彩的名词，是因为我们除了使用“中国美学”这个词外，找不到可以具体指称在中国发生的具有国际影响的美学现象。比如某某学派的美学，某某主义的美学。事实上，中国美学在整体上缺乏原创，甚至连原创性的命题都很少见得到。我们在跟风随潮。美的回潮，不论它是中国风，还是国际风，就如当年发生在中国的知识青年上山下乡一样，潮起潮落。中国美学何时才能不跟风？

中国美学在回潮或回归的路上，其窘境愈发凸显。表现为美学原创性的衰微和美学学科的虚胀。与中国美学博士点和美学研究中心、美学研究所雨后春笋般的建立相比，中国美学一直被“是中国美学还是美学在中国”的问题所困扰。此问题之要害在于怀疑中国有美学。同样，与目前中国的图书中只要有一种行业，就有一种美学的繁荣相比，中国美学并没有因为这种杂美学而步入学术的殿堂，也没有像迪扎英、包豪斯那样有效地服务社会。相反，有的只是教人感到，美学的书是什么人都可以写的。这并非后现代的解构，而是自己糟蹋行当。这种外延广大而内涵微小的中国杂美学无处不透露出美学学科的

虚胖和美学原创的羸弱。人们为什么会怀疑中国美学的存在呢，原因在于中国美学几乎没有中国思想和中国特色，完全是西方的五花八门的主义的传声筒。

造成这种现象的原因有四个。

1. 理论的时代意识不强，很容易盲从。面对汹涌而入的西方美学，中国美学界鲜有考虑中西方在现代性上的代差，即我们同时处在现代、后现代以及前现代中，由于这种代差必然带来西方理论不适应中国的问题。但现实却是，对西方论著的争相翻译、争相介绍、争相诠释、争相推广，丧失了自己的理论出发点和理论立场，完全跟着西方潮流走，不断地被西方的理论所忽悠。当我们还在被行为艺术的理论搞得一头雾水的时候，那种回归原始的陶罐、碗碟又展现在了我们面前。在农民感到没什么了不起的时候，我们的艺术家和美学家们却感到了惊讶。这显然是跟风而落伍的时代笑话。这种误解将导致跟不上却反而要跟的恶性循环。

2. 理论建构的意识不强。中国美学中关于美学理论研究的文章和书籍很多，尤其是关于西方美学家及其理论的研究很多。但是，中国美学家大都是从事美学理论研究，而没有自己的理论建构，如像西方美学家那样堂而皇之地提出一种理论、一个主义来。理论建构的意识是理论建构的原初，没有这个原初，哪来自己的理论？由于我国哲学社会科学界的思想解放还没有达到个体要当思想家和理论家的自觉程度，因此，只有理论研究而无建构自己理论的意识也就在所难免。

3. 理论原创不足。由于理论建构意识不强，只在做一些诠释理论、推介理论的工作，因而没有原创性的理论。在面对诸如后现代的反本质说、超越论时，不能及时地从理论的高度予以回应，而是停留在转述和引申上，替西方后现代美学背书。

4. 美学上没有形成主义。西方的美学是以主义和流派而彰显和传播的。当然，也有以个人名义命名的美学，如康德美学、黑格尔美学等，但他们名字的背后都有主义的支撑。如康德主义、新康德主

义；黑格尔主义、新黑格尔主义；等等。而放眼中国美学，则很难找到由中国人创建的主义的美学①。就是像李泽厚这样被国际承认的大家，论起主义来也还是交白卷。没有了主义，就没有了标杆，更谈不上高度。因而在西方主义的高度面前，许多美学家也就只有二传手的份儿了。

中国美学和文艺学的功绩实则是仰仗“拿来主义”的福利，与自身的原创少有联系，这与经济大国的向全世界输出劳力、资本、产品极不相称，但又很难改变。原因在于我们拿惯了，根本想不到给予，也给予不了。但中国美学要急刹车，从为西方美学背书、张目中解放出来，另辟蹊径，走一条新的现代美学之路。这种新的现代美学是不同于前现代美学、现代美学、后现代美学的新思维、新境界、新理论、新名词、新主义。既有形态的识别，又有主义的建构。不仅是中国特色，而且有志于在后现代之后引领世界美学研究的风潮。

中国美学要摆脱因循、模仿西方美学的老路，就要有超前的观念，要有预想、要有谋划。要在后现代之时想到后现代之后，做到未雨绸缪。古人说：“凡事预则立不预则废”，只有把眼光放远一点，问题想多一点，才能有望摆脱替人背书、唯西方马首是瞻的尴尬局面。

要用后现代的思想和方法解剖后现代，解构后现代，批判后现代，利用后现代的思想成果，在后现代的思想高度上达到新的思想高峰，超越后现代。这个新的思想高峰暂时可以被称之为“别现代主义”，处在这一思想高峰上的美学应该称之为别现代主义美学。

别现代含义丰富。在古汉语中，没有“另”字，“另”字的含义都用“别”来表达。如《史记》中的“使沛公、项羽别攻城阳”。就是另外去攻打城阳的意思。《五灯会元》“拈花微笑”中的“不立文

① 王建疆：《中国美学：主义的喧嚣与缺失——百年中国美学批判》，《探索与争鸣》2012年第2期。

字，教外别传”，就是另传的意思，而非不传的意思。现代有“别开生面”“别动队”等，都不是不要开、不要动的意思，而是另外的意思，是相反的意思。“别现代”可以在另一种现代之外被误读为“不要现代”“告别现代”，类似德里达式的后现代的意义延异和释义无限的思想特征。但别现代最为确切的含义是关于现代、前现代、后现代三种形态的混合以及对这种混合状态的超越。因此，别现代主义具有思想建构和观念创新的能指。这种能指正是我们建设新观念、新思想、新美学的工具，应当珍惜并利用。

我之所以反对西方后现代的回归说，提倡别现代主义，就是因为中国有着与西方不同的文化背景、时代特征和思维方式，西方的后现代无法成为我们的思想指导和精神旨归。在西方后现代美学要大举逃离理论和思辨的时候，我们仍然在为理论的贫乏而犯愁。这就如西方从20世纪70年代开始高举生态主义大旗而批判人道主义一样①，我们那个时候恰恰遭遇人道主义缺失的灾难，我们渴望人道主义但却连人道主义的名字都不敢提，哪里还有超越人道主义的问题？中西方的差别不仅仅是前现代与后现代之间的，还有大家都身处同一个信息时代而文化差异却如此巨大的问题。因此，切勿被西方后现代的所谓超越论和回归说给忽悠了，自己没有理论，就搞什么日常生活审美化去了，糊里糊涂也不知道谁的生活审美化了，日常生活审美化就成了口头禅。

我提出的这个别现代不同于西方后现代的解构经典，相反，是要大力提倡建立理论体系，打造新时期的美学经典，反后现代之道而行之，建构美学思想，将具有原创性和中国特色的美学理论推向世界。

那么，在后现代之后建立别现代主义美学是否具有可能性呢？我

---

① ［美］戴维·埃伦费尔德：《人道主义的僭妄》，李云龙译，国际文化出版公司1988年版。

认为是肯定的。

一是中国的美学家中已经不止一人有了建立中国特色美学的野心，理论建构的意识已经觉醒，对主义建立的认识趋于积极，而且蠢蠢欲动，从而有了建构别现代主义美学的主观动力。

二是我们有丰富的不同于西方美学的思想、艺术、审美资源，成为建设别现代主义美学的文化资源和思想基础。中国特有的思维方式，如建立在天人合一基础上的返本主义思想；实践理性主义传统，如中国美学很少空洞地思辨，而是知行统一，这一点可以克服西方美学尤其是黑格尔美学从概念到概念推演的弊端，如什么艺术终结，人类美学史只是什么和谐与崇高的变奏等；中道思想的美学理论能够在理论与实践两个方面保持平衡。天人合一、知行统一、儒道互补、中庸之道、道法自然等，都是中道的哲学思想，便于守正。在后现代背景下，如果汲取后现代的反向动力精华和标新立异的创新思维，就会在传承与发展、守正与创新方面把握中道，提炼出符合中国审美实际，又有思想高度的美学思想和美学理论来。

三是由于中国独特的审美形态，可以从中提炼出不同于西方美学的新的理论。西方所有的审美形态中国目前都具有，而中国特有的审美形态如意境、气韵、空灵、飘逸等，则不为西方所有。但是，中国这些独特的审美形态，却是当代中国学者建构的修养论美学理论、自调节审美理论和内审美理论产生的根据。因此，从不同的审美形态出发，经过深入研究，就会得出不同于西方的美学结论，创造出新的美学理论。

四是在中国具有三驾马车并行的特殊情况，这就是前现代、现代、后现代并生并举，极易产生大的思想空间，在对立的结构中产生张力，产生关系质或系统质。有的学者说："对中国人而言，现代性只是一个国家的概念，而非一个新的时代的概念。后现代只是现代的一个可供选择的版本。代替对于现代的基本的批判和对现代性的决裂，后现代被认为是更新的现代性的版本。先锋艺术在中国也就因此

而变成了现代和后现代的双头怪。”① 但何止是双头怪，再加上前现代，何尝不是三头怪呢？可见，由于中西方在现代化方面存在着代差，西方的理论就不一定适合于中国，中国的美学家更不应该推崇西方后现代理论，做削足适履的事。面对西方的现代、后现代理论，我们的确没有充分的思想准备和足够的理论资源，因此，当务之急是进行原创性理论的建设，而非匆匆跟着后现代“回归”。相反，我们需要在否定中融合，在融合中否定，大大地扩展后现代之后的思想空间，研究建构中国美学的策略方式。

中国当代美学在思想建构方面有着严重的缺失，具体表现在缺乏理论，缺乏主义，缺乏原创性。与西方后现代的反本质主义及其厌弃理论、解构理论相比，中国不是理论过剩，而是理论贫乏；不是本质主义过度，而是本质研究不足。因此，应该借助新一轮改革的历史机遇，确实解放思想，建构理论，发展理论。使带有民族主义色彩的“中国美学”在当今一代美学家的手中，变成某某人的美学，某某主义的美学，某某学派的美学。只有这些个体化了的思想载体在中国真正出现的时候，所谓的中国美学才会引起国际美学的关注和重视。相反，如果没有主体性，现代派来了跟着现代派走，后现代派来了又跟着后现代派走，那我们将永远是学术上的随从了。

总之，美学之外也好，后现代之后也好，在别现代主义看来，都要从中国的实际出发，而不是盲目信奉和追随。在中华文化复兴的历史进程中，新的思想、新的美学必然诞生，与西方美学、哲学、思想的对话、争辩在所难免。在这样一个大的历史背景下，任何美学都将经历一场新的洗礼。这场洗礼是在诸多对立范畴交互运动中的搓洗，有的理论被搓得稀烂，有的被洗得纯净甚至发亮。

① Gao Minglu, Post-Utopian Avant-Garde Art in China, Postmodernism and the Postsocialist Condition, ed. Aleš Erjavec, the Regents of the University of California, 2003.

第六章

别现代：人生论美学的学科边界与内在根据*

近年来人生论美学在中国受到更多的关注。四川师范大学、浙江工业大学和中华美学学会就分别于2011 年和2014 年举行过全国性的人生论美学研讨会，并邀请我在大会上做过专题演讲。现在我就把自己的一些新的想法奉献给大家一起讨论。

第一节　人生论美学的学科边界

目前，在后现代思潮影响下，突破学科边界的跨文化或泛文化研究很盛行。自沃尔夫冈·威尔施提出美学要在美学之外的超越论以来①，重构美学或解构美学之风日盛。国内也有学者提出要超越经典美学，让美学回到自然和社会中去。为此，需要建立一种突破原有学科边界的“杂美学”②。这种杂美学就是与经典美学的纯美学相对的。

但就中国美学的实际而论，人生论美学的研究应该反其道而行

---

* 本章发表于《文艺理论研究》2016 年第2 期，《高校社科文摘》2016 年第6 期转载，《人大复印资料．文艺理论》2016 年第10 期转载。

① Wolfgang Welsch, *Aesthetics Beyond Aesthetics*, book of abstracts, 19th International Congress of Aesthetics, Krakow 2013 Poland, www. ica2013. pl.

② 高建平：《美学的超越与回归》，《上海大学学报》（社会科学版）2014 年第1 期。

之，原因在于，与西方美学的后现代特征相比，中国处于现代、前现代和后现代交织的别现代①，因此，其美学研究应该具有别现代特征。实际上，不是人生论美学的学科边界限制了美学思想，或者需要被突破、被超越，要回归社会和自然，要变成杂美学。相反，是人生论美学的学科边界在中国从来都是模糊的，是跨界的，是杂乱的。这种现状很不利于人生论美学的研究。有不少人把社会美研究和伦理美研究当成了人生论美学，把美育研究当成了人生论美学，也有人把所谓的生命美学也当成了人生论美学，似乎只要有社会和伦理、教育存在，就有人生论美学；只要有生命存在，就有人生论美学②。这种跨界的、甚至是望文生义的人生论美学研究，确实是将人生论美学的边界搞乱了，焉能不影响到人生论美学的深入研究。因此，我认为，与后现代的 cross border（越界）不同，人生论美学的研究首先应该确立学科边界。要把被混淆了的人生论美学从其他学科中分离出来；要把被肢解了的人生论美学重新还原，恢复其本来面目；要从杂乱无章的状态中走向纯粹。

人生论美学是在同社会美研究、自然美研究、艺术美研究的比较中独立出来的。同时，人生论美学也是在同人生主题研究、美育研究、人生境界研究的甄别中彰显自己的。

人生论美学的研究对象不同于社会美的研究对象，不是研究作为集团或大的系统的人及其社会行为、事迹，而是研究在社会中，在集团或大的系统中个人的行为，个人的人生体验和人生境界以及由此而产生的审美经验。社会美研究中的人的道德风范之美、人的言行之美、人的风韵之美、人工产品之美、人的技能之美、人造景观之美、广场艺术之美、园林艺术之美、大阅兵之美等，都是社会组织和社会

---

① 王建疆：《美学之外与后现代之后——对沃尔夫冈·威尔施引领的一种美学思潮的反动》，《上海师范大学学报》（哲学社会科学版）2015 年第 1 期。

② 许应行《人生美学》："因为从根本上讲，凡是与人类生存与发展相关的一切内容都应直接或间接地纳入人生美学的研究视野。"浙江大学出版社 2004 年版，第 7 页。

分工以及科技进步的结果，也是社会系统中的美，都具有外在的形象之美和形式之美。而建立在个体人生体悟基础上的人生论美学，就如大阅兵方阵中正步行走的每个士兵或专心敲鼓的鼓手一样，他只有个体的心灵的感受，而无整体的队伍行进的印象，那种整体的印象只来自观众和首长的对于社会组织之美和群体气势之美的外在观察。因此，人生论美学虽然其根基在社会系统中，其对象处在一个大的形象体系中，但其真谛却在个体的感受和体悟中。所谓存在与在者的关系，就是通过这种社会系统中个体的审美经验而获得证明的。也许在大阅兵中，每一个游行者个体或鼓手都因为整齐和规范而无个性特征，从而不会给观众留下印象，留给观众的只是外在的整体的风貌，但对每个游行者个人或鼓手来说，他在这次活动中获得的最深刻而且终身难忘的印象和感受就首先是他自己的而非别人的。人生论美学就与这个大阅兵中的每个游行者和鼓手一样，它是关于个体经验的记录、说明、阐释、抽象和理论化。人生论美学的这种个我体验性有时是通过文艺作品加以表现的，但人生审美与社会性审美和艺术性审美还是有着明确的边界。唐代诗人张若虚的《春江花月夜》表现了月夜江边的意境美，历来对这一意境的绘画表现和音乐谱曲演奏也都体现了艺术美，而其景观和人的情感表达又具有社会美的要素。但在艺术美和社会美之外，那种“江畔何人初见月，江月何年初照人？人生代代无穷已，江月年年只相似。不知江月待何人，但见长江送流水。白云一片去悠悠，青枫浦上不胜愁”的天人之问和个人感怀，却是人生的意义之问，是心灵境界的内审美。与这首诗歌之流传，与其相关的绘画和音乐的流传相比，这种天人之问，并不具有可视可听的广泛性，但它却是最能勾起生命之思和人生意义的名句，具有一般社会美和艺术美所不具有的内在性和个我性。这种内在性和个我性就构成了人生论美学的内在实质。

人生论美学不同于政治伦理美学。政治伦理美学建立在善的基础上，着重研究人与人之间、人与社会之间的关系。《论语》里讲“里

仁为美”，就是说有仁有德就美。这里的美实质上是善。政治伦理美学就是研究这种善的美学。在人类美学思想萌芽之时，美与善往往不分。表现为伦理学与美学的交织。近代美学的最大进步就在于区分了伦理学与美学的界限，从而保障了美学的深入研究。政治伦理美学的主要研究对象是人类和人类系统中人际关系所表现出来的美，研究人在处理人与人、人与社会关系时的言语之美、行为之美、风度之美和道义之美。而人生论美学，虽然也离不开人的伦理道德的支撑，但他的研究对象不是伦理关系和道德行为，而是个人的人生感受、人生体验和人生境界之美。

人生论美学的研究对象不同于自然美的研究，不是关注自然的外在形式和自然发育、自然发展，而是研究处在自然中的人的内在情感、内在感受和内在体验。作为西方近代自然主义美学的研究对象，主要是这种人与自然的关系变化，研究自然美的生成发展，最终给诸如“什么是美”这样的难题提供一个来自自然历史的说明。而人生论美学面对天人合一或征服自然的命题，其理论兴趣或关注点主要在于人的内心对于自然的了解，即所谓的知天；对自然的崇敬，即所谓的事天，顺应自然；与自然亲和，即所谓的乐天，从自然中得到快乐；与自然融为一体，成为大全的一分子，即所谓的同天①。这里所说来自中国古人境界说中的知天、事天、乐天、同天，都是个人的主观感受，是孟子所说的“尽心”“知命”，完全是一种内心的觉悟，一种人生境界，完全不同于对自然的观赏，不同于如柏拉图所说的濒临大海的凝神关注以及获得知识的快乐，或如自然主义美学大师桑塔耶那所说的美感皆因自然的色形音而起，而是无对象或者只有想象之天或内宇宙之天的感悟，而非对于自然外在形式美或外宇宙美的研

① 《孟子·尽心上》：“尽其心者，知其性也。知其性，则知天矣。存其心，养其性，所以事天也。殀寿不二，修身以俟之，所以立命也。”“万物皆备于我矣。反身而诚，乐莫大焉。”“夫君子所过者化，所存者神，上下与天地同流。”《孟子·梁惠王下》：“以大事小者，乐天者也。以小事大者，畏天者也。”

究。人生论美学也研究人与自然的关系，但不同于历史唯物主义美学观研究自然美的历史生成和流变，尤其是注重研究人与自然关系中“自然的人化”和“人化的自然”的双向运动，而是注重个体感受的当下性特点和对个体感受的理论概括。

人生论美学不同于艺术美的研究，它揭示的是人生智慧而非艺术技巧。艺术美时刻离不开对于艺术形象和艺术形式、艺术技巧的研究。但人生论美学并不必然面对形象、形式、技巧这些传统美学中的美的要素，而是研究脱离对象、没有形式、远离技巧的内在体验。过去台湾教授张先曾提出过“无对象审美”。李泽厚对无对象审美进行过积极的评价。实际上，《论语·侍坐章》中“吾与点也”的赞叹就是无对象审美的典型例证。康德的崇高感也来自对形式和形象所构成的对象的超越。我把这种无对象审美概括为内审美，我们可以在《论语》《老子》《庄子》及佛禅经教以及康德的崇高感论中找到无数这方面的例证①。这些例证都被认为是人生论美学的范例，而与艺术美研究无关。

人生论美学不同于文艺中的人生主题研究。把人生论美学等同于人生主题研究，无异于将人生论美学混同于人物传记和小说描写。例如，《人生》《活着》等就是典型的人生主题，但能说它们是人生论美学吗？不能。因为，人生论美学是对人生体验和人生境界的理论概括，而非小说那样是对人生过程的描述。美学永远是抽象的，是概括的，是理论的，而非感性的，具体的，描述的。

人生论美学不同于人生境界问题研究。人生境界是人生论美学的重要内涵之一，但人生境界是人的心理觉悟程度，而非对这种觉悟程度的理论概括。同时，除了人生境界，人生论美学的研究对象还有人生修养、人生感受、人生体验等，这些都是人生境界形成的基础，但

---

① 参见王建疆《修养·境界·审美——儒道释修养美学解读》，中国社会科学出版社2007年版，第12—25页。

人生境界并不能替代它们、涵盖它们。所以，人生论美学可以包括对人生境界的研究，但不能等同于人生境界研究。

人生论美学不同于美育研究。美育也叫审美教育。主要是通过艺术教育达到美化世界和实现美好人生的目的。相对于人生论美学，美育只能是一种手段，而非目的。而人生论美学不同，直接联系着人生目的，而且未必需要通过美育的手段来实现。美育可以通过艺术教育，对人的心灵进行熏陶，对人格进行塑造。但并不涉及人的世界观问题。涉及人生观研究的应该是人生论美学，而不是美育研究。人的世界观与最高的人生境界相联系，也与人生的终极关怀相关。而美育更侧重于艺术教育或审美教育。美育可以影响人的人生观，但它本身不是人生观，而且也与人生观无必然联系。相反，近代以来提倡的美育不仅没有关系到世界观这样根本的问题，而且有的学者如蔡元培甚至提倡要“以美育代宗教”。这都说明，美育尚未达到人生境界和人生目的的高度，也不可能具有人生论美学的目的体验层次。

人生论美学不同于生命美学。生命的本质是蛋白质，是生物体的存活状态。人生却是生命的运动过程，是生命的意义展现过程。因此，生命美学旨在突破理性对自然情感和本能欲望的压抑，解放身体，解放感官，在日趋异化的当代有其积极的意义。但生命美学以生物体的存活的合理性来与现代理性的压迫相对抗，本身并不具有人生意义的高端水平。人的修养、人的境界，虽然都建立在生命的基础上，但又因为超越了生命而具有意义。所谓舍生取义、杀身成仁，就都是在强调人生的意义，揭示人生要超越生命的道理。因此，建立在人生意义基础上的人生论美学，无疑因其处在生命存在和发展的高端而与处于低端的生命美学判若两仪。

总而言之，人生论美学确切地说是一种人生观的美学，是目的论美学，是超越形象、形式、技巧的美学，是形而上的美学。从审美形态上讲是内审美。人生论美学虽然不可能凭空存在，与自然、社会、艺术、科技活动保持着千丝万缕的联系，但真正构成人生论美学的仍

然只是个体的人生修养、人生体验、人生境界建构和内审美那种高深的精神感悟和形而上学的思辨，而不是浅表的审美教育、道德体验、艺术体验、自然美感、社会景观和生命情怀。

第二节　人生论美学的形态标志

形态学（morphology）是关于地形、语言形式和生物样态的科学。地形、语言、生物都不是靠内涵来标志的，而是靠形态标识的。如英语和汉语在表达同一个意思时，就不存在内涵的差异，而只有形态的差异。这种形态包括符号系统、词汇系统、语音系统、语法系统等，标志明显，难以混淆。同样，地形形态是不关地质构造和地壳运动的，它只提供地表信息，以地图的形式加以标识。至于生物形态就更是如此，是人还是狗，并非从感情特征和智力特征以及所谓的社会关系这些内涵方面去确认，而是从形态上加以区别。形态学就是这样，到了你不得不重视的程度。

在美学上，区别不同形式、不同风格的审美，应该称之为审美形态。在此基础上建立的学说叫审美形态学。用审美形态（aesthetic formation in morphology）的概念取代日益混杂的所谓“审美范畴”（aesthetic category），在当今的美学研究中不无意义。审美范畴与审美形态是两个不容混淆的概念。审美范畴是指美学研究中所有大的具有节点功能的概念，这个概念包括了审美形态，但除了审美形态，还有美的本质、美的特点、美的规律、美的形式、美的内容、美的生成、美的发展、美的风格、美的欣赏、美的创造、审美、审美活动等一系列范畴。而审美形态却专指悲剧、喜剧、优美、崇高、意境、神妙之类具有体裁特征、风格特征和文化特征的概念。因此，审美范畴与审美形态之间是有大小之分的，混在一起使用，就会冲淡并模糊审美形态的存在。

审美形态是人生样态、人生境界、审美情趣、审美风格及其体裁

的感性凝聚和逻辑分类，是美学研究的具体内容，也是美学多样性和民族性的重要标志。相对于西方美学的悲剧、崇高、荒诞，中国美学的意境、气韵、飘逸、空灵等，就显示出美学的民族性和多样性，具有明显的识别标志。因此，研究人生论美学，就必须首先既注意它的形态学特征，又要注意审美形态的民族文化背景和民族性以及差异性。

审美形态除了按美的分类标准和文艺体裁划分之外，还可以从审美的类型加以划分。如李泽厚所讲的悦耳悦目型、悦心悦意型和悦神悦志型。除此之外，还有一个以前未被学界发现的种类，这就是我提出的内审美。这个内审美之于人生论美学研究更是息息相关。

所谓内审美，是指不依赖外在感官和外在对象的内视型、内景型、境界型审美。如道家的“玄览”或“玄鉴”，由“心斋”“坐忘”引起的“吉祥止止”；儒家的“孔颜乐处”“风乎舞雩”，“无万物之美而可以养乐”；佛禅的“喜俱禅”“乐俱禅”“禅悦之风”；中国文人描述的“思接千载”“视通万里”“神与物游”，“内乐”“内景”“内游”“胸中之竹”；西方文艺心理学中的“内觉”“内心视觉”“内在感官”“内模仿”“内化”“内倾”“内在自由”“内在时间”；普通人的憧憬、回忆、想象等。其中有些是有内在形象相伴随的，如玄鉴、坐忘、禅悦、内景、憧憬、想象等，有些是没有形象的悦志悦神，如“游心于物之初”“孔颜乐处”等。

内审美概括了人类审美的普遍经验，因此，内审美被认为是“立足于美学史的一个创造”①。非常符合人生美学中人生感受、人生体验、人生境界的描述。孟子的“以大事小者，乐天者也”（《梁惠王下》），庄子的“无言心悦”（《庄子·天运》）的乐天境界，“天地与我并生而万物与我为一”（《庄子·齐物论》），以及“上下与天地同

---

① 朱立元为王建疆《修养·境界·审美》一书所做《序》，中国社会科学出版社2003年版。

流”（《孟子·尽心上》）的同天境界，就都是建立在内心体验基础上的内审美，无法通过感官型审美来显示并验证，但又是有大量文献和事实支撑的特殊审美现象。

在内审美理论提出之前，中国哲学界已经具备了这方面的思想准备。战国时代荀子就有“无万物之美而可以养乐”（《荀子·正名》）的命题。当代台湾张先教授提出的无对象审美，李泽厚所言美感三层次等。其中的无对象审美属于内审美的基本形态，而悦志悦神就是人生论美学的高级体验层次。人人都有人生过程，都有人生体验以及与此相伴生的内在审美经验，因此，内审美是人生美学的常态。虽然内审美中的内景型审美如中国古代的“内视”和内照，即塞米尔·泽基（Semir Zeki）所谓“内视”（inner vision），并非普遍，这涉及个体的大脑机制方面的差异，但由于人人都可能具有回忆、记忆、内省、内悟、境界、内心体验等心理过程，因而都有可能具有境界型内审美体验。正因为如此，我认为，人生论美学研究不应该脱离内审美体验，相反，应该利用内审美作为审美形态的高端存在这一事实，将内审美作为人生论美学的坐标。

把内审美理论运用到人生论美学的研究上，就必然带来人生论美学研究的突破。内审美给人生论美学一个本质的界定，不仅厘清了学科边界，而且抓住了人生论美学的本质特征，为人生论美学的进一步深入研究奠定了基础。中国古代有关圣贤的记载，就有许多内审美的特征。司马迁在《史记·孔子世家》中说：“余读孔子书，想见其为人。”更进一步，宋代理学家程颐、程颢说：“仲尼，天地也。颜子，和风庆云也。孟子，泰山岩岩之气象也。观其言皆可以见之矣。仲尼无迹，颜子微有迹，孟子其迹著。”[①] 与魏晋时期人物品藻的注重风姿神韵不同，也与我们从古籍里看到的孔孟的画像不同，这种对已故圣贤的“观其言皆可见之”的审美，是脱离了对象和感官的审美，

① （宋）程颢、程颐：《二程集》，王孝鱼点校，中华书局1981年版，第76—79页。

是一种超越了道德评价的想象或神游的、神交的内审美。借助内审美，将会极大地拓展人生论美学的视野。一个人的人生经历会构成这个人的人生感受、人生体验和人生境界，一个伟人或圣贤，他自己的人生感受、人生体验和人生境界往往为大众所景仰，使人们心向往之、行效尤之。但这种向往效尤的最佳途径还是内审美。这是因为，伟人的或圣贤的人生经验，只有通过内审美才能体会得到、感悟得到。也就是说，对于圣贤或楷模的心向往之和行效尤之，只有在内审美的层次上才更容易得到沟通，从而更容易实现。司马迁、二程对于圣贤的描述，将人们对于圣贤的景仰和效尤带进了内审美的境地，不仅扩大到了人的精神领域，而且还以内景的方式展示了圣贤和楷模的人格魅力，为内审美的研究提供了典型的例证。正是借助内审美，才使人生境界的美学研究别出一路，独具一格。内审美理论之于人生论美学研究的最大贡献在于，确立了人生论美学的形态学特征，找到了人生论美学的识别标志，从而将人生论美学从社会美研究、自然美研究、艺术美研究和伦理美学的藩篱中独立出来，成为一个专门的研究领域，从而有利于人生论美学的确立和发展。

内审美理论并不因为其内省性而不具有被验证的可能性。相反，内审美现象已得到美国神经美学的证明，这就是内视现象的存在。塞米尔·泽基在他的著作《内视》（*Inner Vision*）中表明，画家的内视现象说明画家是在用大脑而非用眼睛来创作。画家的内心形象是外在的艺术作品形象的胚胎，决定并制约着视觉艺术作品的创作。他通过许多实例证明，内在视觉是存在的。甚至画家大脑皮层的意外受损也往往成为画家取得惊人成就的原因。莫奈的印象主义杰作《睡莲》等作品中极其光炫的色彩并不是画家本人的直接的外在视觉印象，而是在画家本人失明的情况下依靠大脑的内视画出来的世界名作。塞米尔·泽基没有内审美的概念，但他的内视的研究成果已经为中国古代记载的内视、内景、内游等找到了根据。这就是大脑的机制，而非人为的杜撰或神秘主义的宣传。这种来自科学研究的发现，对于内审美

来说，无疑是一个很好的证明和支撑。

实际上，内审美现象并非画家的专利，亦非圣贤的独享，也不局限于内功修养的实绩，而是日常生活中普遍存在的审美形象。所谓的余音绕梁，历历在目等，都是内审美的表现，也都是人生感受、人生体验和人生境界的表现。

人生论美学的研究领域要比人生经历范围小得多。原因在于，人生经历可以无限丰富，构成了历史学、社会学、文学、传记学的研究内容和表现内容。但内审美只是一种人生的内在感受、内在体验和心灵境界，这种感受、体验、境界是如此的个我和独特，以致有时很难作为普通经验得到大众的共享。陈子昂《登幽州台歌》中“前不见古人，后不见来者，念天地之悠悠，独怆然而涕下”就不是对幽州台这一景观的欣赏，而是个我的无对象审美，是一种建立在人生感悟基础上而又超越了人生经历的内审美体验。内审美建立在修养学基础上，思古之幽情不会发生在自然境界、功利境界和道德境界的人身上，而只能发生在具有天地境界的人身上。内审美是一种完全内在的、封闭的、个我的内在修养。而人生之广大，经历之丰富，除了修养之外还有更多的顺习而为，因此人生论美学是内涵丰富而外延有限的美学。也正因为如此，宋明理学中那些“吟风弄月而归”“绿满窗前草木不除”（周敦颐）和“闲来无事不从容，睡觉东窗日已红”的闲散之人，可能要比身经百战的将军们更能体会“道通天地有形外，思入风云变态中”（程颢《秋日》）的人生境界。

人生论美学虽然较之人生经历要小得多，但其建立在人生修养基础上的内审美体验，却以获得人生最高境界为旨归，因而，人生论美学处于美学研究的高端，甚至由于其研究的人生境界处于封闭而又神秘的状态，其研究难度无异于哥德巴赫猜想。老子“涤除玄鉴”到底玄鉴到什么？庄子坐忘到底坐忘了什么？孔子乐在其中，到底乐在哪里？孟子上下与天地同流如何见得？这些都是海里的冰山，不潜入水中是得不到答案的。因此，人生论美学研究一定是不同于艺术美

学、社会美学和自然美学等显性研究的深潜研究，需要更大的勇气和更全面的知识，尤其是要有内审美的视域超越。

人生论美学从本质上讲，属于内在精神实践范畴。与外在实践相比，更注重内在实践及其结果——内审美。科学的实践观既注重人的社会实践，又注重人的精神实践，注重艺术创作的特殊性，注重审美的特殊性。马克思主义注重发挥人的主观能动性的说法，就是注重人的精神创造。审美活动、艺术活动，虽然并非物质实践，但仍然是属人的精神实践活动。而在这种精神实践过程中，内审美就最具内在精神实践的特性。人生论美学建立在内审美形态基础上这一事实决定了它自己不仅是物质实践的产物，而且更重要的是内在精神实践的结果。正是这一特性，将它与政治伦理美学、自然环境美学、艺术美学、科技美学等划清了界限。人生论美学的内在实践性，是内隐，与艺术美、社会美、自然美等感官型审美的外秀形成对比。

建立在内审美基础上的人生论美学的确立，不仅意味着人生论美学研究有了新的对象和新的方法，而且意味着整个美学史的写作也要重新考虑。要改变以往那种只以外在物质实践为实践，以感官型审美为审美，而没有意识到内在精神实践的存在和内审美存在的偏差，建立健全合理的、全面的美学理论和美学史观，将内审美这一美学史的重要线索予以确立，使之成为美学史写作的另外一条重要线索，与以往美学史研究中建立在感官型审美经验基础上的线索一起，达到“双峰并峙，二水分流”的美学史理想形态。同时，在美学理论研究上，也将随着内审美理论的建立，将人类的审美理论大大地拓展，概括总结出新的理论来，从而将美学研究向前推进一大步。

第三节　人生论美学的中国背景和特征

内审美西方也有，但与中国不同。西方的内审美一是建立在认知真理的基础上，也就是洞察本质或本体或“理念”的基础上。二是

建立在基督教信仰的基础上。前者如柏拉图所说在对美的“凝神关注”（《会饮篇》）中领悟到的同一的绝对美，都是领悟知识所带来的快乐。这一点虽被后来的康德美学中审美不同于认知的原理所超越，但在认知本体世界的过程中获得快乐却一直是西方美学的传统。认知本体世界就要超越现象、超越视听，要在内视、内省中获得真理。胡塞尔的现象学、海德格尔的存在论，都强调对于真理的洞见，在洞见的过程中达到澄明之境，这种澄明之境与内审美有一定的相同之处。三是建立在救赎的基础上。受基督教影响，西方文化是一种信仰文化。这种信仰建立在人类原罪的基础上，认为只有救世主才能替人类赎罪，因而，人的修养并不重要，重要的是跟着耶稣走，因为《圣经》中耶稣讲他自己就是道路，就是真理，就是生命。这样一来，西方文化就成了建立在他力基础上的救赎文化。其悦志悦神的审美，实际上就是奥古斯丁描述的与上帝面对面的一种超验。超验是非经验的，也是神秘的。而中国的内审美却是建立在人的修养基础上的一种经验，是经验型内审美。中国古代也有形而上哲学和超验体会，道家对于道的论述就是地道的形而上。但这种形而上的超验体会，是在经验的基础上展开的。老子讲涤除玄览、致虚守静、归根复命，但首先都是一种经验，一种致虚守静的功夫，而不是没有经验基础的玄想。宋明理学中的“道通天地有形外，思入风云变态中”，非常形而上，但是，它的前提是“闲来无事不从容，睡觉东窗日已红。万物静观皆自得，四时佳兴与人同”。这里的“静观”和“佳兴”就是由行为与结果构成的体验过程，是在闲暇经验中体会无形的道，在有中感受无。这与所谓的跟上帝在一起的外在超越相比，完全是一种个体活动基础上的内在超越，是一种经验后的超验，而非经验前的先验，具有实践性。

与中国文化中的内审美相伴，产生的是一种内乐。老子所谓涤除玄鉴、庄子所谓心斋坐忘，吉祥止止；孔门所谓“孔颜乐处”，孟子所谓“上下与天地同流”，荀子所谓“无万物之美而可以养乐”；还有禅宗的“禅悦之风”等，都是建立在个人修养基础上的内在实践、内在审美，内在体验，与对知识的习得和对真理的洞见无关，也与宗教的他力救赎无关。

李泽厚将中国文化概括为乐感文化，并与西方的悲感文化和日本的耻感文化相区别。这种乐感文化在明代被概括为“乐学”，也堪称快乐的学说或内审美的学说。这种内乐的学说既是对中国文化审美特征的揭示，也是对内审美的肯定。建立在人生修养基础上的中国美学，实质上就是建立在内审美基础上的人生论美学。这种人生论美学具有以下特征。

1. 内在实践的①，而非外在实践的。外在实践是指人类借助工具所从事的生产劳动、科学实验和社会活动。其过程是实在的，其结果是可见的。而内在实践却是内心活动，其过程是精神的，其结果具有可见与不可见两种。可见的是指艺术品，不可见的是指精神境界。人生论美学的研究对象既不是可见的外在实践，又不是作为精神实践产品的艺术，而是研究不可见的精神过程和精神境界以及由此而产生的内审美形态。长期以来由于人们对实践的了解过于狭隘，仅仅局限于物质实践，而忽视或贬低了精神实践的重要性，造成的结果就是无视内审美的存在，将人生论美学完全变成了政治伦理美学或美育的附庸。现在，随着内审美的发现，人生论美学的内在实践性得到了证明。

2. 自力的而非他力的。儒家和道家本身并非宗教，因而没有贬低人本身而皈依神主的企图，相反，儒家主张通过自身修养，达到修齐治平的人生目的。道家更是主张“与万物为春”的人与自然的平等和天道自然的人与人之间的平等，因而并没有对于救世主的期待。至于佛禅虽然强调对于神佛的皈依，但又认为，佛是由人修炼而成的，不是被某种外在的主宰所授予的。因此，“佛由性中做，莫向身

① 刘冠军：《论内在实践和外在实践》，《天津师范大学学报》1997 年第 3 期。

外求”（慧能《坛经》）就成了佛禅的基本信念。这一信念说到底还是肯定人自身的本体性即“自性”，肯定人的内在修养。正是儒道佛禅这些支撑整个中国文化的思想体系，使中国的文化成为一种自力的文化，一种修养文化，一种自主人生的文化，而与西方建立在神主他力救赎基础上的文化判若两仪。因此，中国的人生论美学就具有明显的自力特征。

3. 内在经验的而非外在超验的。经验是人生体验的记录。中国古代文人的人生经验比较丰富。既有事功事利的积极进取，又有急流勇退恬淡虚无的逍遥自在，形成所谓的儒道互补，进退裕如。这种人生经历都是世俗的，也是经验的，都有现实的基础和可以操作的路径。尽管道家的玄览守静、心斋坐忘，有其超乎寻常的体验方式，但在既定的程序下进行修炼，还是可以得到大致相同的体验。而西方基督教信仰所导致的与上帝面对面的体验却是撇开修炼、无路径可循的形而上信仰，本身更具有超出经验范围的幻觉性。当然，经过文艺复兴和启蒙运动，西方的宗教有所衰微，不再政教合一，但作为基本信仰，仍在西方国家具有不可动摇的地位。西方的美学思想有很大一部分就来自这种信仰文化。其外在超验性构成了西方内审美的重要特征。相反，中国人生美学的内在经验性，更具有中华文化的识别标志。

4. 内乐的而非外喜的。过去人们有种误解，似乎审美只是面对某个对象进行的情感活动，如无对象则无审美。但内审美的发现正在改变这种认识上的偏颇。与外在流露的喜悦相比，内审美更具有内心深处的、持久的心理效应。喜形于色，这是对浅表快乐的描述。这种浅表的快乐很可能来自利益的满足。当然，有些浅表层面的审美如轻喜剧、逗乐、观花赏景等，都会引发喜悦，产生悦耳悦目的审美效果。但内乐却是一种悦心悦意的、悦志悦神的审美快乐。孔子曾说观《韶》乐而“三月不知肉味”，显然是在脱离了对象之后的内心体验。这种体验长久而且具有排他性，使得口福之乐受到排挤，连肉的香味

都没有感觉了。孔子这种感受就是典型的内审美。人生体验中那些天人合一的境界，那种“游心于物之初”的感受，就是以内乐为特征的内审美。庄子把这种由内审美引起的内乐称为“至美至乐”（《田子方》），明代泰州学派的王艮做《乐学歌》，认为“人心本自乐”“乐是学，学是乐”，无所不乐，将乐心灵化，这种内乐直接与内审美相通。内乐与中国文化的含蓄内敛相联系，构成了中国美学的一大特征，中国的人生论美学就是一种内乐的美学。

构成中国人生论美学以上特征的原因有三。

1. 儒道佛禅思想成为中国人的精神支柱和思想指南，为中国人的人生观奠定了人本位思想。儒道思想是中国本土占统治地位的思想。其实质是人本位的思想，即从未有过因为外在的目的比如物质需求或神的存在而将人视为工具或奴婢，相反，认为天地人并称“三才”。孔子有过这样的记载：“厩焚，子退朝。‘伤人乎？’不问马。”即把人看作第一位的。孟子有着更为明显的人本主义倾向，这就是“人皆可以为尧舜”。道家也是重视人的地位。老子说“故道大，天大，地大，人亦大。域中有四大，而人居其一焉”。肯定人与自然与道的平等。庄子的“与天地并生而与万物为一”的思想，明确强调人与天齐。较之西方基督教将人视为上帝的婢女，将人视为无知的羔羊来说，是一种人本体思想而非神本体思想。这样的思想成为中国古代的主要思想，必然会形成中国人注重人生意义和人生境界的传统，为人生论美学思想奠定坚实的人本体思想基础。至于外来佛教思想能在中国扎根，还是因为佛教中的因果观、善恶观符合中国人的现世要求，而非来世关怀。而且，佛的境界是可以通过修养来实现的。这就是以顿悟或渐悟的方式来实现。还有一点，佛的境界是心灵觉悟的程度，是建立在对人生意义、人生真理的领悟的基础上的。虽然佛教的世界观是颠倒了的世界观，但其注重“做一个纯粹的人，一个高尚的人，一个脱离了低级趣味的人”的主张，与世俗的人生实践和人生境界息息相通。正因为儒道佛禅的人本体而非神本体性质，使得中国人

的人生论美学具有境界修养学的特点，是修养美学的实绩。

2. 儒道佛禅确立了中国人的人生目标、人生境界和修养方式。儒家的人生目标是分阶段的修身齐家治国平天下，道家的人生目标是反其道而行之，要返璞归真，逆炼归元，在社会方面和人的身心方面都脱离现有的知识体系和道德规范，重新回归自然而又清明的社会。儒道两家一进一退，一加一减，貌似对立，修养方式也完全不同，但在寻求理想的人生样态和合理的社会方面却有着一致的目标。佛禅在人生目标方面更进一步，这就是人生是有因果的，人生不只此生，还有来生，因此，人应该参透生死，超越自我。所谓“舍弃小我成大我，舍弃大我成无我，无我方为永恒我”，就是其人生目标和人生境界的写照。不同的人生境界和不同的修养方式，都在围绕提升人自身而展开，这样一来，无论儒道，还是佛禅，都把人生定位在修养和境界上。这种人生自我超越、自我完善的定位，超越单独的道德善和认知真，而与审美相沟通，是真善美的统一。

3. 受儒道修养文化熏陶，善于自我调节，在天人之间、内外之间、阴阳之间、道艺之间把握平衡、达到和谐。老子说：“功成、名遂、身退，天之道也。”孟子说：“达则兼济天下，穷则独善其身。”道家讲究功成身隐，儒家主张进退自如，这些都是典型的自我调节策略，使自己处于相对自由的境地。不仅在为人处世方面属于自我调节，而且在天人关系方面讲究天人合一、道法自然、与物为春；在内外之间讲究外圆内方，即以正直的心理看待事物，但又以周全的技巧处理事务；在阴阳之间坚信一阴一阳之谓道，坚守负阴抱阳，冲气以和；在道与艺之间认为道从技艺中升华出来，需要把握两方面的平衡。儒道文化的这些进退平衡之术，为中国人的身心自我调节和保持一种理想的人生状态提供了文化基础、思想指导和智力支撑。中国的人生审美为什么这么发达，原因就在于中国人生的张力很大，进退、荣辱，甚至生死，都可以通过心理的自我调节得到解决。当然，这种自调节审美也带来了文艺中悲剧的隐退和生活中自我满足的膨胀。但

从人生论美学的角度看，却是一种自足性的封闭式审美，与几千年来封闭的封建社会正相和谐。

4. 内向内敛的民族性格所致。老子就主张处下怀柔，“不敢为天下先”。孔子讲“吾日三省吾身”，都是主张在内求诸己的过程中，实现内在超越。魏晋玄学主张在超像中获得真谛，实现审美。汉民族的性格不是积极对外扩张的性格，而是保守的、含蓄的、内敛的。这一点可以从中国第一部诗歌总集《诗经》中那些用比兴表达的一唱三叹、回环往复的情感就可以看得很清楚。当然，骚体诗人反其道而行之，善于夸张，直抒胸怀，但就大的方面而言，由于多用比喻和象征，仍不失含蓄的一面。就中国文学和写意画注重含蓄和内秀而言，含蓄内敛仍不失为最大的特点。在现实中，中国式的求爱方式、表达方式等也都具有含蓄内敛的特点。这一民族性格带来了中国人生方式的内向性特点和在审美方式上的内审美特点。内审美就来自儒家反思自我、反省人生的修为和道家、佛禅反观内照的功夫，是一种人生修养中的内功，是人生境界中的内景。

总之，人生论美学具有其形态学特征和民族文化背景，需要在确立学科边界、揭示形态特征、展现民族文化背景方面下大力气进行研究。只有在把握形态特征的基础上才能确立人生论美学的学科边界；只有在了解民族文化背景的前提下才能揭示人生论美学的内涵。内审美是人生论美学的本体形态，中国的修养文化是人生论美学的本根所在。

第三编

别现代评论

第一章

别现代时期“囧”的审美形态生成*

我们正处于现代、前现代和后现代交织在一起的社会历史时期，无法用单一的现代或前现代或后现代来概括，只好用别现代称呼。“别”的“别裁”“别体”“别传”的古义，虽然在今天容易产生误读，表面上看类似解构主义大师德里达生造的词“différance”（延异），但却有着明确的含义，这就是对一种杂糅社会形态的虚妄的所谓现代性的概括和对别样现代性的期许、建构。

别现代的时代特征从经济基础到上层建筑，再到意识形态，无所不有、无所不包。中国社会日趋发达的物质现代化和对西方教育、科学、民主、法制的借鉴，前卫艺术和知识精英对后现代的认同，以及社会制度、思想意识方面的前现代元素，无不相互交织在一起，构成了这个历史时期的文化景观。

别现代具有由多维制度空间、物质空间和意识空间构成的既和谐共谋又内在紧张的多重复杂属性。包括时间空间化属性、多元并存属性、和谐共谋①属性和内在张力属性、多变量属性、难以预测属性等。

---

* 本章曾发表于《南方文坛》2016 年第 5 期。

① 别现代的“和谐共谋”包括现代、后现代与前现代之间的彼此适应、和谐共处；没有边界、放弃原则、妥协、交易（权钱交易、权色交易、权法交易、行贿受贿）、媾和；不断更改规矩、实行潜规则；有选择地遗忘和遮蔽历史、造假畅行无阻等，前现代的思想观念和行为方式因现代制度的缺位而由后现代的跨越边界（cross border）、解构中心、消解原则来加以表达，形成混沌的和谐，可以浑水摸鱼，这一点在当今那些高智商、高学历、高级别、受过现代教育、出过国、留过洋但又贪污腐化、身败名裂的贪官污吏身上得到了最为集中的表现。

别现代的前现代、现代、后现代并存现状，导致时代的空间化，在这个空间形式中，现代与前现代的天然对立、现代与后现代的相互矛盾、后现代与前现代的文化隔膜，都被某种黏合剂黏在了一起，因而表面上看是多元并置、和谐共处，但是，骨子里还是潜藏着多重对立。因此，跟西方断代式的现代、后现代相比，与其说中国是现代与前现代的“双头怪”，还不如说是现代、前现代、后现代媾和共谋的“三头怪”，是一个共谋而又内在分裂的共同体，往好里说是三驾马车并行，往差里说是南辕北辙，恰如柏拉图《斐德若篇》中所说的灵魂奔向天国的途中那架由良马和劣马一起拉着的难于驾驭的马车，其运行轨迹和发展前景充满变数，难以预测。这种既内在分裂又和谐共谋的结构特征，决定了别现代时期文学和艺术的多元共谋与内在紧张。事实上，反思和批判前现代的具有现代性的批判现实主义文学和艺术不绝如缕，同时，怀旧复古、粉饰太平的具有前现代特征的伪古典主义、伪浪漫主义及神剧的伪崇高等仍有很大市场，而解构崇高、消解英雄、展现丑恶的后现代文学和艺术也方兴未艾①。这种多元共谋和内在张力的并存，使得别现代不仅具有别现代特点，而且具有阶段性特点，如和谐共谋期、矛盾冲突期、超越更新期。目前正处于别现代的和谐共谋期。这种和谐共谋正在影响着社会生活、意识形态、文学艺术、伦理道德、审美形态等各个方面。本文将用审美形态学的方法，解剖具有别现代特征的囧类现象，尤其是其代表囧类电影，以期获得对于特定历史时期中国文学、艺术和审美文化的宏观把握。

第一节 “囧”现象的别现代文化内蕴

徐峥导演、主演的囧类电影具有非常鲜明的别现代文化内蕴和审美特征。

① 王建疆：《后现代语境中的英雄空间与英雄再生》，《文学评论》2014 年第 2 期。

囧类电影中反复出现的前现代的贞操观、香火观、迷信观遇到现代社会层出不穷的随机干扰，于是，吃醋、愤怒、离异、以死相逼等极端表现应运而生，又在随机生成的偶然事件中喜出望外地回归前现代的大团圆结局，表现为一种产生于前现代的中和的审美观。《人在囧途》中隐隐约约的“小三”在窘途之末，只因一次偶然的道德发现而退出了角色。《人再囧途之泰囧》中被误会和醋意折磨得离异的夫妻最终由于事业追求的虚无而破镜重圆。《港囧》中在跟妻子造人和与二十年前的初恋约炮交织在一起而又充满了各种险情的随机故事中，最后以夫妻从高楼坠落而为一夫一妻制正名。这里的生活场景都是现代的，是现代化的，甚至是超级现代化的，但故事内容的意旨却是前现代的血缘宗亲观念、贞操观念和庇佑观念。而在这种前现代与现代的剧情冲突中，将其润滑、戏剧化、喜剧化、娱乐化的却是后现代的艺术手法戏仿、戏谑、消解崇高、无厘头等。如对原有目的回家、争夺专利、造小人人的不断消解，总是通过一个形影不离的愣头青（王宝强、包贝尔分别饰演）在制造了无数的窘态和笑料后，将困窘之路消解而代之以光明炯途。徐峥的电影《人在囧途》《人再囧途之泰囧》《港囧》都因其抢眼而获得了票房的巨大突破，并形成了囧类电影的艺术风格。但是，囧类电影的出现并非徐峥一人的天才所致，而是近年来囧文化兴起的结果。

囧文化的兴起起始于古代汉语的今用。囧的本义是光明。在汉语中有“囧”和“冏”两个字，“囧”和“冏”在《辞海》中的解释如下：“囧”同“冏”。见“囧囧”。“囧囧”——明亮貌。江淹《孙廷尉绰杂述》诗：“囧囧秋月明。”①“冏”本作“囧”，像窗口通明，引申为有光貌。《艺文类聚》卷九引郭璞《井赋》：“乃回澄已静映，状冏然而镜灼。”“冏冏”光明貌。韩愈《秋怀》：“虫鸣室幽幽，月吐窗冏冏。”② 从《辞源》中，我们也可以看出“囧”和“冏”都有

① 夏征农主编：《辞海》，上海辞书出版社 2001 年版，第 921 页。
② 同上书，第 240 页。

“光明”“明亮”的意思，且二者意思相通。但在当今网络流行语中，“囧”又通“窘”，又通“炯”，前者是“窘迫”，后者是“光明”，因而具有多义性。随着网络的兴起，大量的网络语言应运而生。“囧”由于适应了现代网民表达的需要而成为网民不断追捧的网络词汇之一。在网络语言中，“囧”的内小“八”字视为眉眼，“口”视为嘴。它的内涵就是：1. 作为头。表达沉重的思想。2. 作为脸。表达浪漫与激情。①

囧从原初意义到现代网络意义的生成，从一个生僻字到一个流行语演变，不是简单的一时兴起，而是一个复杂的过程。一般认为，囧的流行，必须要提到“Orz”。“Orz”这种看似字母的组合，但不能念成一个英文单词，而是一种象形的符号。在日文中原本的意义是“失意体前屈”，代表一个人面向左方、俯跪在地，O 代表这个人的头，r 代表手以及身体，z 代表的是脚。中国台湾的网民受到“Orz”的启发，用“囧”替换掉了“O”，使得日文中的失意体前屈的头部具有了更加写意的表情，写作“囧 rz”。② 因此，根据囧的表意形状，“囧”被赋予郁闷、尴尬、悲伤、无奈、困惑、无语等意思。“囧”也指处境尴尬、为难。同“窘”一样表示在特殊情况下的一种极为窘迫的心情。“囧”从 2008 年开始在中文地区的网络社群间成为一种流行的表情符号，成为网络聊天、论坛、博客中使用最为频繁的字之一，“囧”也被形容为“21 世纪最牛的一个字”。③

在当下，囧的风行催生出囧文化的流行，囧文化几乎席卷了人们的整个生活，从虚拟到现实处处可以看到囧的影子。网络上出现了与囧相关的文学如：打油诗、绕口令、囧字体、囧字操。现实中产生了由囧衍生的文化产业。一是囧文化的产生，如：囧东西网站的创建、

① 见百度百科“囧”词条。

② 同上。

③ 同上。

囧字舞的出现、囧游戏的开发、囧电影的拍摄等。二是在囧文化的指导下而推出的一系列囧商品，如：李宁囧字鞋、囧字T恤、晨光囧笔以及一些囧科技产品。三是有的人甚至将囧应用到人生的解读中，如“囧事”“囧途”等。甚至这种对人生的解读会与商业广告合谋，借助文学的手法表达一种诗意。如晨光囧笔的简介：“囧是一种明亮而不刺眼的光辉，囧是一种圆润而不逆耳的音响。囧是一种不再察言观色的从容，囧是一种停止申述求告的大气。囧是一种不理会哄闹的微笑，囧是一种洗刷了偏激的淡漠。囧是一种无须伸张的厚实，囧是一种并不陡峭的高度。囧是一种新人类的热忱和气度，囧是一种对新生命的爱惜。囧是一种态度，囧是一种艺术，囧是一种内涵，囧是一种哲学。囧是平凡的，但是囧然一看，却又包含着万般语言。囧是神奇的，囧中有着对世界的探索。囧是伟大的，囧需要顶礼膜拜。晨光囧笔，囧出风格，囧出气质。”①

在囧如此具有文化意义的当下，我们不禁要问，曾经与囧一样非常流行的“酷”“炫”“帅”“靓”怎么就未能像囧那样形成一种电影艺术类型，为什么偏偏一个歧义纷呈的囧会在当下一直流行呢？不仅在网络，而且在电影，在现实生活中，在商业活动中囧都火起来呢？原因可能很多，而其关键在于我们这个由现代、后现代、前现代既和谐共谋，又内在紧张对立而构成的时代，本身就具有奇异性或奇葩性，同时也因为多元并置于和谐共谋而具有模糊性，似乎人们的思想和情感如不借助于随机、朦胧、奇异、歧义、多义的词语就难以表达。而囧相对而言就具有十足的模糊、朦胧、奇异、歧义、多义、奇葩和随意的特点，与当下时代特点和人们的认识相吻合。而其他流行语作为形容词可能是非常新鲜、非常准确、惟妙惟肖的，但作为思想的容器却不能胜任，因为它们都因其明确无误和单一含义而缺少内在的张力。因此，可以说，囧在当下的流行深刻地表明囧已经不再是单

① 见百度百科“囧”词条。

纯的一个词语，而是人们在当下的时代特征、文化内蕴、人生样态和审美形态的展现，是一种别现代的语言创造。囧作为艺术符号和诗意表达，其魅力就在于囧作为审美形态契合了人们的言说方式和审美心理，能够确证当下人生的微妙存在。

囧系列影片虽然表现的是平凡人的遭遇，讲的是普通人的故事，但是我们同样可以找出囧特有的文化意味。囧本身就是一种人生存在的方式，因而饱含着人生的哲理性。囧途通过窘与炯的歧义并呈，展现的是人的动态存在，其中蕴含着在路上和回归两大人生主题。《人在囧途》和《人在囧态之泰囧》无论是表现中国国内的旅行还是异国他乡的旅途，都经历了一个从亲情破裂到亲情回归的过程，都展现了挣脱物质的羁绊重获精神自由的过程。而《港囧》在回归初恋还是回归家庭上的折腾，也是当下人生的随机选择。因此，囧类电影在一定程度上具有人生的哲理意味。这种哲理不是剧作家或导演赋予的，而是在一个充满了既和谐又对立的复杂社会形态中个体谋求存在的真实写照：前途到底是炯还是窘，谁也不知道，人就是这样仿佛被抛在了路上，一切的计划、打算、规划，都显得不是无用就是多余，似乎一切都是被随机性和命运暗中操作着的，但总还不至于绝望。即便是妥协，即便是共谋，即便是无奈，也总有归途。甚至在某种意义上说，囧类电影往往通过单纯、幼稚、无知的配角，展示受随机性和命运控制之人的随遇而安，却较之聪明人（主角）的事业追求和爱情追求更容易获得幸福感的结局，将追求、目的、崇高等一一消解，这种对主角的解构和由此而造成的中心的离散，实在是别现代时期现代与前现代、后现代和谐共谋的人生宿命的隐喻。正是这种隐喻，使得囧类电影成了囧文化别现代特征的代表。

第二节 “囧”作为一种新的审美形态

《港囧》《人再囧途之泰囧》《人在囧途》等数部囧系列影片在中

国电影史上都获得了空前的成功，这不仅仅是动辄十数亿的票房收入，在国内领先，而且形成了囧剧的途中类型电影，在电影史上有其特殊的贡献。因此，囧系列影片的成功就非常值得探讨。囧类电影除了时代特征、文化内蕴外，还由于其凝聚于“囧”的鲜明的特征而构成了新的审美形态，因此，将它作为审美形态进行研究也是十分必要的。

审美形态是指特定人生样态、人生境界、审美情趣、审美风格、体裁的感性凝聚和逻辑分类。[①] 审美形态学从艺术分类和艺术风格的角度对色彩斑斓、变幻无穷的艺术样态和审美现象进行透视和分析，从而把握其内在的精神气韵和风格特征，并揭示其生成原因。由于审美形态的研究能够显示特定文化的识别标志，[②] 如中国的审美形态气韵、意境、神妙、空灵、飘逸等较之西方的审美形态悲剧、喜剧、荒诞等，就不仅是艺术种类和审美风格的区别，而且还是文化上的不同。尤其是新兴的审美形态的出现，会成为时代的风向标。如现代西方出现的荒诞、媚世、堪鄙等审美形态，就不同于古代的悲剧、喜剧、崇高等，是西方现代社会文化嬗变的写照。因此，从审美形态的角度看问题，囧作为别现代时期出现的新的审美形态，其文化意义和美学意义都非同一般。

从审美形态学看，囧类电影或囧剧具有以下特点。

首先，囧类电影中囧的意义生成所彰显的正是别现代时期和谐共谋与紧张对立的矛盾结构，具有疑似中和的特点。“囧”，最初的含义是光明的意思，与“炯”近义。但从目前日常生活和网络使用的情况看，“囧”已经成为“窘”的同义词。但在囧类影片中所表现出来的囧却是两层意义皆有，并在语义的不断转换中获得了内在的张

---

① 王建疆：《审美形态新论》，《甘肃社会科学》2007 年第 4 期。又见由王建疆负责修订的朱立元主编《美学》2006 年版第三编“审美形态论”中关于审美形态的界定。

② 王建疆：《中国审美形态与中华文化特性》，《西北师范大学学报》2016 年第 1 期。

力。2015 年前的两部囧剧都以旅途为题材，总是通过旅途中两个主角的相遇，引发旅途上一连串的悲喜。虽然到了《港囧》，主角是去同城的一个会展约会初恋的情人，但总的来说，故事发生在途中的模式并没有因此而改变，囧的主题意义的生成性也没有改变，尤其是在窘与炯的对立统一中构成中和的结构特征依然故我。

生成，英语 becoming，是跟现成相对的，指走向目的地，走向成功，但尚未到达，尚未成功，也就是方兴未艾，在路上的意思。囧剧不是单纯地表现“炯”或“窘”，而是表现“炯”与“窘”的交织、纠葛、转换，在意蕴上历经了一个不断生成的过程，即由古义的光明到现代的窘迫最后又回到了光明，成了别现代时期人生道路上从希望到失望，而后又重拾希望的隐喻或从内在紧张到和谐共谋的象征，从而具有一定的张力，避免了大光明结局的单调和浅薄。这种内在张力会形成囧剧蕴藉的审美形态特点，生成一个严肃的主题，从而也对囧剧自设的诸多俗浅的搞笑有一定的超越。囧的意蕴生成，是通过情节的随机性或诸多的巧合与悬念来实现的。囧系列影片在喜剧形式的外衣下裹着的同样是富有戏剧性的内容和主题。人在囧途，虽然表现的是“行路难”这一传统的主题，但囧的美学意蕴要比行路难丰厚得多。它把人生的无奈以冷幽默的方式形象地表现出来，取得了“行路难”的直白所不具有的审美效果。《人在囧途》和《人在囧途之泰囧》通过不同交通方式的换乘，不单单地表现了路途之艰难，而是表现了人在旅途中的各种奇妙遭遇，将酸甜苦辣的人生滋味一股脑儿地端出，在不断生长的看点中获得了既搞笑又蕴藉的喜剧效果。

囧系列影片在出人预料、波澜起伏的故事情节中，仍然回归到一个中国传统的大团圆结局。结局最后，没有人受到伤害，人人都有所得。尽管人物历尽千辛万苦，人物矛盾不断激化，但最后一切都得到解脱，没有偏离大众预想和期待的审美轨道，营造出人人都乐于接受的审美效果。虽然这种大团圆结局难免中国前现代审美文化中的心灵鸡汤之嫌，但囧的美学意义却在于囧途之人的窘境已到

了观众忍受的极限，就在将成为苦戏的刹那出现了转换，给人一种惊喜。这里固然有囧剧情节的意料之外和结局的情理之中的张力结构设置，也有中和的大团圆结局，但值得注意的是，囧类电影的中和色彩，已不同于传统意义上的中和，即用理性和礼法对自然情感的节制，所谓“发乎情而止乎礼义”，相反，是将窘境无限放大，甚至像《港囧》那样将窘境放大到险境，不惜使用现代电影的惊悚手法使其达到极致，然后用一个后现代的搞笑（从高楼坠落后夫妻叠合在警察早已铺好的充气救生垫上）使危险和紧张涣然冰释。因此，如果说囧剧具有中和色彩的话，那么，它也只能是一种疑似中和，而非传统意义上的中和。这种疑似中和的产生，无疑跟别现代时期现代、后现代与前现代的内在矛盾没有爆发，相反，三者之间仍处于和谐共谋，三者分别以占比、占股的杂糅方式存在有关。这种杂糅或混血所导致的疑似中和，不可能在现代、后现代、前现代的某一个方向上取得突破，只能在疑似中和的结局和由导演设置的爆笑中获得一种大众共谋的狂欢。

其次，囧类电影既含有中西共享的滑稽，又凸显了中国式的冷幽默。囧剧导演明确地把喜剧作为其体裁和风格类型。徐峥认为：“喜剧的东西是他的包装，是它的形式，好玩。各种错位，俏皮话，没有人真正受到伤害，最后每一个人都有小小的实现，有所失，那边必须有所得。”① 喜剧一般都要通过滑稽和幽默两种审美形态来表现。囧类电影所表现的囧既包含了中西方共有的滑稽，同时含有中国式幽默，是冷幽默和热幽默的结合，而以冷幽默最有特色。正是这种多元素的融合，既使囧剧手法多样，又表现出情感的丰富，形成了独具特色的中国喜剧类型——囧喜剧。

就滑稽而言，囧系列电影中表现出来的滑稽既有西方式滑稽，又有中国式的滑稽。西方的滑稽来自喜剧。亚里士多德认为，“滑稽

---

① 参见《凤凰网·非常道》第236期，http://ent.ifeng.com/fcd/special/xuzheng/。

的事物是某种错误或丑陋，不致引起痛苦和伤害”①。囧系列影片正是通过剧中人物一系列倒霉透顶的遭遇，展现了剧中人物的力量的渺小，他们不断被作弄，唤不起同情却显得荒唐可笑，营造出可喜可乐的喜剧效果，同时也在一定程度上肯定了人们的弱点的合理性。中国的滑稽起源于模仿和取乐，离不开动作。影片中将中国式的滑稽表现得淋漓尽致，通过一系列行为动作散发出大量的笑点。例如，《人在囧途》中王宝强饰演的牛耿在登机时由于飞机上不能携带牛奶而将一桶牛奶当着检票员的面一饮而尽，并在检票员面前痛快地打嗝儿，爆出笑来。这种滑稽的行为同时给电影中的人物和观众都制造了笑点。《泰囧》中王宝强饰演的王宝同样在偷高博的东西时，因被高博发现倍感紧张。但是影片戏剧性的错位，将王宝推向了一个按摩师的位置。王宝将按摩的动作改换为做葱油饼的动作，并在做葱油饼的过程中乐在其中，同样冲淡了电影中的紧张气氛，使影片的节奏变得轻松愉快，观众也被这种滑稽的动作逗得捧腹大笑。这些看似滑稽的动作使囧剧中的矛盾冲突走向消融，能够产生一种奇妙的喜剧效果。

就幽默而论，幽默是与滑稽不同的另一种喜剧表现形式。与滑稽的借助于动作不同，幽默更多地借助语言表现出来。幽默是通过诙谐的语言来对人生的遭遇进行一种评判，最终的效果是引起忍俊不禁的笑，获得一种审美愉悦。幽默可分为热幽默和冷幽默。热幽默通常是笑点就在话语中，听后直接让人捧腹；而冷幽默则是指听完或看完后要思索、回味一番才能体会出其中的诙谐之处。如《人在囧途》中牛耿（王宝强饰）与李成功（徐峥饰）过长江时的一段对话就是典型的冷幽默：

牛耿：老板，你看这黄河多黄？

① ［古希腊］亚里士多德、［古罗马］贺拉斯：《诗学·诗艺》，罗念生等译，人民文学出版社1962年版，第16页。

李成功：大哥，这是长江啊。（用冷幽默来暗讽环境污染）

热幽默表现为温馨赞美，冷幽默表现为冷嘲热讽，也多少有点幸灾乐祸的味道，但总体上还是善意的，给人以快乐，是人与人、人与社会尚未尖锐对立的产物。虽然囧剧的冷幽默非常突出，但又不同于西方现代主义美学的黑色幽默。黑色幽默表现出来的无奈往往连带着绝望的心理和幸灾乐祸的虐待，而非善意，给人以黑色的窒息感，如摔断左腿的一位患者逃过医护的监护去参加圣诞夜的狂欢，就在向别人吹嘘自己逃脱监护的能耐时却不小心脚底打滑摔断了右腿！一般来说，囧类电影的热幽默随处可见，而其中的冷幽默则不易被发现。《泰囧》通过一个以徐朗为典型的“聪明人”和一个以王宝为典型的“愚人”之间的对话，通过运用语言的错位、俏皮话等各种手段，将人生进行了各种冷幽默的处理，使愚与智易位，贵与贱颠倒，也使原本尴尬沉重的人生获得了轻与重、喜与悲相互融合又相互转换的审美效果。《港囧》中小舅子蔡拉拉（包贝尔饰）愣头青式的捉奸戏，以及“你们俩这么恶心，怎么会怀不上孩子呢。（嘲笑徐来夫妇的夫妻‘恩爱’）”更是建立在一系列随机事件基础上的冷幽默。由于别现代时期和谐共谋与对立冲突的交织，冷幽默成了社会情绪宣泄的艺术方式，虽然未必能够达到马克思所说的喜剧能使“人类能够愉快地和自己的过去诀别”① 的效果，但却无疑使囧剧获得中国观众的喜爱。可以说，正是囧类电影中冷热幽默的结合，使囧剧具有了新的审美形态的质素。

第三，以俗取乐的俗乐形态特征。在谈到《人再囧途之泰囧》的主题时，徐峥导演说：“这就是我想做一部主流的喜剧片，它的主题必须够俗，够世俗，因为只有世俗，才能涵盖的人群面够广，才能为

---

① 马克思：《黑格尔〈法哲学批判〉导言》，见《马克思恩格斯文集》第1卷，人民出版社2009年版，第7页。

大部分的观众所接受，这是他电影里的主题。"[1] 事实上，囧类电影展现的是现实生活中的人生百态，通过艺术手法对现实人生进行喜剧化处理，获得了大众普遍接受的审美效果。大众性不仅表现为题材上的世俗性，而且还表现为人物故事情节的民间性。如《人在囧途》以众人皆经历过的春运为题材，将春运中的囧通过两个人物形象的经历展现出来，真实地表现了当下社会的现实，因而能够获得广泛的群众基础。再如《港囧》中的婚外约会与小舅子蔡拉拉的捉奸，也都是现实俗众最感兴趣的事儿，是看点，也是卖点。虽然徐峥明确地说，喜剧要俗，但由于囧剧中窘与炯的内在张力，使它自身并没有一俗到底，而是乐从俗来，以俗取乐，凝聚为俗乐，这种俗乐构成了囧类电影审美形态的共同特征。

以俗取乐是一个很值得研究的审美现象。它的前提是，俗是否也能代表徐峥所说的"主流"？是否还存在着以雅取乐的方式？若是，若有，为什么不选择以雅取乐呢？若非，若无，是否意味着以俗取乐就是喜剧的唯一法则？这个问题的答案仍然在特定历史时期的现实中，在雅俗观众的占比中，而不在美学本身。以雅为乐者在别现代时期仍然是个很小的占比，而以俗为乐者却是徐峥所说的"大部分的观众"，因此，这种占比分析的背后仍然是资本现代性的支配权。决定以雅为乐还是以俗为乐在美学上不具有选择的绝对性，但在经济学上具有绝对性，因为这涉及票房价值和囧剧的再生产。因此，以俗取乐，尽管目前是一种不错的电影产业的经营方式，而且也不是俗不可耐、一塌糊涂，相反，俗得适中，俗得可以，俗得审美，但以俗取乐，能否长久，能否伟大，这却是一个超出了经济学的问题。仅就俗乐在别现代时期的普遍流行而言，俗乐的确是我们这个时代新的审美形态的特点。

总之，具有内在张力的疑似中和，与中国式的冷幽默和俗乐，共同构成了囧这种新的审美形态的整体。

---

① 参见《凤凰网·非常道》第 236 期，http：//ent. ifeng. com/fcd/special/xuzheng/。

第三节　囧类电影的前现代文化根基

囧剧的疑似中和色彩，以及冷幽默、俗乐的审美形态特点，尽管立足于现代生活场景，具有后现代大众文化的特点，也掺杂了后现代无中心的无厘头元素，但是，这种审美形态的精神内涵还是植根于前现代中国的文化土壤中的。因此，囧有自己的形态特征，跟西方20世纪以来形成的新的审美形态范畴媚世有所不同。媚世被认为是“1. 廉价且大为流行；2. 溺情而难称真情；3. 无品而自我品味”①。

囧也广为流行，甚至耳熟能详，但与媚世的区别却在于：以俗取乐而不媚俗，抚慰心灵而不放任欲望，没有批判但有嘲讽，虽有俗乐而不自恋。构成这种区别的原因是在对人生旅途的描述中给人以希望，给人以快乐，而非简单地迎合人们庸俗的甚至俗不可耐的欲望，更非为自己的媚俗而自我感动。这里有着深刻的文化背景。

囧作为一种新的中国审美形态，其现代、后现代、前现代的时代烙印都比较明显。但就其文化根源来说，虽然后现代手法于囧剧中随处可见，但是，中国古代“和”的思想，包括中和、和合的思想，以及中国特有的乐感文化却是其疑似中和、冷幽默和俗乐等审美形态元素的精神命脉。

1. 和合文化的影子。

就中和审美形态而言。《礼记·中庸》中说：“喜怒哀乐未发谓之中，发而皆中节谓之和。”中和作为中国传统的审美形态范畴，在人生样态、人生境界、艺术风格、审美情趣中得到了充分表现，也在戏剧、园林、诗歌等艺术形式中普遍存在。作为审美形态，中和的思想基础和思维方式建立在和合文化的基础上。这种和合包括人们熟悉

① 张法：《媚世（kitsch）和堪鄙（camp）——从美学范畴体系的角度看当代西方两个美学新范畴》，《当代文坛》2011年第1期。

的天人合一，都对中国封建社会的思想和审美形态产生了深远的影响。和合文化不仅为封建社会家天下的皇权统治提供了“君权神授”的信仰依据，而且也为社会的稳态发展提供了思想基础。在这种和合稳态的社会中，“哀而不伤”“乐而不淫”的诗学标准和大团圆的戏剧观都在强化着中和这种中国式的审美形态。儒家讲天人合一，过犹不及，讲中和。道家也讲天人合一、与物为春，甚至“与天地并生而与万物为一”。实际上就如道家阴阳图所展现的那样，也是一种和合文化。中国历史上的儒道互补，更使得这种和合文化具有兼容并包的特点。所谓的“三教合一”，也是一种典型的中外文化和合。产生于别现代时期的审美形态囧，同样具有鲜明的合和特性。不管是囧的语义上的含蓄蕴藉，还是审美风格上的兼容并蓄，都表现为疑似中和的审美形态特征，以审美形态上的和合兼容，暗示现代、后现代、前现代的和谐共谋。

首先，囧审美形态通过象形的方式传达出和合的思维方式。囧通过它的内小“八”字和“口”来象征眉眼和嘴，表达出多义的内涵。作为头。表达沉重的思想。作为脸。表达浪漫与激情。囧将看似不同的含义融合到一起，获得了语义的含蓄蕴藉。有人在谈到“囧”的流行时，认为“这只能说明汉字本身的魅力。今天有些文字里的信息已经被渐渐丢掉，汉字的原生态思维也在一点点被丢掉了，这种返璞归真的趋势值得肯定”①。这也从囧的语义生成上，为囧的古今语义的和合性提供了一个传统文化的例证。

其次，在审美风格上，囧类电影的喜剧性效果建立在悲喜交替、彼此消长的剧情中，不同于西方戏剧那样的悲喜分明，而是将喜和悲在西方看似对立的两种形态，像道家的阴阳图一样，融为一体，从而形成囧的悲喜不断转换和交融的喜剧特点。

---

① 邵宇峰：《在网络上很流行的“囧”到底是个什么字?》，《杭州日报》2008 年 5 月 13 日第 18 版。

最后，囧在思想内容上也表现出儒释道传统文化的兼容并包。囧系列在主题上或通过亲情的破裂走向亲情的回归，或通过由初恋旧梦引发的疑似出轨到最终得以澄清，都是从欲望和争名逐利的痛苦挣扎中回归家庭，体现出儒家特有的重视亲情家庭等道德伦理层面的意义。同时《囧途》和《泰囧》在剧情上通过两个人物的相遇展现出大智若愚的辩证思维，以徐朗为代表的聪明人看似聪明却因物质的羁绊而屡受挫折，在精神上显得不足。而以王宝为代表的傻子看似愚笨却因精神的自由变得乐观强大，聪明人在傻子的指引下获得了精神上的觉悟，这其中大有道家文化中"大巧若拙""离形去知"的智慧品格。此外，囧还有佛禅文化的影子。佛禅认为人人皆可成佛，讲求顿悟，囧系列影片通过在人生道路上的种种遭遇，使人历经劫难，在一瞬间产生顿悟，获得智慧。《泰囧》中，徐朗和高博在寻找和抢夺油霸的过程中历尽了苦难，终于得到了想要的授权书，但徐朗在看到授权书后，却了悟人生的真谛，放弃了对名利的追逐。

以上诸多的和合，也许会因为杂糅而变得模糊，也许会因为共谋而失去了锐角，但前现代的观念在现代社会背景和后现代文化背景下就是如此强大，而且又能为广大的俗众乐于接受，就只能说是别现代时期的审美风貌原本如此。

2. 乐感文化的灵魂。

中国传统文化的突出特征除了和合之外就是乐感。乐感文化说是李泽厚先生的发明①。乐感与基督教文化的罪感和日本文化的耻感相对。乐感文化延续至今，构成囧类电影能够以俗取乐的文化基础。而且不仅如此，乐感文化已经成了徐峥囧类电影的灵魂。囧从窘向炯的转换生成，这个不变的囧主题，在囧类电影那里是被乐感文化主宰着的现代和后现代的践履。

首先是无所不乐的俗乐。中国人不讲求西方宗教基于赎罪基础上

① 李泽厚：《中国古代思想史》，安徽文艺出版社1994年版，第304—313页。

的受难，而要关注现实人生的及时行乐。囧系列影片受到中国乐感文化的影响，将囧这一人生样态进行了乐感文化的浸泡，使囧脱离了一个单线的苦难或者快乐的人生历程，变成一个希望与失望并存的丰富人生。囧片中的艰难不是救赎的磨难，也不会产生任何耻感，相反，只是“梅花香自苦寒来”的必要过程，无疑在暗示人们一种积极乐观的人生态度，只有历经苦难才能收获人生的希望和快乐。囧剧中的人物虽然遭受不同程度的尴尬和痛苦，但都能默默忍受，最后靠着随机的命运，幸运地得到心灵的满足。在这一点上，囧剧与于丹给听众提供的“心灵的鸡汤”一样，都是在消解崇高后的一种贫亦乐，穷亦乐，无所不乐的“炯”途，已将片名中的“囧”抛之九霄云外，获得了大众的俗乐。《泰囧》中王宝虽然经济贫困，母亲有痴呆症，仍然能每天笑容灿烂，在受到别人欺骗时还能笑脸相迎，已将俗乐进行到底。

其次是大团圆的结局。中国传统文化的心理特征是乐感心理，因此也在艺术表现上给人一个快乐的结局。西方的救赎文化很容易导致剧情的毁灭性结局，产生巨大的悲感和震撼。囧剧只有紧张而无震撼，只有快乐而无悲伤。在终遂人愿的大团圆结局中，总有主配角们的一幅幅快乐得蹦跳起来的亮相。尽管囧系列影片的结局也并非俗不可耐，也俗得审美，但是，这种受到观众捧场的大团圆结局，再次告诉我们，尽管人们赋予“囧”以现代的意义，但是，囧的前现代文化根基、思想根基、审美根基，依然故我，而且借助现代电影的科技手段和后现代的搞笑手法，与现时代人们的审美情趣和审美理念沆瀣一气。

正是囧背后的中国文化根基，决定了囧作为审美形态的与西方的媚世的不同。但是，囧毕竟是以俗取乐的俗乐，因此，尽管俗得可以，俗得审美，但永远不可能俗得伟大。也许只有起始于俗而又超越了俗，才可能有伟大。但这将是中国艺术、中国电影将要面对的另外一个话题，也许只有到了别现代社会之后才可能实现的理想。

第四节　余论

囧虽然比较集中地表现在囧类电影中，但囧作为审美形态，不止于电影，而是渗透在人生和艺术的各个方面。

囧这一审美形态的生成，是前现代审美文化在当代的复活，是掺杂着现代、后现代和前现代文化精神的当今人生境界、审美趣味、人生样态和审美风格的感性凝聚。透视和解剖囧这一审美形态，至少可以让我们看清这个时代的面貌，了解国民的审美品位，捕捉到当今人们的精神境界、现实吁求和心理轨迹，从而能为心灵的调节找到另一种审美的方式。当下的社会中，囧为什么能够获得大众的接受，原因即在于囧刻画现实人生的存在样态，迎合了主流的审美心理。囧的受欢迎，说明当前观众期待抚慰的愿望和别现代时期的诉求，即一种回避囧的由窘途带来的崇高而分享欢笑的集体无意识。囧这一审美形态，正是通过艺术的方式来表现人生存在的状态，用艺术来消解人生的苦难，并给人们提供智慧和启迪。

囧的窘炯互通，本身具有人生的全息性。中国人的人生观是“过日子”“好死不如赖活着”，人们都明白“人世难逢开口笑”“人生不如意事十之八九”“千金难买一笑”，只要过得去就行，过不去则不行。囧剧十分切合中国人过日子的脉搏，总是从人在旅途的窘迫开始，最终进入光明囧照的结局。虽然现实中的囧事太多太多，囧类电影又在强化着这种囧事，但囧剧让观众不虚此观的地方就在于总还是能够让人们笑起来，而且笑得开心，笑得停不下来，在笑中得到纾解和愉悦。尽管并不高雅，但也实用，地地道道地帮我们过日子。就这样，囧的俗乐就被老百姓所喜闻乐见。过日子的主题也就是活着的主题。但相较于余华的《活着》的悲剧性存在方式，囧是另一种活着的方式。也许相较余华式的活着而显得肤浅，但毕竟没有沉重和痛苦，还有片刻的欢乐，因此，囧的炯就这样在不知不觉中完成了对于

囧的窘的置换。

囧具有内在的张力和丰富的内涵，通过各种悬念和误会，历经各种人生窘境，制造了令人忍俊不禁的喜剧效果（我在上海闵行区的世纪影城看《港囧》时，同场观众至少爆发出12次大笑），把一个严肃的人生主题浸泡在一个轻快的喜剧形式中，制造了很多笑点，具有很强的艺术表现力。极端的痛苦和极端的滑稽加在一起释放出中国式冷幽默的审美功能，这种冷幽默在制造笑点的同时也能勾起人们对于人生窘境的思考，总有可以回味的地方，这大概就是囧的魅力所在，也是它对中国审美形态的奉献所在。

囧这一审美形态的生成对中国美学研究具有一定的启发意义。中国美学作为舶来品，在思想上、理论上、范畴上一直追随西方美学，虽有不满，并对“中国美学还是美学在中国”的疑问难以释怀，但一时又很难找到突破。其原因就在于对我们今天所处的时代特征缺乏认识，进而对这个特定时代的审美风貌缺乏了解，无法找到中国美学的立足点。这个立足点实质上就是指不同于西方的独特的话语系统和形态特征。如果我们从别现代研究中国审美形态，就会发现中国审美形态的别现代特征，就如我们对囧的疑似中和、冷热幽默和俗乐的发现一样，对这些特征进行概括提炼，就可以形成新的美学思想和美学理论，这些新的美学思想和美学理论既与西方美学思想和美学理论相联系，又有诸多不同，从而有助于我们建立中国特色的美学思想和美学理论。事实上，囧作为审美形态兼具现代、前现代和后现代的综合形态，但又无法将之简单地归为其中的任何一种形态。因而，确切地说，囧作为一种正在生成的审美形态，具有别现代的综合性审美功能。可以说，囧的审美形态发现，使我们进一步明确了时代特征、文化传统以及多元文化杂糅对于当下审美形态范畴生成的意义，从而为中国美学研究找到了新的增长点。

第二章

别现代："消费日本"与英雄空间的解构*

我们正处于现代、前现代、后现代交集纠葛的时代。具有现代性的制度和思想正在建立中，但前现代的制度和观念仍根植于现实的社会和人生中，同时，后现代的文艺思潮和美学思潮已在中国泛滥。这种现代、前现代和后现代并置的现象在断代式的欧美国家并未出现，因此，很难有个现成的名词对这种现象予以概括，无奈之余只好将之称为"别现代"（Bie-modern；Bie-modernism；Bie-post-modernism 等）。别现代既涉及现代、前现代，又涉及后现代，但它既不是单一的现代，又不是单一的后现代，更不是单一的前现代，因此，只能是别现代。别现代只是借用了"现代"这个词，而非别现代就是现代的一种，也不是说，别现代属于复杂的现代性。因为，中国的现代性尚在路上、尚不具足。除了现代性的因素外，还有前现代性和后现代性的同时存在，所以，所谓复杂的现代性并不能概括别现代的非现代性。相反，别现代却恰当地涵盖了现代/现代性、后现代/后现代性、前现代/前现代性交集纠葛的"非标"状态。因此，别现代就是别现代，不是英语表述中的可选择的/另类的现代性（Alternative modernity）或其他现代性（Other modernity）所能概括的。从哲学上而非字面上讲，别现代包含了虚妄不实的现代性和期

* 本章曾发表于《中国文学批评》2017 年第 2 期。

许建构别样现代性的思考和主张，因而既是对社会形态的描述和概括，又是一种价值倾向和主义主张，是在概括别现代现状之外对别现代的一种更新和超越。

如何准确地把握这个时代的特点，对我们正确地认识和评价现代化生活中的文化现象、审美现象、文艺现象不无裨益。正是本着这个思想，我们愿就现实社会和文艺作品中同时存在的“消费日本”现象和英雄空间现象进行考察，试图提供一个新视角和新话题。

第一节　别现代时期的“消费日本”现象

别现代时期是现代、前现代和后现代的和谐共谋期，其“共谋”表现在社会生活的方方面面。

就社会的经济形态而言，各种所有制和谐共处，国有、私企、外企并驾，现代化大工业、家族企业和私人小作坊齐驱，计划经济与市场经济混合。

就社会的管理制度而言，具有现代意义的法律和管理制度正在建设中，但同时，与现代法律和管理制度相矛盾的现象比比皆是。或没有原则，没有法规，或有法不依，没有边界、放弃原则、妥协、交易（权钱交易、权色交易、权法交易、行贿受贿）等；不断更改规矩、实行潜规则；有选择地遗忘和遮蔽历史、造假畅行无阻等，前现代的思想观念和行为方式因现代制度的缺位而由后现代的跨越边界（cross border）、解构中心、消解原则来加以表达，形成混沌的和谐，可以浑水摸鱼，这一点在当今那些高智商、高学历、高级别、受过现代教育、出过国、留过洋但又贪污腐化、身败名裂的人身上得到了最为集中的表现。

就社会的文化形态而言，一方面是传统文化与当代文化之间的矛盾，中国文化与西方文化之间的矛盾；另一方面是现代、后现代与前

现代之间的彼此适应、和谐共处。

就社会的文艺现象而言，异彩纷呈。现代的场景、背景、技术，与前现代的理念和后现代的手法同台亮相。现代的场景、背景、技术自不用说，前现代的香火观念、专制思想、迷信思想等影响仍在，后现代的戏仿、恶搞大行其道，英雄和英雄空间①都被以戏仿、娱乐、恶搞的方式解构。

但别现代诸多特征中一条贯穿性的主线是消费。这种消费似乎在印证着后现代消费理论的正确性，但在中国，这种消费是一种非常复杂的现象。比如，物质消费与精神消费之间的差异，实体消费与虚拟消费之间的不同，实物消费与象征消费之间的区别，不同阶层之间的不同消费，以及不同阶层的不同形式的消费等，很难用西方现有的理论来解释。如果套用当下正流行的鲍德里亚符号消费理论来解释中国的消费现象，会认为中国人目前的消费也是对符号的消费，而非对于实体的消费，因而是一种浪费。但是，在中国，现阶段的消费首先是对物质的消费，是对质量比较高的生活必需品的消费，是一种实实在在的消费，而非显富摆阔式的以商品为富有象征的消费。这一点，只要看看电商网购那些超低折扣对亿万消费者的吸引力和数百万游日旅客对日本原产商品质量的信赖及抢购，就可以明白，中国人当前的消费并没有脱离物质消费，没有进入后现代的符号消费阶段，而是前现代物美价廉观念的延续而已。因此，中国迫切需要来自中国现实和解释中国现实的消费理论，而非来自对西方现实概括总结的西方消费理论。

近年的中国消费，以电商网购和消费日本最为引人注目。电商网购是利用互联网廉价消费吸引亿万消费者，而消费日本却是要到日本去消费。据日本观光厅数据显示，2015 年有近 500 万中国游客赴日

① 参见王建疆《后现代语境中的英雄空间与英雄再生》，《文学评论》2014 年第 3 期。

旅游购物，花费近800亿人民币①。除此之外，消费日本就是观赏抗日题材的影视作品。虽然物质上的消费日本现象看起来要比电商网购原始一些，但消费日本却因中国影视观众对于以“抗日神剧”为代表的涉日题材的青睐而具有了超出物质消费的更多含义，比如情结的释放、情感的愉悦、无聊的打发、肾上腺素的分泌等，更具有精神消费的特点。

由于日本与中国在文化上的历史渊源和现代纠葛，中国人对于日本的消费就显得格外引人注目。就物质消费而言，中国人到日本旅游并“扫货”，与中国部分民众不时自发兴起的反日情绪，如抵制日货等，判若两仪。但日益火爆的赴日游和不可思议的“扫日货”现象，却一直在刺激着中国人的神经。从媒体对这一现象的高频次报道中，不难看出中国人在消费日本中的这种纠结。这一纠结是现代与前现代某些观念在消费中的妥协、共谋与和谐，也体现出后现代解构中心观念下离散的、随机的消费模式。这种消费模式集中体现在：消费日本现象中上述两方面都不再是具有独立支配意义的中心，也不再是单一的、排他的主宰，相反，二者完全可以含混并置，从而形成和谐共谋的平行观念或交叉观念。可以说，在消费日本现象的背后，是物质消费与精神消费的合谋。

就精神消费而言，消费日本未必要去日本，只要在家中打开电视热播节目，总有抗日题材的作品可供观赏。不管是日本人出演的“日本鬼子”，还是中国人出演的“日本鬼子”，都已成为地道的精神消费品。这种对日本的精神消费，虽已持续多年，但观众、编导和出品人的兴趣并未随着岁月的流逝而减弱，相反，有着“心潮逐浪高”的势头。往往是那些骂着“弱智”的观众，说起“抗日神剧”来头头是道，比一般观众看的“神剧”更多，也有更深的体验。甚至，

① 陈杰、左婧远：《去年内地赴日游客人数同比翻倍》，2016年1月21日，http://www.bbtnews.com.cn/2016/0121/137111.shtml，2017年3月8日。

现在推荐看“神剧”的是愈来愈多的女性观众。总之，消费日本正在成为别现代时期的奇葩现象，也正在成为不断成长的基金，不仅中国人投注，日本人也在投注。①

精神消费远比物质消费复杂得多、深奥得多。也许有人会问，看电视也叫消费？是的。从购买电视机之日起，为电视节目付费已成事实。消费的实质是商业、商品与消费者之间的和谐共谋。商业、商品、消费者缺一不可，这才构成消费。但是，以电视机为播放器、以文艺为载体的消费日本现象，却要比一般的文艺作品消费复杂得多、纠结得多。因为这里不是简单的消遣和纯粹的文艺鉴赏，而是有着民族无意识的集体记忆和不言自明、难以了断的情结，是一种别现代式的对前现代历史的回顾和对后现代戏仿恶搞的勾连。

消费日本中的精神与物质这两种情况之间颇具张力。一种情况是在游日的过程中给日本的 GDP 做贡献，已然与抵制日货等反消费行为构成矛盾，形成现实主义消费与对日复杂情绪之间的巨大张力。另一种情况却是在消遣、娱乐的过程中宣泄情绪，形成消费主义与道德主义之间的张力。尽管这两种情况看起来截然不同，但在消费的意义上没有太大的区别。有的只是支付方式的不同，而无性质的不同。一个支付的是钞票，一个支付的是精力。只有财力和精力同时充裕的人才可能全面地消费日本。

消费日本是个特殊的时代现象。一方面，消费日本是中国改革开放以来经济发展的结果。在这之前，中国的普通民众何尝会想到去日本旅游并大宗地采购，将其看中的存货买光呢？也只有到了 21 世纪 10 年代后才有了这种消费日本的现象。相较于改革开放前的物质贫乏与经济拮据，这种现象可谓“天翻地覆慨而慷”了。另一方面，

① 比如 2015 年中国曾播出一部由日本 TBS 电视台制作并播出的《红十字——女人的入伍通知单》（日文名为“レッドクロス～女たちの赤紙～”），该剧是日本为纪念世界反法西斯战争 70 周年所做，播出后引起了中国网友的关注与热议。该剧从侧面描写了日本对中国的侵略战争，不禁让人好奇日本人到底会怎么拍摄这部抗日战争题材的剧集。

世界上还有其他曾经遭受过侵略的国家，如波兰。虽然该国首都华沙的博物馆、大商店，甚至首饰店里播放着当年反抗德国侵略的纪录片、故事片等，但与中国的交集纠葛不同，波兰与德国的经济合作却是若即若离的，不像中国这样与日本有着非常紧密的经济与文化合作。对日本的物质消费与精神消费表面上看来完全是两股道上的车，互不搭界，一股道是买你的东西，一股道是表达我对你复杂的情感。但是，这两股道之间之所以构成了一种张力，就在于它们之间既紧张对立，又和谐共谋，不会因为购买你的商品而放弃观看“神剧”的痛快，同样，也不会因为宣泄情感而放弃对你的消费。也许，这是一个民族逐渐走向成熟的标志，但是，首先应该说明的是，这是现代中国人多种需要的消费化表现，是现代、前现代、后现代时间空间化带来的必然结果。

消费日本是对前现代神武英雄的钩沉和打捞。很难想象，在民族观念和边界概念式微的欧美国家，还会出现这种对于曾经的敌对国的精神消费，还会出现反抗侵略的神武英雄。事实上，欧洲自詹姆斯·乔伊斯（James Joyce）的意识流小说《尤利西斯》出版后，英雄已成过去。美国人于 1990 年编写的《当代全球英雄》，已然没有战斗英雄，有的只是职业英雄（professional model）和民主斗士。① 因此，正是中国社会现代、前现代、后现代的交集纠葛所构成的别现代才孕育了消费日本的物质与精神两束奇葩。说它奇葩，是因为在抗战“神剧”中，前现代的神武英雄又从脱魅中重新复魅，如“手撕鬼子”的情节就是对隋唐英雄李元霸“手撕英雄”的拷贝，神武英雄从经典的陈潭中被打捞出来。

对日本的精神消费有着比对日本的物质消费更为深刻的原因。也许有人误认为“抗日神剧”是随着中国人民抗日战争胜利 70 周年纪

---

① 参见 RB Browne, GJ Brown, KO Brown and DG Brown, eds., *Contemporary Heroes and Heroines*, Detroit: Gale Research, 1990。

念活动才开始热播的，实际上从2000年开始，“抗日神剧”就逐渐走红了。其直接的原因似乎是钓鱼岛争端，但深层的原因却在于中国的爱国主义、民族主义，而最深层的原因却是出于凝聚人心的需要。这些深层原因较物质消费而言是更为复杂和深刻的。通过战争回忆把整个民族重新唤醒这种现象，只有在现代、前现代、后现代交集的国家才会发生，才会产生巨大的精神能量，而在美国、英国这些“二战”时期日本的敌对国和战胜国身上，都不可能发生。但是，同样作为战胜国的中国，为什么会出现以文艺的形式消费日本这一现象，这应该是一个深刻的课题，其中深藏着民族情结的密码。

消费日本现象需要新的消费理论。按鲍德里亚的说法，在消费社会，随着媒体的发展，“已经没有意识形态这样的东西，只有拟象”①。电视剧自然是拟象，而非现实真实的记录，但电视剧包括“抗日神剧”消费能否否定意识形态、遮蔽意识形态、消解意识形态，至少在消费日本现象面前是值得怀疑的。因此，针对消费日本现象建立一种新的中国式的消费理论也是势在必行。

新的中国式消费理论就建立在社会形态基础上民众消费与意识形态之间既和谐共谋又矛盾对立的辩证运动中。一方面，在别现代时期，无论物质消费还是精神消费，都形成了对民众的主宰，但是，另一方面，消费并不可能抛弃意识形态，相反，在别现代时期，意识形态对于精神消费的制导作用从来就没有消失过。不仅没有消失过，相反，会随着消费的增长，愈加明显。在消费的主宰和意识形态的制导之间，任何一方的超强，都会导致另一方的衰弱甚至失效，即形成了替代。因此，二者之间需要和谐共谋。但是，二者之间也不可能合二为一，相反，是要保持距离，保持对立的状态，相互制约，形成一种张力。只有这样，双方才会独立存在。这种张力的存在将导致消费日

① 让·鲍德里亚：《象征交换与死亡》，马海良译，汪民安、陈永国、马海良编：《后现代性的哲学话语：从福柯到赛义德》，浙江人民出版社2000年版，第304页。

本现象，即物质消费与精神消费共存现象的长期存在，从而形成具有中国特色的消费理论和中国特色的意识形态掌控理论。

消费与意识形态二者之间既可分，又可合。分则构成意识形态与消费现象的对立，合则构成意识形态与消费现象的和谐共谋。因此，别现代时期的中国消费理论应该是对法国消费理论的修正，不再是消费与意识形态的分裂，或与意识形态无关，相反，而是消费与意识形态的分合共管。正是这种分合共管，构成了我们这个时代文化产业的双重使命，既要保证消费量的不断增大，又要严格的意识形态主旋律控制，从而使民众消费，尤其是消费日本现象，总会在物质与精神的悖论中存在，不断地生长出奇葩来。

第二节　英雄盛筵与欢乐神话

消费是工业文明的标志，虽然中国尚未完全进入消费时代，但是，随着投资、外贸和消费“三驾马车”中消费占比的日益提高，中国完全进入消费时代已是预料中的事。在现代、前现代、后现代交集的别现代时期，消费正在成为主旋律。在别现代的消费中，英雄也难逃厄运而成了消费品。

别现代的英雄消费，具有盛筵的特点。爱国主义的、民族主义的、民粹主义的、人道主义的、普世主义的、救世主义的、神秘主义的英雄观多元并置导致了多种英雄谱系的并存。但所有谱系一旦被试图导向神坛和复魅时，就被菜谱化、消费化了。当张艺谋导演的电影《英雄》中刺秦而又最终放弃刺秦的残雪（李连杰饰）甘愿自己受死时，当电视连续剧《二炮手》中那位二流子（孙红雷饰）竟然成了抗日“神人”时，当《王大花的革命生涯》中的王大花（闫妮饰）以一己之文盲而使日本特高课、共产国际远东情报组织和中共地下党都围绕着她而奔忙时，英雄的崇高已被莫名其妙的转换和滑稽逗乐的表演所替代，成为快乐消费的增长点。别现代时期影视剧就如现实社

会中那样“英雄辈出”却难定于一尊，即使是那种“数风流人物，还看今朝”的豪迈超拔的英雄，充其量也就是英雄盛筵中的一道菜，这一道菜不可能取代其他菜而独霸宴席。这就如今日普通百姓餐桌上的菜碟，早已告别了单一和贫乏一样。

在别现代语境中，英雄正在被英雄空间所代替。所谓英雄空间，就是由多元英雄观构成的巨大的想象空间和塑造空间。在这个空间中，人们都可以根据自己的价值观和审美观想象自己心目中的英雄，塑造自己心目中的英雄。因此，这个英雄空间就是英雄盛筵，包括经典英雄、当代英雄、道德英雄、职业英雄、神武英雄、平凡英雄、恶魔英雄、游戏英雄等。随着全球化的推进，人类英雄谱系从未像今天这样庞杂过，彰显着英雄空间的巨大无比。在这个巨大无比的英雄空间中，既有欧洲尤利西斯式的委顿英雄，也有美国式的科技生物英雄；既有反法西斯的战斗英雄，又有恐怖主义的反人类英雄；既有脱魅平凡的职业英雄，又有为国家争光的民族英雄。但无论人类的这个英雄空间如何巨大，其英雄的存在还是在于被消费，尤其是通过文艺的审美来消费而非被崇拜、被模仿。

消费时代的英雄消费，是一种审美的消费，是对政治伦理压力的缓释。英雄虽然只是凤毛麟角，但具有全息能性质，集中体现了不同的核心价值观。美国的职业英雄、社会主义国家的战斗英雄，恐怖主义的反人类英雄，都凝聚了人类的多元价值观，使英雄更具有意识形态属性。但同时，作为审美消费对象的英雄，由于其戏剧化、戏谑化、滑稽化、神秘化处理，而具有了艺术魅力。《二炮手》（孙红雷主演）中的主角劫财、撬别人的未婚妻、与首长争风吃醋，但打起“日本鬼子”来干净利落无往不胜，可以说虽然没有文化，但样样不落，本来是道德谴责和政治打压的对象，却因抗日而获得了光环并独享尊荣，又因其随身遍布的笑点而获得了审美的价值。还有瘸子英雄、厨子英雄、戏子英雄等，都是在缓释政治伦理压力的情况下，凸显神奇，从而超越了生理的、政治伦理的缺陷而高大起来。同时，各

路英雄的卖萌、诙谐、搞笑，无不强化了审美的消费主义倾向，其好看之处，正是其政治伦理受到调侃和挤压之时，也是消费者为之而感到愉悦的地方。当二炮手从晋军团长手里撬拐其未婚妻时，当二炮手与战功赫赫的八路军司令争夺情人而取胜时，英雄就已然是被消费的对象而非被崇拜的对象，英雄已然是英雄盛筵或英雄空间中一道色香味俱全的上品佳肴。

别现代的英雄消费有其自己的特点。就其消费日本中的“神剧”而言，可以说前现代遭遇了现代，然后又遭遇了后现代，从而造就了国民的消费对象——欢乐神话。一场起初以大刀长矛对付坦克大炮的战争，本身是前现代的不幸，但这种不幸却因后现代艺术的包装而有了亦真亦幻、亦悲亦喜的欢乐神话的审美消费特点。

神话是人类脱魅前的事，但在现代政治伦理理念的驱使下复魅并非不可能。如果这种复魅是一本正经地进行，可能会引人厌恶。这方面，马克思曾说过：“任何神话都是用想象和借助想象以征服自然力，支配自然力，把自然力加以形象化；因而，随着这些自然力之实际上被支配，神话也就消失了。”① 因此，上古英雄、中古英雄的不断脱魅是历史的必然。但是，由于人们心中对于英雄的集体无意识情结，总会给英雄的复魅留有广大的空间。中国古代的“五虎上将”及其神勇就曾在多部历史小说中出现，并一直延续到抗战时期国军的“五虎上将”。如果这种复魅借助了后现代的反宏大叙事和去崇高化，如戏仿、搞笑、恶搞等，就有可能形成欢乐神话。欢乐神话的最大特点就在于不是以平庸表现伟大，而是以崇高表现滑稽，从而将英雄解构，将崇高娱乐化。近年“抗日神剧”吸引眼球的地方在于：

一是削平崇高的娱乐化。“神剧”的卖点即在“爆笑”，即大笑的被引发。引起爆笑的原因或在于语言的幽默，或在于动作的滑稽，

---

① 马克思：《〈政治经济学批判〉导言》，《马克思恩格斯选集》第2卷，人民出版社2012年版，第711页。

或在于表情的有趣。为获此效果，往往选取有生理缺陷或道德缺陷的角色，与其英勇神武的表现形成强烈的反差，从而产生引人发笑的效果。《我的兄弟叫顺溜》就选取以“土得掉渣”又憨得可爱、外傻内秀而知名的王宝强做主角，在其时不时出人预料的言语中引爆笑点。其他的瘸子、戏子、痞子、二流子等，都是以其生理缺陷或道德缺陷与其抗日本领形成强烈的反差而引人注目的。有时还要佐以无知的聪明，像《王大花的革命生涯》中的王大花那样，无知却能背着“戏匣子”（发报机）而调动东亚几大间谍、特科、情报系统围着自己转。这种巨大的反差最容易产生幽默、滑稽的效果。但这里的幽默滑稽并非正戏，而是欢喜剧，是制造看点和制造笑点的精心设计，其戏剧效果并无悲剧的悲壮，亦无喜剧的暴露和批判，有的只是笑点的被引爆，产生为之一笑的娱乐效果。这种娱乐效果具有审美的属性，但属于浅层审美，即娱耳悦目之类。因为在此娱乐中，英雄的神圣和崇高被解构，英雄成了搞笑的元素。王大花无意中帮了中共地下党，在不知道毛泽东是何许人物的情况下非要找他去讨公道——以加入中国共产党来作为对她的报答，在凸显英雄性格的同时，已将崇高削平，将英雄搞笑，成为娱乐的对象。

二是惊悚化。神武英雄能够做出一般战士做不出来的动作，构成惊心动魄的情节，吸引观众眼球，加速观众肾上腺素的分泌。王大花给日本特高课课长下药，以文盲之身偷拍自己根本就不认识的日军文字情报；《异镇》中中统特勤人员在被活埋的瞬间做出的反制等，无不令人惊叹唏嘘。这大概也是“神剧”人“骂”之而又人看之的原因吧。我们的生活太单调贫乏，如果不打游戏，看看“神剧”也不失为一种消遣和调节。

三是引人入胜的随机化故事。近年来“抗日神剧”的主人公大多是在无知的情况下凭着阴差阳错的运气而干出惊天动地的大事的。王大花偶然间从自己的情人口里得到日、苏、中三大谍报系统寻而不得的“戏匣子”如此，牙医王天桥（《虎口拔牙》）得到日本特高课、

国民党军统和共产党地下组织都在搜寻的印有 14000 多件国宝藏地图标的胶卷亦如此，都是天上掉馅饼、掉机缘的事。仿佛倒霉的日本侵略军走错了路，一头撞到了遍布“神功异能”和得道多助的华夏神州，只有被戏耍、宰割、消灭的份儿了。这些随机化的故事在应验中国古代“无巧不成书”的理念时，平添了许多悬念，使故事情节波澜起伏，惊心动魄，看点频出，引人入胜。但这类故事情节毕竟是建立在随机性基础上的，因而能将崇高和伟大轻掷，不必有声，看完之后能够一笑了之。这大概就是后现代去除了崇高这种与惨厉相伴随的审美形态之后而产生的另一种审美效果，仿佛在小吃一条街上徜徉，随时随地都可以得到口福之乐。

别现代时期，消费不仅主导着国民的社会生活，而且主导了意识形态和文艺作品。消费日本现象中“抗日神剧”的英雄塑造犹如菜谱迎合观众的口味而风行起来。“抗日神剧”作为消费品，不乏为商业的明智之举。因为它“为老百姓所喜闻乐见”，于是就有市场，有票房，就有艺术生存的土壤。但随之而来的代价却是违背了塑造英雄、宣传英雄的初衷——崇高被随意化和娱乐化，从而去除了其意识形态的教化功能。

“抗日神剧”完全是消费时代的产物，在它的背后有一种主导性的力量。表面上看是艺术迎合了主流意识形态和审片规则，但实际上却是在迎合消费市场。在市场起主导作用的情况下，爱国主义的精神指导正在被文化消费所浸透、所改造、成为消费的另一盘菜，这就是解闷、释放欲望、调节肾上腺。在这种情况下，英雄的塑造完全是为迎合观众的口味而定制的。“抗日神剧”中的“手撕鬼子”“裤裆藏雷”“子弹拐弯”等情节，虽然过于玄幻而被观众吐槽，但更多的离奇情节还是被观众所接受，而且近来“神剧”之“神”正在升级，已由拙劣的“裤裆藏雷”“手撕鬼子”“子弹拐弯”升格为由中国共产党主导中国国民党军统（《虎口拔牙》）、主导国民党中统（《异镇》），甚至主导日本谍报系统特高课（《王大花的革命生涯》）。这些

颇有浪漫主义色彩的影视片并不因为其新的历史知识而吸引观众，而是由于情节的引人入胜和演员的优秀表演而吸引观众。正应了消费时代里“消费者是上帝”的这一说法，是一种编导与观众、文化产业与大众文化消费之间的和谐共谋。

消费日本中人们到底消费了什么？也许有人会说，影视作品里的“日本鬼子”并非真正的“日本鬼子”，而是拟象，是符号，而非真人，因此属于鲍德里亚所说的符号消费。但是，消费日本具有多重的含义。到日本去消费，表面上看是在消费日本的物质和商品，实际上也是为日本的商业和经济做贡献，因为这是由需要主导的实实在在的消费，而非鲍德里亚所说的浪费，也不是为了显示财力而消费符号。但在影视中对于日本的消费，却并不为日本的 GDP 做贡献，而是观众自己在消耗自己的精气神，是在无聊中打发日子，过日子，但这些实际上只是观众对自己的消费，与一海之隔的日本并无关系。因此，这两种消费日本现象，性质截然不同，而且与鲍德里亚的符号消费理论相对照，并不合辙。鲍德里亚关于消费是浪费，是对符号的消费这一说法可能过于欧洲化，没有看到中国在现实消费中消费者的上帝身份和在精神消费中对自我的消费这些情况。

总之，在别现代时期，虽然英雄依然是人类的精神食粮和崇拜对象，但难以逃脱精神消费的魔咒，处在英雄空间和英雄盛筵中的英雄不再是被崇拜的对象和被效仿的楷模，而是成了被消费的对象，成了消费品。当英雄的复魅遭遇后现代的洗礼后，欢乐神话的出现就成了必然，而“抗日神剧”只不过充当了欢乐神话的一个角色而已。

第三节　后现代之后的英雄空间

利用英雄的复魅创造“神剧”，会产生一种消费的快乐，带来焦虑和苦闷的暂时消除，这是英雄被塑造和被消费的心理原因，也是中国人“过日子”的现实依据。“抗日神剧”持续走俏，就说明了它的

市场需要有多大。但“神剧”走俏的同时，批评和嘲讽如潮，这本身就是在英雄被解构之后英雄空间的扩张。较之“文革”时期全国人民学唱革命样板戏、学习革命样板戏英雄来，我们的时代的确进步了不少。

但是，“神剧”之殇在于现代文化工业的复制。这种复制不是拷贝，而是不同剧组对类型题材没有太大差别的制作，因而难免雷同。有个叫于震的演员，被称为“神剧专业户”，他领衔的“神剧”连续剧在电视频道上已不下两位数。也许是面熟了，觉得他和他的剧组就那么一套，比画出来的神武，装出来的威风，没有什么新奇的。而且在这种复制中，前现代的情结和观念几乎无一例外地贯穿其中。有一部叫《大秧歌》的“神剧”，主角拿着狼牙棒给日本军官行家法，较之《我的兄弟叫顺溜》中顺溜非要将盛有侵略者骨灰的骨灰盒击碎，的确有着独到的构思，但其前现代的精神轨迹已然历历在目，跟无以计数的“神剧”如出一辙。可以说，复制的“神剧”已经覆盖、遮蔽了《亮剑》等电视剧精品的光环，成为一个娱乐搞笑的代名词。

与媒体的伪事件（广告、报道）相似，影视正在制作伪英雄，即工业文明时期的神武英雄。但吊诡的是，这种伪英雄远胜于历史上的真英雄，更容易被消费者接受。这可能是美学对于媒体的胜利，也是浪漫主义对现实主义的超越，是后现代艺术化处理对于影视写实的胜利。事实上，古希腊罗马的阿喀琉斯、斯巴达克斯，中国的关羽、张飞等世界英雄影视形象，似乎远不如中国“神剧”的伪英雄们吸引眼球。在消费时代，伪英雄因为美学而被欣赏，而不是历史人物作为真实英雄被崇拜、被模仿。由此可见，好像媒体之“伪”之余仍有美学之真。这种美学上的真就是消费者对于英雄的不必认其真的审美消费，是一种观赏的辩证法。因为欢乐神话从来就不是神话，也不是现实，就是用来娱乐搞笑的，是一种审美消费，因此，审美消费本身就是一种真实，是在崇高与鄙俗、高雅与低贱之间人们活着的方式之一，而且是较有滋味地活着的方式之一，因而有其合理性，不应该被

谴责、打压、甚至剥夺，但也不应该被赞颂。就像活着一样，任其自然，当然在“尘世难逢开口笑”的现实中爆出一点笑来，就更能喜出望外。这大概就是被称为俗美学的、甚至是非美学背后的美学意义。

真实的英雄和媒体制造出来的英雄以及艺术化了的英雄，共同构成了英雄空间，使得英雄被多极化消费和多极化处理成为可能。古典的、现代的、后现代的英雄可以同时亮相，可以同时展谱，形成了突破时空界限的英雄空间。如还不够，可以来个穿越，创造更大的英雄空间。中国的穿越剧正在进行着英雄空间的扩张，现时代的人们可以穿越到先秦时代做将军，当英雄了。因此，消费时代，英雄空间不仅不会萎缩，反而会进一步扩大。事实上，中国前现代的三国英雄已经通过《三国杀》桌牌/网络游戏而被赋予了兼具主公、忠臣、奸臣、反贼四种可能性的生成性角色，而不再是现成性角色，这部英雄游戏已将经典的、固定的英雄模式打破，其影响亦不仅限于中国，它已经成了美国伯克利分校的文化选修课。这些现象都在说明别现代时期英雄空间的解构与建构已不再局限于一个国家和一个民族，而具有了走向全球的可能性和世界意义。

英雄空间的解构与建构是个要比英雄的解构和建构本身更为复杂的问题。这是因为英雄空间要比英雄大得多，同时可以涵盖多元英雄价值观，形成英雄空间的压缩与扩张、解构与建构。人类历史上希特勒、墨索里尼、日本天皇等人的反人类英雄观导致人类英雄空间的解体，但也告诉人们，借助于国家机器，可能会在短期内形成某种英雄类型的独尊、独大，但这种情况不能长久，最终会被人类进步的、普适的英雄观所淘汰。美国的抗日大片《血战钢锯岭》写的是一个参加战争但抗拒带枪的医疗兵的真实故事。影片效果很震撼，也很血腥，也是“神剧”的味道。主人公就凭着对于耶稣的信仰和一遍一遍的祈祷，在日军的眼皮子底下，从悬崖上救下来 75 名重伤员，从而成为在战场上不拿枪的英雄。但这个“神剧”给人一种心灵的震

撼，而非神奇、喧嚣、娱乐的浅表审美效果。由此可见，普适的英雄观还是存在的，随之而来的英雄空间的跨地域解构和跨地域建构也是完全可能的。

按照英雄空间理论看问题，对待过去的日本军国主义英雄观的最佳方式就不是“你用刀，我用棍，你用拳，我用腿”，更不是“你用飞机坦克，我用大刀长矛”，不是用前现代的家法或神武英雄通过“神剧”来征服对方，而是唤起这个民族最为敏感的东西——耻感。人类学家鲁思·本尼迪克特（Ruth Benedict）曾在她的《菊与刀》一书中将日本文化概括为耻感文化。① 李泽厚也曾引用过这种观点来说明中国文化是乐感文化。② 眼下的状况似乎并非如此，中国的“神剧”是不是正在通过神武英雄唤醒和激活日本的武士道精神呢？是智是愚，是善是恶，明眼人自有公论。

虽然，到目前为止，“抗日神剧”仍如日中天，消费日本也方兴未艾，但是，复制不可能长久，“神剧”消费总有尽头。因此，当下的编导们应在此时实现跨越式停顿，③ 换位思考，另辟蹊径，在现代、前现代、后现代的交集纠葛中寻找更大的创造空间和解读空间，而不再囿于前现代的神武记忆。

别现代既是对杂糅的社会形态的概括，又是对别样现代性的期许和主张，是对别现代社会形态的更新超越，而非对于别现代社会形态的固守。作为更新超越的别现代主义，不同于前现代英雄的复魅，不同于现代英雄的凡俗化和职业化，也不同于后现代的解构英雄，而是要建构新的英雄空间。这个新的英雄空间就是别现代之后的英雄空间。就消费日本而言，就是要把人们从目前在观看“神剧”时对自我的消费中解脱出来，达到对对象的消费，比如对民族精神塑造的消

---

① 鲁思·本尼迪克特：《菊与刀》，南星越译，南海出版公司 2007 年版，第 272—273 页。

② 李泽厚：《中国古代思想史论》，安徽文艺出版社 1994 年版，第 308、309 页。

③ 参见王建疆《别现代：跨越式停顿》，《探索与争鸣》2015 年第 12 期。

费，而不再是对欢乐神话自娱自乐式的消费。因此，别现代的英雄空间解构与建构将指向未来，超越现在。这个“未来”，在西方是后现代之后，在中国就是别现代之后。因为，别现代中包含了后现代因素，因此，别现代之后的主张就是别现代主义对现代、前现代和后现代的整体超越。

由于前现代神话和神武英雄的历史性消失，英雄空间建构当然应该不仅体现在当下，而且要指向未来，再加上西方后现代的式微，考虑后现代之后①的事已属必然。后现代之后随着人类与星际之间关系的进一步确定，另一个世界的开创将被提上人类未来的议事日程。随着对另一个世界的开创，人类英雄空间将别有洞天。也许新的创世纪正在酝酿中，后现代之后的英雄空间将搁置上帝创世纪的神话，也会淡忘前现代的神武记忆，在现代、前现代、后现代的交集纠葛中超拔出来，开创地球人的星际英雄时代。这看起来似乎又是神话，但愈来愈多的科幻影视、三体小说正在进行着世纪英雄的更新和英雄空间的扩容。

艺术的创新在于换一种方式，艺术风格和艺术流派的形成都是跨越式停顿的产物。在艺术上没有永远的神圣，正如生活中没有永远的英雄。

---

① 参见王建疆《别现代：美学之外与后现代之后》，《上海师范大学学报》（哲学社会科学版）2015 年第 1 期。

第三章

别现代：艺术的发言*

——写在别现代作品展前

别现代作品展于2016年9月至10月在上海师范大学举办，展出的同期正值“艺术与美学的话语创新暨别现代高端专题国际学术研讨会”召开，海内外的知名专家和艺术家专就话语创新和别现代的问题进行研讨。也是2016年，国家社科基金办公室批准了我将我主持的国家社科基金项目改名的申请，将“后现代语境中英雄空间的解构与建构问题研究”改为“别现代语境中英雄空间的解构与建构问题研究”。虽然从“后”到“别”只是一字之差，但语境变了，时代变了，社会背景变了，看问题的角度也不得不变。

第一节　别现代是社会形态

从这次别现代作品展中我们看到了来自绘画、雕塑、建筑、装置艺术、电影海报招贴画、门神画等多种体裁的视觉艺术，这些作品的共同特点正如每件作品的中英文简介词中所说的，具有别现代的时代特征、社会特征和风格特征，是别现代的形象展现，是别现代的艺术盛宴。

---

* 本章曾发表于《美学与艺术研究》第7辑，武汉大学出版社2016年版。

别现代这个日渐成为热词的学术术语①，是对历史发展阶段和社会形态的概括，是一种哲学界渴望的“涵盖性理论”。

我们的时代具有现代、前现代、后现代交集纠葛的特点。现代性的制度和思想尚在建立中，而前现代的制度和观念仍牢固地扎根于现实的土壤中，不时地以人治而非法治的方式表现出来。同时，后现代的文艺思潮和美学思潮也在中国泛滥。这种在欧美国家不可能出现的现代、前现代和后现代并置的现象，没有现成的名词，“别现代”（Bie-modern；Don’t be modern；Bie-postmodernism；Bie-modernism；etc.）于是做了最好的替补②。别现代既涉及现代、前现代，又涉及后现代，但它既不是单一的现代，又不是单一的后现代，更不是单一的前现代，因此，只能是别现代。别现代只是借用了“现代”这个词，而非别现代就是现代的一种或云选择性现代性、另类现代性（alternative）。关于中国的现代性，有人认为是复杂的现代性。但我并不同意这种观点。因为，现代性就是西方的科学、理性、人权、自由、民主、法制，再加上现代福利制度，本身一点也不复杂，十分明确，耳熟能详。而中国的现实情况是，除了现代性的因素外，还有前现代性和后现代性的同时存在，所以，所谓复杂的现代性在法理上并不能成立。相反，别现代却恰当地涵盖了现代/现代性、后现代/后现代

---

① 潘黎勇：《“‘别现代’时期思想欠发达国家的学术策略”高端专题研讨会综述》，《上海文化》2016年第2期。“不服来辩”，《探索与争鸣》“学术争鸣”栏目（2月—4月）别现代讨论征稿，2016年2月3日。《别现代：基于中国现实的主义?》，《探索与争鸣》2016年11月7日。李小佳：《用西方话语解释中国现代性很尴尬？“别现代”来了》，《上观新闻》2016年9月28日。《“艺术与美学中的话语创新暨别现代问题”学术研讨会举行》，《社会科学报》2016年9月28日。Wang Weiyu, *International Academic Seminar on Discourse Innovation and Bie-Modern Problem in Art and Aesthetics*, *International Association for Aesthetics*, Volume 48, 10, 2016. 王维玉：《艺术和美学的话语创新暨别现代问题高端专题国际学术研讨会》，《上海文化》2017年第6期。王维玉：《艺术和美学的话语创新暨别嫌的问题高端专题国际学术研讨会综述》，《当代文坛》2016年第6期。

② 分别对应王建疆《别现代：主义的诉求与建构》，《探索与争鸣》2014年第12期，《人大复印资料·社会科学总论》2015年第12期；《别现代：美学之外与后现代之后——对一种国际美学潮流的反动》，《上海师范大学学报》（哲学社会科学版）2015年第1期，《社会科学报·学术文摘》2015年4月9日第3版，已引起讨论。

性、前现代/前现代性交集纠葛的特点。因此，别现代具有唯一性，它本身就是他自己，就是别现代，不是英语表述中的 Alternative modernity（另类现代性，或另现代），Other modernity（其他现代性）所能概括的。

别现代时期是现代、前现代和后现代并置而且和谐共谋的时期，这种和谐共谋表现在社会生活的方方面面。

就社会的经济形态而言，各种所有制和谐共处，国有、私企、外企并驾，现代化大工业与家族企业和私人小作坊齐驱，计划经济与市场经济混搭。

就社会的管理制度而言，具有现代意义的法律和管理制度正在建设中，但同时，与现代法律和管理制度相矛盾的现象不时涌出。或没有原则，没有法规，或有法不依，没有边界、放弃原则、妥协、交易（权钱交易、权色交易、权法交易、行贿受贿）、共赢、媾和；不断更改规矩、实行潜规则；有选择地遗忘和遮蔽历史、造假畅行无阻等，前现代的思想观念和行为方式因现代制度的缺位而由后现代的跨越边界（cross border）、解构中心、消解原则来加以表达，形成混沌的和谐，可以浑水摸鱼，这一点在中国当下不断加大力度而起案的那些高智商、高学历、高级别、受过现代教育、出过国、留过洋但又贪污腐化、身败名裂的人身上得到了最为集中的表现。

就社会的文化形态而言，一方面是传统文化与当代文化之间的矛盾，中国文化与西方文化之间的矛盾；另一方面是现代、后现代与前现代之间的无间道，即彼此适应、和谐共处。这在别现代作品展中得到了形象的展示。

就社会的文艺现象而言，异彩纷呈。现代的场景、背景、技术，与前现代的理念和后现代的手法同台亮相。现代的场景、背景、技术自不用说，前现代的血缘宗亲观念、香火观念、专制思想、迷信思想

借尸还魂，后现代的戏仿、恶搞大行其道，英雄和英雄空间①都被戏仿、娱乐、恶搞的方式解构。

就哲学思想而言，或平庸或虚无，缺乏原创，或犬儒主义盛行，歌德美学独统，以致连“是中国美学还是美学在中国”“是中国哲学还是哲学在中国”的问题至今也搞不清楚，混沌中的和谐却在“过日子”的策略中在国内学术界独步六合。

但正如医患冲突所显示的那样，建立在红包基础上的和谐共谋，终因医术的有限和人的贪欲的无止境而归于破灭，于是医患冲突成为替代和谐共谋的新阶段。在不少的医院候诊大厅，防范暴恐的举措正在诠释着和谐共谋阶段终结后的新的步履，一个当代寓言正在艺术地发言。

别现代的内涵以及发展阶段等问题不是本文要阐释的，但是，按照马克思主义的观点，任何观念、意识形态都离不开其社会的现状及其组织结构和发展阶段，因此，本文也如其他已经发表过的论文那样，还要不厌其烦地重申一下别现代的性质和特定。

事实上，别现代是一个正在生成的术语。起初，我觉得它是别裁、别体、教外别传，但现在看来，它超出了所有“别”的汉语界定，容易使哲学家们想起了德里达的“différance”（延异）。但别现代并非现代性别体，而是前现代之未脱，现代之未至，而前现代又隔着现代与后现代勾肩搭背，是个多级杂糅体。

第二节　别现代是哲学

别现代的“别”耐人寻味，现代的学者马上想到的是告别、不要这些现代意思。事实上，关于别现代，国内外已经发表过的我的文章中，英译“别现代”就有《探索与争鸣》的 don’t be modern，《上海

---

①　王建疆：《后现代语境中英雄空间与英雄再生》，《文学评论》2014 年第 3 期。

师范大学学报》的 Bie-postmodernism，《上海文化》的 Bie-modern，和欧洲《哲学杂志》（*Fiozofski vestnik*）的 A theory of the new times and the new historical development stage。相比之下，我更倾向于使用欧洲《哲学杂志》的译法。

汉语词汇十分丰富，而其词义表达充满魅力。中国古代没有“另”字，另字的意思全用“别”来表达。如《史记·项羽本纪》中的“使项羽、刘邦别打荣成。”就是作为另一支部队去攻打荣城，而非不要去打荣城。再如文论界熟知的《沧浪诗话》中的“诗有别材，非关书也；诗有别趣，非关理也。”其中的别材、别趣，就是指另外一种才能和另外一种情趣。至于《五灯会元》中佛祖拈花，迦叶微笑，佛祖所讲“不立文字，教外别传”中的别传，就是用一种特殊的传教之法，而非不要去传。虽然现实中人们都在讲“别墅”“别动队”，但讲到别现代时，总是跟古代的用法联系不起来，这样一来反倒是别现代有了过目不忘的功能。

虽然别现代之“别”词义丰富，但其语源在于古代汉语，其流变也从未脱离汉语表意的规律。正因为别现代是多义的，才具有词义生成的特点和表现差异的哲学功能。法国思想家德里达为了表达差异，自造了“différance”这个词，表示永无止息的歧义生成。别现代不用生造词汇，从古代汉语中信手拈来，就有了在功能上不亚于 différance 的术语。这对鼓吹哲学帝国论而无中国份的理查德·舒斯特曼来说也好，对宣传中国没有哲学的雅克·德里达来说也好，对其远祖黑格尔来说也好，中国的文字中既然有哲学，又何能被忽视呢？实际上，如果深入透视别现代时期的中国社会，再加上我们自己的具有无限可能性的价值判断，那么，现代性、后现代性、前现代性与告别现代性、不要现代性、另一种现代性，以及要与不要、不要与要，再加上这一种、那一种，这个占比、那个成分，是与不是，等等，都构成了对别现代的可能性的无止境的解释，具有话语增长的巨大潜力。因此，从这个意义上说，别现代可以说是立足于汉语的对后现代解构主义的改

造、升级和超越。

别现代的提出，看似对于汉语哲学功能的激活，实则乃中华文化复兴之时社会现实对于话语创新的吁求。别现代是对现实的概括，是对现实的认识，而别现代主义却是对别现代的改造。

从现代文化创造的意义上讲，名宾实主的观念已被名主实宾的思想所替代。如果不服，你看看商标法、授权生产法、域名权等现代名词，你肯定会生成现代哲学理念。在社会转型、时代变革之时，新语汇的出现其革命性意义更加明显。王国维早在 1905 年就公开提倡"造新语"，即创造新的话语、新的术语、新的名词，以弥补汉语表达在面临西学时的明显不够用。原因在于古代汉语多用单纯词，无法准确地表达新的概念。而来自日本的"日源新语"亦日显不够，因而"造新语"已迫在眉睫。而于当今西方话语霸权之际，话语创新更是刻不容缓。

别现代具有明确的话语识别功能。如法国新马克思主义思想家阿尔都塞提出过"另类现代性"（Alternative modernity）概念，是对毛泽东思想及其毛泽东发动"文化大革命"的定义。但这个另类现代性只是特指毛泽东的所谓现代性思想，并不能概括中国社会形态和历史阶段，是一种误读。还有英语表达中抽象的"另一种现代性"（Other modernity），也无法确指哪一种现代性。至于西方众多的现代性，如艾森斯塔特所谓的多元现代性，吉登斯的反思的现代性，齐格·鲍曼的流动的现代性，C. 詹克斯的"新现代性""新现代主义""晚期现代性"，贝尔所谓的"第二现代性"等，都是针对西方现实而提出的现代性划分，与别现代针对中国的社会形态和历史阶段而进行的界定不是一回事。至于中国学者提出的复杂现代性，也是沿着西方思想家的路数对现代性的界定的多种说法所做的概括，但不符合现代性的单一明了性特点，而且更主要的是这种所谓的复杂性概括还不能一目了然地揭示中国社会的形态和发展的历史阶段，尚处于混沌状态，而未达区隔状态。再说，别现代由于涉及多种社会形态的交织、

对立、互补，因而内在的紧张所形成的力度也是西方断代式现代性、后现代性不再遭遇的。因此，别现代的话语创新是肯定的。

别现代作为哲学，仅仅具有话语创新是不够的，还要看其思想内涵。别现代的现代、前现代、后现代交集纠葛或三位一体，从哲学上看就是时间或时代的空间化或共时态。于是，时间的空间化就成了别现代的思想基础。

习惯于引荐而非原创思想的当代中国哲学界和美学界个别学者，小学的功夫倒也不错，他们会不厌其烦地考证这个时间的空间化来自西方的哪位大师或哪位大神。时间的空间化很容易使人联想到法国的列斐伏尔、福柯，英国的哈维，美国的杰姆逊等人的空间理论。但是，既然时间的空间化是现代、前现代、后现代的杂糅，就与西方断代式的历史观形成了强烈的对比，西方那种历时性理论就不符合中国的共时态现实。因此，别现代就是别现代，别现代的时间的空间化就是对中国特殊社会历史阶段和社会形态的理论概括和理论表达，而非对西方理论的生搬硬套。

当然，时间的空间化只能是别现代思想的现实基础或灵感之源，而非其思想内涵的全部。如果别现代就此打住，完全空间化了，停滞了，凝固了，那么，不就在新的历史时期印证了黑格尔所说的中国没有历史或中国历史停滞论吗？事实上，我在本文第一部分里讲的那个始于红包终于医患冲突的故事，就是别现代历史阶段论、发展观和前景的隐喻，容当别文展开。

除了时间的空间化和发展阶段论外，别现代的思维方式是跨越式停顿。这个观点发表后被人大复印资料《哲学原理》转载，《探索与争鸣》杂志社也在全国征稿讨论。其核心在于，在发展的顺风顺水之日，或者如日中天之时，当作断然的停顿。这不是脑筋急转弯之类的教学法或滑头主义，而是对于增长的极限的预知和对终极结局的了然于心，从而改弦易辙，谋求更大的发展空间和最佳的生存之道。中国古人有这种智慧的，叫作急流勇退，也叫作本来无一物、何处惹尘埃。现代社会中人类急剧膨胀的野心就如不断增速的高铁，正在“向死而生”，不知危险。因此，跨越式停顿也就是停顿式跨越。专制与集权盛行的亚洲国家和地区，按跨越式停顿办事的不少。中国台湾地区、马来西亚、缅甸、越南等就是甩开惯性制导的先例。

与跨越式停顿相联系的自然是自然发展观。这是老庄的路数，但别现代将其做一番跨越式停顿的功夫，使其在与科学发展观形成的张力中，给中国，也给人类以生存之道的启发。

别现代还有自己的美学观，如在别现代的和谐共谋期和对立冲突期，提倡冷幽默而非黑色幽默；在精神文明建构中提倡自调节审美；在审美形态方面主张内审美；在艺术创新方面提倡艺术再生；等等。这些美学观点都早已出版、发表过。

总之，别现代既是对社会形态和历史发展阶段的概括，又具有自己的哲学思想和美学理论，因而愈来愈为学界所关注。

第三节　别现代是艺术在发言

此次“别现代作品展”具有明显的别现代社会背景、别现代哲学思潮和别现代艺术的识别标志，也是对西方哲学和西方当代艺术批评对中国哲学和艺术的批评的最好回应。西方美学家总是认为，中国的美学家不懂艺术，甚至对于当代在海外流行的中国先锋艺术是无知的。① 因此，举办别现代画展，并把他们的作品以图文的方式收进来予以展出，就可以展示中国美学对于当代中国先锋艺术的认识和研究，可以为中国美学和与中国艺术的关系辩护。另外，这些在海外产生很大影响的先锋艺术家们，受到了来自欧美艺术批评界的严厉批评

① Aleš Erjavec, Zhuyi, From Absence to Bustle? Some Comments to Jianjiang Wang's Article "The Bustle or the Absence of Zhuyi", *Journal of Art + Media Studies*, 2017, 13.

和指责，说他们的作品是对西方艺术的拙劣的复制、模仿，甚至剽窃。[①] 这样的评论影响很大，杀伤力极强。别现代美学作为一种以时代命名的主义，不得不予以关注。举办这次别现代作品展，就是要从全球观众眼中的中国海外先锋艺术那里思考当代艺术存在的合法性问题，以及艺术发展的关键问题，在客观上回应当前国际艺术评论，进入先锋艺术视野。

作品展第一部分是水墨艺术[②]。不同于水墨作为中国传统绘画的主要表现形式，水墨艺术是指一切在水墨元素基础上所进行的艺术创作，它不仅包括传统意义上的水墨画，也包括抽象水墨、表现水墨、都市水墨、新文人画等，同时还包括以水墨为媒介的装置艺术、行为艺术以及观念艺术等。徐冰的“新英文方块字”系列，将英文的二十六个字母转换成汉字的偏旁部首，然后将其组装成中国的方块字的形式；岛子的“圣水墨”以中国的水墨表现西方的基督形象以及信仰；张卫的“齐白石 vs 梦露”系列将齐白石的水墨人物画与梦露的照片拼贴在同一个画面当中，表现了西方对于中国传统的观照；黄一瀚的《我们都疯了》以水墨的方式将持手枪的中国青年与持枪的麦当劳叔叔放置在同一个画面当中，表现了西方文化已经将中国的青年同化。以上例证所示，当代水墨艺术具有明显的别现代的杂糅、混搭的特点。

水墨艺术中的实验水墨，争议最大，它包含多种艺术形式，抽象水墨、水墨装置艺术、水墨行为艺术以及水墨影像艺术等。但有一点值得注意的是，实验水墨艺术家的跨越式停顿思维。即从最早的对于传统水墨和传统文化的反叛，到欧美旅程中的困惑和反思，反过来在传统中寻求自己的立足点。像徐冰的“新英文书法”系列，岛子的

---

① 《中国当代艺术侮辱了人生》，中国南方艺术网转载，2014. 2. 19。

② 水墨艺术是以中国传统水墨为介质的绘画创作，但又佐以拼贴、装置等西方后现代手法。

《苦竹》，还有《我们都疯了》所显示的那样，艺术家预见到了传统艺术的不断消解以及修养缺失对原创带来的危害，因而自觉放弃了对西方的模仿与追随，通过寻求传统资源来反观自身。这种停顿之后的变化不仅有可能使得中国艺术在世界上引起关注，而且也是对中国传统修养、信仰丧失的一种反思以及救赎。

展品的第二部分是陈箴的装置艺术图集。在陈箴的装置艺术作品中我们随处可见别现代社会的隐喻，如完成于 1996 年的大型装置艺术作品《日咒》由 101 只按照战国编钟方式排列的墩形老式木马桶组成一个乐器装置，其中的一部分马桶还被改装成音响，播放着电视广告人声音与刷洗马桶时的混合声。作品中间部分是一个巨大的地球仪，里面充斥着现代社会产生的典型垃圾：键盘、显示器、电线……旧式马桶隐喻前现代时期，作品中央的一大堆工业垃圾象征着现代时期；将代表中国古代礼乐制度最高形式的编钟与代表中国世俗文化中最污秽之物的马桶并置，用一大堆工业垃圾填充进被誉为人类母亲的地球之中，则是一种后现代的祛魅。然而，要对陈箴艺术特征进行总体概括，非别现代莫属。因为这里虽然有着现代、前现代和后现代的

图一　《日咒》

艺术元素，但又非其中任何一种简单的元素可将其概括净尽，只有别现代才是最恰当不过的表述。

在思想内涵方面，陈箴作品最为典型的作品或许是他的《早产儿》。陈箴回国探亲时目睹了这样一句口号："2000年有一亿中国人拥有自己的汽车，欢迎来中国参与汽车工业竞争！"颇感担忧，因此在其装置艺术作品《早产儿》中表现了这一灾难式的场景：无数自行车内胎缠绕成龙形，龙头是残破的自行车，龙身爬满了被漆或被染成黑色的玩具小汽车，巨龙在展厅上空摇摆，看似凶悍威猛，可它扭曲的姿态和胀裂的腹部告诉我们它已如负载过重的高架桥，无法消化迅速增长的车辆。在该作品中，陈箴终止了线性思维，消除了肯定—否定，前进—倒退等庸俗的辩证法，他将过去（自行车）、现在（汽车）和可能到来的未来（姿态扭曲、腹部欲胀裂的龙）置于一个平等、共享的空间重新谋划。在这种过去、现在、未来的多种维度中，陈箴颠覆了线性思维的统治，为思维的跨越提供了可能，为我们能更好地反思中国在城市化进程中遇到的各种问题，提供了艺术的智慧和美学的反思。

图二　《早产儿》

作品展的第三部分是别现代的建筑艺术。其中，某省会城市里美国白宫与北京天坛和合的阴阳式电影城建筑外观图，中国公务机构的红顶子建筑，致富了的村舍以西方洛可可风格与镇宅、镇妖、镇河等观念混搭的建筑，似乎都在图解着别现代的理念。

作品展的第四部分是对别现代电影如穿越剧和囧类别现代电影的剧照展。虽然不如美术和建筑那么醒目，但这些已经受到别现代评论的影视作品还是能够以图文并茂的形式加强别现代艺术给人的映象。

作品展的第五部分是本展的重头戏，即别现代波普艺术。展出了徐冰、王广义、张小刚、岳敏君、方力钧、曾梵志等“四大天王”“五虎上将”的代表性作品。他们的作品吸收了美国现代波普艺术大师安迪·沃霍尔同像复制的手法，主要表现中国的“文革”记忆和世代忧虑，时代感很强，政治寓意深刻，是用现代观念反思前现代历史，并通过后现代政治波普的杂糅、拼贴、复制等手法，共同创造了别现代艺术。

作品展的第六部分是别现代民俗画展，主要是门神画展。通过将现代地产大亨、武装力量入画门神，彰显了新财神替代旧财神的别现代过程。这一过程也是神化金钱和武力的过程。

作品的第七部分是别现代装饰艺术。通过上海松江钟书阁书店将西洋画与中国古代训诫拼贴的装饰风格，进一步说明别现代的时代混搭和艺术杂糅。

作品的第八部分是别现代系列论文发表、会议讨论的情况介绍。

总的看来，这个展览具有令人耳目一新的感觉，符合别现代的别开生面、别具一格、别出一路、别有洞天的别格特质。同时，此展还具有一定的学术意义和艺术意义。

首先，这次的别现代作品展，第一次以艺术的形式展现了别现代的本质特征；也对中国当代美术作品尤其是华裔欧美艺术家作品的后现代称谓予以否定，而冠之以别现代，以正视听；作品展将揭示中国当代艺术中的发展趋向，纠正了以前的习惯性说法，从此艺术地翻开

了别现代的第一页。

其次，将回应西方艺术评论界对中国当代艺术包括华裔海外艺术家的批评。2008 年美国最著名的自由主义言论旗舰刊物《新共和》（*The New Republic*）杂志发表了批评家杰德·珀尔（Jed Perl）抨击中国现当代艺术的报道“毛疯狂”（“Mao Craze”），点名道姓地批评当代当红中国海外艺术家的作品过时落伍，思维狭隘，拙劣地滥用“文革”和“文革”领袖形象并以此为中国的全部而向西方世界示丑。更为甚者，不少所谓的华裔大艺术家明显地抄袭西方艺术家的作品，或者拙劣地模仿西方艺术家的作品。最后的结论是这样的：“这批艺术家不但侮辱了艺术，也侮辱了人生。那些吹捧叫卖的策展人、批评家和收藏家，也一样侮辱了艺术，侮辱了人生。我们所见到的，是一场轰轰烈烈的昂贵的广告和邪恶的宣传。”这种批评是致命的，受批评者起来反击亦属正常。但有关剽窃的事我们却不能因为民族感情而下断语，这毕竟涉及法律取证问题。但是，《别现代作品展》在这种激烈的中西对话中，能够回应珀尔的批评的地方在于：虽然别现代的杂糅时时显露着由于观念的混沌和拿来主义所导致的边界不清及其涉及第三者利益的嫌疑，但中国别现代现实、中国元素以及中国传统根基的不可动摇性，却是别现代之所以为别现代的根据；数百年来的“中体西学”“洋为中用”和“拿来主义”等大词在同化个体的过程中，已将原则变为手段，且习以为常，不自觉中构成了无数的涉三方利益的案例；面对批判和讨伐，别现代海外艺术家们亟须进行的不再是模仿和山寨，而是跨越式停顿或停顿式跨越；别现代艺术家亟须在传承与创新之间，在借鉴与创新之间来一个切割，而不是混搭，只有切割，才有自己的领地，才有自己的独创，这种切割也就是跨越式停顿的具体运用。总之，别现代思想在艺术实践和思辨逻辑的展开中，将升华为别现代主义。

最后，回应了亚里士多德、德里达、朗西埃、艾尔雅维茨等人的声音（voice）与语言/发言（speech）相区别的观点。这里，我将著名美学家艾尔雅维茨对我发表在欧洲《哲学杂志》上的英文文章①的批评辑录如下，看看他说了什么，我们又能做些什么：

> 在我看来，当代中国的主义、艺术和理论（涉及美学、哲学和人文学科）在许多方面都与西方目前或者近来的情形截然不同。如果说几十年前，西方的文化对抗和竞争主要出现在美国和欧洲（特别是法国）之间，那么现在这种两极的趋势已转变为一个四边的较量。我们仍然见证着美国和欧洲文化的蓬勃发展，但是现在有一个全新的竞争者参与其中，它就是中国。曾有一段时间，人们认为这个新的竞争者似乎应该是苏联国家，但遗憾的是他们未能承担重任。所谓的"第三世界"再次从角逐中逃离并继续保持"沉默"，而中国正在努力获得一种"声音"，这种声音诠释了当代法国哲学家雅克·朗西埃的观点。在《政治学》一书中，亚里士多德宣称人"是一种政治动物因为人是唯一具有语言的动物，语言能表达诸如公正或不公正等，然而动物所拥有的只是声音，声音仅能表达苦乐。然后整个问题就成了去了解谁拥有语言，谁仅仅拥有声音？"②

我不想在此回答艾尔雅维茨关于声音（voice）和语言/发言（speech，也可译为"发言"）的区别和归属，因为，《别现代作品展》就是最好的回答，是艺术在发言。而且9月份在上海举行的"艺术与美学的话语创新暨别现代问题国际高端专题学术研讨会"上，组委会就是让艺术来发言，然后才是西方的哲学家、艺术家和国内的美学家们发言的。

---

① Wang Jianjiang, "The Bustle and the Absence of Zhuyi. The Example of Chinese Aesthetics" *Filozofski Vestinik*, Letnik, XXXⅦ, 2016.

② Aleš Erjavec, Zhuyi, From Absence to Bustle? Some Comments to Jianjiang Wang's Article "The Bustle or the Absence of Zhuyi", *Journal of Art + Media Studies*, 2017, 13.

第四章

别现代：话语创新的背后*

“别现代”首先是在沪上学术圈中流传起来的。

乍一听，好像是不要现代，但马上又有人说是要告别现代……但别现代所到之处总能引起人们的兴趣，因而能被人们记住，并进而传开了。这与自20世纪文艺学方法论热之后人们对于中国学者创造的新概念总是嗤之以鼻的习惯判若两仪，也算对治学者的一种安慰。

第一节　别现代的提出与进展

2014年上半年，《上海大学学报》的曾军先生把该刊发表的朱立元先生和高建平先生的关于现代、后现代与中国文论和美学的关系的文章寄给大家讨论。读过这两篇文章后产生一些想法，正好上海市美学学会要在上海师大开一次美学和艺术学的讨论会，组会者安排我做大会发言。

我在会上针对美学的现代性的问题提出，中国美学的问题不是现代性的问题，而是别现代的问题。因为，任何问题都是特定社会形态中的问题，是特定历史时期的问题，而中国正处于特定的历史时期和特定的社会形态中，这里既有高度发展的现代化物质基础，又有前现代的意识形态和制度设施，还有后现代的解构思想，三位一体，和谐

---

* 本章曾发表于《上海文化》2015年第6期。

相处。因此，中国美学的问题就不是西方的现代性问题，也不是西方的后现代性的问题，而是别现代的问题。

别现代就是既不同于现代、后现代、前现代，但又同时具有现代、后现代和前现代的属性和特征的社会形态或社会发展阶段。因此，别现代就是别现代，不是现代，也不是后现代，更不是前现代，是一个特殊的历史时期和特殊的社会发展阶段。在别现代时期，社会需要、时代问题、文化背景、思想话语都具有自己的特点，不可能把西方的需要当成自己的需要，把后现代的问题当成自己的问题，其文化背景、思想话语一定是不同于西方的。事实上，当以德国著名美学家沃尔夫冈·威尔施为代表的超越经典美学、重构美学理论、回归自然和社会以及让美学走向行动的风潮席卷全球之际，中国美学还在为“是中国美学还是美学在中国”而烦恼，为自己没有美学上的主义而惭愧。与整个西方已进入“后理论”相比，中国美学不是理论过剩，相反，是理论贫乏，主义缺失，尚处于“前理论”时期。因此，跟着西方美学走，把西方美学的话语当成自己的话语，难免邯郸学步。正如我国从20世纪50年代开始直到80年代，都在从阶级政治的高度批判人道主义、人性论，而西方已从那个时代超越了人道主义，是从生态主义出发反思人道主义一样，由于社会形态的差别和发展阶段的不同所造成的错位，甚至南辕北辙，都在为别现代的确立提供着现实的根据。

这次会议发言取得了较好的反响。几位与会学者表示，别现代这个词很新颖、很有趣，具有巨大的思想空间和话语潜力。某编辑部也预约要刊出这个发言稿。不过，当《上海师范大学学报》2015年第一期特别推出我的《美学之外与后现代之后——对一种国际美学潮流的反动》一文时，已经晚了半拍。2014年第12期的《探索与争鸣》已发表了我的《别现代：主义的诉求与建构》。这两篇文章发表后，分别为《社会科学报》和《人大复印资料·社会科学总论》转载。批评沃尔夫冈的那篇文章还引起了讨论、争鸣。

2014年年底，在中央编译局、上海交通大学联合举办的《经济全球化与中俄文化现代化比较论坛》上，我的大会发言讲到别现代文化问题，引起热烈反响。与会的俄国专家有数人跷起大拇指为别现代点赞。大会总结时，别现代议题被会议主办方认为是“本次会议的重要收获”。中央编译局的学者们认为，别现代是中国话语创新的一个非常好的尝试，表示愿意将别现代的系列成果翻译到国外去。2015年10月在复旦大学“法国文论在中国、北美的影响国际学术会议”上，我的发言指出，别现代看似一个具有“延异”功能的术语，但它是对法国解构主义大师德里达的“différance”（延异）的超越，是根据汉语语源和中国现实提出来的学术术语，代表了中国接受法国文论影响中的创新派的原创性，是对法国文论影响的负相关。又在稍后的复旦大学“中国美学的现代性”会议上指出，中国美学貌似具有现代性，实际上是被现代化了，是被赋予了现代性。同时，中国美学的这种疑似现代性，实质上是别现代性，具有很大的阐释空间和很多的发展路径。还针对与会的著名美学家理查德·舒斯特曼将中国哲学纳入实用哲学美学的发言提出了批评，实际上是现代、后现代美学与别现代美学的一次初步的对话。

10月底，在上海音乐学院举行的“音乐美学的传承与创新暨上海市美学学会年会”上，学者们就西洋乐器与中国传统乐器的合成问题、西方画法与中国传统画法的兼容问题、现代设计的文化背景及其导向问题展开辩论。大会主持人要求我将我的别现代观点介绍给与会者。我的发言认为，处于别现代时期，中国当代艺术兼具现代、后现代和前现代的特征，在中西古今之间，融合具有必然性，而且构成了我们这个时代艺术和审美的主要特征。当根据传统经典小说《西游记》改编的电视剧主题曲用现代电子琴的“嘣嘣”拟声表现时，其审美效果是传统的民乐或西洋乐都无法单独达到的。而上海人徐峥的囧类电影，其别现代的鲜明特征也是他当下走红的原因。这种将别现代跟艺术结合起来的做法，引起与会者的讨论，觉得按照别现代的理

论，许多过去看来光怪陆离的艺术现象和审美现象就似乎显示出存在的合理性，而且还会启发人们从新的角度去思考艺术和审美现象。

别现代之所以叫得响，有人听，我想还是跟国际大环境有关。“二战”之后，民族国家的兴起和后殖民时代的来临，使现代性问题成为绕不过去的话语。而在全球化背景下，具体的、有价值的、与人们的生存发展紧密相关的话语，总能引起人们的关注，而那些既有价值又有意味的话语则更能引起人们的兴趣。别现代就是对于当下问题和现状进行思考的话语凝聚，因此，引起关注和兴趣并不奇怪。

别现代不仅是一个新词，而且相关的论文都在说明它是有内涵的。同年发表的《思想欠发达时代的学术策略》（中国社会科学杂志社《中国社会科学评价》2015 年第 4 期），《别现代：跨越式停顿》（《探索与争鸣》2015 年第 12 期），《别现代时期中国影视艺术的囧与神》（全国“艺术：形态 精神 创意”学术会议论文）等都在使别现代成为一个有内涵、有思想的术语，而非简单的标新立异。

别现代理论提出后，很快在国内和国外引起讨论，并随着国内外别现代专题研讨会的召开而得到了进一步的深入开展。国内的王宏岳教授、陶国山副教授、夏中义教授、刘锋杰教授纷纷撰文与我商榷，对别现代主义提出学术上的批评，我尽量回应他们，展开讨论，从而使别现代理论得到了深化。其中，王宏岳关于跨越式停顿需要跨越式转型的补充的说法，夏中义反对建设主义的说法，都是需要进一步辩驳的，因为这些话题能够深化别现代主义。

在国外，首先对我提出的主义和别现代理论进行评论的是世界著名哲学家、美学家阿列西·艾尔雅维茨。他在评论我的观点的同时，把主义的问题和别现代的问题嵌入了欧洲哲学史，从而使得别现代主义问题获得了广阔的世界哲学背景。接着是欧内斯特·曾科教授从朗西埃的观点评述我与艾尔雅维茨之间的争论，使得别现代问题成为一个可以与西方当代哲学对话的命题。同时，美国雕塑家基顿·韦恩从中国和美国当代艺术的比较中评述别现代理论，认为，别现代问题也

是美国当代艺术的问题。由于中国和美国的文化土壤和文化背景不同，同样的波普手法，在中国艺术家那里和在美国艺术家那里却会产生完全不同的意义。这三位欧美学者的文章正在陆续发表，相信会引起对于别现代的进一步的讨论的。与欧美学者对话，曾经是中国学界梦寐以求的，现在，通过别现代这条路就通了。这正好应证了欧内斯特·曾科所说的，别现代是中西交流对话的桥梁。

第二节　别现代的话语创新

别现代虽然歧义纷呈，但其语源在于古代汉语，其流变也从未脱离汉语表意的规律。但正因为它是多义的，才具有词义生成的特点和表现差异的功能。法国思想家德里达为了表达差异，自造了“différance”这个词，表示永无止息的歧义生成。别现代不用生造词汇，从古代汉语中信手拈来，就有了在功能上不亚于 différance 的术语。实际上，如果深入透视别现代时期的中国社会，再加上我们自己的价值判断，那么，现代性、后现代性、前现代性与告别现代性、不要现代性、另一种现代性，以及要与不要、不要与要，等等，都构成了对别现代的可能性的无止境的解释，具有话语的巨大张力。因此，从这个意义上说，别现代可以说是立足于汉语的对后现代解构主义的改造、升级和超越。

别现代的提出，表面上看只是对汉语的巧智的发挥，但实际上却是中华文化复兴之时社会现实对于话语创新吁求的结果。

从现代科学意义上讲，名词的诞生往往都是发明创造的结果。就人文社会科学而言，在社会转型、时代变革之时，新语汇的出现往往具有革命性意义。20 世纪初，王国维就针对张之洞等重臣宿学借故来自日本的对于西方的学术术语的表达不符合古汉语习惯，而反对新术语、新名词倾向，提出“造新语”的主张。这里的“造新名”就是对各种科学发明、学术发现、人文创见的命名。如果没有好的名

称，再好的思想也会被淹没，再好的理论也终将离散。在当今西方文化霸权时代，思想原创尤其应该与话语的原创同步。就如生活中自己的孩子应该有自己的名字，而不能用隔壁邻居家孩子的名字一样，别现代一词就是对我们的当下现状的一个命名，是一种完全意义上的话语创新。

别现代的话语创新来自理论创新和主义建设的需要。与中国在经济上、科学技术上、军事上的突飞猛进相比，中国当代哲学和学术思想的发展仍居于第三世界学术思想欠发达国家之列。原创性的哲学、主义、理论很少见到，国际影响力不强。哲学、美学上的“是中国哲学/美学还是哲学/美学在中国”的疑问不绝于耳。造成这一现状的原因很多，如思想的不够解放，未得到解放等，但对于中国现实中社会形态和发展阶段的认识局限，也是一个重要的原因。我们的学者往往热衷于谈论后现代，对西方思想家的话语跟得比较紧，但对中国的别现代属性没有认识，因而学术研究往往替西方背书。而对社会形态和历史阶段的概括，首先需要“涵盖性理论”，需要叫得响、传得开的名词。即思想的创新首先在于话语的创新。话语的创新具有导向新思想的功能。因此，别现代绝不是为了造词而造词，而是顺应时代的呼唤和理论创新的需要。

别现代（Bie-modern）具有明确的话语识别功能。如法国马克思主义思想家阿尔都塞提出过“另类现代性”（Alternative modernity）概念，就是以中国某一个特殊历史阶段的特殊人物的思想特征来概括整个中国的现代性的，难免失之偏颇。还有英语表达中抽象的“另一种现代性”（Other modernity），也无法确指哪一种现代性。至于西方众多的现代性，如艾森斯塔特所谓的多元现代性，吉登斯的反思的现代性，齐格·鲍曼的流动的现代性，C. 詹克斯的“新现代性”“新现代主义”“晚期现代性”，贝尔所谓的“第二现代性”等，都是针对西方现实而提出的现代性划分，与别现代针对中国的社会形态和历史阶段而进行的界定不是一回事。至于有的中国学者提出的复杂现代

性、混同现代性、新现代性等，也是沿着西方思想家的路数对当代中国所做的概括。但是这种概括还不能一目了然地揭示中国社会的形态和发展的历史阶段，尤其是中国的现代性尚在路上的实际情况。而且，别现代由于涉及多种社会形态的交织、对立、互补，因而内在的紧张所形成的力度也是西方断代式现代性、后现代性所无法比拟的。因此，别现代的话语创新是纯粹的。

话语创新的第一步是划定和坚守语言边界。语言边界简称语界，是民族独立、思想独立的前提。语界建立在语言、宗教、社会形态和文化类型的基础上。语界的模糊和消失，意味着被同化的危险。文化人类学的研究认为，语言是文化的识别标志，没有识别性语言的文化是最容易被同化的文化。我这里讲的别现代“语界”，就是一个在全球背景下用于表示民族文化、时代差异、思想边界的一个超大概念。这个超大概念就是能够指证现代、后现代、前现代和而不同的概念。由于在全球化背景下中国当代文化中语界的不够清晰，甚至存在着“失语症”，因而现实中极具特色的中国当代文化却无法在文化的而非政治统治的意义上进行自我表达，相反，却是在听从西方后现代主义者的摆布，难免迷茫。但是，这种现象只是特定历史时期的产物，随着大国文化复兴意识的觉醒，模糊的甚至是消失了的语界最终会被找到，有涵盖性和统摄性的创新性的理论和概念最终帮助我们赢得话语权。事实上，别现代理论通过同艾尔雅维茨等西方学者的对话，赢得了他们的尊重，他们已将中国哲学纳入世界哲学四边形中，从而突破了德里达的中国无哲学和舒斯特曼的哲学帝国论中无中国的说法，给中国哲学的世界地位一种期许。这不能不归结为别现代话语创新的实绩。将目前流行的“在西方主流话语中注入中国元素”的自豪，改造成为“在中国主流话语中注入西方元素”，别现代就是这样的语界标识，它不仅是汉语的创造，而且还是主义的建构。

第三节　别现代的思想创新和文化意义

在全球化背景下，文化的全球趋同与文化的地域特色之间的张力正在加大。按照理查德·舒斯特曼的说法，在全球化时代，哲学将由几个“哲学帝国”生产，帝国之外的国家只能去认同和传播哲学帝国的哲学。但在舒斯特曼的哲学帝国中，中国并未忝列其中。2001年，德里达在沪上的演讲就认为中国有思想，但中国没有哲学。虽然后来他解释说中国没有西方式的哲学，这样可能会更好，但就中国哲学界、思想界来说，无疑是个很大的震动。在别现代理论讨论之前，著名美学家阿列西·艾尔雅维茨也同意这种看法，认为没有哲学传统的国家和小国家，只能建立由哲学帝国派生出来的学派，不可能形成原创性的哲学。就美学而言，艾尔雅维茨曾在我主持的上海师大的学术演讲中公开讲，美学就是美学，不应该存在哪一个国家的美学，也不应该讲中国美学。虽然一如前述，艾尔雅维茨已经开始逐步改变这种看法，但是，这些来自西方哲学家和美学家的看法，无疑是对建立民族哲学和民族美学的挑战。

哲学、主义、思想、理论，是一个国家软实力的标志，尤其是如果缺乏哲学和主义，这个国家要想独步于世界舞台是不大可能的。而哲学和主义的建立既在于对传统的传承和创新，也在于对社会形态和历史阶段的认识和把握。

别现代的提出始于对学术思想欠发达现状的忧虑，力图在全球化背景下建立中国语境，摆脱欠发达现状的尴尬。别现代首先是对社会形态和历史阶段的认识和把握，是对前现代、现代、后现代三种情况并存的社会结构和时代特征的认识和把握。别现代是由多种社会形态交织、矛盾、互补所构成的张力性结构。其中充满着随机选择性和结果的难以预测性。建立在别现代基础上的别现代主义则是对别现代的价值倾向，是对别现代的统御，目的在于超越别现代，达到更为理想

的存在状态，进入更高的发展境界。

别现代的哲学基础是时间的空间化。现代、后现代与前现代共时存在，本身就是时间的空间化。时间的空间化带来别现代的多重张力结构。在这个张力结构中，现代、前现代、别现代中的任何一方都有可能导致社会向着自己的方向发展。就如我们司空见惯了的，封建意识、贪污腐败将会使别现代时期更具有前现代的色彩。相反，科学思想、民主制度将会使别现代时期更具有现代社会色彩。因此，如何把握别现代的张力结构，使其发挥正能量，就是别现代主义的历史使命。但别现代的时间空间化哲学并不是一个封闭自足的概念，而是一个开放的、发展的理论，具体体现在对别现代四个时期的揭示和界定，从而时间的空间化有了历史发展的可能性，别现代具有了自我更新、自我调节、自我超越的结构和功能，从而别现代主义才有可能成为不仅是解释世界而且还能够改造世界的理论。

别现代的思维方式是跨越式停顿，即在事物发展到高潮时，在如日中天之时，突然停顿，另辟蹊径。这种思维方式貌似中国古代的急流勇退，实质上是对事物发展有限性的认识。是在跨越式发展达到一定程度后，对于更高境界的追求。事实上，跨越式发展一味追求增长的思路正在被生态学和可持续发展的思路所矫正，跨越式停顿正在通过世界无水日、无车日等仪式而得以表现和强化。当今世界的许多弊端，尤其是在自然生态被破坏、文化中断、制度解体方面，都无不打上了跨越式发展的烙印。揠苗助长、违背规律，陶醉于一时的得意，而不知道自省、自拔、自主性停顿，就只能被动地接受由此而造成的不良后果。同样，别现代并不追求别现代时期的永垂不朽，相反，而是知道增长的极限和发展的尽头，因此，总是把跨越式停顿作为必要的调节手段，以便获得稳态发展。

别现代主义总是期待着别现代时期的结束和更理想社会形态的出现。而对更理想社会形态的期待，就是别现代的“后现代之后”的思想。后现代之后就是在我们尚未完全进入后现代之时，思考后现代

之后的事情，试图从后现代之后反观或回望我们今天的时代，从而做出对当下更有利的处理。这看起来不可思议。但是，现在是什么呢？不过就是过去的未来，或者现在就是未来的过去。在时间空间化的别现代看来，跨越、穿越、回望，没有什么不可能的。在时间的空间化中，别现代正在突破西方话语制约，建立中国式的话语场、思维场。

在中国学术思想崛起并走向世界的过程中，必然会遇到阻力和困难。在本书我对艾尔雅维茨先生的回应中可以看出，他在质疑我们发出的主义和别现代的声音到底能否成为“语言”，因为西方哲学自亚里士多德开始，就一直以“语言”和“声音”的不同来区分人与动物的不同。如果我们仅仅满足于发出别现代的声音，还是远远不够的。但我相信，别现代作为对特定社会形态和社会历史阶段的概括是有根据的，因而是有说服力的。而建立在别现代现实基础上的以改造别现代为己任的别现代主义，也会因其符合社会历史发展的必然趋势而具有生命力，会迟早被西方学术界所理解和接受的。到时候，什么语言与声音之别，这种西方中心主义设计的框框，将不再是西方话语对中国话语的屏障。

从美国教授基顿·韦恩那里得到的消息称，2016 年美国佐治亚州西南州立大学通过了建立当代中国别现代研究中心（CCCBMS）的决定，目前正在筹建中。这个研究中心的英文名称是 the Center of Contemporary Chinese Bie-modern Study，简写为 CCCBMS。希望从此以后，世界上有更多的国家和地区研究别现代、传播别现代的思想。

相信随着艾尔雅维茨等著名学者参加到别现代的讨论中，以及欧美学术界对别现代的逐步认可，中国学术思想欠发达的问题，中国美学是否存在的问题，都会涣然冰释。

第五章

别现代：跨越式停顿与文化艺术创新中的切割理论

——兼回应王洪岳教授

王洪岳教授第二次与我商榷，已由对我讲的主义的问题转向对我提出的“跨越式停顿”[①] 问题。而跨越式停顿，恰好又是“主义”或别现代主义话题的延伸。虽然这两个问题有所不同，但是这两次商榷都是在先肯定我的基本观点的同时提出改进意见。如第一次说，建立美学上的主义没有问题，关键是要从德国思想中汲取营养，而非我说的首先要从中国传统中找资源；[②] 第二次说，跨越式停顿是对的，但跨越式转向更好。[③] 可见，洪岳对我的学说不乏建设性的善举，堪称友善的“修正主义”。这在学术写作已沦为自说自话的当下有一种话语共享、和而鸣之的感觉，使人感到搞学术研究也不寂寞。但洪岳这种善意的修正主义是否符合我的本意，是否可以成立，我想再发表一点看法与洪岳讨论。

第一节　跨越式停顿的本体性、断代性和革命性

跨越式停顿是与跨越式发展相对的哲学范畴，有哲学的思维、方

---

① 王建疆：《别现代：跨越式停顿》，《探索与争鸣》2015 年第 12 期，《人大复印资料·哲学原理》2016 年第 3 期，《探索与争鸣》编辑部全国征文讨论。

② 王洪岳：《精神建构的彷徨与出路》，《探索与争鸣》2012 年第 4 期。

③ 王洪岳：《“别现代”理论的模糊性及反思》，《探索与争鸣》2016 年第 7 期。

法、范畴、对象。属于哲学中与存在论相对的发展论和发展中的突变论范畴。它的立论和反论对象都是跨越式发展论。跨越式停顿是针对跨越式发展提出来的，它的有效论域是讨论发展问题。同时，跨越式停顿是建立在现实需要基础上的哲学理论，因而与现实必要性紧密相连。没有现实中对于跨越式停顿的需要，任何有关跨越式停顿的理论、主张、思想、主义，都没有意义。相反，如果现实需要跨越式停顿，那么，跨越式停顿就获得了哲学的价值和生命。正是跨越式停顿的论题有效性和现实必要性，决定了跨越式停顿命题本身的不可动摇、不可改变、不可修正的本体性。就比如医生针对癌症病人，就是想方设法如何根治癌症，阻绝疼痛，至于癌症根治后的其他事情则不在医生的关注范围，这就是本分和本体，而非旁枝斜逸。洪岳在我的跨越式停顿之后再加个跨越式转型、转向、拐弯等，看起来是在拾遗补阙，实际上已经超出了跨越式停顿本身要关注的根本问题，而把话题引到了另一个论域。

跨越式发展与自然发展相对。自然发展是个循序渐进的过程，不存在跨越式发展的问题，因此，也就没有跨越式停顿的必要。但在跨越式发展的轨道上，跨越式停顿不仅必要而且有效。这样讲最为直接的原因不仅仅是理论思辨的需要，更主要的是来自社会现实中社会制度和人与自然关系方面的经验与教训。

跨越式停顿针对跨越式发展的弊端而立。跨越式发展的恶果有二，一是对制度和文明（文化）阶段的跨越导致目的与过程背反、动机与效果脱离，欲速而不达，直至自我解体；二是无视自然规律的跨越式发展，虽逞一时之能和一时之功，但揠苗助长，违背规律，破坏基因，最终导致对自然资源和自然生态的破坏，不仅危害当代，而且祸及子孙。在全球化背景下，这两个恶果所带来的惨痛教训日益彰显。前者表现在苏联的解体上，后者表现在中国严重的大气污染、土地毒化、食品不安全以及自然资源枯竭、生态恶化上。但是，面对这两个恶果，俄国和中国都有自己的应对方式，都在跨越式停顿方面做

了杰出有效的工作。就面对第一个恶果而言，俄国，其前身——苏联的解体就是跨越式主动停顿的结果，是主导性力量的所谓“新思维”取得胜利，从而主动终止了病入膏肓的苏联。而在中国，之所以能够避免苏联的解体，就在于从制度上对跨越式发展教训的吸取和跨越式停顿的及时到位，及时地进行经济基础的改革，已从对资本的全球性开放中得到了维系社会稳定的制衡力量，实现了社会结构的根本改变和社会的稳态发展。而面对第二个恶果，虽然苏联的切尔诺贝利核电站事故至今仍令全世界谈虎色变，但俄国地广人稀，其面对的自然报复问题并没有中国那么严重。相反，中国近 14 亿的人口和逐渐放开的生育政策，其面对的自然的报复可以说压力山大。但当中国面对来自跨越式发展和大自然的报复之间的巨大历史难题时，是继续进行跨越式发展，还是进行跨越式停顿，已经迫在眉睫，刻不容缓了。正是从这个意义上讲，跨越式停顿不仅是哲学，而且是社会发展学；不仅是方法论，而且是战略学；不仅是理论，而且是实践。它具有自己的论域和对象，有着因与现实的紧密联系而得到的定位。因此，无限定的对其进行修正、改造，或者善良的修正主义，都有可能使其问题论域被转换，问题焦点被离散，问题意义被消解。

跨越式停顿除了自身的本体性不可被支配被转换外，还具有断代性和革命性。这种断代性和革命性表现在以下几个方面。

首先，跨越式停顿具有断代性。与西方社会历史发展的断代性不同，即西方现代中断了前现代，后现代又超越了现代，中国当代社会是现代、前现代和后现代的杂糅，这种杂糅用哲学术语表达就是时间的空间化。在这个时间的空间化中，现代、前现代、后现代是以既和谐共谋又内在对立的方式存在着，因而具有全新的社会形态特征和历史阶段特征。这种特征被称为别现代。别现代若用上海话说就是杂糅在一起的“拎不清”。但是，如果按照马克思主义的观点，哲学的使命不仅是认识世界，而且要改造世界，那么，别现代的拎不清并非理想的社会存在，而是有待被改造、更新的时代，这种改造和更新也就

是目前我国深化改革所要进行的工作，也就是要拎得清的过程。这个改革的过程或拎得清的过程，就是戛然终止别现代时期还在和谐共谋、浑水摸鱼的前现代的思想、制度，从而趋向和实现真正意义上的“自由”“民主”“法制”这些写进社会主义核心价值观中的现代社会。因此，在别现代时期，我们需要的就是这种断代式的跨越式停顿。它要中断前现代的思想意识形态和制度延续及影响延续；中断前现代性；中断虚假的现代性而代之以真实的现代性；中断别现代的杂糅性而代之以现代的单纯性。

其次，跨越式停顿具有革命性。别现代主义不同于别现代的对现状的客观描述，而是对它的前现代占比的革命性批判和全方位改造。革命不同于简单的转向、拐弯，而是中断前现代的历史，就如欧洲的文艺复兴和启蒙运动中断了政教合一和封建专制的前现代一样，跨越式停顿就是对前现代的终结。而所谓的跨越式转型或跨越式拐弯，则可能只是一种被迫的调整或有意的规避。现实中，面对日益强大的环保监控压力，跨越式转型或拐弯已经露出了尾巴。如电脑病毒的不断变形升级造成了“道高一尺，魔高一丈”的现实；为了规避检查而继续跨越式发展或跨越式发财，利用高科技的高压泵将工业污水成功地注入地下腔体，就不仅可以危害当时，而且祸及千秋万代。此两例可被视为跨越式转向的反面例证。但就跨越式转型、转向的正面例子而言，如洪岳所说的东亚、南亚的民主转型，因其还背负着前现代的包袱，没有革命式的中断而与前现代告别，因而问题多多，并没有实现完全意义上的转型。《红楼梦》里有诗“世人都说神仙好，惟有功名忘不了”。这种“斩不断，理还乱”就是没有灵魂深处的革命所致。因此，跨越式停顿就是对前现代的革命性改造，而非目标不明确的充满随机性的跨越式转向。

由于中国迈向现代性的伟大改革尚在试步阶段，前现代往往借助现代和后现代将自己伪装起来，在思想意识、制度建设、依法治国、科学管理等多方面搞和谐共谋，浑水摸鱼，混淆视听，因而对它实行

跨越式停顿势在必行、刻不容缓，不容它搞什么跨越式转型或跨越式拐弯。跨越式停顿在面对日趋严重的大气污染、生态破坏、土地毒化、食品变异之际，需要当头棒喝式的停顿而不允许它搞什么转弯转型。

总之，跨越式停顿具有话语和命题的本体性，不容改造；跨越式停顿具有时代的断代性，不去维系时间空间化所带来的杂糅形态，而是努力改造它；跨越式停顿具有自我革命性，即主动地而非被动地终结别现代时期的前现代性，通过改革进入理想的社会形态。

第二节　跨越式停顿的不可替代性与阶段性策略

跨越式停顿是在现代、前现代、后现代的交集纠葛的社会形态和历史阶段中的基本框架内进行的，是在寻求对于前现代的中断和终结中进行的，因而，跨越式停顿也可以被表述为别现代断代或停顿式跨越。因为只有别现代在中断了前现代之后，才会实现前现代向现代的跨越。否则，所谓的跨越，总会因为被前现代扯着后腿而无法实现。

既然跨越式停顿是在现代、前现代、后现代的交集纠葛中进行的，那么它的适用范围和前进方向一开始就是明确的，这就是在现代、前现代、后现代的不同占比中，通过对于前现代的终结、归零，而使三者之间的占比发生革命性的变化，从而将别现代社会导向真正意义上的百分之百的现代社会中去。可见，跨越式停顿的论域是清晰的，价值倾向是确定的，发展方向是明确的，不会向其他社会形态转型、转弯。而所谓的跨越式转型或转向、转弯，则或者已被包含在跨越式停顿的论域中，或者没有跨越式停顿这样明确的方向和论域。就以跨越式转向论所乐道的东亚和南亚的民主制度而言，实际上就属于现代性的一个重要方面，也是别现代占比中的一个重要成分，是别现代消除前现代占比走向现代的重要一环，本身已在别现代跨越式停顿的论域中，不需要转型、转向、转弯。相反，是如何中断前现代、终

结前现代的问题。如果忽略了跨越式停顿的停顿所在，就很容易放下或避开断绝前现代的核心问题而进入一个技术调节的转型、转向、转弯范围，但与别现代的跨越式停顿的哲学理念愈行愈远。

中断与转向不是同一个问题。跨越式停顿就是对前现代的根断和根绝。在未经历过文艺复兴、启蒙运动这样的真正意义上的文化大革命的社会，前现代的噩梦时刻萦绕着它，就像癌细胞那样寄存于现代性的机体中，又与后现代的解构中心、跨越边界合谋，堂而皇之地在别现代时期招摇过市，如果不能根除阻断前现代，只是做一些转医转院的工作，那么这个癌细胞迟早会扩散致命的。因此，决意根除前现代的跨越式停顿，就是做根绝前现代的手术，如果中断得不彻底、根绝得不干净，仍然背着前现代的包袱，如何实现历史性转向或转型、转弯？因此，跨越式停顿就是要断得彻底、断得干净，只有这样，才能拎得清，才能有进步、有发展。

脱离跨越式停顿断代的所谓转型、转向、转弯，究竟要转到哪里去？转向前现代？这是逆历史潮流而动，早已有了前车之鉴。转向现代？转向后现代？我们就在现代和后现代中。所以，所有的问题都不在于如何转向现代和后现代，而在于根绝前现代。别现代的问题不是转向问题，这是因为在别现代社会形态中已经无向可转。别现代主义的使命就在于甩掉历史的包袱，根绝前现代弊端，进而结束别现代时期而进入理想境界。正是在这个意义上，跨越式停顿具有话题的不可替代性。

跨越式停顿除了对于前现代的根绝阻断外，还有一个人与自然关系的面对。相对于跨越式发展的一路高歌，跨越式停顿是对危机的预测和警告，面对跨越式发展的惯性，跨越式停顿则是以急刹车的方式避免危机。盲目的为欲望冲动指使的无止境的跨越式发展，终有一天会把这种跨越者引向深渊。因此，及时的停顿无可争辩。至于停下来干什么，这是另外一个问题。比如相对于现代性，停下来进行现代性的补课；针对人对自然的破坏和自然对人的报复，停下来治理、排

毒、进行生态修复等，都是针对性很强的非常具体的问题。但无论如何，其前提仍然是跨越式停顿。停顿就是阻绝、就是革命、就是更新、就是超越。

在跨越式发展中，现代、前现代、后现代的和谐共谋并未得到改变，而是变本加厉。同时，现代、前现代、后现代的纠结所导致的内在矛盾冲突终会爆发，从而伤及社会的稳态发展。因此，相对于跨越式发展已经凸显的种种弊端和危害，及时地进行跨越式停顿，乃为正解。否则，任何的发展和转向也只能是戴着脚镣跳舞或者带着癌细胞狂欢。

回过头来再看洪岳所讲的跨越式转型和他所乐道的东南亚的宪政民主制度，是否就是跨越式转型、转向的力证呢？当今世界，在欧美之外的许多国家实行了宪政民主制度，这些都成了洪岳跨越式转型的力证。但是事实证明，欧美之外许多实行宪政民主制度的国家很快又恢复了专制，甚至更有甚者，政变、内战由此而生。原因在哪里呢？首先，在欠发达国家，恰好由于前现代的包袱太重，影响到宪政民主的内核和根基，因而一有风吹草动，专制复辟，民主难以为继。因此，欠发达国家民主制度夭折的历史和现状值得反思。我认为，其根本的原因在于缺乏跨越式停顿的革命，没有根绝和阻断前现代的影响，没有断代发生。也就是说，在欠发达国家和地区，比民主转型更重要也更迫切的是对于跨越式发展的跨越式停顿。欠发达国家宪政民主制的挫折也再次证明社会制度和文明阶段的不可跨越，只有在对前现代的跨越式停顿之后，才有真正成熟的民主制度的建立。无论是缅甸和非洲等低端欠发达国家，还是埃及、土耳其等高端欠发达国家，都依然是民主与专制的混合体，并非真正意义上的标准的民主国家，其政变、内战的可能指数仍然很高。因此，跨越式转型看起来似乎是跨越式停顿的升级版，看起来似乎是百尺竿头、更进一步，但由于其与前现代的藕断丝连，因此并不是现阶段历史的选择，也不会成为宪政民主的圭臬。

当然，我也注意到了跨越式停顿后的走向问题，我举了中国古代急流勇退后的归隐，和后现代之后的星际移民，但作为阶段性考虑，目前我们还是要从根本上进行跨越式停顿。否则，当了隐士后还会在宗教团体内实行宗法制，到了外星际还要去做独裁，这种转型我们需要吗？在某种意义上没有跨越式停顿的转型或转向，只不过是像病人转医转院一样，并不是对病症的根治。相反，跨越式停顿则是对病症的根治。

跨越式停顿不同于停滞，而是为了寻求更大的发展而做出的必要的调整、甚至必要的牺牲，也就是列宁所说的退一步进两步。因此，跨越式停顿因其所处的别现代现实而具有了阶段性策略。

别现代来自对时间空间化的现实的概括，但是，这个时间的空间化并非时间和空间的凝聚，相反是在空间化现状中各种元素既和谐共谋，又相互纠结相互矛盾斗争中所产生的动力结构，从而将这种空间化结构导向解体，即通过和谐共谋期、对立冲突期、和谐共谋与对立冲突交织期，最终主导性力量依靠自身的变革和更新进入自我更新超越期，从而结束别现代时期①，进入新的理想的社会形态。但是，这里每一个时期的结束和向更高形态的发展，都是跨越式停顿的结果，而不可能是轻松转向的结果。

在别现代的不同时期，跨越式停顿有着自己的特点和使命。如在和谐共谋期，面对和谐假象所进行的揭露和批判，包括文艺的现实主义揭露和批判，拆穿和谐假象；面对对立冲突期的对于崇高和悲剧等审美形态的张扬，并通过文艺和审美做抚慰心灵的工作；面对和谐共谋与对立冲突张力所进行的冷幽默讽刺，以释放和减缓社会紧张；面对自我更新超越期而进行的全面创新和范式制定等，虽然这里所举大

① 王建疆：《时间的空间化与别现代主义》（《当代文坛》2016 年第 6 期）：“别现代中现代、前现代、后现代既和谐共谋又内在分裂的结构功能和矛盾运动以及主导性力量的出现，构成了别现代的阶段性特征，这就是和谐共谋期、对立冲突期、和谐与冲突交织期、自我更新超越期。”

多为文艺和美学，但都是别现代主义跨越式停顿的阶段性策略，都有着针砭时弊，驱邪扶正、聚集正能量的与前现代诀别的性质。

跨越式停顿尽管面临种种阻力，但现实的需求最终会导致它的成功。我之所以强调跨越式停顿，就在于跨越式发展惯性思维的根深蒂固和对跨越式停顿的罔顾。尽管我们在跨越式发展中有着非常深刻的历史性教训，但对这个历史性教训的总结和汲取目前尚未进行。虽然跨越式发展带来的问题有些已经积重难返，跨越式停顿面临重重困难，但由于跨越式停顿是针对这些严重而迫切的社会问题而提出的，因此，它在实践中最终会取得成功。全球有名的甘肃省省会兰州市，就通过整顿吏治，以壮士断腕的方式，断然诀别了重污染历史，成为跨越式停顿的典型例子①。因此，面对由跨越式发展引发的重大社会疑难问题时，就不再是转向、转型、转弯、转院，而是当机立断，根绝和阻断那些前现代的权大于法、和谐共谋，进行跨越式停顿，实现停顿式跨越。

第三节　跨越式停顿与文化和艺术创新中的切割理论

洪岳在他的大作《“别现代”理论的模糊性及反思》② 中举了两个例子，一个是北京的建筑，一个是莫言的小说。给我留下了深刻的印象，颇有启发，但也不无遗憾。启发者在于，北京的建筑、莫言的小说都是现代性、前现代、后现代杂糅纠结的最好例证，而且与别现

① 2015 年 12 月 14 日《甘肃日报》《甘肃新闻网》：甘肃省会城市兰州，曾经是全球污染最为严重的工业化城市之一，但是，近年来经过兰州市政府的大力整治，情况根本好转，已于 2015 年 12 月在联合国应对气候变化巴黎大会上荣获由联合国气候变化框架公约组织、中国低碳联盟、美国环保协会和中国低碳减排专委会联合颁发的“今日变革进步奖”。兰州市主要领导面对污染难题，敢动真格的，撤免了 3 位治污不力的环保局主要领导，29 名干部因治污不力而受到免职、降级和处分，从而使得兰州的污染得到根本解决。

② 王洪岳：《“别现代”理论的模糊性及反思》，《探索与争鸣》2016 年第 7 期。

代及其跨越式发展紧密相连。遗憾处在于，在洪岳的笔下只有所谓的新的现代性，并没有与跨越式停顿挂起钩来。

说到北京的建筑，洪岳认为：

> 然而，就在中国建设现代化的民族民主国家目标之际，西方后现代思潮大肆进入，而且在90年代与本土保守思潮合流，对现代化建设造成了严重的干扰。仅以北京建筑为例，国家大剧院、鸟巢、水立方、央视新大楼等后现代建筑，矗立于京城各处，同故宫、四合院、民国建筑、五六十年代苏式建筑、80年代集合了欧美和中国传统建筑精华的北京图书馆新馆、香山饭店等杂陈在一起，形象地呈现出当代中国社会和文化形态的无序性。本来一个拥有深厚底蕴的北京古代建筑完美和谐地留存到20世纪中叶，然而在50年代之初，拆城墙后苏式建筑在京城大行其道，就已经在破坏老北京城市建筑的和谐之美；90年代以来"奇奇怪怪"的后现代建筑混杂其间，再一次破坏了和谐的城市天际线。

通过与巴黎建筑的比较，洪岳指出造成这种现象的原因在于前现代建筑拥抱西方后现代建筑，而唯独无视或抛弃了体现现代性建筑的精髓。这是一种非常深刻的见解。但在我看来，北京市建筑是中国古代和苏联现代以及西方后现代的混合，是典型的别现代建筑。这种建筑中的别现代问题并非转型或转向的问题，而是跨越式停顿缺位的问题。如前所述，跨越式发展适用于经济、技术、军事，不适合社会制度、文明（文化）形态和自然形态。北京建筑恰好是在文明（文化）上搞了个跨越式发展，将现代、前现代和后现代的建筑杂糅在了一起，因而受到的批评也就不绝于耳。如果北京建筑不搞跨越式发展，而是来个跨越式停顿，即将作为前现代遗产的紫禁城来个停顿、区隔、固化，作为文化遗产保护起来，另外再造新城，就像罗马古城之

外再建新城一样，城市形态学效果可能就会今非昔比了。由于跨越式停顿是在跨越式发展基础上而言的，因此，及时地终止那些有违北京总体建筑风格的方案和建设，可谓亡羊补牢，未为晚矣。我相信，跨越式停顿的思维方式会使首都北京更具魅力。

说到莫言的小说，我特别欣赏洪岳下面这段话：

> 在莫言的小说中，带有前现代性色彩的信仰，包括万物有灵论、自然神论、鬼神崇拜，儒释道以及基督教等多种信仰的杂糅，深深地打上了中国传统文化的烙印。同时，莫言小说对于自50年代以来连续不断的乌托邦冲动和对精神之理性与非理性维度的深度揭示和描述，体现了莫言小说世界的现代主义的精神向度。因此，莫言并没有放弃主体性的担当意识和开拓情怀，他常常用“个性化”来表达其主体性诉求，对于自由民主的企望在其访谈录和对话录中时常出现。因此，社会现代性是莫言小说世界的一个底色和基调，只不过他并不刻意地或抽象地谈论，而是渗透于其整个精神结构之中，渗透于其整个小说艺术世界的营构当中。他充满机智地调动了反讽和戏仿技巧，对现代社会时间性的空间化处理，叙述视角的自由转换和游移，混淆你我他的多元的叙述视角，从而创造了一个融合了现实和虚幻的“高密东北乡”文学共和国。

这不就是我说的别现代——现代、前现代、后现代的杂糅或小说叙事中的时间的空间化吗？至于“莫言并没有放弃主体性的担当意识和开拓情怀，他常常用‘个性化’来表达其主体性诉求，对于自由民主的企望在其访谈录和对话录中时常出现”。不就是别现代主义的立场吗？至于洪岳所言“这不是欧美或标准的现代主义，也不是后现代主义的，更不是现实主义或浪漫主义的，而是杂糅和融合并超越了所有这些元素的一种新型现代主义，或者说是现代主义的中国化的实

现。”云云，这种所谓的“新型现代主义”难道不就是别现代主义吗？为什么我们非要用西方人造的词来表达自己的思想，而不能用自己的话语创新来表达自己的意思呢？

虽然莫言的小说我看的不如洪岳多，但莫言对于令人惊悚和令人发指现象的揭露直指人性的弱处和痛点，尤其是那些发生在当代的前现代事件，更能激发读者对于一个世界的厌恶和恐怖。通过莫言的小说，我们感到了前现代必须被终结的合理性和迫切性，是一种以文学的方式表达的跨越式停顿，因此非常契合我们这个时代的吁求，在此我还要感谢洪岳提供的以上两个典型的别现代艺术例证。

由以上洪岳提供的两例可以看出，现代性已经成了我们考察文化和艺术不可脱离的坐标。那么，作为别现代重要理论支柱的跨越式停顿在文化和艺术上又有什么用场呢？

跨越式停顿很容易被误解为文化中断论。如说，“五四”就是对传统文化的中断这难道还不够吗？但是，我认为，恰好相反，不是跨越式停顿导致了对传统文化的中断，而是跨越式发展跨越了中国文化发展的自然阶段，通过“砸烂孔家店”等否定本民族文化的方式而与西方文化对接，从而对传统文化造成了毁灭性的伤害，以致对于一代又一代的青年来说仿佛断了文化上的香火。这一后果的直接原因就在于我在前面提到的，跨越式发展只适应于经济、技术、军事，而不适合的社会制度和文明（文化）形态的跨越上。而跨越式停顿就是要在已经产生严重后果的跨越式发展中来个急刹车，从而回到正确的轨道上去。

跨越式停顿不是发生在自然发展阶段的事，而是在跨越式发展阶段的事。在自然发展阶段，一切都是按部就班、循序渐进的，因此没有跨越式发展，从而也就不需要跨越式停顿。在自然发展状态下，继承、发展成为文化发展的常态。而一旦在文化上搞跨越式发展，那么，继承已被抛弃，建立在继承基础上的革新也就失去了根据，剩下的就极有可能是对外来文化的对接、拥抱、传播。“五四”新文化运

动就是中国文化上跨越式发展的典型例证。因此，在文化发展上，要严防跨越式发展。在别现代时期，不去补现代性的历史课程，而是直接与西方后现代拥抱，只能导致社会形态的更加拎不清。苏联时期的未来主义，中国“文革”中的“砸烂一个旧世界创造一个新世界”，就是违背文化发展规律的大跃进式的文化跨越式发展，其结果是对民族文化的巨大伤害。文化上的跨越式发展，最直接的结果就是民族文化上的虚无主义和崇洋媚外。“文革”中在党报上被不断痛批的“崇洋媚外”到“文革”结束后很快就变成了真正的举国崇洋媚外，似乎外国的月亮也比中国的圆了。而且，对文化不加区隔、分层的跨越式发展，最容易造成对传统文化从精神到器物的全方位摧毁。这也是国人在全球重视文化遗产的今天常常扼腕叹息的原因所在。

与文化上的跨越式发展不同，文化上的跨越式停顿就是将前现代的具有历史记忆和审美元素的文化遗产做一个区隔，将它保护起来，成为研究对象，成为观赏对象，固化为展品。而对其制度文化和观念文化要有更为清醒的认识和更为严格的批判。前现代的制度文化的腐朽自不用说，就前现代的观念文化而言，也有许多愚昧落后有碍现代化进程的东西，如血缘宗亲文化、帝王江山文化、专制独裁文化、神秘腐朽文化、等级门第观念等，在跨越式发展中是容不得它的转向的，而是要将它阻绝、固化、化石化、展品化，而非让它转向、转弯，或换一种面孔，借尸还魂，或披着非遗、优秀传统的面纱进入我们的社会运行之中。它们只能作为被研究的对象、被揭露的对象、被批判的对象、被展示的对象，而不能成为要拯救的对象、要组合的对象、要传承的对象。在对前现代文化的研究的过程中，甄别那些于今还有现实意义的元素，对其进行传承，并在传承的基础上推陈出新、传承创新，在创新的基础上发展，在发展的基础上跨越，这与停顿式跨越的主题并行不悖。原因就在于跨越式停顿并非不发展，相反，是要谋取更大的发展。这一点，我已在拙文《别现代：跨越式停顿》中讲过了，此不赘。

跨越式停顿与跨越式转型（向）在曾经热闹了一阵的“古代文论的现代转换”中，孰优孰劣已经得到了证明。中国古代文论其产生于前现代的文化基础、语汇表达、问题意识、范畴界定等，在很大程度上已很难适应现代文艺现象和现代文艺理论，如果不是将其区隔开来，采取分类取舍的方式分别进行借鉴或封存或展示，而是一味地向来自西方的文艺理论转向、转型、转弯，势必强古人所难，削足适履。事实上，中国古代文论的现代转换并没有进行下去。尽管还有不少学者至今还在试图进行古代文论关键词的转换工作，但面对“这就是中国古人的意思吗”的质疑难于跨越。原因很简单，前现代文化在现代社会只配跨越式停顿，而无法进行跨越式转型、转向、转弯，从而进行跨越式发展。所谓的转型、转向、转弯，就是让中国古代文论去适应西方话语。但话语是权力，具有规训、指导的作用，将自己的知识谱系纳入别人的话语，就只有被改造、被规训的份儿了。因此，前现代文化及其文艺理论、美学思想等一旦脱离本土语境而进入跨越式发展的转型转向，势必迷失自己，只有跨越式停顿，才有可能展现自己本有的独到的价值。

跨越式停顿在宗教发展上也有其特别的意义。作为前现代信仰产物的各种宗教，在现代社会只能做跨越式停顿而非跨越式发展或跨越式转型。原因很简单，随着科技进步带来的祛魅和脱魅的普世化，政教合一的宗教模式和精神统治的意识形态总要受到现代社会的遏制，主动式的跨越式停顿势在必行，表现为信仰与存在的分离与并存，即政治家、科学家可以同时成为牧师，牧师也可以成为政治家、科学家。但在政府、学校、公共场所与在教堂不同，都必须在俗与教的不同场合说不同的话，做不同的事，这就是对宗教传统的政教合一和信仰大于一切的跨越式停顿。如果没有这种跨越式停顿，那么，宗教存在于当代的合法性将受到挑战。就一些还在政教合一与政教分离之间徘徊的国家为例，如土耳其，它的不放弃宗教在国家统治中的地位，不愿对政教合一进行跨越式停顿，同时又要

进行民主改革，想在欧亚两大洲左右逢源，但结果却是成了伊斯兰世界和欧盟国家都不待见的国家。因此，跨越式停顿是文化上的革命，是断代式的历史跨越，是拎得清，而不是投机主义的转型、转向。在对文化的选择上，骑墙、含混、杂糅和拎不清的结果反而使投机主义者自己成了受害者。

跨越式停顿在文学艺术中的表现最为突出。通过描写荒谬、残酷、杀戮、苦难、恐怖、困惑、忧伤等，揭示造成这些苦难的深层原因，目的还在于引起对于痛苦的疗救。鲁迅的小说如此，莫言——这位洪岳教授所乐道的作家亦如此。他们在自己的小说中已经无力告诉人们生活应该是什么样子的，也无法描述该如何进行转型，但是，与他们所描写的这种非人的残酷现实的诀别，即跨越式停顿却是一目了然的。他们不需要转型，而是要进行彻底的诀别，仅这一点就足以成就他们的高大。

跨越式停顿在当代中国艺术的发展中具有特殊的意义。中国当代艺术的一个最大特点是传承和借鉴有余而创新不足，没有主义、流派或方法。其根本原因就在于只知道传承——创新（纵向）或借鉴——创新（横向），而不知道在传承与创新之间、在借鉴与创新之间，还需要一个跟被传承对象、被借鉴对象之间的切割。没有切割的传承就只会沦为因袭，没有切割的借鉴就会跌入“拿来主义”的陷阱。

浏览人类艺术史发现，艺术风格、艺术流派的形成都有着跨越式停顿的前提。这种前提具体体现在传承—创新和借鉴—创新之间的切割上。杜夏与超现实主义的崛起就在于与传统绘画手法的切割，终止了绘画无法表现运动的观念，而大胆地画出了《下楼梯的女人》系列，通过绘画表现出运动感，从而自成一派。而杜夏将人工器物带到画展上去的做法，更是与整个人类的艺术观念做了切割，中断了手工雕塑才是艺术的常见，而将批量生产的器物引入艺术，小便壶因画家的签名而成为艺术，从而形成了现成主义艺术流派，不仅彻底颠覆了

人类的艺术观念，而且使得“什么是艺术”和“艺术不是什么”都成了艺术的和美学的长达一个世纪的难题，而且这个难题至今无解。杜夏的绝活不是他的画，更不是他带给艺术展的夜壶，而是他对传统艺术观念的切割、阻断、根绝，这种切割、阻断、根绝拉开了人类艺术的新纪元，因而实现了伟大的跨越式停顿，而这个伟大的跨越式停顿成就了他的伟大的停顿式跨越。

通过跨越式停顿来创造风格、形成流派和方法的例子太多了，不胜枚举，印象主义、立体主义、超现实主义、达达主义、现成主义、合成主义等，哪个不是跨越式停顿、阻断、切割、根绝前代的脐带而自成一体、自成一家、自成一派的呢？

相比之下，中国当代艺术的尴尬，就在于跨越式停顿的缺乏，在于前现代、现代、后现代的勾肩搭背中从来就拎不清，从来就没有形成自己独立的风格、流派、主义。相反，是现代、前现代和后现代的杂糅与和谐共谋。长此以往，不仅影响到中国艺术的原创性，而且中国当代艺术市场也将遭受灭顶之灾。海外华人画作在拍卖价1000万元港币以下时，好评如潮，但当拍卖价突破2000万元港币时，却恶评不断，如说什么海外中国先锋艺术沦为“抄袭”“剽窃”“侮辱了人生”“侮辱了艺术”① 等。但由于中国海外艺术家并未形成抱团的流派，也没有自己的主义和方法，没有自己的理论，因而面对责难却无力反驳，任由人家评判，其结果会是什么，就是作品将变得一钱不值。造成中国当代艺术影响力和自我保护力阙如的原因即在于“停”“断”意识的缺乏。即没有跨越式停顿的思维方式，将自己与西方艺术手法和流派做一切割、区隔开来，没有在模仿西方的老路上来一个及时的跨越式停顿，没有断开西方艺术的影响，因而被扣上了抄袭和剽窃的大帽子。

---

① ［美］杰德·珀尔（Jed Perl）：《中国当代艺术侮辱了人生》，《新共和（*The New Republic*）》，纽约，2014.2.19. 中国南方艺术网转载。

总之，跨越式停顿的思维就是断代式的、格式化的、革命性的思维，要拎清现代、前现代、前现代之间的界限，切割、斩断与其他的主义和流派、方法的勾连，独树一帜，从而别出心裁、别开生面、别出一路、别具一格、别有洞天，为中国艺术张目、为中国文化立标、为艺术家立言、立身、立威。

后　记

“别现代”是本人首次提出并论证的新概念，起始于我在2014年春天上海市美学学会主办的一次学术会议上的发言，不经意间引起了学者们的注意。而真正引起反响却是在同年年底由中央编译局和上海交通大学联合主办的中俄高层文化论坛上。

别现代理论在不断引起国内外关注和讨论的过程中逐渐积淀了它的内涵。由于别现代理论所反映的社会现实具有交集纠结的特点，因而对它的理解、界定和翻译都多有不同。但作为学术探讨，本书抛出别现代问题的主要目的在于另辟蹊径，对一些哲学的、美学的、文艺学的问题进行新的更为深入的探讨。这种探讨是无止境的，本书也只是开了个头而已。

在全球化背景下，学术话语的封闭已经难以想象，相反，对某一话题的关注度和关注范围，也将会成为学术评估的重要参照。因此，本人非常感谢所有关心别现代问题并为别现代理论发展给予帮助的新老朋友们。

特别感谢那些撰文与我讨论并将这场讨论引入国际学术界的欧美哲学界、美学界、文学界、艺术理论界的学者（按参加讨论先后顺序）：

阿列西·艾尔雅维茨、恩斯特·曾科、基顿·韦恩、麦克·兰特、兰斯·斯特拉特、洛克·本茨先生。

特别感谢积极参与别现代问题学术讨论的国内文学界、哲学界、

美学界、经济学界、法学界、艺术理论界的学者（按参加讨论先后顺序）：

黄海澄、朱立元、杨金海、陶国山、夏中义、张法、周宪、程金城、许明、周海敏、苏宏斌、刘毅青、何云峰、林少雄、夏锦乾、钟仕伦、孙逊、于光荣、汪行福、陆扬、吴炫、李春青、刘锋杰、王洪岳、徐碧辉、夏述贵、张隆溪、邓晓芒、庄志明、李大勇、马正平、肖明华先生。

尤其是邓晓芒先生和孙逊先生关于“别样现代性”的不同看法，给我更多的启发。

特别感谢为别现代提供英译参考意见的中央编译局秘书长杨金海博士、香港中文大学的张隆溪先生。

特别感谢首发别现代论文的叶祝弟、秦维宪先生。

特别感谢建立全球第一个“中国别现代研究中心”的美国佐治亚州西南州立大学的 Keaton Wynn 先生。

特别感谢为“别现代”设计 logo 的刘宇襄先生。

特别感谢中国社会科学出版社的责编刘艳女士。

正是因为他们与我之间无私的讨论所贡献的智慧，才不仅使得我们之间因为有了共同的话题而成为同道，而且在学术研究已经沦为自说自话的当下重启了真正的思想市场。

虽然本书的大部分内容都已公开发表过，但本书在论文的基础上做了较大调整和提升。因此，专业引述亦可根据注脚查阅已发表的论文互参。

作者

2017 年 6 月 20 日于沪上古美斋